Evidence for Truth: Prophecy

Evidence for Truth: Prophecy

Victor Pearce

B.Sc., Dip.Anth.(Oxon), M.R.E., D.Ed., F.R.A.I., C.F.

Series Editor: David Page

eagle

Guildford, Surrey

Other books in this series by Victor Pearce:

Evidence for Truth, Vol. 1: Science
Evidence for Truth, Vol. 2: Archaeology
Evidence for Truth, Vol. 4: Miracles and Angels

Other titles by the same author:

Who Was Adam?
Origin of Man
The Science of Man and Genesis

Copyright © Victor Pearce 1999

The rights of Victor Pearce to be identified as author of this work has been asserted by him in accordance with the Copyright, Design and Patents Act 1988.

British Library Cataloguing in Publication Data. A catalogue record for this book is available from the British Library.

This edition, 2000
Published by Eagle, an imprint of Inter Publishing Service (IPS) Ltd,
PO Box 530, Guildford, Surrey GU2 4FH.

Scripture quotations: unless specified, Bible quotations are the author's own translation from the Greek or Hebrew text.

Typeset by Eagle
Printed by CPD, Wales
ISBN No: 0 86347 265 6

CONTENTS

LIST OF ILLUSTRATIONS

THE PRINCIPLES BEHIND THIS SERIES

THERE IS MORE EVIDENCE today that the Bible is true and accurate than ever before, but the facts have been denied to the public and even to many church people. Evidence and the Bible text have convinced Dr Pearce that the Bible is true from the beginning. It is his purpose to reveal all the undeniable facts:

- That the Creator of the world is also the author of the Word. He fully inspired all the 41 writers of the Bible who contributed to the sacred Scriptures over a span of 1,500 years. This is the only explanation for the accuracy and cohesion of the Bible.
- That the message in the Bible concerning spiritual truth is true, as is also its history, cultural details, prophecy and science. All are completely true, reliable and factual. This has been confirmed by research.
- That those who doubt, do so because they do not have the facts, or do not wish to have them or believe them.

Those who have attended the author's lectures have included atheists and agnostics who thought that they had explained everything without God, but as the result of his teaching, have become convinced and converted and blessed.

Dr Pearce has found it is possible to explain science, archaeology and prophecy in simple ways which thrill the student.

- Psalm 119:160 – 'Your Word is true from the beginning.'
- Psalm 119:18 – 'Open my eyes that I may see wonderful things out of your law.'
- Psalm 119:42 – 'Then I shall have an answer for him who taunts me.'
- 1 Peter 3:15 – 'Be ready to give an answer to everyone who asks you for a reason for the hope that is in you.'

The Creator is seen in his works and has spoken in his Word.

ABOUT THE AUTHOR

DR VICTOR PEARCE had factory experience as an apprentice and later as a personnel officer and so knows the type of discussion typical of the factory floor and in the office. His experience as a teacher in comprehensive and grammar schools, and his training and lecturing in universities, gives him additional insight. He became an honours graduate of London University in anthropology, through University College, and specialised at Oxford in prehistoric archaeology. He travelled for archaeological digs and research around the Mediterranean, including Turkey and The Levant and also in the USA. He read theology at the London College of Divinity; is a Prebendary of Lichfield Cathedral; was Rector of one of the largest Anglican parishes in England; has had 25 curates, built two churches and several halls (one by voluntary labour). He was a member of the Diocesan Synod; was chairman of an *ad hoc* committee of the Education Council for a new religious syllabus and a visiting lecturer in two Bible colleges. Because this combination of skills with geology and fieldwork is unusual, Victor Pearce is able to offer a unique ministry. He has been much used of God in the conversion of atheists and agnostics who become surprised and fascinated by the facts which previously had been denied them.

He is author of *Who was Adam?*, *Origin of Man*, *The Science of Man and Genesis* and a contributor to the *Dictionary of the Church* and writes in various periodicals. He has lectured on evidences in university unions and schools. He was a broadcaster for Hour of Revival and Transworld Radio for 18 years and now broadcasts daily throughout Europe for United Christian Broadcasters. One of his main subjects is the accuracy of the Bible as corroborated by the science of man (anthropology) and archaeology.

PREFACE TO THE FIRST EDITION
WHAT THIS COULD DO FOR YOU

LET ME ASSURE YOU from the outset that there is abundant evidence available which can establish you in a triumphant faith in God and help you to convey it to others. In this series, I recount **evidence for truth** from science, archaeology and fulfilled prophecy and relate this evidence to the Bible in considerable detail.

In Volume 1, I considered the abundant evidence of **science** in relation to Scripture. There is much scientific background in the Bible which can be accounted for only if the author of the Bible is the Creator of the universe. In speaking of science, I mean that science which has general consensus of agreement arising out of empirical investigation, not changing theories. I give you many examples.

Likewise, **archaeology** has confirmed that all the written history in the Bible is true, accurate and factual. Tablets, mounds and pottery dug up from past civilisations confirm this, especially when the Bible dates for events are accepted. All this is covered in Volume 2.

Above all, the Bible contains the **prophecies** by God of future history right from the beginning. God foretells to the prophets at each stage all that is to happen and why, and all that will happen. In this way, God proves that he is unfolding a remarkable plan for the future happiness of the world and for you. This plan could have unfolded without suffering had not mankind rebelled against God, but now, even by suffering, especially through that of Jesus Christ, those purposes will be fulfilled. In Volume 3, we discover the evidence for Bible prophecy past, present and future.

The facts which will be brought before you can give you a firm, practical faith to face life and to convince friends.

Victor Pearce
Kidsgrove, England
Autumn 1992

PREFACE TO THE SECOND EDITION

In addition to all the events I outlined in this volume in 1992, significant developments in the world have been taking place. The fulfilment of prophecy in Europe and Israel today is a most powerful witness for truth both to believer and unbeliever. Significant things have happened. Europe has moved towards a single monetary system with all that the Bible says about the future for that. The Common Market began with ten countries of the old western Roman Empire as anticipated from Scripture by the famous scientist Isaac Newton and is now being joined by other sovereignties eastwards – bits of the empires before Rome.

On the Israel front, the diamond jubilee of the creation of the State of Israel has been celebrated. Many seem to have forgotten the significance of that. Jesus said that Jerusalem would be governed by 'Gentiles until the times of the Gentiles are completed'. That was fulfilled when, for the first time for over two and a half thousand years, Israel once again ruled in Jerusalem.

Also, the trouble it is causing was anticipated in the Bible when God told Zechariah that before the Messiah descends from heaven (when every eye will see the wounds of his first coming, 12:10) Jerusalem will become an insoluble problem. In fact, everyone who tries to solve it will injure himself like a man trying to move a heavy boulder would rupture himself (12:3).

Significant events will continue with the power which occupies the river Euphrates (Iraq), as prophesied in so many scriptures. Meanwhile, nothing will prevent God gathering his ancient people back 'one by one' (Isaiah 27:12) which has increased dramatically over recent years. Israel may even benefit from peace pacts, but note that Israel is instructed to treat the Palestinians fairly (Ezekiel 47:22,23). But it is their coming Lord Jesus who will ultimately bring peace to them and through them to the whole world.

In applying scriptures to contemporary events, it is important to make sure we are doing so in the context of the surrounding passage. I believe that I have explained all these prophecies in their correct contexts as given to Moses, Hosea, Daniel, Peter, John and others. They are the 'signs of the times'.

Victor Pearce
Kidsgrove, May 1998

FOREWORD

This book by my good friend and colleague Dr Victor Pearce about Prophecy is the third in his Evidence for Truth series. Although it is quite different from the first two volumes both in subject and content, I highly recommend it.

We should be knowledgeable about what the Bible has to say about the age we live in, the future and the end times. We may not have all the answers, but that does not mean we should avoid the subject.

Dr Pearce's book, *Prophecy*, is based upon the Bible, Middle-East and European history both past and present and is a real insight into the significance of current events.

Dr Pearce has kept an honest and open mind, and challenges us to consider a complex subject whilst not losing sight of the focus – the relationship between man and God. It is well worth reading.

Gareth Littler
Managing Director, UCB Europe

EDITOR'S NOTE

It gives me great pleasure to commend to you this last book from the writings and broadcasts of Dr Victor Pearce.

In our work together whilst compiling this series, we have spent many happy hours discussing how best to express the wonderful insights to God's words which have been handed down to us over many thousands of years. This whole series of books is the outcome of a life-long study to correlate the evidence of different life-sciences and pieces together the jigsaw of life's origins, development and purpose. The Bible is full of scientific and cultural detail, which is being verified today through modern research techniques. In so many disciplines we find full corroboration with Scripture: geology, astronomy, archaeology, anthropology, palaeontology, palaeobotany, palaeomagnetics, genetics, atomic physics, tectonics, etc, etc. The historical and cultural understanding of the last 10,000 years has been captured by Victor in his first two volumes, but additionally, Volume 3 points to biblical **evidence for truth** of a prophetic nature.

Victor's studies have taken him into many universities, museums, laboratories and archaeological sites the world over and he has received much support from many scientists, archaeologists and theologians. He has also aroused criticism inside and outside the Church among those who resolutely deny the existence of a Creator behind the truth that is revealed for all to see and which continues to be discovered and fulfilled around us today.

As you complete this trilogy, you will have gained a truer perspective of the Creator, the Judge and the Saviour of mankind who one day soon will return in flesh and in glory with spectacular consequences. Furthermore, you will grow in confidence to dispel doubts and lies which have been perpetuated in the media and in many churches over the years. This will in turn enable you to gain fresh ground in God's Kingdom for yourself and for others, whilst there is still time in the darkening age we live in. Good reading!

But please remember that the knowledge gained by science and archaeology is not truth of itself: absolute truth is the inspired and prophetic Word of God. This alone gives insight and meaning to the discoveries and postulations of mankind which, in the right hands, help to reveal the divine origins and destiny of life.

David Page
Series Editor

1 THE IMPORTANCE OF EVIDENCE FROM PROPHECIES
THE SECOND COMING, EUROPE AND ISRAEL

WHY IS PROPHECY HUSHED UP?

Once I had a surprise visitor. It was a bit 'hush-hush'. She was from abroad and so she asked me not to mention her name or country.

Why had she come to see me? It was to tell me that my broadcasts on prophecy had brought her to full faith in the Lord Jesus Christ. She had to listen secretly to the broadcasts and fortunately her husband did not interfere. He asked her to stay indoors and not to let others near her radio or do things which would make it awkward for him. In spite of this, their marriage relationship greatly improved.

But she could not keep the good news to herself. All her relatives came to tell her not to forsake their beliefs. She wondered whether to keep quiet, but she opened her Bible at random and read, 'A city set on a hill cannot be hidden . . . let your light so shine before men'.

Another woman was brought to trust in Jesus as a Living Saviour – a Saviour who was coming again. She had come over to England to tell me of the power of the prophetic word. She could not keep quiet. I thought, 'Isn't it sad that people in England keep quiet about the return of the Lord Jesus Christ?' People often say to me, 'Why don't we hear more about the second coming of the Lord Jesus Christ? The message is so powerful and relevant.' Of course, this important subject is given its just place in many churches. Why is it not preached about in others?

There are big contrasts. I was preaching once in a cathedral and the organist said, 'That's the first time I have heard anything about the second coming. Do you really believe it will happen – how extraordinary!'

I said, 'You speak about it every Sunday when you say the creed, "He will come again at the end of the age to judge the living and the dead." '

This situation of unbelief is actually one of the signs of Christ's return. 2 Peter 3:4 says that in the last days there will be those who say, 'Where is the promise of his coming?' The reason for their doubt is that they do not believe God can step into history, either by creative acts or by destructive acts like the Flood. One excuse for only passing references to the second coming is that there are differences of opinion about the glorious return of Christ. This is not a valid reason because there have been differences of opinion about other doctrines which have not prevented full reference to them. But when it comes to the subject of the second coming, people just shrug it off and say, 'Are you a pre-millennialist or post-millennialist or an a-millennialist?' Such a theological choice does not invalidate the second coming. Whether the Lord comes before or after the 'millennium' does not alter the fact that he is coming. ('Millennium' here and elsewhere in this book refers to the biblical millennium mentioned in Revelation 20:1–15, and not the new calendar millennium commencing in the year 2000.)

Concerning such matters, Paul's words are relevant. He wrote, 'If I have the gift of prophecy and have not love, it profits me nothing' (1 Corinthians 13:2). We should remember also that the disciples did not understand all the details immediately. Even up to the ascension they were asking, 'Will you restore again the kingdom to Israel at this time?'

A lady once remarked to me, 'Isn't it tragic that we hear little about the second coming just now when the signs show that it is near?' Yes, there are so many unmistakable signs. It is an impressive list which is powerful for convincing the casual enquirer, so in Chapter 2, I will list them under the acrostic SIGNS.

He Thumbed a Lift

One is cautious these days to whom one gives a lift. He looked a respectable young man – about 30 years old. He stood on the grass verge of a heavily trafficked road. Could I draw on to it without being bumped in the rear by some determined driver? I pulled over and released the door.

Where do you want to go?

'Derby or Nottingham.'

I can drop you off at Derby.

'OK. Thanks a lot.'

Actually, I was going on further to Nottingham, but I wanted to see if his company would be pleasant enough before committing myself. (Eventually I did take him on to Nottingham.) He settled in and belted up and I was soon speeding into the run of traffic.

'Thanks a lot!' he said again. 'I am a police cadet and need to get to my station.'

I looked quickly at my speedometer and was gratified to see that I was within the allowable speed limit.

He chatted pleasantly and then noted a leaflet sticking up in the dashboard. It was one which a zealous friend had given me and I had stuck it there temporarily. It announced that everything happening in the world today showed that Christ's coming was near.

'What is happening to show that?' he asked, pointing to the leaflet.

I remembered he was a trainee policeman, so I volunteered: *Lawlessness, vandalism, terrorism, break-up of home life and many other social evils.*

'Well, there is certainly plenty of that, but there has always been some, though I admit we are in a pretty bad patch at the moment. What other things are there?'

Many scriptures prophesy that Europe will unite into a sovereignty of nations with a single market system. Many Christians have read these prophecies and foretold this for the last century. The widely-held view is that the countries involved would be those which were former-ly in the old Roman Empire.

'That is certainly happening,' he remarked, 'and a single market is due soon. Where does it say that in the Bible?'

In Daniel and Revelation. God showed Daniel the future history of empires down from Daniel's day, six centuries before Christ, to the last days. The European amalgamation and single market is interpreted as the last stage before Christ's descent from heaven. My passenger's interest was deepening.

'Any other signs?' he asked.

Oh, plenty. Widespread fear at the possible destruction by nuclear warfare, the return of Israel to Palestine.

'The Israel problem is causing a lot of trouble!' said the cadet. 'I wouldn't have thought that that was an event to be happy about.'

That is exactly what the Bible says. God told Zechariah that it would cause an insoluble problem which only Christ's return would solve.

'I don't see how Christ's return would solve it. His gentle teaching wouldn't be taken any notice of. Why, there was a man the other day claiming to be Christ.'

Jesus said there would be, I replied. *False christs, he called them, and said his second coming would be quite different. It will be with power. He will descend from heaven suddenly to judge the nations and stop the world destroying itself.*

This young man became so interested that he asked me to send him something I had written. The following is what I sent.

PROPHECY AND EUROPE EAST AND WEST

What tremendous happenings there are today! Did you know that it is all working out as prophesied in the Bible?

In my writings, I have outlined these events. I do so before some of them have actually happened, because they are in the Bible before they happen. It shows that God has a purpose in history, a purpose which leads up to the second coming of Christ. He will set the world right. In fact, he is the only hope for the world. And he told Isaiah that this is what proves that he is God – his ability to foretell the future, because he has planned it. 'I am God; there is no other. I am God and there is no one like me who declares the final things from the beginning; and from ancient times, the things that are not yet done. I have spoken it, I will also bring it to pass. I have purposed it; I will also do it' (Isaiah 46:9,11).

Have others recognised these prophecies? Yes, many have. I am not the only one who has related present happenings to the fulfilment of Bible prophecy. Many others have read those prophecies. They show that Christ's second coming is near. The Bible foretold many things. One was that happenings in Eastern Europe and Russia were antici-pated; another that Europe would unite in a common market. Those prophecies about the European Common Market are in the book of Daniel and in the book of Revelation. Let us look at these first.

The European amalgamation of kingdoms was foretold in Daniel chapters 2 and 7. Daniel lived in 580 BC. He was told that there would be a succession of political powers down the next 2,500 years from his time. That brings us down to our days. He was told that the last sce-nario would be the European Amalgamation of Kingdoms and Revelation 13 shows it would be a single market. The single market agreement was signed on 31st December 1992. I wrote the year 1992 in the margin of my Bible some twenty years before, worked out from those strange figures God gave to Daniel.

In the words of Revelation 13, 'None would be allowed to buy or sell unless he had the number of his name.' All those plastic cards and cash points are leading up to this! All the check-out points which read the coded price of your goods are leading up to this. This number is given in Revelation 13:17,18. The European Commonwealth was inaugurated by the Treaty of Rome. Rome is described in Revelation 17:9,18, as the Seven Hill city.

Israel is one of the main signs of Christ's near return, and what is happening in Europe and Eastern Europe and the Middle East is all part of the scenario described in the Bible.

Are there other signs prophesied by the Bible? Yes, there are lots. The great increase in science and knowledge and travel (Daniel 12:4). The outburst of lawlessness (2 Timothy 3; 2 Thessalonians 2). The for-bidden dabbling with the occult and zodiac horoscopes (1 Timothy 4). The fear of nuclear warfare (Luke 21:26). The increase in education, but also of scepticism (2 Peter 3:3).

Children's programmes on TV show cartoons of all sorts of funny beasts. You get them too on national flags – the Welsh dragon; the English unicorn. They are called mythological animals. God likes to make reading easy; so in Daniel and Revelation, he illustrates the future by a lopsided bear, a deflated lion, a leopard with wings and animals with many heads and horns, as we shall see; which reminds me to give a piece of advice. *Always let Scripture interpret Scripture. Don't let your imagination do it.* Some thought a lion in the book of Revelation meant Britain and that a bear meant Russia, but God himself tells Daniel that the lion meant Babylon (in Iraq) and the bear meant Persia (Iran), the leopard symbolised the Greek Empire and the animal with iron teeth is Rome; the ten horns are the European Sovereignty of nations which arose out of the former Roman Empire.

Europe and the Antichrist

Interpret Revelation 13 by Daniel 7 and what do you find? As a matter of fact, it shows that the European Sovereignty of nations will be joined by the former Babylonian area in the latter days, then by modern Persia (Iran) also by the Eastern European countries and they will join the economic monetary amalgamation of Europe. Why? Because Revelation 13 says no one will be able to buy or sell unless he has the marketing number of the European economy represented by the ten horns, and that economy will also include the leopard of Eastern Europe in the old Greek Empire, the bear's feet of the former Persian Empire and the lion's mouth of the Babylonian area (Revelation 13:2). It is Daniel 7 which identifies the animals and countries they represent. No doubt oil revenues will have a lot to do with the economy.

The fact that Europe is an amalgamation of several sovereignties ,instead of the old Roman Empire, is illustrated by Revelation 13:1, where the crowns of sovereignty are upon each of the ten horns, whereas before, only the Roman beast was crowned with one single crown. I have always said, therefore, that Europe would not be a revived Roman Empire, but an amalgamation of sovereignties of European countries with a single monetary system.

So you see, this means that the countries of Europe will each be given their **separate sovereignty** because, in this symbol of the ten horns, each horn is separately crowned. In other words, each European country joining the European economy is given separate sovereignty. Then the leopard of Greece in East Europe joins up, then the bear's claws of ancient Persia and then the lion's mouth of Babylon in Mesopotamia (Revelation 13:2).

This could mean that in these latter days, the European countries of the former Roman Empire will be joined by the earlier Greek Empire area, then what remains of the former Persian Empire (the claws) and then what remains of the former Babylonian Empire area – the mouth

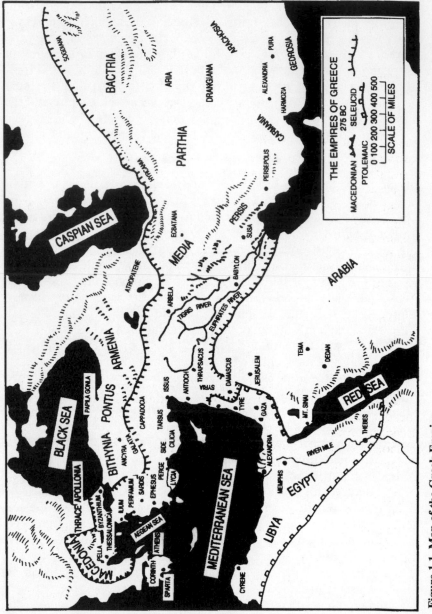

Courtesy: Unger's Bible Dictionary

Figure 1.1. Map of the Greek Empire.

(all talk?). Does this mean then that economic Europe will be joined by Eastern Europe, by old Greece and then all the Middle East will join the economy? I think it does, but we shall see.

Politicians will rise and fall according to how they help on this process, even as politicians rise and fall according to how they help or hinder Israel. That has happened in the USA where unexpectedly, contrary to expectations, a President more helpful to Israel was elected. For Revelation 17:17 says, 'God will put a plan into their minds, a plan which will carry out his purposes. They will agree together to give their authority to the beast, so that the words of God will be fulfilled.'

Then the antichrist will arise out of Europe and the false prophet will arise out of the Middle East and both will be destroyed by the descent of Christ from heaven. This harmonises with Daniel's Image where it will be in the days of the sovereign European states that Christ will come to set up his Kingdom which will never be destroyed.

But what about the events in Eastern Europe and Russia? What I want to tell you now is that not so many have noticed that the Bible also speaks of the break-up of Eastern Europe which is happening now, then their eventual formation into another power bloc. It had to start with the re-uniting of East and West Germany which I wrote about before it happened. Then south-east Europe had to disintegrate.

It is those last five chapters of Daniel which make the events of Eastern Europe significant. They don't speak only of Palestine. They speak of the area occupied originally by the Greek Empire. It is that area which would eventually concern Jewish history after Daniel's day. That area stretched from eastern Europe to Iran and Pakistan; from Yugoslavia to beyond Iraq, the eastern power bloc. It highlights the significance of what is happening in all those East European countries. The old Greek Empire, invaded by Turkey, included those eastern European countries of former Yugoslavia, Albania, Bulgaria and extended eastwards through Turkey, Jordan, Iraq, Iran to Pakistan. Chapter 10 enlarges on this.

The Greek Empire is clearly named in Daniel 8:21, even though by Daniel's time it had not yet come into being. Parts of it had been ruled first by the Babylonian Empire, then Persia, then Greece. The Greek Empire had the largest geographical area and was the only one which included eastern Europe. It was this area which became the eastern Roman Empire or Byzantine Empire which lasted a thousand years after the western Roman Empire had fallen. It was this which was eventually conquered by the Turkish (Moslem) power in 1453 as anticipated by these chapters in Daniel, and described in Revelation 9.

As a matter of fact, other prophets add further information. They are Isaiah, Jeremiah and Ezekiel. They even give significance to the recent Gulf War. Isaiah 27:12 says that God will beat out all opposition to the restoration of Jews to the Holy Land. Iraq declared that its projectiles would demolish Israel, but God said in Isaiah 27:12, 'I will beat out all that area of the Euphrates so that my people Israel can go back one by one.' What a beating-out Iraq has experienced from the air!

Figure 1.2. Tigris-Euphrates basin.

Courtesy: Unger's Bible Dictionary

But did this refer to our times? These chapters say yes. It would be near the day of resurrection at the coming of Christ. 'He will swallow up death for ever (for the Christian). The Lord God will wipe away tears from all faces. Thy dead shall live, their dead bodies shall rise.'

Furthermore, it is Isaiah and Ezekiel who add further information to Daniel's – all about the last days. Ezekiel adds further information about the northern power bloc from Germany through to Russia.

'All Israel Gathered Together'

What effect are the events here having on the Jewish nation today? It is releasing the two million Jews living in Russia to return to Israel. Before that, the Soviets stopped Jewish migration, but as Jeremiah 31:8 says, 'Behold, I the Lord will bring them from the north country and gather them from the farthest parts of the earth.' The country to the far north of Israel is, of course, Russia. And meanwhile, Jews have been returning to Israel from other countries around the world:

During the 50 years since the birth of the state of Israel in 1948, approximately 3 million Jewish immigrants have come from some 70 countries around the world – the greatest number of all, 900,000, from the former Soviet Union. The momentum is increasing – nearly 1 million in the last decade alone . . . A massive airlift was carried out by the Israeli Government between 1984 and 85 to rescue 10,000 Ethiopian Jews from civil war and . . . in 1991, 14,200 Ethiopian Jews were daringly airlifted out in a single day. As the scripture says, 'I will bring your children from the east and gather you from the west. I will say to the north, Give up, and to the south, Keep not back. Bring my sons from afar, and my daughters from the ends of the earth!' (Isaiah 43:5,6).

David Hathaway, *Prophetic Vision*, Vol 8, 1998

Jews are now flooding into Israel at a rate of over a thousand a day. But some ask, Did these prophecies refer to an earlier return in 530 BC, the one after the exile? No, those prophecies spoke only of Judah and Benjamin returning, not the whole twelve tribes (read Ezra 1:5) and only a proportion (remnant) of them. These prophecies speak of all the twelve tribes of Israel returning from a worldwide scattering after about 2,500 years. God told Hosea that, eight centuries BC; God told Isaiah that, seven centuries BC; God told Ezekiel that, five centuries BC.

Here is God's word to Hosea (1:11): 'And the two tribes of Judah and the ten tribes of Israel shall be gathered together under one head.'

Here is God's word to Isaiah (11:11,12): 'In that day, the Lord will extend his hand a second time [that is, in addition to the exile], and will bring together the outcasts of Israel (the ten tribes) and gather the dispersed of Judah (the two tribes) from the four corners of the earth.' That is why the State of Israel calls itself 'Israel' and not 'Judah'. Only Judah was gathered after the exile.

Here is God's word to Ezekiel (37): 'Behold, I will take the stick of the ten tribes of Israel . . . and I will join with it the stick of Judah's (two tribes) and make them one stick, that they may be one stick . . . thus says the Lord God, behold I will gather the people of Israel from the nations among which they were scattered and will gather them from all directions and bring them back to their own land and I will make them one nation in the land.'

Now, in our own days, God has done this very miracle. We see on our maps the State of Israel. The Bible says they are being gathered back to meet their Messiah, Jesus Christ, when he descends from heaven to Jerusalem.

The Bible says that this creation of the State of Israel will cause a lot of problems to nations around – which it is doing, isn't it? Jerusalem will be an insoluble problem. (So Mr Foreign Secretary, look out!). Politicians will fail if they don't solve it God's way! But eventually only Christ's return will solve the problem.

Fashionable Fallacies which Blunt Perception

There are three main fashionable fallacies which hinder some from seeing the significance of what is happening all about us. They are:

1. The assertion that the disciples expected Christ to return in their lifetime, while ignoring statements that it would be after a long time, together with blindness to prophecies which say that 2,520 years would elapse before Israel's return to Palestine;
2. Teaching that God has abandoned Israel, and that now all the promises refer only to 'spiritual Israel', i.e. the Christian Church;
3. That the return from the exile (533 BC) satisfies all the prophecies, which is coupled with a failure to note all that the Scriptures say about the *Diaspora,* the period of the Jews living outside of Palestine.

Unless I deal with those points first, the impact of the list of signs happening in our time will have been lessened. So we will take those points in order.

When scrutinising the first fallacy, let us consider the problem that the Lord Jesus himself faced. He had to keep his early Church alive with expectancy for his coming. The Church which said, 'My Lord delays his coming', would fall into drowsy spiritual sleep (Matthew 25:5). If he had revealed that 2,000 years would elapse, their expectancy would collapse.

So, very cleverly, Jesus gives enigmatic sayings which fulfil two needs. The need for Christians down the centuries and insight for those near the end of the age.

'After a Long Time'

Q Where then are the hints that Christ's return would be after a long time?

The following is taken from my booklet *Advent or Atom.*

Even if the disciples expected Christ to return in their time, it would not contradict Christ's promise to return. It would merely mean that they were looking for the signs foretold by the Lord. And it confirms that those signs were definitely foretold. They are actually happening today as never before and are significant because *they are accompanied by certain long-term prophetic processes which are also terminating in our times.*

Besides, it should be noted that Jesus and those who record his teaching clearly indicated that it would be after a long time. In Matthew 24:4, Jesus said, 'Take care that no one deceives you, for many will come in my name saying, I am Christ, and shall deceive many; and you shall hear of wars and rumours of wars, but see that you are not alarmed, for all these things must come to pass, but the end is not yet. The gospel must first be preached in all the world for a witness to all nations and then shall the end come.' There are still tribes today which have not heard the gospel and in whose language no portion of Scripture has yet been printed.

The Lord then outlined a process of history in which the fall of Jerusalem would happen as it did in AD 70. Then the Jews would be scattered among all nations and Jerusalem governed by Gentiles (which ended in 1967), see Luke 21:24. He spoke also of the rise of the false prophet of the desert (Mohammed, AD 604) and of a head of false Christianity in the 'inner rooms' (Matthew 24:26). These deceptions concerning false christs and false prophets continue down the centuries until the end times after the Israelites regain Jerusalem. The end times become marked by fear at the release of cosmic powers and a banding together of nations to find solution. Deceptions will continue to the end, and will 'deceive even the true elect if that were possible' (Matthew 24:24; Mark 13:22).

In Matthew 25:5, Jesus shows that because the Bridegroom (Christ) seemed to delay his coming, the Church would fall into spiritual slumber, which it did in the Middle Ages. The delay of Jesus was 'like a man travelling away into a far country' (v 14) and, only *'after a long time'* (v 19), the Lord would return to reckon with his servants.

A Thousand Years as One Day

This is again emphasised by an earlier parable told in Luke 19:11, because the disciples thought the Kingdom was to come immediately. 'A certain nobleman went into a far country to receive for himself a kingdom and to return.' Again in Matthew 24:48 there is a warning against backsliders because Jesus 'is a long time coming'. In Mark 13:34, Christians are to watch whether their master comes in the evening or at midnight or in the morning. In 2 Peter 3:8, we are reminded that a day in the sight of the Lord is as a thousand years, and a thousand years as one day, so do not question 'Where is the promise of his coming?'

Peter said in Acts 3:21 that heaven had received Jesus at the ascension 'until the time of universal restoration' spoken of by the prophets. One prophet, Hosea, said this would be two days after the ascension (Hosea 5:15 – probably meaning millennial days of 1,000 years each) before the resurrection of his people (6:2) for 'his coming is as assured as the dawn' (6:3).

So Paul writes to the Thessalonians (2 Thessalonians 2:2) concerning the coming of our Lord Jesus Christ, to tell them 'not to become
easily unsettled or alarmed by some prophecy, report or letter supposed
to come from us, saying that the day of the Lord is at hand. Don't let
anyone deceive you in any way, for that day will not come until the
falling away from the faith comes first and the lawless one is revealed,
the son of perdition' (like Judas Iscariot, who misused his bishopric,
Acts 1:20, John 17:12, cf. 2 Thessalonians 2:3). This turned out to be
a long process of history. See Dr A.J. Gordon's *Behold He Cometh*
(Thyan, 1934). The Early Fathers of the first centuries prayed that the
Roman Empire would continue as the restraining power, because when
the last Roman emperor disappeared (as he did in AD 610), a worse
power would possess Rome and corrupt Christianity from within; the
deception being subtle enough almost to deceive the elect (Matthew
24:24–26), and certainly to deceive the insincere (2 Thessalonians
2:10,11). This power would first be curbed by the return to the
Scriptures and finally destroyed by Christ's return (2 Thessalonians
2:8, Revelation 19:12–21).

Thus the knowledge that the period between the Ascension and the
Return would be a long one is inherent in many scriptures. However,
the real reason that the sceptical cannot see the promise is that they do
not believe it can happen. As Peter goes on to say, they hold a materi-
alistic theory of evolution which denies to God the power to intervene.
'All things continue as they were from the beginning of creation.' St
Peter continues that they would be wilfully blind to the fact that creation was by God and deny that he interrupted history by the Flood
(2 Peter 3:3–6).

HAS GOD ABANDONED ISRAEL?

The prophecies that Israel would be dispersed in the *Diaspora* are dealt
with in Chapters 7 and 11. God reveals that all Israel would be dispersed (hence the name *Diaspora*), but that only a remnant would
return after the exile. The rest would return 'at the end of the age'.

St Paul refers to the born-again Christian believers as spiritual children of Abraham, but does that mean that Israel has been deleted from
God's purpose for Israel? The importance of the question is whether
we see significance in the amazing reappearance of Israel in Palestine
today.

Paul himself, however, refutes that misunderstanding. In Romans
11, he says that only a remnant of Israel would believe on Christ, but
at the end 'all Israel' will be grafted back, 'so all Israel will be saved'.

Paul is referring to Old Testament promises. In the Old Testament
those very prophecies which said Israel would be cast out, also say
very clearly that God will never abandon Israel. God told Moses this.

He told Hosea this. He told Jeremiah this. He told Ezekiel this.

In Leviticus 26, God describes the 2,520 years of *Diaspora* which Israel has experienced. Then at the end of that long list of punishments, God says in verses 44 and 45, 'Yet in spite of this, when they are in the land of their enemies, I will not reject them or abhor them so as to destroy them completely, breaking my covenant with them. I am the Lord their God. But for their sake I will remember the covenant with their ancestors whom I brought out of Egypt in the sight of the nations to be their God. I am the Lord.'

This is repeated in Deuteronomy 28. To Jeremiah, when that dispersion was commencing, God said that the sun and moon would cease before God would even think of abandoning Israel. 'If these depart from me, says the Lord, then the seed of Israel shall also depart from me.'

Then God says, 'If you can measure endless space, then I will cast off Israel'. He repeats the assurance in chapter 33. If day and night ceases, then he will cast off Israel.

Once when I was in Palestine a man said to me, 'Those Israelis called Zionists think that the prophecies about their return refer to this century, but of course they were only about the return from the exile.'

I replied that Isaiah 11:11 says *God will bring them back a second time*. However, I added hastily, don't forget that in those prophecies *God instructed fair treatment to the Palestinians* (Ezekiel 47:21–23).

The Limited Exile

Those who say that God's promises to restore Israel referred to the end of 70 years exile (five centuries before Christ), fail to see the greater overall picture.

After the exile, only the two tribes of Judah and Benjamin returned. This is clear from Ezra's record of it. In Ezra 2:1 and 4:1, it clearly states that it was only from the tribes of Judah and Benjamin that a remnant returned to Jerusalem. The rest of the twelve tribes remained and spread worldwide. They made pilgrimages to Jerusalem only for the main feasts. That is why at Pentecost, when Peter preached, Israelites had come from all over the world. 'There were staying in Jerusalem, Jews, devout people out of every nation under heaven.'

Then a list of 15 tongues was given. They had been placed by God in their 15 different countries to be the start points for the gospel. Paul always went first to the synagogues. Most of Peter's first converts were from the Gentile proselytes in those synagogues. At the end of the age, Isaiah was told that this *Diaspora* would be gathered into a State of Israel, 'from the four corners of the world' (Isaiah 11:12).

So let the scales drop from your eyes as you recognise the significance of the presence on the map of the State of Israel. 'When you see this,' said Jesus, 'know that my return is near.'

It is stated in Daniel 12:12 that the Israeli who reaches the year 1335 will be blessed. Dr Richardson commented, 'Our year 1917 is the year 1335 in the Mohammedan calendar when the Balfour Declaration established a home in Palestine. Just before Jerusalem fell, newspapers published in that city bore the date 1335 AH on one side of its heading, and the Western date AD 1917 on the other.'

In 1886, thirty years earlier, Dr Grattan Guinness correctly read these prophecies and wrote in *Light for the Last Days*, 'There can be no question that those who live to see the year 1917 will have reached one of the most important of these terminal years.'

Tantalising Technique

Here in the book of Daniel, God used a technique similar to that of Christ's. Daniel was anxious to know 'how long it would be' before the end of the age. If God had said, 'Not for another 2,500 years', Daniel would have despaired. Instead he is given mysterious figures which looked as if it would not be too long, but if those figures meant years and not days, it would bring it to our times.

God said that those living in those times 'would understand', but until then, 'the meaning of the words were shut up and sealed until the time of the end' (Daniel 12:9). God has now given that insight as we shall see. Remember that the Bible believer on his knees can see farther than the Bible sceptic on his tiptoes!

S U M M A R Y

EFFECTIVENESS OF EVIDENCE FROM PROPHECIES

Two benefits of evidence from prophecy:
1. For Christ's first coming it proves his claims, prophesied by many prophets.
2. For Christ's second coming, it is topical and makes the Bible relevant for non-Christians today. They see that events prophesied are today's world news.

Fashionable fallacies which blunt perception to significance of modern events:

1. That disciples expected Christ's return in their lifetime. Reply:

- They were intended to so that their hopes were kept alive. Acts 1:6,7; Jn 21:21,23; Dan 12:8,9,13.
- Enigmatic metaphors intended to keep expectancy alive, e.g. Mark 9:1–2 says they will not die until the Kingdom comes with power. Next verse shows Transfiguration as a fulfilment and Luke 9:28 connects the two. Power came to spiritual Kingdom at Pentecost. Also, e.g. John 21:21–23. John corrects wrong impression in v 23.
- 'Certain things'. Jesus did not know actual date (Mk 13:32), but he knew it would be after a long time: Matt 24:4 'These things must first be fulfilled but the end is not yet . . . gospel first to all nations'.

2. That God abandoned Israel in favour of the Church. Reply:

- Rom 11:24 Israel to be grafted back in. Lev 26:44; Jer 33:24–26.

3. That Israel's return refers to end of 70 years exile. Reply:

- From exile only two tribes returned (Ezra 2:1, 4:1).
- From the *Diaspora* all tribes are to return (Is 11:12, Ezek 37:16–24, Hos 1:10,11).

What things were actually prophesied?
- Fall of Jerusalem AD 70, scattering of Jews (Luke 21:24)
- Rise of Mohammed (Matt 24:24).
- The return of Israel after 2,520 years from 603 BC.
- Matt 25:5 Coming delayed so Church falls asleep (v. 48). Luke 19:12 'Far country'. 2 Thess 2:3 falling away first.
- Two thousand year-days Hosea 5:15; 6:2; 2 Pet 3:8.

2 SIGNS
A USEFUL ACROSTIC

'When you see these signs,' said the Lord Jesus Christ, 'know that my return is near.' So let us take the word 'signs' as an acrostic to use when discussing them with a friend:

- 'S' for Science;
- 'I' for Israel;
- 'G' for Gospel;
- 'N' for Nations and Nature;
- 'S' for Society.

'S' IS FOR SCIENCE

'Science and travel shall greatly increase.' That is what God told Daniel in chapter 12 verse 4. Every time you pass a travel agent, you can say to your friend 'Daniel 12:4!' Every time an airliner flies over your head, you can point up and say, 'Daniel 12:4'.

'What do you mean?' he will say, and there is your subject opening up the curious enquirer. The two are tied together. Science led to travel. Travel for the masses. 'Many', says the verse. Two hundred years or so ago, very few moved any farther than to the next village. In social geography, students learn that the first invention to make the boys visit the lasses in the next village was the boneshaker bicycle, and later the motorcar for the select few. Now, 400 passengers in one aeroplane at a time speed through the air all over the world.

Another verse you can have up your sleeve is Isaiah 60:8,9. 'Your sons and daughters shall come from afar flying like a cloud'; or Isaiah 31:5, 'The Lord shall deliver Jerusalem like birds flying'. Both allude to the aeroplane. In 1917, the Turks fled out of Jerusalem when the British planes flew over the city. Not a shot was fired and the migration of Jews back to the land began as prophesied.

However, increase in science and knowledge also brought bad results. With the increase in education came many unbelieving teachers. That too was prophesied. 'They shall be for ever learning, but never come to the knowledge of the truth' (2 Timothy 3:7). That will be in the last days when perilous times will come.

'There will be a strong delusion, so that all who do not want to be saved will believe the devil's lie' (2 Thessalonians 2:8–11). We have seen in Volumes 1 and 2 how the devil's lie of evolution is propagated

at every level. This has brought lawlessness and massacre, often justified as operating the 'survival of the fittest' theory. 'Don't give them
hospitals or social help,' said Herbert Spencer, 'otherwise the unfit will
not perish.' 'The master race must dominate by war,' said Haekel to
Darwin's horror and Hitler's delight.

Figure 2.1. 19th-century cartoons of Darwin.

Source unknown

Nuclear Fission

Worst of all, the very existence of our planet has been threatened by
the science of nuclear fission. The release of sub-atomic forces within
the elements is triggered off by uranium. The horrific forces within
uranium are released by separating Uranium 235 from Uranium 238.
God put them together to stabilise them.

Jesus gave this peril as a sign. In the Greek, all three Synoptic
Gospels report, 'The forces that are within uranium shall be released'.

That will cause 'men's psyche to fail with fear' (phobias). Peter, learning from Jesus, wrote, 'The elements shall melt with fervent heat'.

The *Dictionary of Science* defines element as 'A substance consisting entirely of atoms of the same atomic number'. Uranium is an element. The old Greek word *stoicheia* used by Peter and translated 'element' has exactly the same meaning. The word 'atom' was an equivalent used by Leucippus 400 BC. Uranium from which atom bombs are made is an element.

Peter speaks of the terrific heat wrought by the release of power within uranium as 'fervent heat'. It approaches that of the sun. One exploded in the Mexican desert and fused the surrounding sand into a sea of glass.

The use of the word *uranos* by the Lord seems to be the Lord's foreknowledge of future events which would lend deeper meanings to the prophecies Daniel was told. It was more than coincidence which made the German scientist call it uranium when it was discovered in 1784. The word *uranos* in Luke 21:26 is etymologically the same as uranium, according to the *Oxford Dictionary*.

'I' IS FOR ISRAEL

Scores of prophecies have said that God would bring Israel back to their ancient land after two-and-a-half thousand years scattering. Some have blunted the impact of this amazing miracle by saying that God was only referring to the return from exile. But only remnants from the tribe of Judah and Benjamin returned from the 70-years exile. Read Ezra 1:5 and 4:1.

God told Isaiah, Jeremiah, Ezekiel, Amos and Hosea that it will be all the reunited twelve tribes who will return before the Lord comes. Paul sums it up in Romans chapter 11 by saying, 'So all Israel shall be saved'.

Another theological fashion which blunted the impact of prophecy in Scripture was to say that Jesus was referring only to spiritual Israel, namely, the Church. But, inasmuch as Jesus said that Jerusalem would fall and his nation would be 'led captive into all nations', so, just as realistically as a people, Israel would be brought back. They would be scattered among the nations only 'until the Times of the Gentiles are completed'. Jerusalem would be ruled by Gentiles, that is non-Jews for that two-and-a-half thousand years.

It was in 1967 by the 'six day war' that Israel actually regained rule in Jerusalem. This was for the first time in 2,520 years.

Hosea was the first prophet to be told by God that both the ten tribes (Ephraim) and the two tribes (Judah with Benjamin) would return united in the last days. Hosea's warning in 770 BC was primarily to the ten tribes. They are often called Israel when it should be Ephraim (Hosea

11:8) which represents the ten northern tribes. Judah had not become so wicked by that time. In Hosea chapter 2, God says that the ten tribes of Israel (Ephraim) will be utterly taken away. Judah will be spared until later, but both Ephraim and Judah will be brought back together.

'Then shall the children of Judah and the children of Israel [Ephraim] be gathered back together and appoint themselves one head' (Hosea 1:11). Yes, there is only one government over Israel today and one Prime Minister.

Next it was Amos (9:8,9) in 750 BC who was sent by God to warn the ten tribes to repent or they would be the first to be scattered. 'I will cause you to go into captivity, says the Lord.' 'The sanctuaries of Israel will be laid waste.'

Then comes this amazing prediction, 'Behold,' says the Lord, 'I will command and I will sift the house of Israel among all nations just as corn is sifted in a sieve, yet shall not one least grain fall to the ground.' In other words, Israel will never be wiped out in spite of many Hitlers and in spite of scattering among the nations.

Indeed, to Hosea, God had said that they would be scattered for over two millennial days (6:2) and exist without a king, without a prince, without temple sacrifices, without idolatry, without priests wearing ephod robes, and without an idol. A rabbi of a London synagogue identified that for me as what they called the *Diaspora* of the last 2,520 years.

Yet, even though they have been without a country or king or priest or sacrifice, yet purified from idolatry, 'Afterwards shall the children of Israel *return* and seek the Lord their God . . . in the latter days' (Hosea 3:4,5).

God told the same to Amos (9:14,15): 'I will bring again the captivity of my people of Israel and they shall build the waste cities and inhabit them. They shall plant vineyards and drink its wine. They shall make gardens and eat their fruit. I will plant them back upon their own land and they shall never again be up-rooted out of their land which I have given them, says the Lord your God.'

The sceptical critics said Amos could never have written that because he was only bent on forecasting Israel's doom. Events have revealed how wrong they were. Other prophets have said how Israel's deserts would be made to blossom again as a rose. Vast irrigation plans have enabled Israel to produce and export to the shops of the world the fruits of their land.

Judah Next

When Judah also forsook God over 100 years later, it became their turn to be warned by the prophets and scattered from 603 BC onwards. But

God told those same prophets also that it would be the united twelve tribes which would return.

Isaiah was first told in chapter 11 verses 10–16, 'It shall come to pass in that day, that the Lord will set his hand the second time to restore what is left of his people. He will set up a flag of all the nations [the world surrounded by the olive branch], and shall assemble the outcasts of Israel, and gather together the dispersed of Judah from all over the earth . . . Ephraim [10 tribes] and Judah [2 tribes] will not vex each other' but be united. They shall fly down the Gaza strip (literally 'upon the shoulders of the Philistines towards the west'), frustrate those in the east (like Saddam of Iraq) and the kingdom of Jordan (children of Ammon or Amman) will be neutral or be quiet.

Jeremiah and Ezekiel, who prophesied during the exile of Judah, were also told by God that Judah and Ephraim would return united in the last days. Jeremiah makes the distinction between the 70 years exile of Judah and the return of all the Diaspora.

Ezekiel is told in 37:19–22, 'Take two sticks, one to represent Ephraim's ten tribes and one to represent Judah's two tribes. Join the two sticks together, because I will make them one nation on their land. They shall not be divided into two kingdoms any more.' That is the significance of the presence of the new nation of Israel.

'It is causing great difficulties,' someone objected. That also is a sign. The opposition from ethnic groups around is clearly foretold. 'Jerusalem shall become a burdensome problem,' God told Zechariah, 'like a heavy stone which anybody trying to lift will rupture himself.' (Zechariah 12:3) Only the return of Christ to reign in Jerusalem will solve that problem, when all nations will come before him for judgement on how they treated his brethren (Matthew 25:32). 'They scattered my people and divided my land' (Joel 3:2).

The nation of Israel will be converted to Christ when they see him descend to the Mount of Olives. They will see the wounds of his crucifixion (Zechariah 12:10 and Revelation 1:7) and mourn deeply that this was the Saviour they rejected.

'G' IS FOR GOSPEL

How is the gospel progressing? That is the key to history. It is an eye-opener to many when they realise that history is overruled by God according to how the gospel is reaching earth's millions.

This is the great contribution which the historic interpretation of the book of Revelation made. We shall explore this at the end of this book, but it is expressed by the Lord Jesus in Matthew 24:14. 'This gospel of the kingdom will be preached throughout the whole world, as a testimony to all nations, and then the end will come' (RSV).

Notice that the good news is to be preached as a witness (*marturi-*

Figure 2.2. Satellite winged angel? Literally 'messenger flying in mid-heaven', Revelation 14:6. Today's gospel messages radiate from satellites and bounce off the ionosphere in mid-heaven.

on). The name 'martyrs' comes from this word. It does not mean that all nations will be converted. It means that the witness must come to all nations.

How is the witness to reach every nation? Jesus goes on to say it will often be through believers being arrested and dragged before anti-Christian authorities. This has been so down the ages and even now a large percentage have shut their gates to the gospel. Christians witness at the peril of their lives, but the Holy Spirit, said Jesus, will make the truth indisputable.

A modern means of bouncing belief over the boundaries is by radio. A clear hint of this is seen in Revelation 14:6. The proclamation is from 'mid-heaven'. 'Then I saw another messenger flying in mid-heaven with the eternal gospel to proclaim to those sitting upon the earth and to all ethnic groups and to all families and tongues and people; and saying in an amplified sound, "Fear God, and give him glory, for the hour of his judgement has come and worship him who is the maker of heaven and earth, the sea and the sources of water." '

This is a very free translation, but justified by the root meanings in the Greek. *Aggelos* means 'messenger', but can also be translated 'angel'. *Kathemenous* is from *kathemai* meaning to sit. Dr Marshall translates the phrase *epi tous kathemenous* in his *Greek New Testament* (Bagster) as, 'over the ones sitting on the earth'. We can see the picture of individuals and families sitting to listen to the gospel.

What is mid-heaven? It is the ionosphere. This is what bounces the radio-waves around the world. Without it, the radio programmes would reach no farther than 30 miles at ground level.

Another 'winged messenger in mid-heaven' is the radio and television satellite whose programmes are received by dishes for those 'sitting on earth' around their sets. You have, of course, seen pictures of this 'winged messenger' (Fig 2.2).

Is there an indication of when this would particularly apply? There are two things. Judgement is near, and it is at a time when the role of God as Creator has been widely questioned. See *Evidence for Truth, Volume 1: Science*. Christian broadcasts on evidence for creation are therefore very relevant in reply to atheistic propaganda.

Satan's propaganda through the media is graphically pictured in Revelation 16:13–16. From the mouth of propagandists, 'uncleanness' is poured out from three main sources – the old pagan dragon; the beast and the false prophet. When? Verse 16 says, as Armageddon approaches. That is the last battle of the age. But God has his answer to the 'Prince and power of the air' who is Satan (Ephesians 2:2). The gospel sound, *phthongos*, went into all the earth and their words *hremata* (active words) to the ends of the earth. Romans 10:18 quotes from Psalm 19:

> The heavens declare the glory of God, and the firmament shows his handiwork. Day unto day utters speech and night after night shows knowledge. There is no speech or language where their voice is not heard. It is beamed out through all the earth, and the words to the ends of the world . . . The doctrine of the Lord is perfect, converting the soul.

Does not all this highlight the words of Jesus? 'This gospel of the kingdom will be preached throughout the whole world, as a testimony to all nations, and then shall the end come.' As this is the prime purpose of God, should it not be ours also?

'N' IS FOR NATIONS AND NATURE

All that is happening among the nations today is fully pictured in the prophecies concerning the near return of Christ. First the agony to find a solution to the problems. Jesus said, 'Upon the earth there will be distress among the nations with perplexity' (Luke 21:25).

The picture is of nations coming together in organisations to seek for solutions. Indeed, the word in the Greek which is translated 'distress' is a secondary meaning to the word *enoche* which was used for a club or organisation.

The title, United Nations Organisation, is fully anticipated here. It is also in Isaiah 11:10–16 which also speaks of the troubles caused by Israel's return. 'He shall set up a flag for the nations and shall assemble the outcasts of Israel and gather together the dispersed of Judah from the four corners of the earth.'

The Role of UNO in Prophecy

The United Nations Organisation plays a big role in modern affairs. Many of us think it is referred to in this chapter 11 of Isaiah. First let us put it in the right context. Does it refer to the latter days? The answer is yes, it's all about the millennium, the rule of Christ, also peace in the animal kingdom. It tells how it will be brought about. Verses 10 to 12 show that it would be when Israel is restored to Palestine. The flags or ensigns of powers are involved in the process. By God's overruling, they will feature in the restoration of Israel and the conflicts which should result.

As we read this chapter and give these peoples their modern names, we realise how the prophecy describes the whole scenario being played out in the Middle East.

Verse 12 says that one of those two flags will be for the nations. Notice the plural; so it means nations united for action. What is the emblem upon the United Nations flag? It is planet earth surrounded by olive branches. This is the flag then that verse 2 says God will raise for the nations to assemble the ten Ephraim tribes and the two Judean tribes, making twelve tribes of Israel reunited (just as God also told three other prophets) and they would be 'gathered from the four corners of the earth'.

That happened in 1947. When Britain was preventing Jews from returning, UNO took over the responsibility and, to the surprise of all, signed the document creating the State of Israel. This was implemented the following year and Israel has now celebrated its Jubilee.

What is that second flag? It is the flag of Israel (Isaiah 11:10). What is the emblem foretold for it? It says it shall be the root of Jesse. What is the emblem of Israel's flag today? It is the Star of David, the son of Jesse. Jesse is the root from which the tree of the royal house of David sprang. Under the flag, verse 11 says the Lord will bring back the people 'for the second time'.

The reaction to the new State of Israel is then described in verse 14 concerning the invasion by the surrounding peoples during the Six Day War and Israel's counter attack. They swooped down the Gaza Strip in the west and devastated the attackers on the east, but the king of Jordan, in capital Amman, became neutral. Egypt was routed right to the Suez Canal (v 15) and later Iraq, astride the Euphrates, was scorched. All this was so that Israel could continue to return. So the Arabs will not stop Israel, yet God says he will bless them as well as Israel.

When the root and Branch of Jesse, Jesus Christ, reigns, all the peoples (Gentiles) will seek him and the earth will be at rest in the millennium (Isaiah 11:1–9).

The Role of Europe in Prophecy

The formation of a States of Europe is also a sign indicated in Scripture. It has been so clear in Holy Scripture that believers have written about it for the last hundred years, e.g. the fourth empire of Daniel's image in chapter 2 is widely held as the iron Roman Empire. This divided into two as depicted by the two legs, the western and the eastern empire; then the ten toes depict an amalgamation of those countries in the last days.

It is soon before the return of Christ, because God said, 'In the days of those kings, he will set up a kingdom which will never be destroyed.' How? It will be by the stone uncreated which will descend from heaven and smash the image on its toes.

This amalgam of European powers will be that of separate sovereign states, because it says, 'In the days of those kings'. Note the plural. That is why when the picture is repeated in Revelation 13, the one crown is taken from the one emperor and placed as separate crowns upon each of the ten heads of the beast. It is interesting that even European nations which have no king as such, still refer to themselves as sovereign states.

We have heard a lot about monetary union and single currency and opposition for and against. Monetary union is clearly depicted in Revelation 13.

'The beginnings of sorrows' in Matthew 24:6–8 are identified with the world wars. Before the First and Second World Wars, battles were merely the matter of professional armies, but the new feature was that whole populations were involved. All were recruited. 'Nation shall rise against nation and kingdom against kingdom.' Before that, the population only heard reports of battles, 'rumours of wars'. Note that reporters were called 'Reuters' or reporters of rumours.

'N' can also stand for natural signs, because the Lord Jesus goes on to say that there would be 'famines, epidemics and earthquakes in many places'.

People ask whether there has been an increase in these things or is it just that the media is able to tell us more about them? The answer is that records show a very big increase. I give figures in Volume 2, Chapter 20, on 'God is a Geologist', showing that the increase had been tenfold. Concerning famines, we have no need to emphasise the scale of these sad events.

'S' IS FOR SOCIETY

Many scriptures speak of stress, vandalism, terrorism, lawlessness and the increase of wickedness which would characterise 'the last days'.

2 Timothy 3:1–6 reads like a daily press report. In fact, when one

man in prison heard the passage read out, he asked, 'What paper was that in?'

> In the last days there will come times of stress, for people will be lovers of self, lovers of money, proud, arrogant, blasphemous, disobedient to their parents, ungrateful, unholy, cruel, refusing reconciliation, slanderers, sexual libertines, fierce, haters of good, treacherous, reckless, swollen with conceit, lovers of pleasure rather than lovers of God, holding a form of religion but denying its power. We should avoid such people and desires.

This prophecy then moves on to the feature of increased education which does not promote God's revealed truth.

> They will be for ever learning but can never arrive at the truth . . . opposing the truth, men of corrupt minds and counterfeit faith . . . evil impostors, from bad to worse, deceivers and being deceived . . . people will not endure sound teaching . . . teachers will turn it into myths.

It is this unbelief and perverting of the truth which is the cause of our social ills today. Young people are not given guidance from divine authority which promises, 'Do these things and you will prosper in a good and happy life'.

An increasing number are accusing the Bible of being a collection of myths in spite of evidence to the contrary. As Peter prophesied, 'They will run greedily into error'. Even blatant attacks have been made upon the beautiful character of the Lord Jesus Christ. Films have been made with this object, but perhaps the most fantastic has been the books by Dr T. She wrote, *The Gospels and Qumran*, in 1981, *Qumran Origins of the Christian Church*, in 1983 and *Jesus the Man*, in 1988.

She said that the Gospels were so much myth that they were all in secret code. They had double meanings behind everything. The Dead Sea Scrolls helped her to crack the code. This was further developed. She said Jesus was the 'wicked priest' of the scrolls who opposed John the Baptist. Jesus was crucified in Qumran by the Dead Sea, not in Jerusalem, and Pilate went to Qumran to condemn him. The two thieves were also crucified in Qumran and their names were Judas Iscariot and Simon Magus of Acts 8. Simon Magus was also ascribed to four other characters in the New Testament. He was also Simon the Leper of Matthew 26:6; Lazarus, raised from the dead; Lazarus in Abraham's bosom of the parable; also the high priest Ananias. Multiple personalities were also extended to the Virgin Mary; Dr T's secret code found she was Dorcas whom Peter raised from the dead. The final touches, however, were that Jesus married Mary Magdalene, had two sons and one daughter, but divorced her and married again. Who was Mary Magdalene? she asks. She was Jairus' daughter (age 12) whom Jesus raised from the dead. She was also Rhoda who opened the door to Peter, but she was 'mad', so this is why Jesus divorced her.

Degrading and Destructive Fantasies

All this would be painful if it were not so ridiculous and without a shred of evidence. But in 1990, Australian TV made it into a programme for Palm Sunday. It seems to me that Dr T's last fantasies were transferred from the book of Hosea to Jesus. That prophet experienced an unhappy marriage with one who became a prostitute. As a result, he divorced her after he had had two sons and a daughter. As Dr T transfers the date of the scrolls from two centuries BC to the first century AD, she would include Hosea whose prophecy is among the Qumran collection. Her date is impossible, however, because all the Old Testament had been translated into Greek in 288 BC. That included Hosea.

Unfortunately, the general public today knows so little of Scripture that it is gullible to the tales of the myth-makers, thus their books are selling like wildfire worldwide, especially since the TV programme. If you are confronted with such fantasies, you may find the most effective reply is to use it as evidence and say, 'Yes, prophecy says that that will be a sign of error in the last days'.

You could also quote 2 Thessalonians 2 which says that God will allow a strong delusion for those who do not want to be saved so that they will believe a lie. That passage also speaks of the widespread lawlessness as a social sign of the times. This would arise from a 'falling away from the faith'. The word actually means apostasy. That word includes those within the Church who 'deny the Lord who bought them'. The media makes good capital out of leaders who let the Church down.

More damage is done by one sceptical bishop than the good done by 50 good bishops and there are many very good bishops, learned stalwarts of the faith. An example of a sceptical bishop, is one that says the biblical stories of Jesus' birth are 'midrash' meaning fanciful stories which were not meant to be taken literally. This again can be turned into prophetic evidence. 1 John 4:1–3 says:

> Beloved, believe not every spirit, but test the spirits whether they are of God, because many false prophets have gone out into the world . . . Every spirit that does not confess that Jesus Messiah has come in the flesh, is not of God. This is the spirit of antichrist that you have heard shall come.

Along with Jesus, Paul and Peter, John says that such would come from within the Church (1 John 2:18–23).

It really depends upon who is speaking the truth. Which would you rather believe? Bishop S, who disbelieves Christ's miracles 2,000 years on from when they happened or Luke who records eyewitnesses of them in AD 54? Contrary to Bishop S, Luke claims his records to be factual: 'They were delivered to us by those who were *eye-witnesses* from the beginning . . . It seemed good to me having followed all things accurately to write an orderly account . . . that you may know the *certainty* of these things.'

What does John mean by 'test the spirit: believe not every spirit'. He does not mean be a medium for that is strictly forbidden throughout Scripture. He means that behind twisted doctrines is an evil spirit influencing the mind of sceptics. A doctrine has to be tested by the Scriptures which were inspired by the Holy Spirit.

Jesus warned that false christs and false prophets would arise and deceive many, especially the false prophet of the desert (Matthew 24:26).

Society does not realise how much damage has been done by the occult. A number of cases of rampage by a civilian with firearms has been the result of occult coaxing by evil spirits. This has been admitted by such cases as the one at Hungerford where a youth shot down some 16 civilians walking along the street outside his house. This increase in tampering with the occult is also a sign. 1 Timothy 4:1 says: 'The Holy Spirit expressly says that in the latter days many will depart from the faith and give heed to deceitful spirits and doctrines of demons.'

Why are the evil spirits getting more active and deceiving people? The demons themselves let out the reason when Christ was casting them out. 'Are you come to destroy us before the time?' They were confused. Was this the first coming of Christ or was this the second coming? They knew that when Christ came to judge, they would be destroyed in hell fire.

Now, as his return is getting near, the evil spirits and Satan know 'that their time is short' (Revelation 12). Their judgement and punishment for the disasters they have brought to God's good creation and mankind, is near, so they are having their last fling.

So then, I have given you a succinct summary under the acrostic SIGNS. There will be an enlargement upon many of the themes mentioned, but meanwhile the acrostic will help you to remember some of the main points for your use in conversation about contemporary catastrophes.

As a starter, write a potent prophecy opposite each letter. Then from memory add all the other references I give you below. Then mark all those references in your Bible.

SUMMARY

USEFUL ACROSTIC ON SIGNS

'When you see these signs, know that my return is near'

'S' for Science
- Knowledge of travel increased (Dan 12:4).
- Ever learning but erroneous (2 Tim 3:7).
- Strong delusion to believe evolution (2 Thess 2:8–11).
- Air travel from afar (Is 60:8,9).
- As birds flying (Is 31:5).
- Nuclear fission (Mk 13:25, 2 Pet 3:12).

'I' for Israel
- The re-united 10 and 2 tribes will return in the last days as Israel (Is 11:10–16; Jer 16:14–16).
- After a long time without a country (Hos 1:10,11; 3:4,5; Ezek 37:20–28; Amos 9:9–15.
- Moslem date 1335 = AD 1917 (Joel 3:1,2; Dan 12:11,12).
- Nailprints to convert Israel (Rom 11:25,26; Zech 12:10).

'G' for Gospel
- All nations must hear as a witness (Matt 24:14).
- The ionosphere is in mid-heaven for radio waves and gospel proclamation (Rev 14:6).
- Mouth of propaganda by Satan (Rev 16:13).
- Christian radio penetrates closed countries (Rom 10:17,18).

'N' for Nations and Nature
- Old Roman Empire now European Sovereign States before Christ descends to rule: Dan 2:28–45; Rev 13:17,18.
- United Nations flag regulates Israel's return; Gentile nations ruled Jerusalem until 1967 (Lk 21:24,25; Is 11:10–16).
- World Wars (Matt 24:6,7).
- *Natural Signs*: Increase in earthquakes, famines, diseases (Matt 24:8).

'S' for Society
- Stress, vandalism, terrorism, lawlessness (2 Tim 3:1–6).
- Truth forsaken by teachers (2 Tim 4:3,4).
- Occult dabbling increase (1 Tim 4:1,2).
- Lawlessness (2 Thess 2:7–9).
- Wickedness increases (Lk 21:34–36; Dan 12:10).
- Wickedness decreases love of truth (Matt 24:9–13).
- Fears and phobias at society's unrest (Lk 21:26–32).

Now mark the texts in your Bible so that you can use them easily.

3   WORLD HISTORY FORETOLD FROM ABRAHAM TO ZECHARIAH
OLD TESTAMENT A TO Z OF PROPHECY

WHAT GOD FORETOLD TO ABRAHAM 2000 BC

Abraham had a horrific nightmare. It arose out of two fears. One was that,in obeying God's call, he had mortgaged his property to a certain Eliezer of Damascus. The second fear was that he had no son or heir. Now Abraham was very old and, according to the laws we know of those times, that would mean that all his property would be forfeited to Eliezer.

It was in the agony of such thoughts that God said to him, 'Don't fear, Abraham. I am your protecting shield and your tremendous reward. Eliezer won't grab your property and home. Your wife, Sarai, will give birth to your heir even though she is over 80 and descendants from her will multiply more than the number of stars.'

Because God himself pledged this impossibility, Abraham believed him. That act of faith God 'reckoned to Abraham instead of righteousness'. By that faith, God said that Abraham was saved.

But the strain had been great. The sun was going down amidst an angry red sky. Abraham fell into a deep sleep in which a horrible dense darkness burdened down on him. He was startled as he heard God speak to him.

The good news is that a great nation will spring from you and Sarai. The bad news is that they will be slaves in a foreign land for 400 years. But the good news is that I will deliver them and they will come to this land I promised with great wealth. They will be used by me to punish the Amorites who by that time will have become so foul that their cruelty and blasphemy will cry to heaven. Indeed, it is the cry of helpless babes which will come to me. Babies which they are burning alive in fires to Satan. Judgement must come to stop it.

The sun sank red and angry and thick smoke belched out from a pottery kiln, blacking out the stars. But something caused the horror to shrink away. It was a lamp of bright hope. It began to move between a sacrifice until the darkness fled (Genesis 15:17). Then the Lord made a covenant with Abraham. The Light of the World would come through Abraham and Sarai's seed.

'I give my guarantee of this land to you,' said the Lord. 'See, it is confirmed by the legal seal of sacrifice.'

But another ten years passed and no heir was born, so Sarai said, 'I'm 90 years old and you are 100 and still we wait. The law says you can have an heir through my servant.'

So Ishmael was born to Sarai's servant and grew to early teens. Abraham was so fond of him that he said to God, 'Let the Messiah come through Ishmael.'

But God said, 'No, through Sarai's son I will send the Messiah. I will bless Ishmael certainly and make him a great nation, but Sarai will bear a son next year and call him Isaac. It is through Isaac's descendants that all the world will be blessed by the Saviour.'

So God knew the future and overruled history. The horror of 400 years slavery was fulfilled. The Promised Land was given. The Saviour did come; so that 2,000 years later Matthew opened the New Testament with these words, 'These are the ancestors of Jesus Christ, a descendant of King David and of Abraham'.

WHAT GOD SAID TO MOSES ABOUT HIS TIME PLAN

How appropriate it is that God's time plan is based upon your time piece, your clock or watch. Did you know that what the Lord Jesus called, 'the Times of the Gentiles' is based upon a very old system of time calculation and goes back beyond the time when God spoke to Moses 3,500 years ago? This system of time-keeping goes back to the Sumerians who lived 5,000 years ago soon after the Flood. Indeed, evidence exists that it was based on the 360-day calendar year which existed prior to the Flood. See *Evidence for Truth, Volume 1: Science*, Chapter 13. It is important to grasp this time concept because it reveals to you that God is God of the Ages. In his pre-announced purpose, he planned to implement it over long periods of time.

Archaeology has revealed that our time pieces and compasses were founded all that time ago. Why has your watch got 60 seconds to the minute? Why has your watch got 60 minutes to the hour? It is because the Sumerians calculated that way. They even added up in columns of 60. They also divided up the circle into 360. We still use 360 degrees for a circle and the compass maps out the globe on that basis.

God mapped out his time plan on that old method. He told Moses in Leviticus 26:18,21,24,28, that Israel would be scattered among the nations for 'seven times' and then return to God's ancient land.

Your question now will be. 'Seven times what?' Let me explain. *One 'Time' was an actual measurement of 360*. It could be days, years, or anything. In this case, it referred to years. Therefore, multiply 360 by 7 and that equals 2,520 years. That is the length of time Israel has been expelled from Palestine. They were first expelled in 603 BC and a home was granted them in 1917 by the 'Balfour Declaration'. That is, 2,520 years. Since then, the Israelis have been restoring the land to prosperity as God said they would. Seven times have passed since Israel's first scattering and lo and behold, they are back in God's land. There's evidence for you! And what an easy talking point when you show your watch to your friend!

There are two things to be clear on. One is that it is not dates which matter so much as time scales. The Jews were dispersed more and more during a period following 603 BC and so, in similar stages, they are being restored more and more during a period following 1917.

Second, this prophecy is about the return of Israel, not about the return of Christ. Jesus warned us against dating his return. Only the signs would show if his second coming is near.

So then, in Leviticus 26 God tells Moses about the 2,520-year dispersion. He does so in four places.

Four Examples of Seven 'Times'

In verse 18 of Leviticus 26, God says that if Israel forsakes God, disobeys his commandments and despises his statutes, 'they will be chastened for seven times' and the Promised Land of milk and honey will become barren.

In verse 21, God says, 'If you walk contrary to me and refuse to listen and ignore my health laws, your children and farm animals will suffer diseases for seven times.'

In verse 24, God said, 'If you still refuse to repent, you will be delivered into the power of your enemies for seven times.'

In verse 28, God says, 'If you still will not listen to my word, then for seven times I will destroy your false religion, your enemies will destroy your cities and you will be scattered among all nations and the sabbaths which you profaned will have rest in my land.'

You will notice that some translations have added the word 'more' to say 'seven times more'. There is no word 'more' in the Hebrew. This is a misunderstanding of the text. It does not mean that God will punish seven times more than they deserve. *The translators did not know that it was a period of time referred to based on the ancient measurement of 360.* **One 'Time' in Bible prophecy = 360 years.**

Four Examples of Year-day Prophecies

Concerning prophecy, there is a neglected area which is very effective in convincing the unconcerned. Many Christians don't even know about it. Yet God gave it as a special proof of truth for those living 'at the time of the end' (Daniel 12:9,10). Neglected Bible-believing scholars were Dr Adam Clark, Dr Grattan-Guinness and Dr Basil Atkinson. The witness of Christians would be greatly strengthened again today by getting to know about their findings.

God told Daniel that the believers living in the end times would understand something which was concealed even from Daniel. What is it that God wants us to know which is special for those living in the end times?

Daniel asked when these things will end. He asked about times and seasons. It wasn't good for him to know. We can see that it would have been discouraging for him to know that the glorious climax to God's plan was still 2,520 years off. So he is given a mysterious number and figures which he didn't understand. Those living in the last days will understand, God said. To Daniel it was sealed up, but in Revelation 22 it is unsealed for those living when the second coming of Christ is near. 'Behold I come quickly,' said Jesus. 'Do not seal up the meaning of these words.'

If the Lord made special provision for us to understand, it is surely wrong to ignore what he intends for the believer today. This is not to be avoided merely because some have misused these figures. Some foolishly predicted the date of the Lord's coming. Those who did were disobedient to Christ's words. 'The day and the hour no one knows.' But observe the signs.

How are we to apply these mysterious numbers? It was in the nineteenth century that Bible-believing scholars were given the clue. *They noticed that, in various places in Scripture, God made one day stand for a year.* There are five such cases in the Bible. They were to do with the spies, Moses' warnings, Ezekiel, Daniel and the Lord Jesus.

First, the spies. Their faith failed when they reported back that Palestine was impossible to conquer. They took 40 days to spy out the land, so Israel's punishment would be extended to 40 years wandering in the wilderness. I quote: 'Each day for a year,' says the Lord.

Who were the spies? How was it that 40 days spying led to 40 years wandering by Israel? The Israelites had been delivered out of slavery in Egypt. They were making their way across the desert to south of the Promised Land. At that time, the land was lush and fertile through rain and sunshine and rich soil. Twelve men were sent to spy out the land. The fruit was so large that the samples they brought back included a huge branch of grapes carried on a pole between two of them. After 40 days they returned, but they reported giants in the land and high city walls which ten of the spies said were too powerful to overcome.

The Israelites were frightened. They revolted and appointed a leader to take them back to Egypt. God was angry at their feeble faith. Moses pleaded with God to forgive them. 'This is the tenth time you have refused to listen,' God said. It was obvious that this rabble of slaves needed many years' training and learning to trust in the God of miracles. Yet, through those frightened, feeble followers, God would bring the world's Saviour. It was in this context that God uttered those beautiful words sung now in many a church: 'As truly as I live, all the earth shall be filled with the glory of the Lord'.

But the first stage was to take 40 years. The spies took 40 days to give a bad report. God was to take 40 years to turn a rabble into reliable believers. In Numbers 14:34, he said, 'According to the number of days in which you spied out the land, 40 days, for every day a year, you shall bear your iniquity for 40 years.'

This then is the background to the first of five instances where God shows that each day means a year. As these year-days unfold, they bring nearer that purpose just quoted, 'As surely as I live, says the Lord, all the earth will be filled with the glory of the Lord'.

This declared purpose was first given when that principle of prophecy was first declared – one day represents one year.

Secondly, this was enlarged upon when God told Moses about a measurement of seven 'times' duration as we have seen above. As each day equals a year, that means that Israel would be scattered from the Holy Land for over 2,520 years. For 2,520 years, Israel and then Judah were dispersed among the nations. Only a small percentage (remnant) returned to Judah after the exile; the rest still remained in various countries. They are called by the Jews themselves, the Diaspora or the dispersion. In Paul's day, they had set up synagogues all over the world. That is why Paul could travel along Roman roads and find a synagogue in most towns. Even as they were dispersed in various stages, over 2,500 years ago, so they would be regathered in various stages, as has been happening in our days.

An early stage in this resettlement in Palestine was revealed to Daniel in chapter 12. He was given the figure of 1335, but he didn't know where the starting date for that would be. This led to that remarkable fact that when the Turks were driven out of Jerusalem in 1917, the newspapers had two dates on them. In one corner was the Western date 1917 and in the other corner was the Eastern date – the figure given to Daniel, 1335. It was then that the Jews were granted a home in Palestine.

Now, Dr Grattan Guinness, writing in the 1880s – over 100 years ago – said that 1917 would be a very significant year. Dr Adam Clark, writing even earlier, over 150 years ago in 1830, worked on another figure. This was given in Daniel 8:14. He said this would be of great significance and worked it out at 1966 to 1967. What happened then? Israel re-occupied the Wailing Wall and governed the old city for the first time for 2,520 years. Clark also gave another date. He said that in

1947, Israel would replace Gentile government. That was the year in which the State of Israel was agreed to and the next year it was implemented.

Now some readers of prophecy got very excited about these dates and foolishly said that these figures indicated the year of Christ's return. It was nothing of the sort! They were ignoring Christ's warning that no one would know the day or hour of his return. What were the prophecies really about? They were referring to the re-gathering of Israel in various stages. Unfortunately, their foolishness discouraged many from studying God's timing of prophecy, yet God stated that he gave this insight especially for the last days. By not using it, effective proof of Bible truth is neglected.

Thirdly, Ezekiel. Where else does God show that one day stands for one year in prophecy? He gave it to Ezekiel 800 years later when Moses' ancient warning was about to be implemented. Israel would be scattered if they forsook God and sacrificed to devils. Alas, the day came when it happened. They had backslidden to idolatry and such horrible practices that at last God had to say 'Enough! I've had enough! I have sent you prophets to warn you, yet you persisted in burning your children alive to the heathen god Molech. In spite of my long-suffering, you killed my prophets who warned you against immorality, homosexuality, mugging and downtreading the poor. Ezekiel is my last prophet I send before I let you be invaded. If you don't listen to him, the warnings of Moses (in Leviticus 26) will be implemented. You will be scattered, you will be hounded from country to country. Your country will become desolate, yet you will never cease to be a nation and at the end I will bring you back to my land, but before that you will suffer terrible things – that is, unless you respond to my last warning through my prophet Ezekiel. To catch your attention, I have told him to do dramatic acts – acts in public places, things to make you stop and take notice! Ezekiel, lie on your side in front of a model of the city of Jerusalem for 390 days. Ezekiel, lie on your side before the model for 40 days. Each day represents a year.'

You will find this in Ezekiel 4:6, '40 days I assign you, a day for a year – each day represents a year.'

The **fourth** example of collating years with days is from the Lord Jesus himself. He referred to his ministry as being three-and-a-half days long. He did this to conceal when his crucifixion would take place. The Pharisees tried to scare him away. They said, 'Make yourself scarce because Herod is after your blood.'

Jesus replied to the effect that, 'It would not be fitting for any prophet to perish away from Jerusalem. Nevertheless, go and tell that fox, Herod, that I have ministered for two days, and will for tomorrow, but the day after, I will be offered up.' Thus Jesus prophesied a three-

and-a-half day-year ministry.

It is well known that Christ's ministry lasted three-and-a-half years, but Jesus called it three-and-a-half days. In so doing, he applied the prophecy in Daniel 9:26,27. Here Daniel was told that the Messiah would be cut off in half a week of years, but not for himself. It would be for others and his sacrifice would cause all other sacrifices to cease as unnecessary.

Let me give you the **fifth** example. Earlier in that chapter, Daniel was told that the Messiah would come in 70 weeks' time. The critics agree that each day of those weeks meant a year, and that therefore the prophecy meant that the Messiah would come in 490 years' time from Daniel's starting date – 70 x 7 = 490.

If you recognise this principle, it will open your eyes to the time plan of the God of Ages, and you will be one of 'the wise who understand, the time of the end' (Daniel 12:9,10).

WORLD HISTORY FORETOLD

A. Messiah to come through Isaac, Gen 17, through Judah, Gen. 49:10, succeeding Moses, Deut 18:15, through David, 2 Sam 7:16, through Zerubbabel, Zech 4:7, through Mary, Luke 3:27.

B. The order of events given to Joel, Ezekiel, Daniel and Zechariah:
(1) Israel will return in the latter days.
(2) When Israel is settled they will be invaded.
(3) The Lord will descend to judge the nations.
(4) The Lord will then rule over all the earth.
Note the order of events. The N.T. agrees with this order, e.g. Matt 25:31,32; 1 Cor 15:23–28; Rev 19 to 20.

C. Prophetic Time Span: The 7 'Times' or 2,520 years of dispersion of Israel among the nations.
(1) 360 degrees or periods come from Sumerian time unit of 360, Lev 26:18,21,24,28.
(2) Each day represents a year; Num 14:34, Ezek. 4:6, Luke 13:32,33, Dan 9:26.
• Therefore 360 x 7 = 2,520 years.
• Also, Daniel 1,260 x 2 = 2,520 years.
• First capture of Jerusalem 603 BC to AD 1917 = 2,520 years.
(3) In 1917 Balfour Declaration opened Palestine to Jews. 1917 was also Moslem year 1335, see Dan 12:12 (Dr Grattan Guinness calculated correctly 31 years before fulfilment).

Learn Numbers 14:21: 'Truly as I live, all the earth shall be filled with the glory of the Lord.'

WHAT GOD FORETOLD TO HOSEA

The northern ten tribes were the first to backslide into heathenism so, as the time drew near, 775 BC, Hosea was sent to give a final warning (Hosea 3). God foretold to Hosea that the ten tribes of northern Israel would be the first to go into exile. God told him that northern Israel would be without a country, without a king, without temple sacrifices, without idolatrous images, for a long time. After that, they would return.

God would not abandon Israel because of his covenant promise to Abraham. At the end of that terrible chapter, Leviticus 26, he said to Moses in verse 44, 'Yet for all that, when they are in the land of their enemies, I will not spurn them, neither will I abhor them so as to destroy them utterly or break my covenant with them, for I am the Lord their God; but I will, for their sake, remember the covenant with their forefathers.'

So, as you look at your watch (which is based on ancient time-keeping methods involving multiples of 60) and look at Israel back on the map of today, thank God that he kept his promise (even though it is 4,000 years old) to Abraham and that the seven 'times' are ended (see Chapter 10).

WHAT GOD FORETOLD TO AMOS

God could not find anyone faithful enough to take his warning to the ten tribes of northern Israel. None of the professionals, none of the priests, none of the politicians. So he sent a man who was a fruit picker and herdsman to warn them that the seven 'times' of Moses would start if they did not repent.

> Hear this word that the Lord has spoken against you people of Israel . . . 'You, only, have I known of all the families of the earth, therefore you are more responsible for forsaking the truth . . . Truly the Lord God does nothing without revealing his secret to his servants the prophets . . . The Lord God has spoken! Who can but prophesy?' (3:1–8)

One hundred and fifty years had passed since Israel had split into two. The ten tribes called Ephraim had strayed from the truth quicker than the two tribes called Judah. 'Therefore,' saith the Lord, 'they shall be the first to go into captivity' (6:7).

Judah was still more faithful under their King Uzziah, and would last another 150 years. Ephraim did not repent of her false religion and godless life; so the invasion came from the Assyrian Empire in north Mesopotamia in 722 BC. Yet God in his mercy told Amos at the end of his prophecy:

1. That the ten tribes would never be lost (9:9). There is no such thing as 'the lost tribes'. *They would be scattered through the nations, like seeds sown worldwide to establish synagogue centres, to be go-areas for the gospel later* (Acts 13:5; 14:1; 18:4). 'Sifted like a sieve but not one grain lost.' This was all fulfilled.
2. They would return to Palestine, and rebuild and plant and prosper: that in spite of opposition, *they would never be expelled from God's land again* (9:11–15). This is being wonderfully fulfilled today.

WHAT GOD FORETOLD TO JOEL

Joel was a successful prophet. His blowing the trumpet in Zion, Jerusalem, had successfully called both priests and people to repentance and prayer (2:17–23). 'Then the Lord had pity on his people.' This had saved Judah's two tribes from the fate coming to Ephraim's ten tribes. 'Fear not, O land; be glad and rejoice for the Lord has done great things' (2:21).

But there would be an early and a latter rain experience for Judah, even as there were two rainy seasons in Palestine. God foretold (probably 740 BC to 720 BC) that his Holy Spirit would be outpoured during the spring rains at Pentecost and, as there were two rainy seasons (v 23), there would be an outpouring when Judah and Israel were 'restored to the land after being scattered among the nations' as well.

The 'terrible day of the Lord' would be Armageddon and the judgement of nations. This would be heralded by the mushroom columns of nuclear explosions (2:30). The Lord Jesus referred to the signs in the sun and moon before his second coming in Matthew 24:29, Mark 13:24, Luke 21:25, where he uses the Greek word for uranium.

We saw in *Volume 2*, Chapter 20, the Great Rift Valley of Jordan will extend to join the Mediterranean to the Red Sea (3:18, Ezekiel 47, Zechariah 14:8) and the Lord will rule from Zion in Jerusalem (3:21).

S U M M A R Y

OT PROPHETS AND PROPHECIES

What God told Abraham 2,000 BC (Genesis 15:13–21).
- Israel would suffer 400 years' slavery in Egypt.
- Messiah would come through Isaac, not Ishmael (17:18–21).

What God told Jacob.
- Messiah would come through the kingship of Judah's tribe (Gen 49:10) (not through Joseph, his favourite).

What God told Moses 1,440 BC before entering Palestine (Leviticus 26:18,21,24,28).
- Israel to be dispersed worldwide for 2,520 years, then return.
- The Law operative until Messiah (Deut 18:15–19).

What God told Hosea 775 BC before the ten tribes were invaded.
- Israel would be on probation for 2½ millennial days, then return (Hosea 3:3–5; 5:15–6:3).
- The return will include both ten tribes and two (1:11; 2:23).

What God told Amos 750 BC, before the ten tribes were invaded.
- The ten tribes would be the first to go into exile (6:7; 7:11,12).
- They would never be lost (9:9); they would return, build and plant and never be expelled (9:11–15).

What God told Joel probably 740–720 BC (2:30–3:21).
- The Holy Spirit would be outpoured at Pentecost.
- Judah would return in latter days.
- Jerusalem would be invaded; God would judge the nations.
- The Lord would then reign from Zion.

What God told Isaiah 740–700 BC.
- After Ephraim (10 tribes) are scattered, Judah will be spared (7:8b).
- Judah will become deaf and therefore removed (6:9–12).
- UNO flag will authorise return of united 12 tribes (11:11–16;17:12).

What God told Jeremiah 625 BC onwards while Judah (2 tribes) was being invaded.
- God would never abandon Israel (5:18; 31:35–37; 33:19–22).
- They would return (32:37–42) first with pleasing prospects, second by persecution (Hitler's gas chambers) (16:14–16).

(Continued)

What God told Ezekiel during the exile 592–570 BC.
- That in prophecy a day can equal a year (4:3–8).
- One third will survive in exile; a remnant will return; but majority will spread throughout world and not return until the latter days. Those who return from exile, will again be scattered (i.e. AD 70). Both ten tribes and two tribes will return as Israel in latter days (37:15–28).
- When Israel is resettled safely, they will be invaded (38 and 39, Armageddon?).
- God will come and judge the nations and rule the earth (43:47).

What God told Daniel during exile 587–530 BC.
- History of empires down to European Single Market (ch. 2 and 7), then the Lord rules the earth.
- Three successive abominations on temple site 168 BC, AD 70, AD 638, and possibly one during the tribulation.
- The 2,520 years *Diaspora* again, giving 'Home for Jews' in 1917 (12:6–12).

What God told Zechariah 518 BC during return of some from exile.
- The agony of Lebanon when Israel returns (10:8–11:3).
- Jerusalem will be an insoluble problem (12:3).
- Invasion results. Christ descends to Olivet with the saved.
- Israel converted when they see the Crucified One (12:10; 14:4).
- Christ will judge the nations and rule the world (14:2–9).

Make your Bible your very own by marking in it all the 30 points above.

N.B. Try to avoid the bad habit of saying, 'The prophet said so-and-so', when usually it was what God told the prophet.

4 CHRIST'S CLAIMS PROVED BY OLD TESTAMENT PROPHECIES
CREATOR; DIVINE; VIRGIN CONCEPTION

What religion are we to follow? What sect are we to believe? Which founder of religion is the right one? These are the questions confronting you today. There is one sure answer. It is this. Only Jesus Christ was prepared for by prophecies all down the centuries before he came. Only Jesus was prepared for by God. The Creator told all the prophets of his plans to send Jesus to be the Saviour of the world. As the centuries passed by, more and more information was told to holy men who wrote it down in the books of the Old Testament – all the details about the Messiah's divine origin, the virgin conception, his ministry, crucifixion, resurrection, ascension and second coming.

That is why the risen Christ was able to show to his astonished disciples that he was foretold in all the Scriptures from Moses to Malachi. All those 39 books spoke of Jesus Christ.

> Jesus said to them, 'O foolish men, and slow of heart to believe all that the prophets have written' . . . And beginning with Moses, and all the prophets, he showed to them in all the Scriptures the things concerning himself. (Luke 24:25)

Later he reinforced this evidence to all the disciples:

> 'Everything written about me in the Torah of Moses, and the prophets and the psalms must be fulfilled.' Then he opened their minds to understand the Scriptures and he said to them, 'Thus it is written and thus it was necessary for Christ to suffer and to rise from the dead the third day, and that repentance and forgiveness of sins should be preached in his name among all nations.' (24:44–47)

The disciples and early Christians followed Christ's example of proving him from the prophets and it is your most effective tool as well. That is why we shall look at those prophecies together and find how astonishingly detailed those prophecies were of every aspect of the Lord.

The Dead Sea Scrolls prove the prophecies concerning Christ were not added later, as some allege – see the end of the chapter.

HIS DIVINITY FROM ETERNITY

When you remember the insistent monotheism of the Old Testament, it is even more astonishing that it should declare that the Messiah is divine. Take the well-known statement by God to Micah 760 BC, 'Thou, Bethlehem in the south, though you are but little among the families of Judah, yet from you shall come forth for me One who is to be ruler in Israel *whose origin is from everlasting*' (Micah 5:2).

A quite astonishing statement was made to Isaiah in chapter 9, verse 6. It is that the child born would be the Son given whose name shall be called Wonderful Counsellor, Mighty God, Everlasting Father, Prince of Peace. In that prophecy, 730 BC, all the attributes of the Holy Trinity are named. No wonder Jesus was able to say, 'He who has seen me has seen the Father. I and the Father are one' (John 14:9). That is why when the virgin bore a child (Isaiah 7:14), his name would mean 'God with us'.

Incidentally, critics contended that the word *parthenos*, 'virgin' meant only a young woman, so do not quote this as your strongest text. Isaiah 9:6 is much more indisputable. Nevertheless, it has since been found out that *parthenos* did mean virgin at that time.

The Creating Word

The New Testament makes the clear claim that Jesus was actually the Creating Word in creation. John's Gospel opens with this (NKJV), 'In the beginning was the Word, and the Word was with God, and the Word was God. He was in the beginning with God. All things were made through Him and without Him nothing was made that was made . . . and the Word became flesh and dwelt among us.'

Revelation chapters 1 and 22 agree (Revelation 1:11 NKJV), 'I am the Alpha and the Omega, the First and the Last'. Verse 17: 'I am the First and the Last. I am He who lives, and was dead, and behold I am alive for ever more.' Revelation 22:13: 'I am the Alpha and the Omega, the Beginning and the End, the First and the Last.'

Where in the Old Testament do we find this confirmed? In Isaiah 48:12 (NKJV) Jehovah says, 'I am the First, I am also the Last. Indeed my hand has laid the foundation of the earth, and My right hand has stretched out the heavens.'

Isaiah 46:9 (NKJV): 'I am God, and there is none other; I am God and there is none like Me . . . Declaring the end from the beginning.'

We saw in Volume 1 that the scientific DNA code demonstrated that God created by words. That is why the majestic account of creation in Genesis 1 records that God spoke ten times in creation. Psalm 33:6,9 (NKJV) sums it up, 'By the word of the LORD the heavens were made . . . for He spoke and it was done.'

So that is why St John calls Jesus 'the Word', who created all things, and then became flesh and dwelt among us. Paul sums it up in Colossians 1:15: 'He is the image of the invisible God . . . by him all things were created that are in heaven and that are on earth, visible and invisible . . . all things were created through him and for him . . . He is the firstborn from the dead.'

THE VIRGIN CONCEPTION IN THE OLD TESTAMENT

Some critics have spoken about the virgin conception as if it were an optional extra. It is far from that. The cross without the conception would not accomplish complete salvation by a just God. Many prophecies link the two for this reason.

Old Testament prophecy predicts the incarnation in four ways:

- First, it is implied genetically.
- Second, divine Sonship is implied.
- Third, the human sonship is implied by calling him 'the Branch'.
- Fourth, predictions became explicit.

Implied Genetically

'The seed of the woman shall bruise the serpent's head,' announced God to that snake Satan. Our modern knowledge, coupled with other scriptures has brought an exciting insight to this Genesis record. The seed is the genetic code in the sex cells and it is only the mother who passes on a certain code from one generation to another. This is called the Mitochondrial DNA code. It manufactures the power to work the machinery of the cells. Without it no human body would work, but it is not supplied by the human father. It is an exclusive female monopoly. It is this discovery which has made scientists state that the whole human race is descended from one woman. See *Evidence for Truth, Volume 1: Science*, Chapter 4.

So it is this seed's essential constituency which was passed down through the generations from Eve to Mary. It would also be the reason why, in Luke's account, it is Mary's kindred list which is given and not Joseph's. That descent from King David to Mary is different from Joseph's except for one common ancestor named Zerubbabel.

This brings me to another extraordinary fact which no one seems to have noticed. It is this. In the Old Testament, the mother's names of the kings descending from David are always given, but in contrast, they are not for the north Israeli kings. In the succession of kings listed for them, the mother is never mentioned.

For example, in 2 Kings 17:1 we read, 'Hoshea, the son of Elah, began to reign in Samaria over northern Israel'. But in the next chapter, 18:1 we read, 'In the third year of Hoshea, son of Elah, king of northern Israel, Hezekiah began to reign, the son of Ahaz, king of Judah (southern Israel, David's throne). His mother's name was Abi.'

This system of reference to the mother is consistently repeated. Only divine inspiration can explain this genetic anticipation, from Eve to Mary the virgin, through the mothers of David's line, through centuries of prophecy.

Divine Sonship Implied

A divine Sonship could result only by conception in a virgin with no human father. David's psalms anticipated this. Jesus said, 'King David wrote about me'.

In Psalm 2, the divine Sonship of the Messiah is clearly given. 'The nations conspire against the Lord and his Christ . . . He who sits in the heavens laughs; the Lord has them in derision . . . He said to me, "You are my son, today I have begotten you . . . Be wise, be warned O rulers of the earth, kiss the Son lest he be angry and you perish." '

How do we know that the ascension of Jesus was prophesied in Psalm 110? Because Jesus said so. He said the Holy Spirit inspired David to write about him.

This psalm of David, written 1,000 years before it was fulfilled, makes several remarkable statements. It states that Jesus is Lord who sat at the right hand of God when he ascended into heaven after his resurrection. But that's not all. It states that Jesus is King David's Lord. 'The Lord [Jehovah] says to my Lord, "Sit at my right hand until I make your enemies your footstool".' This implies that he is co-equal with the Father Jehovah. This is very remarkable in David's time when great emphasis was placed upon the truth that God is one God. This can be explained only by the Trinity in Unity.

Now let me explain that verse 1 of Psalm 110: 'The Lord said unto my Lord . . .' First, this is an answer to reductionists who water down such prophecies and try to make them refer to David in his kingship. The question of Jesus to the theologians of his day defeats the reductionism of some theologians of our day. Jesus put the teaser to them like this, 'If David calls the Messiah his Lord, in what way is he his son?'

Obviously, his Lord must have been existing in David's day as David's Lord. Christ's Spirit was there. So then, this can be explained only by the incarnation. The pre-existent Jesus took on flesh by the virgin birth and became man, he dwelt among us and we beheld his glory, the glory as of the only begotten of his Father God, full of grace and truth. Only by the virgin conception could the son of David also be his Lord. In fact, because the descendant of David was the one David spoke of a thousand years before the incarnation, it shows that it was the eternal Spirit of Jesus who took on flesh and was made man; but he was already David's Lord sitting at Jehovah's right hand. Only the virgin conception explains that. That is why David, in another psalm, quotes the words of the Spirit of Jesus when he was about to become man.

In Psalm 40:6–8, the Spirit of Jesus said, 'A body hast thou prepared for me. Lo, I come to do your will O God. Animal sacrifices are not sufficient to atone for man's terrible sins.' Only the Eternal One can do it, Jesus is saying, and I am willing, though the cost and suffering will be terrible. (See Chapter 6 for my derivation of these words.)

In reply, Jehovah encourages David's Lord by speaking of the triumph he will have when he has completed our salvation and ascended to heaven. 'Sit at my right hand.' He would do that when the cross was past and redemption completed. 'Jehovah said unto my Lord, sit at my right hand.' Jesus was David's Lord. Is he your Lord?

Human Sonship by 'The Branch'

Jesus is not only divine, the virgin conception made him truly human. His human nature was inherited through the Virgin and the mothers before her to David and beyond.

Little notice has been taken of the remarkable prophecies concerning the 'Branch'. This became another name for the Messiah. It is even mentioned in the Dead Sea Scrolls as the 'scion' or branch of David. Why? Because it looked as if Satan had won after all. In spite of God's promise that David's throne would be for ever, it looked as if the royal tree had been sawn down to the roots. Only the stump remained in the dry ground. For 600 years no king sat on David's throne. From the time Nebuchadnezzar had destroyed Judah, to Christ's day, no descendant of David had reigned in Jerusalem. Herod was only a foreign Edomite king. Yet Mary's lineage was intact to produce a descendent of King David. And yet Jesus would never have been born in Bethlehem had not Joseph's descent also been from David. (See Summary to Chapter 9 of *Evidence for Truth, Volume 2: Archaeology*.) Then, from the dormant stump of David's fallen tree, the Branch suddenly sprang. First it was a shoot and then a branch. The amazing thing is that the 'Branch' prophecies spanned nearly 300 years.

First, it was Isaiah whom God told. He foretold it in 759 BC when the occupants of David's throne were flourishing as a prosperous power. Ahaz had just succeeded Uzziah. It was 'in the year that King Uzziah died' that Isaiah was told that David's tree would become 'a stump remaining when it is felled, but the holy seed would come from the stump' (Isaiah 6:13). This is further explained in Isaiah 11:1. 'There shall come forth a shoot from the stump of Jesse and a branch shall grow out of its roots.'

Figure 4.1. Branch from a tree stump drawn by the author. From Jesse's fallen tree stump there sprang the shoot and branch of David's 'greater son' Jesus Christ

The virgin root of David produced the shoot so green and tender to grow into the strong branch so that 'the earth shall be full of the knowledge of the Lord as the waters cover the sea' (Isaiah 11:9).

Still further is the wonderful theme developed in Isaiah 53. That prophecy which describes all the life and atoning death of the Lord begins, 'Who has believed our report? To whom has the arm of the Lord been revealed? For he grew up before him like a young shoot, and like a root out of a dry ground.'

It is not until 156 years later that God tells Jeremiah of the Branch. The royal tree had just been savagely sawn down by Babylon, but you can't defeat God. Weeping Jeremiah is told, 'Behold the days are coming says the Lord, when I will raise up for David a righteous branch and he shall reign as king. His name will be called the Lord Jehovah, our righteousness.' There in that statement is both the human form from David and the divine from God (Jehovah). Only the virgin birth made that possible.

A hundred years pass, some have returned from exile, but still there is no king on David's throne. A descendant of David called Zerubbabel is made only a governor.

Zechariah the prophet tells in chapter 3 how God stands the high priest side by side with Zerubbabel and declares this is significant. 'I will bring my servant the Branch . . . I will remove the guilt of this earth in a single day' (vv 8,9).

Why? Because later, Mary's line crossed with Joseph's at Zerubbabel's name in those two lists and, as Mary's cousin was a priest, it meant that Jesus would be both Priest and King and, as Priest, his atoning sacrifice would remove the earth's guilt in a single Good Friday.

No wonder that, in chapter 4, there were to be joyful shouts of 'Grace, grace, unto the stone which had become the head of the corner' and Zerubbabel would be the Davidic ancestor 'not by might nor by power, but by my Spirit says the Lord'.

In Zechariah chapter 6, again it is emphasised that 'the man whose name is the Branch who shall grow up, will be Priest-King crowned upon his throne' (vv 12,13).

He would be more than a Levitical priest 'offering sacrifices which could never take away sins'. Jesus was David's son 'after the order of Melchizedek' (Psalm 110) whose one sacrifice atoned for all sins for all time (Hebrews 10:12). That was because 'a body hast thou prepared for me' by the incarnation. Hebrews 10:5 quotes the prophecy of Psalm 40:6,7.

Prophecy Becomes Explicit

After such remarkable anticipations, prophecy became explicit and states outright, 'A virgin shall bear a child' (Isaiah 7:14). 'The child to be born will be a Son given and his name shall be Wonderful Counsellor, Everlasting Father, Prince of Peace' (9:6).

'But,' says a critic, 'that word virgin means only a young woman.' If it did, then Isaiah 9:6 cannot be explained away like that. Opinion (for what it is worth) is changing. A more careful study reveals that the word translated virgin did mean just that. In any case, God's angel Gabriel told Joseph that it did and I would rather believe him than a critic!

The word in the Hebrew is *almah* (virgin). Where used in the Old Testament, it means virgin, e.g. in Genesis 24:43, Abraham's servant is looking for a virgin to be a wife for Isaac and prays, 'Let a virgin (*almah*) come out to draw water. Let her be the virgin whom the Lord has appointed for my master's son.'

The Greek translation made 288 BC uses the word '*parthenos*' for Isaiah 7:14 which means virgin. This had the same meaning in the New Testament where the same word is used and every time it clearly means 'virgin' (2 Corinthians 11:2; Matthew 25:1; Acts 21:9; Revelation 14:4, etc.).

THE PROPHESIED LONG WAIT FOR THE MESSIAH

Some think there is another problem. It is how could the sign of a virgin birth be a sign to King Ahaz and his immediate problem? The problem was a threat from Syria and northern Israel. Syria and northern Israel had plotted to displace David's throne and place upon it a king who was not Davidic, namely, the son of Tabeel (Isaiah 7:6). By doing that, the royal throne would not last until the Messiah.

In effect, the Lord told Isaiah, 'Yes, it will last because a virgin will bear a child who will be the shoot from the root of David already predicted but this will be after a long time. It will be when the whole area will be deported, Syria, Israel, Judah, Assyria and even Babylon, before the virgin-born child is weaned.' It is only a problem if the sign is taken out of this larger context.

It is a mistake, from a casual reading of the passage, to think that the sign of the virgin conception was to happen in Ahaz's time. Between the promise of a sign to Ahaz and the statement 'a virgin shall conceive and bear a son', verses 5 to 8 of chapter 7, Isaiah speaks not only of an invasion of Syria, but also of another 65 years of deportation. Then a further cycle of events is given.

As Dr Kay said, this is part of a larger cycle of prophecy which starts in chapter 6 with Isaiah's commission and does not finish until the fall of Babylon in chapter 14 and even to chapter 27.

What is this cycle? It includes more than the removal of Syria's threat. It is that the whole population throughout the Middle East will be deported and redistributed throughout the whole area.

Isaiah had asked 'How long?' (Isaiah 6:11). The Lord replied, 'Until the cities be waste without habitation and houses without men and the land is utterly desolate and the Lord removes men far away.' It is then that God says, 'But the house of David will not perish' (6:13) and in chapter 7, 'because the virgin conception will restore David's throne through his descendant, the Messiah'. Not only will Ahaz's threat from Syria disappear through an Assyrian invasion, Israel will also be deported, King Ahaz is told, and then even Judah by Babylon, and then even Babylon will be devastated. All this and more will happen before the one born of a virgin will appear on the scene. That was to be 'how long' it would take. That it was more than the immediate threat which would be removed is shown by 7:8: 'Northern Israel will be exiled in 65 years' time.' The Assyrian Empire would disappear and the Babylonian successor would disappear as well as other smaller nations.

All this had happened before Christ came and Jesus actually quoted the reason given in Isaiah 6:9–12. It was because 'this people have ears which are heavy and eyes which cannot see and hearts which do not understand, in case I should heal them'.

Incarnation Necessary for Salvation

That is a tremendous statement in Psalm 40:6,7. It tells us that the incarnation was necessary to provide the only kind of person who would be able to make atonement for our sins.

> Sacrifice and offerings thou hast not desired,
> *But a body hast thou prepared for me.* [Margin note]
> In burnt offerings and sin offerings thou hast taken no pleasure.
> Then I said, Lo I have come to do thy will, O God.
> As it is written of me in the roll of the book. (RSV)

You may have turned to that psalm in another version and found that the second line is not quite right. A marginal note may say 'meaning unknown'. This is one of the few passages where copying and translating down the centuries has confused the meaning.

Fortunately, the New Testament writer has preserved the original (Hebrews 10:15). This is because he quoted from the Greek translation of the Old Testament as the early Christians did. That correct verse is still in the Greek Septuagint. Furthermore, the Dead Sea Scrolls have confirmed it: 'A body hast thou prepared for me' (see Chapter 6 of this book).

Only a God/Man Incarnation Could Atone

Here again is an instance of which Jesus said, 'David spoke of me'. The inspiration of the Holy Spirit showed David that animal sacrifices were only a prophetic symbol of the perfect sacrifice Jesus would make.

Complete sacrifice for sins could be made only by a person who was sinless, yet a man, who was also eternal and therefore God-made-man. This was made possible only by the virgin conception by which God became man. 'A body hast thou prepared for me.' 'The Word was made flesh and dwelt among us, full of grace and truth.'

Where in 'the volume of the scroll' was this written of Jesus? At this time when David wrote the psalm in 1000 BC, he would be referring to the scroll of the Torah, that is, Genesis to Deuteronomy.

Where in this book of Moses would Jesus' incarnate sacrifice be described? It was in the various kinds of sacrifice described and in the shewbread of the tabernacle.

SHEWBREAD SYMBOLISM

The shewbread was the unleavened bread anointed with oil and placed upon the shewbread table. Jesus is the Bread of Life. Bread is grown from the earth and through Mary he was of human origin. But he is without sin. Throughout the Old Testament, leaven or yeast was symbolic of sin and error. That is why the bread had to be without leaven (1 Corinthians 5:6–8). So Jesus had to be a sinless man. To be that he must be divine. Oil anointing was symbolic of the Holy Spirit. The incarnation was by the Holy Spirit. 'The Holy Spirit will come upon you and that holy being to be born of you will be called holy, the Son of God' (Luke 1:35) .

The shewbread table was also a symbol of the Second Person of the Holy Trinity, when 'the pattern of the tabernacle was revealed to Moses'. Why? Because God first gave to Moses three symbolic items of furniture: the ark of the covenant; the table of shewbread; and the seven-branched lampstand. These stood for the Father, the Son and the Holy Spirit. I will show you why. It is unusual to speak of some items of furniture before the house is described.

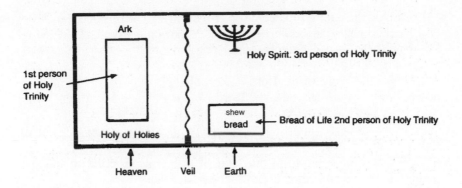

Figure 4.2. The Tabernacle. Plan of the first three-piece suite of furniture?

The details of the tabernacle are next given and the New Testament says that they represented creation. Heaven was represented by the Holy of Holies behind the veil, and earth was represented by the section on man's side of the veil. The three Trinity symbols were given before the tabernacle because God existed before creation. That is why the rest of the symbolic furniture is described *after* the tabernacle, but why the Trinity symbols were given before it. The furniture after the tabernacle has all to do with the redemption of fallen mankind. It represented the sacrifice which the incarnate Jesus was to make upon the cross. This is fully explained in the New Testament book of Hebrews.

Holy but Merciful

Why does the ark of the covenant represent God the Father? One reason is that he is behind the veil and no one could enter his holy presence except the high priest if sprinkled by the blood of atonement. The commandments in the ark box represented God's righteousness. The mercy seat was a lid which covered the laws. Mercy came when the atoning blood was sprinkled on it. The shewbread on the table represented the Second Person of the Trinity because he was to become the Bread of Life as we have mentioned.

Why was that not also placed in the Holy of Holies behind the veil? It was placed in the section representing the earth because the Saviour was to come to earth as man. For bread came from the earth depicting his manhood, but it was anointed by the Holy Spirit who brought about the incarnation. 'I am the bread of life who came down from heaven' (John 6:51). This could only be by 'the Word being made flesh and dwelling among us'.

The Lamps of Holy Spirit Witness

Why did the third item represent the Holy Spirit? The answer is in several scriptures. One is Zechariah 4:2–6. Zechariah is asked, 'Don't you know what that seven-branched lampstand means?'

'No, my Lord'.

'This is the Word of the Lord to Zerubbabel, "Not by might nor by power but by my Spirit, says the Lord of Hosts"' (see also Revelation 4:5).

Why was not the lampstand also placed behind the veil? Because the Holy Spirit was also to come into the world. 'When he has come, he will convict the world of sin, and of righteousness and of judgement. Of sin, because they do not believe in Jesus.'

Sinlessness Symbol

The different animal sacrifices had one common feature. They all had to be 'perfect and without blemish'. The sinlessness of Christ was thus portrayed. As Peter says,

> You know that you were ransomed from the futile ways inherited from your fathers, not with perishable things, such as silver or gold, but with the precious blood of Christ, as of that of a lamb without blemish and without spot (1 Peter 1:19). He committed no sin; no guile was found on his lips . . . He himself bore our sins in his body on the tree [the cross]. (2:22)

So you see how the virgin conception of the sinless God-man was essential for complete atonement to be made upon the cross. It also shows how the Old Testament prophesied it by tabernacle type, by implication and then by explicit description. How wonderfully the whole of inspired Scripture unfolds God's loving plan for you and me.

Did Christ Come from Three Places?

I sometimes illustrate how a person wanting to make Scripture contradict itself could say that one prophecy says the Messiah would come from Bethlehem, and another says he would come from Egypt and another says he would come from Galilee.

Jesus fulfilled all these apparent contradictions. He was born in Bethlehem according to what God told Micah in chapter 5 verse 2, he returned as a refugee baby from Egypt as symbolised by God in Hosea and the light of his gospel first shone in Galilee where he started his ministry, as prophesied in Isaiah 9.

The circumstances in which the prophecies were fulfilled also seemed impossible. Christ's mother lived in Nazareth and Joseph made no preparation to move, but was summoned to Bethlehem to pay his poll tax.

'Out of Egypt have I called out my son,' God said to Hosea, but he appeared to some to be referring to Israel when they were delivered from slavery. However, even as Jesus represented the human race when atoning for them on the cross, so also he represented the delivery from Egypt which a believer experiences when he trusts God's Passover Lamb. 'Out of Egypt have I called my Son.' Hosea's prophecy had a double meaning.

Concerning Galilee, the Pharisees said the Messiah would not come from that despised land (John 7:52). These 'scholars' ignored the plain statements of Isaiah chapter 9 that the 'great light would shine out first in Galilee'. Their scholarly opinion refused to listen to the one whose 'name was called Wonderful Counsellor, Mighty God, Everlasting Father, the Prince of Peace'.

Those in Galilee who swarmed to listen to Jesus were called ignorant because they were not guided by the theological authorities (John 7:48).

It was in the context of this blindness that Jesus said to them, 'I am the light of the world. He who follows me will not walk in darkness, but will have the light of life.' This was a direct reference to this prophecy that the light would shine out from Galilee.

CRUCIFIXION, RESURRECTION AND ASCENSION IN PROPHECY

Evidence for Christ's claims comes, above all, from the many prophecies of his crucifixion, resurrection and ascension. It comes from the types in the tabernacle 1400 BC; it comes from David's psalms 1000 BC; it comes from the prophets 800 to 400 BC. Someone misled by a certain certificate course said, 'David in his psalms was speaking about himself'.

Who Was it that David Referred to?

Did they pierce David's hands and feet as in Psalm 22? Did they cast lots for David's garments? Was it David who cried, 'My God, my God, why hast thou forsaken me?' and then in the last verse, according to the Hebrew, said, 'It is finished'?

In the ascension, was it David who referred to himself when in Psalm 110, he wrote, 'Jehovah said to my Lord, "Sit at my right hand until I make your enemies your footstool" '? Jesus confounded the theologians with this very question.

Was David 'a priest for ever after the order of Melchizedek'? Was David the 'stone which the builders rejected and became the head of the corner' (Psalm 118)? Apparently not, because 250 years later, Isaiah was told about this foundation stone and that he who believed on him would not be confounded (Isaiah 8:14). Apparently not, because 500 years later than David, this stone was still to be descended from Zerubbabel (Zechariah 4:7). It was prophesied that the 'stone' was still to come and be a descendant of Zerubbabel who was an heir of David and ancestor to Christ through his earthly father Joseph (see genealogy in Luke 3:27).

The whole of Christ's life and ministry is described in the servant passages of Isaiah. The famous chapter 53 is one of them. A large part of it is given to prophesying the Saviour's atoning sacrifice: 'He was wounded for our transgressions; he was bruised for our iniquities.'

The scourging for our healing is then described. His refusal to defend himself, his death with the wicked thieves, yet buried in a rich man's tomb; his soul made an offering for sin; and then the resurrection and the preaching of the gospel and winning many to righteousness.

One of the more moderate German Bible critics, Delitzsch, was puzzled. He said he could not see of whom Isaiah was writing. He could not be referring to Jesus because no one could foretell the future!

Philip found no such difficulty in Acts 8. When the Ethiopian asked, 'Of whom was Isaiah writing; of himself or about some other man?' Philip opened his mouth and beginning with this same scripture he told him the good news of Jesus.

Philip had no difficulty about the ability to foretell the future because God had told that same prophet that he planned the future to prove that he was God and no one else (Isaiah 46:10,11).

Proof from the Dead Sea Scrolls

So as to negate the power of these prophecies in pointing to Jesus, some have said that the Hebrew prophecies were altered by the Christians to refer to Jesus. Such an objection is impossible. The Jews had and still have their Hebrew Old Testament intact and unaltered, separate from the New Testament. Besides, the discovery of the Dead Sea Scrolls in 1947 included all the books of the Old Testament (except Esther). These scrolls were copied 200 years before Christ from the originals; furthermore, all the prophetic records are just the same as in today's Bibles. (See *Evidence for Truth, Volume 2: Archaeology.*)

Christ's second coming to reign is described in so many scriptures that the next few chapters will be given to the books of those prophets.

S U M M A R Y

OT PROPHECIES PROVE CHRIST'S CLAIMS

In all 3 sections of OT Christ was described, i.e. in Pentateuch, Prophets and Psalms (Lk 24:25,44)

Divinity described
- 'From eternity' Mic 5:2.
- Son given is part of Holy Trinity (Is 9:6; 7:14; cf Jn 14:9).

Creating Word
- 'I am the first and the last' (Is 48:12; Rev 1:11; 22:13).
- The Word, God said, Gen 1, Ps 33:6,9. 'In the beginning the Word' Jn 1:1.

By virgin conception
- **Genetically** through mothers Eve to Mary. Mitochondrial DNA. Mothers only mentioned in David's kings e.g. 2 Kg 18:1.
- **Sonship, Divine Source:** Proud Father Ps 2:7 'You are my Son'. In Gospels, God speaks three times 'You are my beloved Son' Matt 22:42–46. Ps 110 'The Lord said to my Lord'.
- **Sonship's Human Source:** Body prepared (Ps 40:6–8; cf. Heb 10:5)
- **Branch of Royal Tree.** Is 6:13; 11:1; 53:2. Shoot out of root. Zech 3:8,9. Atones on one day. 6:12,13. Priest-King. (Mary's lineage had priest affinities as well as royal.) Hebrew word '*almah*' Is 7:14 means virgin as in Genesis 24:43 so does '*parthenos*' in the Greek OT translation and 2 Cor 11:2. The virgin birth will be long after the exile (Is 6·11–13; 7·8) Two geno-type sources become phenotypically *one* person.

'Moses wrote of Me'
- Unleavened shewbread i.e. sinless, Ex 25:30 (2nd person of Trinity).
- Lamb without blemish (Lev 23:12; 1 Pet 1:18,19).
- A new covenant (Deut 18:15–19).

Prophets also wrote of Jesus
- To be born in Bethlehem (Mic 5:2).
- As refugee from Egypt (Hos 11:1).
- Ministry to be launched from Galilee (Is 9:1,2).
- Christ's life, death, atonement and resurrection (Is 53).

Psalms
- e.g. Ps 22 'Pierced hands and feet' and gambling for garments could not be referring to David.
- See also summaries to Chapters 5 and 6.

5   JESUS PROPHESIED IN THE PSALMS
PSALMS 2 AND 45 IN DETAIL

I have mentioned a few prophecies of Jesus in the Psalms. They are so remarkable that they are worthy of a chapter on them alone.

These prophecies are not so often studied, yet they are very significant indeed. Many of them were written by David about a thousand years before Christ fulfilled them. Listen to Christ's own opinion about them! He said in Matthew 22:43 that 'David was inspired by the Holy Spirit'. In Luke 24:44 he said that 'everything which had been written about him in the Psalms must be fulfilled'.

There are about ten psalms which prophesy about the Lord Jesus and they give over 30 details about the birth, life, the cross, resurrection, ascension and eternal priesthood of Jesus. That is quite a lot of detail isn't it from a thousand years before they were fulfilled? Each one is remarkable.

PSALM 2: CHRIST ACTUALLY NAMED

The second psalm starts us off with 'The Lord and his anointed' (v 2). Its fulfilment is quoted in verse 7 and in the New Testament letter to the Hebrews 1:5. Did you know that the name of Christ appears first in this psalm? The word 'christ' is the Greek word for 'anointed one'. That is why, in the New Testament, when it is quoted, it says, 'The Lord and his Christ' as we shall see. In the Old Testament your translation probably says, 'The Lord and his anointed'.

In the Gospels you read in many places of people chatting and asking, 'Do you think this is the Christ?' That was the word in common parlance then, but when Jesus asked the Pharisees whose son they thought Christ would be, they knew perfectly well that Jesus was referring to all the prophecies which called him 'the anointed one'. Everybody in Jesus' day used the Greek translation of the Old Testament and that translation had the name 'Christ' where the Hebrew had 'the anointed one'.

The Lord Jesus was indeed anointed, anointed by the Holy Spirit. John said that God did not limit any measure of the Holy Spirit to Jesus. John 3:32 says that 'he who has come from heaven bears witness to what he has seen and heard in heaven. Jesus, whom God has sent, utters the words of God, for it is not by limited measure that he gives the anointing Holy Spirit to him.'

Opposition Foretold

We saw that over 30 prophecies about the details of Christ's life were given in the Psalms written 1,000 years before he fulfilled them. Some Christians are surprised by the opposition they experience as soon as they are converted. The first Christians were not surprised. When Peter and John were discharged from the religious court and ordered not to preach Christ, they fled to prayer and quoted Psalm 2 which prophesied this. They prayed, in Acts 4:25, 'O Lord of creation . . . by the mouth of David your servant, he said by the Holy Spirit "Why did the Gentiles rage and the peoples imagine a vain thing. The kings of the earth set themselves in array and the rulers were gathered together *against the Lord and against his Christ.*" ' Then in their fervent prayers, they added the application, 'For truly in this city there were gathered together against your holy suffering servant Jesus, whom you anointed, the opposition by Herod and Pontius Pilate, with the Gentiles and the peoples of Israel. But they fulfilled only what your plan had prophesied and predestined to take place. So Lord, look at their hearts, and stretch out your hand to heal and do signs and wonders in the name of Jesus.'

No wonder that the place where they prayed shook like an earth tremor and they were all filled by the Holy Spirit and spoke the Word of God with boldness. And no wonder, for they had based their prayer upon God's promise to fulfil his prophecy.

Read Psalm 2 again. It is stirring and strong. It tells you that all down these 20 centuries, various kings and governments will reject Christ and say, 'We will not have this man to reign over us'. Only at the end of this age, at the coming of Christ to reign in Jerusalem, will they be subdued. The psalm says that day is now fast approaching. It will be a great shock to the Christ-rejecting world when Jesus Christ descends with power to reign in Jerusalem.

> The One enthroned in heaven laughs; the Lord scoffs at them. Then he rebukes them in his anger and terrifies them in his wrath, saying, 'I have installed my King on Zion, my holy hill'. I will proclaim the decree of the Lord. He said to me, 'You are my Son, today I have become your Father. Ask of me, and I will make the nations your inheritance, the ends of the earth your possession. You will rule them with an iron sceptre, you will dash them to pieces like pottery.' Therefore you kings be wise; be warned, you rulers of the earth. Serve the Lord with fear and rejoice with trembling. Kiss the Son, lest he be angry and you be destroyed in your way. (Psalm 2:4–12)

How have you kissed the Son of God? Let it not be like Judas the traitor, but instead like Mary Magdalene who kissed his feet because he had changed her life.

The Son of God . . .

That second psalm not only tells you it would be Christ who would come, it also says he is the Son of God. Verse 7 says, 'You are my Son, today I have begotten you'. And again in verse 11, God warns kings and rulers to be wise: 'Serve the Lord with fear and with trembling, kiss his Son's feet lest he be angry and you perish in your political plans.'

Hebrews 1:5 quotes the remarkable prophecy of this psalm. It says, 'To which of the angels did God say at any time "Thou art my Son, this day have I begotten you" or again, "I will be to him a father and he will be to me a son". And again, when he brings the first-born into the world, he says, "Let all the angels of God worship him". Of the Son, he said, "Thy throne O God is for ever and ever, a sceptre of right-eousness is the sceptre of thy kingdom".'

So you see, those last words make it clear that Jesus did not begin his existence when he was born of Mary. He is the Creator from the beginning.

. . . Begotten

This harmonises with Isaiah's prophecy that the child who would be born would be 'the Son who was given' long before. How gracious is God who, in spite of the insults and horrors of mankind, 'so loved the world that he gave his only *begotten* Son, that whosoever believes on him should not perish, but have eternal life' (John 3:16).

Another remarkable prophecy in Psalm 2 is this. It spoke of the divine Sonship of Jesus Christ. In testimony to this, 1,000 years later, God spoke audibly from heaven and said, 'This is my beloved Son'.

But what does Psalm 2:7 mean when it says, 'This day have I begotten you'? What day was that? In several places in the New Testament you are told that it was upon the day of Christ's resurrection. Paul said so in Acts 13:33 when he preached at Antioch on the Turkish plateau. By that ice-blue lake he declared, 'This God fulfilled to us by raising Jesus from the dead as is written in the second psalm, "Thou art my Son, this day I have begotten you".'

Paul says the same in Colossians 1:18, 'He, Jesus, is the beginning, the first-born from the dead, that in everything he might have pre-emi-nence, for in him all the fulness of God was pleased to dwell.'

St John also pinpoints the resurrection as that day. In Revelation 1:5 he says, 'Jesus Christ is the faithful witness, the first-born from the dead and the ruler of kings'.

Now that links up Psalm 2 with its statement that Christ will rule over kings. It is with his resurrection body that he will come again to earth to judge the nations. Every eye shall see him and his body whom they pierced.

Why the first-born? Paul says in 1 Corinthians 15 that the resurrection from the dead has an order of time. Christ, the firstfruits; second, those who belong to Christ; and third, when Christ has reigned on earth, the rest of mankind for judgement.

Now this clears away certain errors. It is obvious that, for Christ to be the first begotten from the dead, it does not mean he did not exist as God's Son before. Obviously he did. He was God's Son during his ministry before that resurrection. God said so. 'You are my beloved Son in whom I am well pleased.'

He was also God's Son before he was born of Mary. That is why Isaiah prophesied, 'A child is born, but it is a son who is given' – not born, but given (9:6). The word 'begotten' does not refer to when he began to exist; so the Creed correctly says, 'Begotten, not made, being of one substance with the Father'.

'I and the Father are one,' said Jesus. This is a profound mystery, but very wonderful. It is similar to space and time. It is beyond the human mind to understand eternity which has no end and no beginning.

Future Earthly Reign?

Many are speculating on what the future may hold. We find that the Bible reveals God's wonderful plans for the future. Jesus reigns in heaven, but will he reign on earth? Psalm 2 says he will. The Lord's prayer says, 'Thy kingdom come, thy will be done on earth as it is in heaven'. Is that prayer ever to be fulfilled on earth? Psalm 2 says it will be.

In Psalm 2:7–9 the Son of God tells you what was decreed to him. He says, 'I will tell of the decree of the Lord. He said to me, "You are my Son, today I have begotten you. Ask of me and I will make the nations your heritage and the ends of the earth your possession. You will break them with a rod of iron." '

Now when does the New Testament say that will be fulfilled – about the rod of iron? At the end of the New Testament, in Revelation 19:15 you read, 'He will rule them with a rod of iron'. That applies the same expression as in the Psalm. When? It is at the second coming of Christ because it follows the marriage of the Lamb. Then the heavens open and Christ comes forth as King of kings and Lord of lords. Satan is thrown into the bottomless pit. They are all the events of the end of the age. Christ's rejecters will experience 'the rod of iron'.

The expression about the kings of the earth making war against Christ also matches Psalm 2 which says, 'The kings of the earth set themselves and rulers take counsel together against the Lord and his Christ' and verse 6 declares that God will set his king on Zion, his holy hill.

This matches the words of Jesus in Matthew 25:31: 'When the Son of Man comes in his glory and all the holy angels with him, then he will sit on his glorious throne. Before him will be gathered all nations . . . then the king will judge them.'

This picture is developed by God for Zechariah and other prophets. They wrote from 300 to 500 years *after* David. Zechariah 14 reads: 'Behold the day of the Lord is coming . . . for I will gather all nations against Jerusalem.' God described how Jerusalem will have become a problem to the nations. There will be agony in Lebanon which we have seen now. Then Christ's descent to the Mount of Olives is described with all his saints. The nations (through television close-up shots, no doubt) will see the wounds of Christ. 'They will look on me,' saith the Lord, 'whom they pierced.' St John repeats this in the New Testament book of Revelation. 'Every eye will see him whom they pierced and the nations will cry with shock.' 'Then,' says God to Zechariah, in chapter 14 verse 9, 'The Lord will become king over all the earth'.

PSALM 45: OVERFLOWING INSPIRATION

I hope your heart has overflowed at the treasures we have discovered!

Our next prophetic psalm is Psalm 45. What a beautiful opening it has. It says, 'My heart overflows with a goodly theme; I address my verses to the king; my tongue is like the pen of a ready writer.'

This expresses the thrill of inspiration of the Holy Spirit. The Bible does not say who wrote this psalm, but what the Lord Jesus said of David's psalms certainly applies to this Psalm 45.

Remember, Jesus said that David was inspired by the Holy Spirit. That was why he was able to reveal 1,000 years before that the Messiah, the Son of David, was David's Lord who would ascend into heaven to sit at the right hand of the Father God.

But whereas David's psalm was about Christ's majesty and divinity, this psalm is about Christ's humility. He humbled himself to become man. As the psalm opens with the inspiration of the pen of a ready writer, let us examine what the Bible says about the nature of inspiration. This is necessary these days as there are too many who reduce the Holy Spirit's inspiration of the Bible to a human level.

Some have put it down to good ideas which a godly man may have. If so, how could Jacob in his psalm before his death foretell the fortunes of the twelve tribes of Israel? How could Moses have done the same?

Read the remarkable prediction in Jacob's psalm about Judah. In Genesis 49:8–12, he foretells that the tribe of Judah will lead the other tribes in spite of the fact that Judah the ancestor was only fourth in seniority, and in spite of the fact that Judah himself was not too virtuous a character, certainly not so noble as Joseph. Yet, in verse 10, the prophecy said that, 'The sceptre would not depart from Judah'. And it was King David of the tribe of Judah who became king 800 years later. And it was to David that God promised an everlasting throne.

Jacob's prophecy also said, 'Until Shiloh come'. That was an early name for the Prince of Peace. He is now the eternal King who will sit upon the throne of David at his second coming. 'Thy throne is for ever and ever', says Psalm 45.

To Jeremiah the prophet, God said, 'I will raise up for David a righteous branch and he shall reign as king' in the last days. Similar promises were made to the other Old Testament prophets.

As Peter wrote, 'Prophecy came not of old time by the will of man, but holy men of God spoke as they were moved by the Holy Spirit.'

That is why, when you read God's Word, your 'heart can overflow with a goodly theme'.

Psalm 45 Foretells His Gracious Words

What gracious words the Lord Jesus said to those in distress; what restoration he gave to sinners seeking him; what great numbers went away with new hope and purpose in their lives and limbs?

Psalm 45 describes his life on earth with a sentence in verse 2. 'Grace is poured into your lips'. How true this was when the Lord preached his first message in Nazareth. Luke 4:22 says, 'All bare him witness and wondered at the gracious words which proceeded out of his mouth.'

He had quoted the prophecy of Isaiah 61 about his ministry. 'The Spirit of the Lord is upon me because he has anointed me to preach the good news to the poor; he has sent me to heal the broken-hearted; to preach deliverance to the captives, and recovery of sight to the blind; to set at liberty them that are bruised; to preach the acceptable year of the Lord.' Certainly 'grace was poured into his lips'.

The police came to arrest him for unauthorised preaching and healing, but they returned empty-handed and said, 'We just couldn't do it. No other man spoke like this man.'

John the Baptist said of Jesus, 'We have all received his fulness, grace for grace. For the law came by Moses, but grace and truth came by Jesus Christ.' Yes, for the woman caught in adultery, the law said, stone her, but Jesus said, 'I do not condemn you, go and sin no more'. Certainly, grace was poured into his lips. Yes, for the woman who wept for her sins and poured sweet, fragrant ointment upon Jesus, the law had a penalty, but Jesus said, 'Your sins are forgiven you'. And to the Pharisee he said, 'She loved much and she has been forgiven much'.

Yes, for financier Zacchaeus, who had appropriated lots of money, the law had a penalty, but Jesus changed him from greed to grace, so that he gave away his money and received Jesus joyfully. Certainly grace was poured into Christ's lips.

The scribes and Pharisees grumbled at him. 'He eats with money-grabbers and sinners,' but Jesus answered, 'They who are in good health don't need a doctor, but only those who are [spiritually] sick. I came not to call the righteous but sinners to repentance.' What grace poured out to them! Grace and truth was costly to him. Through his sacrifice for you and me, salvation by grace without works is available.

Down the centuries, millions have been saved by grace and given new lives. His grace is offered to all. Those faint with frustration he can refresh with grace. Grace is free because he has paid for it. Paid for our free salvation. That is what grace is – free and undeserved – a gift of Christ's love.

From Ivory Palaces

'Out of the ivory palaces, into a world of woe; only a great eternal love, made my Saviour go.' It is from verse 8 of Psalm 45 that this beautiful song comes. The ivory palaces symbolise heaven with all its glory. Jesus was willing to leave all that and come to rescue everyone who would forsake the defilement of this fallen race. He did not need to do it. He could have justly left us to our fate, we who avoid God and run from his loving grace. Out of the ivory palaces he came to a stable and a carpenter's shop to be despised and rejected of men.

Paul's graphic description of the contrast which fulfilled the psalm is written in Philippians 2 verses 5–11. Let me paraphrase it for you:

> Let this attitude of mind be in you, as it was in Christ Jesus. He was in the form of God, and knew it was not robbery to be equal with God. The devil tried to rob God of his glory, but Jesus who had a right to it, made himself of no reputation instead, by taking upon himself the form of a slave, and was made in the likeness of man. And being found in human form, he humbled himself still further by becoming obedient unto death; and what a death – the torture of the cross. Therefore God has highly exalted him and given him a name which is above every name, that at the name of Jesus, every knee should bow. Yes, everything, everything in heaven, everything on earth and everything under the earth, that every tongue should confess that Jesus Christ is Lord.

'They have made you glad,' said God to King Jesus in Psalm 45. 'Yes, it was for the joy which was set before him that the Lord Jesus endured the cross, despised the shame of a criminal's death and has sat down at the right hand of the throne of God.' These words of Hebrews 12:2 echo the prophecy of Isaiah 53 as well as those of the Psalms:

> Yet it pleased the Lord to bruise him. He has put him to grief. When thou

shalt make his soul an offering for sin, he shall see the results; he shall prolong his days by resurrection. He shall see that his travail was worthwhile and be satisfied . . . by many coming to know him.

The Bible ends with a picture of all those ivory palaces. All those who accepted his salvation are seen rejoicing in those streets of gold and jewelled walls with gates of pearl. But the greatest joy of all, it tells you, is the loving Lamb himself, Jesus in the midst of his Father's throne giving light and joy to his redeemed. The ivory palaces of heaven ring with their praises. They had washed their robes and made them white in the blood of the Lamb. They were a great multitude whom no man could number from all nations, colours and families, crying, 'Salvation to our God who sits upon the throne and to the Lamb. Blessing and glory and wisdom and thanksgiving and honour and power be unto our God for ever and ever.'

Christ's Attributes

The words 'anointed one' meaning 'Christ' occur again in Psalm 45. It is verse 7 which states the Lord Jesus was anointed by the Holy Spirit. There are a number of other attributes given in this psalm as well. Verse 6 tells you 'Thy throne O God is for ever and ever'. What a stupendous revelation. Hebrews, in the New Testament, starts by developing this wonderful theme. In Hebrews 1:8–12 it says this was addressed by God to his Son who is Christ (the Anointed One of Psalm 45:7).

To the Son, God said, 'Thy throne O God is for ever and ever; a sceptre of righteousness is the sceptre of thy kingdom. Thou Lord, in the beginning hast laid the foundation of the earth and the heavens are the works of thy hands.' That harmonises with the opening of St John's Gospel. 'In the beginning was the Word and the Word was with God and the Word was God . . . all things were made by him and without him was not anything made which was made.' So this psalm clearly identifies the Messiah Christ as the Creator.

The New Testament develops this mystery in many places. 'I and the Father are One,' declared Jesus. So they are not two persons, but one. Jesus said that when a person believes on Jesus as his own Saviour, the Holy Spirit comes into that one. He also said, 'and the Father and the Son will come in with the Holy Spirit and make our abode in him.'

How is this Trinitarian Unity possible? 'God is light and in him is no darkness at all,' says the Bible. Light is a good illustration of how three can be one. White light splits up into three primary colours and yet it is one. Three in one and one in three. The Bible presents the Holy Trinity as an enlightening personal experience.

The adoration and love of Jesus as prophesied in Psalm 45 just flows out of it. Verse 2 says 'he is fairer than the sons of men'. In the Hebrew, the word fairer is repeated. 'Fairer, fairer than the sons of men.' Some think that the word beautiful would be a better translation – stated twice in the Hebrew, 'beautiful, beautiful'. He certainly is that to those who have come to know him. Beautiful, as mirrored in the Gospel accounts and beautiful in our growing experience of him. He is fairer than the sons of men because he is in a different category. He is a Son of Man and represented us when he suffered on the cross, but he also is the eternal Son of God from everlasting.

It is because of the beauty of his character that this is represented by the sweet scent of his garments in verse 8, 'All thy garments are fragrant with myrrh and aloes and cassia', the Bible urges you to replace unpleasantness by the fragrance of Jesus. The Lord Jesus is precious to God and precious to the believer and these three perfumes tell you why.

Myrrh is given first, because it is by Christ's death for you that he becomes precious. Myrrh was an ingredient in the holy anointing oil and also used for embalming the dead. Jesus was anointed by God to die for your sins.

Aloes is mentioned next. Aloes is a perfume from India and China, an essence and resin which gives out fragrance from the garments to those who are near. 'Your garments are fragrant', this psalm says to the divine Jesus. To those who are near to Jesus, the fragrance of his character makes their life a joy to themselves and to others.

Cassia is from the bark of a plant in China, Malaysia and Sri Lanka. It is often put on cakes to bring out the taste. In Exodus 30, this was put on the cake of bread offering and waved before God, then burnt on the altar. This made its spicy fragrance rise to God. God says it was a sweet fragrance to him. The bread represented the Lord Jesus, the Bread of Life, sacrificed on the cross. When he was tortured, he only gave kindness and forgiveness. God says that was a sweet fragrance to him.

So then, by the myrrh, Jesus was anointed for death, so that by the sacrifice of himself, he brings the fragrance of aloes to believers who are near him and the fragrance of cassia to God for believers. That all changes the odour of our sins into sweet fragrance of changed lives to God and to others – wonderful!

The Arrows of Conviction and Love

Whose is that baby figure on a poster? He is shooting arrows into a target. Yes, we still see cupid represented in pictures. He shoots his arrow of romance into the red heart of one falling in love.

Falling in love in a spiritual way was what those tough disciples found themselves doing as they knew more and more about Jesus. It happens the same way with us.

Here in Psalm 45:5 we read, 'Thy arrows are sharp in the heart of the king's enemies'. What are those arrows?

First, it is an arrow of conviction. It is usually with unwillingness that we find his Word has penetrated our heart. We are not willing to admit that, in God's sight, we are sinners. Yes, it is while we are enemies of Christ that the shaft of conviction drives home. As Romans 5 says, 'While we were still sinners, Christ died for us'. It was while we were repugnant in the sight of a holy God, without anything to commend us, that Jesus laid down his life for us. As one said, 'When I looked at myself in the mirror, I persuaded myself that I was not too bad, but when I looked at Christ on the cross, I realised I was also callous enough to pass him by. His arrow of conviction broke my heart. I realised that my heart was a rebel – an enemy to God's truth.'

The second arrow which penetrates the heart is the arrow of love – in fact, astonishment! Astonishment that my Creator could even trouble himself about me, let alone come to earth to die for me.

If the story was not in the Bible, recorded by eye-witnesses, testified by those won over by his love, it would be a story most incredible. In fact, when a Stone Age man in New Guinea first heard it, he cried, 'It's foolish! foolish! Why should God let man do that to him?'

The kinds of gods that men have thought up have been gods of vengeance, but the character and sacrifice of Jesus planned in the Old Testament and implemented in the New Testament is something man would not have dreamed of or dared to suggest.

The third thing is that it is the heart that the arrows of King Jesus penetrate. Many make intellectual excuses and we often satisfy the brain and give evidence for the truth. In many cases, the first interest is aroused by giving the evidence for truth, but in the end, unless the heart and affections are won to Christ, nothing deep really happens.

Billy Graham has said that the sun hardens clay and melts butter. You can harden your heart against anything and everything that Christ can do for you, but instead, let the sun of love melt your heart to butter as you see a Christ who was willing to take the punishment we rightly deserve. It may seem foolish that he should do it for us, but it is a thousand times more foolish for anyone to ignore this wonderful love and offer of eternal salvation.

> Amazing love! How can it be,
> That thou my God shouldst die for me!
> *Charles Wesley*

Marriage of the Lamb

I am going to tell you of a wedding you ought to attend! The latter half of Psalm 45 is a prophecy of Christ concerning his bride. You thought Jesus never married! No, he did not, not yet! He is getting married soon though; that is what the Bible says.

You see, the story of Jesus is a love story. Those who are won to him are won to him in love. He doesn't force you to love him, he woos your love. All those who have responded and are saved, are won to him by his sacrificial love. So when Christ returns and resurrects those who belong to him, the Bible says they are invited to a wedding feast. All those who have accepted Jesus are called his bride. That is how close the love and joy and relationship gets between every saved individual and his Lord.

What about the love stories which end, 'And they lived happily ever after'? Sometimes they don't, but in this case, they do, once they are married. All the tests and trials and tiffs of courtship and engagement are over. The saved will live happily ever after.

S U M M A R Y

JESUS IN THE PSALMS

Ten psalms give thirty details
- 1,000 years before fulfilment David wrote of me – inspired by Holy Spirit' (Matt 22:43).

Called 'christ' (means anointed)
- Matt 26:63.
- Ps 2:2 'The Lord and his anointed' or 'his Christ' Ps 45:7.

Rejected by earth's rulers
- Ps 2:2; rulers plot against Christ.

Begotten from the dead. When?
- Ps 2:7 'This day' – the Resurrection Day.
- Ps 118:17–26 Rejected stone became head on the Lord's day v 24.
- Will return v 26.
- Col 1:18 'First-born from the dead'.
- Acts 13:33 'This God fulfilled by raising Jesus from the dead, as it is written (in Ps 2), you are my Son, this day have I begotten you'.
- 1 Cor 15:23 First in order of resurrection; 'first-born from the dead'.
- Rev 1:15 'First-born from the dead.'

Pre-existence
- The Son existed before this from eternity: 'I am' Jn 8:58.

Earthly reign
- Ps 2:7–9 'The earth your possession . . . with a rod of iron'.
- 'Rod of iron' to be experienced by opponents of Christ; Rev 19:15.
- Matt 25:31 'He will sit on his glorious throne'.
- Matt 6:10 Lord's Prayer 'Your kingdom come . . . on earth'.
- Ps 45:6 'Your throne is for ever and ever'.

His gracious words prophesied in Psalm 45
- Ps 45:2 'Grace poured into your lips'.
- Lk 4:22 'Gracious words' Jn 7:46 'No one spoke like this man'.
- 'Fairer' Hebrew word means 'beautiful, beautiful'; lovely character.
- 'Sceptre of righteousness' v 6.
- Myrrh anoints for death v 8.
- Cassia anoints bread for lovely taste. Bread of life satisfies.
- Aloes gives personal fragrance to those near Christ.

Marriage of the Bride Psalm 45:9–17.
- Won to Christ, Rev 19:7–9.

6 THE MISSING WORDS OF PROPHECY
PSALM 40 WITH 22, 110 AND 118

Do you enjoy supplying missing words in a competition? I do! Lots of people spend hours supplying the missing letters in a crossword puzzle.

PSALM 40

Did you know that the Bible has a missing words puzzle for you? It is in Psalm 40. The words before the missing words are these. 'Then I said, "Lo, I come. In the volume of the book it is written about me." Sacrifice and offering you did not desire.'

Then some strange words are added; in fact, a strange sentence. A comment on the original Hebrew will tell you that the Hebrew here has got jumbled up. The translators didn't really know what the next sentence was.

What do you do when working on a crossword? You look at the clues! Where should you look for the clues in the Bible? Well, in the New Testament, of course. In this case, you will find the clue where this verse is quoted in the New Testament. It is the letter to the Hebrews 10:5. 'Sacrifice and offering you did not desire'. That's the start clue, so the next words should supply the missing ones in the Old Testament. What are these very important words? Here they are – 'A body you have prepared for me.'

It is the Lord Jesus speaking. He is saying that, when he was born at Bethlehem, God was supplying him with a body to be sacrificed for sin on the cross when he was aged 33.

How remarkable! Remarkable because that Psalm 40 was a prophecy made by David 1,000 years before Jesus came to fulfil it.

But can we be sure that the words in the New Testament were not added after they were fulfilled? Do you know how we can know they were the genuine original words? Because they were in the Greek translation of the Old Testament and this Greek translation was made 280 years before Christ came and that was the version all the people used in Christ's time. Yes, those words are there. 'A body you have prepared for me.' So what a great solution to the missing words. They could be a solution to words missing in someone's life! Could they be these? 'Lord Jesus, thank you for suffering in my place. I accept forgiveness through your sacrifice in the body which was prepared for you.'

Cave Confirms the Missing Words

In our 'competition' for the missing words from Psalm 40, we have found the clue in the New Testament: 'A body you have prepared for me'. And that this was why God needed no other sacrifice to enable him to forgive sins. We saw that the New Testament found the clue in the Greek translation of the psalm made 280 years before Christ came.

Now I am going to tell you that there was still another clue which confirmed and supplied those missing words. This clue was found when an Arab boy threw a stone into a cave. This cave was in the Dead Sea desert. When the stone landed, he heard a shattering of pottery. He knew he had hit something and climbed into the cave to look. He found very, very old copies of the Old Testament Bible. When experts looked, they knew they were copies made a long time before Christ came. They were in very old Hebrew. See *Evidence for Truth, Volume 2, Archaeology,* Chapter 13.

When they examined more and more of these precious copies, they saw how accurate all the copies of the Scriptures were which had been made since. They found something else too. They found the missing words to Psalm 40. They were the same which were supplied by the New Testament 'A body you have prepared for me'.

So you see, not only did the Greek Old Testament supply the missing words which had been copied by the New Testament writers, the Dead Sea cave also supplied them. They told you why God no longer wanted animal sacrifices for sins. It was because God had supplied the Lord Jesus Christ with a body to be sacrificed on the cross:

> Sacrifice and offering you did not desire; but a body you have prepared for me: burnt offering and sin offering you have not required. (Psalm 40:6; Hebrews 10:5,6)

In this Psalm 40, written 1,000 years before Christ, what is it saying? 'Lo I come to do your will O God.' It must be the eternal Spirit of Jesus long before his birth at Bethlehem. So God must have planned our salvation long before Jesus came to fulfil it. In fact, the next words go on to say what was even in the prophecies before David wrote this psalm. It says, 'In the volume of the book it is written of me'. What book was that? It was the earlier part of the Bible written up to that time.

What parts of the Bible had been written by 1000 BC? All the first five books of Moses in one scroll. God said the king must make a copy of these and read them regularly, which David did. Next, there was the book of Joshua which it says was added. Then what Samuel wrote according to 1 Samuel 10 up to the time of David.

Yes, even in these early Scriptures, the Lord Jesus had been foretold and how the sacrifices given to Moses were only pointing to Jesus, the perfect sacrifice, who would be sufficient atonement for sins for ever and sufficient to save us for ever.

Jesus 'Booked'

Have you been booked? It is usually not a pleasant experience. It usually means that a policeman or traffic warden has put your name and number in a book for a fine.

Wherever I have travelled in the world, I have seen this in the cities – a traffic warden with his little book writing out a parking fine whether in Greece, Sardinia, America, Africa, Australia, Palestine – you name it, there is the man with his book.

I mentioned Palestine. There is a record of a man and his book over 1,000 years before Christ. Here it is in 1 Samuel 10:25. 'Then Samuel told the people the manner of the kingdom and wrote it in a book'. In a way that was a booking for an offence. The people demanded a king. No longer would they rely directly on the Lord. Samuel warned that was a second best, but he wrote the rules in a book.

The first king was a failure, but the second king was David. He was a brilliant success because 'he was a man after God's own heart' and kept God's rules. When Samuel wrote his book about kingship, he 'laid it up before the Lord', the verse says. Wherever was that?

When Moses, long before Samuel, finished writing Deuteronomy, he laid it up before the Lord. When Moses finished Deuteronomy, he'd finished the whole five books called the Law, the Torah and laid it up before the Lord.

When Joshua had conquered the Promised Land, he finished his book and laid that up. Where? In the sanctuary (Joshua 24:26).

So you see, when Joshua and Samuel finished their part of the sacred history, they added their record to the writings of Moses. Where were they kept? In the sanctuary. In fact, in the sacred ark, according to Deuteronomy 31:24. This is what it says:

> When Moses had made an end of writing the words of this Law in a book, until they were finished . . . Moses said, 'Take this book of the Law [that is all five books of Moses] and put it in the side of the ark of the covenant of the Lord your God.'

To this, Joshua added his, and then Samuel added his part up to the time of David.

So then, when David wrote about Jesus in Psalm 40, 'In the volume of the book it is written of me', he was referring to those sacred writings. It said that Jesus was prophesied in those books. Yes, Jesus was booked!

Was he booked for an offence? Actually, he was! He was booked for our offences. He had none of his own. That is why he could take the booking for us. Psalm 40 verse 8 says he had no offence against his own name. 'I delight to do your will O God. Your Law is deep within my heart.'

So, he was booked for our offences. Colossians 2:14 says, 'He blotted out the handwriting which was against you . . . and nailed it to his cross, having forgiven you all your offences.'

Remember that, next time you see a traffic warden with his book, Jesus has paid the fine.

PSALM 22

Words from the Cross

Psalm 22 is the most remarkable prophecy of Jesus Christ in the Psalms. It describes minute details of the suffering of Christ on the cross for our sins. Eight or nine details are given and remarkable ones they are. They are also the very words which our precious Saviour utters – yes, that cry of dereliction, 'My God! My God! Why hast thou forsaken me!' and his last words, 'It is finished!'

Sceptics say, 'Oh, David was speaking about himself when he wrote this'. My reply is, 'Was David referring to himself when he wrote in verse 16, "They pierced my hands and my feet"?' Certainly not. Nowhere in the detailed history of David did this happen. They did not pierce David's hands and feet. There are no circumstances in which this could happen.

It is remarkable that this commonplace torture of crucifixion was not invented until 900 years after David wrote this prophecy. The wounds of Christ for us are again prophesied by Isaiah in 740 BC. Then later still, God tells Zechariah, 'They shall look on me whom they pierced'. The Gospel of John quotes this prophecy as he describes the Saviour hanging there upon the cross.

John also says in Revelation 1, that everyone will see those wounds in Christ's hands and feet. 'Behold, he will come [again] with the clouds, and every eye will see him, and also those who pierced him; and all races of the earth will wail and weep because of him.'

Who was it who pierced him?

- First of all, it was the Roman soldiers who hammered in the nails, tearing the flesh of the hands and feet of their Creator.
- Secondly, it was the commissioned officer who thrust his spear into

the Saviour's side and drew out blood and water, the sign of a broken heart.

- Thirdly, the legal court had pronounced Jesus 'not guilty', but then bowed to popular antagonism. Popular opposition dissuades the uncommitted.
- Fourthly, the religious council and rulers had handed over Jesus to be crucified because some did not believe the prophecies and others did not believe in miracles. Is Jesus being crucified again today by the same people?
- Fifthly, it was the crowd who had come up to the feast from every nation of the known world. Were you there when they crucified your Lord?

Forsaken

Have you felt forsaken and derelict? Then Psalm 22 is for you. It opens with a prophecy of the very cry of dereliction and forsakenness which the Lord Jesus felt on the cross.

He uses the actual words of the Hebrew in that Psalm. '*Eli! Eli! lama sabachthani!*' I have just read them to check in my Hebrew Bible of Psalm 22:1. He cried out those terrible words at the height of the day, 12 noon – and immediately afterwards the whole earth was suddenly plunged into the depth of night darkness as verse 2 says.

If ever you feel forsaken, it can never equal that dread and terror of the darkness which invaded the Saviour's soul. He experienced it all for you – forsakenness.

That darkness was actual and physical too. We have testimony from two writers of the time. They tried to explain it away because they were unbelievers. Their names? One was Thallus who lived in Rome. Yes, the darkness reached the city of Rome. So then, the words of the Gospel, that the darkness covered the earth, are to be taken literally.

The other was Phlegon who, in his writing called *The Chronicles*, said, 'During the time of Tiberius Caesar, an eclipse of the sun occurred during the full moon.' Why does he emphasise the full moon? Because an eclipse of the sun is impossible during the full moon. So it was not an eclipse. God must have used some other means. He is correct, however, about the full moon, because the Passover took place at the full moon of Nisan 14.

A striking article appeared in the science magazine *Nature*. It says that astronomical evidence shows that the 'sun was turned to darkness and the moon to blood' on Friday, 3rd April, AD 33. The full moon would have risen looking as red as blood on that occasion. (Peter referred to it later on the day of Pentecost, Acts 2:20.)

What was it that made God forsake Jesus, as prophesied? It was because God transferred your sins and mine on to our substitute, Jesus.

'It Is finished'

In David's prophecy of Psalm 22, the suffering of the Saviour for us is graphically described. David described all the suffering of Christ on the cross which was to happen 1,000 years later. He wrote two of the words from the cross. The second is in the last verse of the psalm. It reads: 'It is finished'. That is what Jesus said as he bowed his head and gave up his spirit and died. These words are not at first obvious in our English translations of Psalm 22. They merely say, 'He has done it', but the Hebrew would be better translated, 'It is finished'.

Because of this, the psalm says this news will be published to the whole world. Because it is finished, David said it will be told even to generations yet to be born. Generation after generation will be told, 'It is finished'. Down the generations of 2,000 years, this good news certainly has been told.

What is it about those last words from the cross which are such good news? What was finished? It was the work of salvation for you and me. It was completed. Those who trust it can be completely saved. You and I are invited to fulfil the prophecy of the last verse. How? By telling future generations about the completely finished salvation.

Scoffing Crowds

On television and in newspapers, we often see many great crowds of people swirling around for some reason or another, some good, some bad. This Psalm 22 prophesied an accurate picture of the crowd reaction to the crucifixion of the Saviour of the world. Verse 7:

> All they that see me laugh me to scorn, they shoot out the lip and shake the head and jeer, 'He trusted on the Lord that he would deliver him, seeing that he delights in him.'

John reports this as an eye-witness, he says, of the actual fulfilment in the very words the scoffers made.

Then the psalm describes the feelings of the one being crucified (even though crucifixion was not known until 900 years later). 'I am poured out like water, and all my bones are out of joint'. (This is the effect of the weight of the body, dragging down on the nails through the hands, unable to support itself adequately because of the nails through the feet.)

'My heart is like wax. It is melted in the midst of my body. My strength is dried up . . . my tongue cleaves to my jaws.' Remember how Jesus cried, 'I thirst'.

'They pierced my hands and my feet, yet I may count all my bones.' Remember how not one bone of Jesus was broken, but they broke the leg bones of the criminals who were crucified on either side of him.

'They part my garments among them and cast lots upon my vesture.' Now listen to John's eye-witness account in John 19:23 onwards, 'The soldiers took Jesus' garments and divided them into four parts, to each soldier a part. But the coat was without seam, woven from the top throughout, so they said to themselves, "Let us not tear it but cast lots for it".'

So then, the prophecy of the callousness of the crowds to the sufferings of the Saviour was fulfilled. Jesus said there would be similar reactions to Christians after him and down the centuries that has been so.

Here is the account of the testimony of a Christian in the second century. She was a slave girl named Blandina. After others had been tortured to death, Blandina was left. She rejoiced to go 'home' as though it were a wedding feast. She was first scourged with the full severity of a Roman scourging over a pillar, then torn and dragged about by the beasts, then roasted in an iron chair, then put into a net and tossed about by a bull to the satisfaction of the cheering crowd, and finally she was butchered by the beast-finisher. Even that brutal audience which had been watching with frantic joy, could not refuse its admiration: 'Never woman in our time suffered as much as this one.'

The the flesh of the Christians was then eaten by dogs and their bones burnt to ashes and swept into the river and the persecutor shouted, 'They trusted in a resurrection, but we have made sure they will never have a resurrection'.

In our next psalm, we will see how the resurrection of Jesus was prophesied even though they thought they made sure of him. How small will any affliction of ours be compared with these!

Te Deum of Praise

How can you attract a big audience? In the early centuries, the Christians did it by being tortured to death. When the thousands gathered to see them die, they heard their testimonies to how the Lord Jesus had saved them; how Jesus himself had suffered for their sins.

One man who was being roasted alive shouted to the emperor, 'I am thoroughly done on one side and ready for turning'. Obviously, he wanted the emperor to turn to the Lord Jesus. The day may come again when Christians will have to gain their audience by being tortured to death.

The more Christians were tortured before those brutal crowds, so the more among the spectators repented of their sins and turned to Christ, until by the time of the Emperor Constantine in AD 300, over half of his empire was Christian. It is thought that that was the main reason he declared Christianity to be the state religion.

Psalm 22 gives a full description of the terrible sufferings of the

Lord Jesus, and then ends with a Te Deum of praise for the great audience who will praise the Lord and 'all the ends of the earth will remember and turn to the Lord'. It was the suffering of Christ on the cross which made all those Christians willing to suffer as well. In the words of verse 20 onwards, 'He saved their souls from the sword, from the dog, from the lions' mouths and from the horns of bulls' by which they were tossed to death to entertain great crowds.

The saying arose: 'The blood of the martyrs is the seed of the church' as recorded by Tertullian (c. AD 160–225). That ancient hymn called the Te Deum, was written after Christianity won the empire over and was in celebration of the martyrs. It was written in the fourth century. May I remind you of some of its words:

> We praise you O God. We acknowledge you to be the Lord! All the earth worships you, the Father everlasting. The glorious company of the apostles praise you; the goodly fellowship of the prophets praise you; the noble army of martyrs praise you; the Holy Church throughout the world acknowledges you.

It was indeed a great army of martyrs. Such great numbers of them had paid the price to witness before hostile crowds. Revelation 6:9 speaks of such sacrifices. 'I saw under the altar the souls of those who were slain for the Word of God and for the testimony they held.'

PSALM 118

The Psalm of Resurrection

What an eye-opener it has been. The whole history of Jesus is contained in the Psalms of David; his pre-history and eternal existence as God the Creator; the virgin conception; his ministry; his sacrifice for sins; his resurrection and ascension; his eternal priesthood and coming again as triumphant King to rule the world. It is all in the Psalms written 1,000 years before Christ.

Now we come to the Psalm of Resurrection. That is Psalm 118. It begins to give a picture of the risen Lord from verse 18 onwards, then in verse 22 we read: 'The stone which the builders rejected has become the head of the corner. This is the Lord's doing. It is marvellous in our eyes.'

The Lord Jesus said this referred to him, and Peter in Acts 4:10 said this was fulfilled by the resurrection of Jesus from the dead. I quote:

> Rulers of the people and elders . . . be it known to you all . . . that Jesus Christ of Nazareth, whom you crucified, God raised from the dead . . . This is the stone which was rejected by your builders, but which has become the head of the corner. And there is salvation in no other name

under heaven given among men by which we must be saved.

Now Psalm 118 goes on to give the reason that Christians from then on always met for worship on the resurrection day – the first day of the week. Verse 24 says, 'This is the day which the Lord has made. Let us rejoice and be glad in it.' That Jesus would rise on the first day was portrayed by the firstfruit sheaf in Leviticus 23. St Paul says it was in 1 Corinthians 15:23. It is clear that it was the first day in the week because the firstfruit sheaf was waved on the day after the Jewish Sabbath according to Leviticus 23. We find that, after the resurrection day, the disciples gathered again on the next first day and the risen Jesus appeared to them again. From then on, this became a Christian Sabbath, 'The day the Lord hath made'.

Paul celebrated the Lord's Supper at Troas on the first day. He told the Corinthians to prepare their tithes and offerings on the first day. St John was in the Spirit the first day (the Lord's Day). In AD 112, Pliny reported to the Emperor Hadrian that all Christians met for Communion on the first day of the week.

Yes, the resurrection was the Lord's doing and is marvellous in our eyes. This is the day that the Lord has made. Let us rejoice and be glad in it.

Peter quoted another psalm about the resurrection, Psalm 16:8–11. 'I saw the Lord always before me for he is at my right hand . . . my flesh will dwell in hope, for thou wilt not abandon my soul in Hades, nor let thy Holy One see corruption . . . in thy presence there is fullness of joy.'

Fullness of joy – so the result for you should be rejoicing in worship on the Lord's Day.

PSALM 110

The Ascension

Have you ever tried to imagine yourself as an astronaut whizzing straight up into space with your body taking the strain of several g's of gravity? We are going to look at God's first astronaut in his space programme.

In the remarkable Psalm 110, there are as many as nine descriptions of what Jesus was going to do and be. Verse 1 speaks of his ascension into heaven. In this psalm we see the ascension from heaven's vantage point. It is God ordering the ascension of Jesus to commence. 'Sit at my right hand until I make your enemies your footstool.' Another psalm says, 'God is gone up on high with a shout!'

In Acts chapter 1, we see the ascension from earth's angle. The crowd of believers were looking up from the ground, on the Mount of

Olives. Jesus was going up from them, far up into the sky until a cloud concealed him. So you see, the angle and direction of the ascension depends upon what position you see it from.

In the 1960s, there was a lot of discussion on where heaven was and why Jesus had to go up to it instead of at an angle. There was a lot of silly talk about it, such as, if Jesus had been in Australia, he would have gone down instead of up. This kind of talk was really aimed at disbelief in heaven. So I asked, 'In what direction do the astronauts have their lift off?' 'Why, up of course!' Does that mean that their destination is straight up? No, of course not! They change to the appropriate direction once they get out into space.

Figure 6.1. Astronaut's rocket. They have to go straight up first! After that, they change direction to their destination.

The famous writer, C.S. Lewis, who was an atheist at first until he found Christ, looked on heaven as a spiritual realm. It has a location, but in a different dimension from space and time. This is very likely because Genesis 1 says that God was before space and time. Even scientists now talk of when there was no space and no time. Science research also tells us that the evidence is that, in the universe, things exist which cannot be seen. They say that there are over nine times more things in the universe than what can be seen or detected materially. (See *Evidence for Truth, Volume 1: Science,* page 54.)

Isn't it fortunate that God has revealed many of them to us through his Word. As Hebrews 1 says, faith in God's revelation gives the evidence for things not seen . . . Through faith we understand that the universe was framed by the Word of God, so that the things which can be seen were not made by the tangible things which appear.

Thus science is getting up to date with that and believes that over nine times as much reality exists in the universe which cannot be seen as that which is detectable.

So trust God's written revelation of those things which cannot be detected by your material senses, but only by God's revelation.

Private Conversation in Heaven

Have you ever been allowed to overhear a private conversation between important persons? David was! He was allowed to hear what God the Father said to God the Son. What a privilege to hear a private conversation in heaven between the Father God and the Son!

This is what those opening words are in verse 1 of Psalm 110. They record what Jehovah said to the Lord Jesus. Listen carefully to those words. 'The Lord [the word is Jehovah] said to my Lord [that's David's Lord, the Messiah], "Sit thou at my right hand until I make thy enemies thy footstool".'

It was at the ascension that the Lord Jesus left this earth and sat down at the right hand of Jehovah God on high to wait until he descends from heaven with power. So King David, 1,000 years before, was allowed to hear this private conversation between God the Father and God the Son. And we are allowed to read of it – what a privilege! We are given an insight into the discussion of plans for the future – God's plans for the future – tremendous plans for the future which affect world history. Jesus is to sit on his Father's throne until the enemies of Christ are defeated.

How did David hear this private planning in heaven? The original Hebrew word tells you that he saw and heard it in a vision. That private conversation in heaven was typical of many a private conversation of Christ with his Father when he was on earth later. We sense the loving fellowship which Jesus had with the Father God in such passages as the following. This one is recorded by Matthew and Luke:

> At that time, Jesus answered and said, 'I thank you O Father, Lord of heaven and earth, because you have hidden these things from the clever intellectuals and have revealed them unto babes. Even so Father, for it seemed good in your sight.'

That too must have referred to an earlier planning discussion in heaven. Then Jesus continues:

> All things are delivered to me by my Father and no man knows the Son except the Father, neither does any man know the Father except the Son, and to whatever person the Son will reveal him.

That is in Matthew 11. You are given more examples of that kind of loving conversation by John in the fourth Gospel. Here is an example in chapter 5:

Jesus said to them, 'Truly, truly, I say to you, the Son can do nothing of his own accord, but only what he sees the Father doing, for whatever he does, the Son does also, for the Father loves the Son and shows him everything he is doing; and greater works than these will he show him, that you may marvel . . . that all may honour the Son, even as they honour God the Father.'

Again in John 17:

These words Jesus spoke and lifted up his eyes to heaven and said, 'Father, the hour has come, glorify your Son so that your Son can also glorify you . . . O Father, glorify me with your own self, with the glory which I had with you before the world existed.

So you see how closely Jesus knew the Father and the Father knew the Son, as both Matthew and John record; but did you notice that remarkable possibility of your joining that divine fellowship.

As God promised in Jeremiah 31:31, even the least important can now know him personally when you receive Jesus as your Saviour and from there go on to converse with your heavenly Father about his plans for you.

The Order of Melchizedek

One of the most astonishing statements is in David's Psalm 110 verse 4. It is extraordinary from many angles and I will tell you why. It is this verse, 'You are a priest for ever after the order of Melchizedek'.

Now in David's day, who could be told that the Messiah was an eternal priest? David said it was God speaking to his Lord after he had ascended into heaven and sat at God's right hand.

However did David come to write those extraordinary words? It was 1,000 years before Jesus fulfilled them. But a further mystery is that David should say that his Lord, Jesus, would not be a Levitical priest, but an order of priesthood unheard of by the Israelites. Their type of priesthood was the Levitical. They sacrificed animals as sin offerings in the tabernacle and the temple. But this Melchizedek did not sacrifice animals at all. He only sacrificed bread and wine. Now who was Melchizedek foreshadowing – one who was to be an eternal priest and who was to bring bread and wine? Surely, it is Jesus. Yet David speaks of him 1,000 years before he became man and calls him his Lord. 'Jehovah said unto my Lord . . . you are a priest for ever after the order of Melchizedek.'

Who was this Melchizedek? He lived 1,000 years before David. He lived in Abraham's time. You will find the record in Genesis 14.

Abraham had a private army. I told you about it in *Evidence for*

Truth, Volume 2: Archaeology. He had a big battle with four kings. You may be surprised to know that this very ancient history was proved true when a record of it was found on clay tablets which were dug up. Well, those four kings kidnapped Abraham's nephew, so Abraham's army chased them and rescued his nephew. It was then, after the rescue, that this mysterious person met Abraham. He is described as: 'King of peace and righteousness, priest of the Most High God, who brought bread and wine and blessed Abraham.' He said, 'Blessed be Abraham by God Most High, Maker of heaven and earth.'

So you see how remarkable is this prophecy by David. It took a mysterious priest, 1,000 years before him, to illustrate the kind of King and Priest Jesus would be, 1,000 years after him. David said that his Lord would ascend into heaven, sit at God's right hand and be an eternal priest after the Melchizedek type. He would not need to offer any animal sacrifice, because he would sacrifice himself and would express its meaning in bread and wine. Now that is inspiration!

Christ's Intercession

Do you feel powerless, overlooked, just a nobody? Then you have a powerful representative in the powerhouse that matters. One who has been through it just like you; one who is ready to act on your behalf. He is a most powerful advocate, who has risen from the depths of suffering to the most powerful place in the universe. He is willing to put your case. He is willing to plead it for you! We read this:

> We don't have one who is unable to sympathise with our weakness, but one who in every way has been tempted like we are, yet without sinning (Hebrews 4:15).

Yes, it is Jesus, your Saviour.

> In the days of his earthly life, Jesus offered up prayers and entreaties, with loud cries and tears to him who was able to save him from death, and he was heard . . . Although he was a Son, he learnt obedience through what he suffered . . . and became the way of eternal salvation to all who obey him, being chosen by God to be a High Priest after the order of Melchizedek (Hebrews 5:6,7).

Our Melchizedek intercedes for us. This is also prophesied in Isaiah 53:12. 'He bore the sin of many, and made intercession for the transgressors.'

When he ascended to the presence of God, he would plead for you and me in God's presence as one who had gone through it all, as you are doing. One who came not to blame, but to bless.

I read in Hebrews 7:25 that, in the Melchizedek role, 'he is able to save for ever those who draw near to God through him, Jesus Christ, because he lives for ever to make intercession for you.'

The fact that the Lord Jesus is our advocate is also spoken of in John's first letter. 'We have an advocate [someone who pleads for us] with the Father, Jesus Christ the righteous, and he is the expiation [payment] for our sins' (1 John 2:1,2).

I have had a lot of phone calls and letters from people who feel that they have nobody to stand up for them. Even God seems distant. Life hardly seems worth living This may be due to a feeling of rejection or worthlessness which comes from a feeling of failure.

Beloved, don't trust your feelings, trust Jesus. He is your advocate, not your accuser. It is the evil one who accuses the Christian. Jesus is your advocate. It was while you were worthless, the Bible says, that he redeemed you.

'We have an advocate who was tested in all points like us' (Hebrews 4:15). He had such agony of depression and forsakenness that he sweated great drops of blood. That is your wonderful advocate. Put your case to him. He will plead it for you with his precious blood.

The Day of His Power

We are coming to the end of this wonderful insight into prophecies of Jesus in the Psalms. It is amazing, isn't it, that those prophecies of David give every aspect of Christ's birth, ministry, death, resurrection, ascension to the right hand of God and his coming to reign and judge.

To complete the many thoughts from this psalm above, we are told that the day of his power is coming. Psalm 110:1: 'Sit at my right hand,' said Jehovah to David's Lord, when Christ ascended to heaven, 'until I make your enemies your footstool.'

The psalm goes on to say, 'Your power will reach out from Zion in Jerusalem'. Christ will rule his foes, but his people will offer themselves willingly in the day of his power. He will execute judgement, and shatter rulers who have opposed him.

There are rulers and governments who have shut out Christ from their nations today. In fact, half the world has done so. That is why the gospel can reach some of them only through the air. The sudden descent of Christ from heaven will shatter them in God's wrath and anger. He will judge the nations, the psalm says. He will shatter chiefs over the wide earth.

Here then, we can turn to the second psalm. 'Be wise therefore O kings! Be warned O rulers of the earth! Serve the Lord with fear, kiss the feet of his Son lest he be angry.' This psalm foretold that at the end of this age, 'The rulers of the earth would set themselves against the Lord and his anointed Christ'. Yes, these are the words written 3,000 years ago. But verse 6 says, 'I will set my king and Christ on Zion, my holy hill' in the face of his enemies.

But what does verse 3 mean? 'They will be willing in the day of his power.' What people are these? Does this refer to Israel? It must do, because his saved ones were willing *before* his day of power. In fact, other scriptures say that they will descend with him in the day of his power. They were willing in the centuries during his rejection. But his ancient people Israel will not be willing until he descends to them in power.

So you who are sharing his rejection now will share in the day of his power.

A vivid description of this was given to the Christians in Thessalonica who were brutally persecuted: 'When the Lord Jesus is revealed from heaven in blazing fire with his powerful angels he will punish those who do not obey the gospel of our Lord Jesus Christ . . . On that day he comes to be glorified in his holy people, and to be admired in all you who believe' (2 Thessalonians 1:7–10).

Lift up your heads – it's a great day that's coming!

SUMMARY

PROPHECY IN PSALMS 22, 40, 110 AND 118

Psalm 40

- Supply the missing words from Ps 40:6 (Jewish Hebrew copy of AD 900 had lost the words).
- 'Sacrifice you did not desire . . . burnt offering and sin offering you have not required.'
- Clue from NT Greek in Heb 10:5: Sacrifice you did not desire *soma de katertiso moi.*
- Clue from OT Greek LXX translated 280 BC; sacrifice you did not desire *soma de katertiso moi.*
- Clue from Dead Sea Scroll 100 BC agrees. So they supply the words which are missing from the Hebrew copy of AD 900. The English translation is: *But a body you prepared for me.*
- Significance of Ps 40: David 1000 BC heard the Second Person of the Trinity prophesy that a body would be prepared for him (by virgin conception) for him to sacrifice for our sins.
- 'And in the volume of the book it is prophesied of me.' What volume was that? Up to David's time it was the Pentateuch, Josh, Jdg to 1 Kgs. Scrolls were by Moses, Joshua and Samuel, all put in the sanctuary (Deut 31:24–26; Josh 24:26; 1 Sam 10:25). Moses wrote of atoning sacrifice and Samuel of kingship.

Psalm 22

- Describes suffering in detail of Christ on the cross. Mark each detail.

Psalm 118

- The joyful Resurrection, The Lord's Day and foundation stone for faith.

Psalm 110

- Ascension to God's right hand until his return and our present advocate.
- It is a private conversation in heaven which David overheard. The Father and the Son were discussing future plans.

7 WHAT GOD FORETOLD TO HOSEA
ISRAEL ON PROBATION

Most Bible commentaries miss the main point of Hosea's tragedy. It is that, even as Hosea placed his wife on probation for a long time, so God would place Israel on probation for over two-and-a-half millennial 'days' in their dispersion if they did not repent. This was fulfilled in 721 BC, when the ten tribes of northern Israel (called Ephraim) were dragged into captivity in Assyria (northern Iraq). That was 118 years before the southern two tribes (called Judah) were banished into captivity.

GOD'S BROKEN HOME

Did you know that God had a broken home and a broken heart? This will help you if you have experienced this close at hand. Today, most families have had an experience of this in some way – either one of their sons or daughters has experienced it, a relative or sadly their own marriage has been threatened.

Yes, I said that God had a broken home. That is what he told Hosea the prophet. 'O the pain of it!' said God. 'I had a wife who left me, her husband and she became a prostitute, not once, not twice, but three times. And now I have still taken her back, but this time I have put her on probation.'

Yes, you are reading right! That is what God told Hosea the prophet to say to the ten northern tribes of Israel.

'But worse still,' God said, 'I have had unfaithful children. I have pleaded with them and I implored them to return to the good ways I taught them, but they have just sneered in my face. Now I have got to give them up. O Ephraim, how can I give you up!' God continued to dictate his feelings to Hosea. 'I remember when you were a sweet child. I jumped you on my knee. I put walking reins on to you to teach you to walk. I dangled you from my hands as you chuckled with glee. But now look at you – a sulky sodden son! Oh Ephraim, how can I give you up!' (Ephraim meant the ten tribes of northern Israel.)

Yes, that is what God told Hosea about his broken home and his disappointed hopes and his broken heart.

'Now, Hosea, your broken home and prostitute wife; your faithless ungrateful children are an experience near to mine as I weep over my unfaithful wife, Israel, and over my rebellious sons, Ephraim and Judah, as I weep over them, I weep over every unfaithful wife. I weep over every unfaithful husband. I weep over every straying daughter and son. I weep over everyone who has strayed from me,' God says.

'But Hosea, you must show compassion and forgiveness for your unfaithful wife; for I will show compassion for Israel, after she has learnt her lesson, after her period of probation. Her period of probation will be 2,500 years and I will bring back her sons. I will not be defeated! I will win them back in the end. Where once I said, "You are not my wife or my sons", there I will say, "My wife" and she will say "My husband".' Yes, God likened Israel to being a wife to him, who had run after others and shamed his name. God likened the sons of Israel, Ephraim (the ten tribes) and Judah (the two tribes) to rebellious sons – prodigal sons; and later Jesus Christ said that all who have forsaken God are like prodigals. The Father God runs to meet the stray as he comes back in his rags. If you are one who is straying, the pain of a good Father is in the heart of God for you.

This is the message of the prophecy of Hosea. As I discuss this series with you, we will see how remarkably prophecy is working out in history. We will look at staggering predictions and fulfilments which so many seem to have missed or were afraid to reveal.

It is a human story; a story of a human tragedy. It is a divine story; a story of a divine tragedy. The story of a broken home and broken hearts; a story of seeking and forgiving love; a story which will snatch you up and involve you in the loving, restoring arms of your Father God. It will amaze you to discover that those arms of God reach down the centuries of history. They reach out to fulfil today what was so remarkably foretold in Hosea's time. That agony of love not only reaches out to embrace again a nation, it reaches out to you, an individual! The prophecy of Hosea dives in at the deep end of sorrow straight away in the second verse:

> The Lord said to Hosea, 'Go and marry a girl who is a prostitute so that some of her children will be born to you from other men. This will illustrate to you the way my people have pained me by being untrue to me and my revelation.'

So young Hosea did just this. He married Gomer, the daughter of Diblain and soon the children began to arrive. The first was named Jezreel, as a warning to Israel that the end was near. The second was named by God by a name which meant 'No more mercy'. The third was named by God *Lo-ammi*, which meant 'Not my people'. This is not my son! These children would also be put on probation. Why? Because they too would forsake their Father God and his truth. They too would cause pain to their loving Father God. And yet, right at the start of these 14 chapters of prophecy, God shows his loving forgiveness and restoration. Yes, he is not going to give them up. He is going to wait patiently until they have learned the hard way. They refused to learn the easy way.

That is so with many of us, isn't it? God has to put us on probation if we won't learn the easy way and the hard way is the painful way for our God as well. Yet, before this first chapter has ended, our loving God promises restoration in spite of our truculent ways. Listen to verse 10:

> It shall come to pass that in the place where I named you *Lo-ammi* – 'Not my people' – there will I rename you 'My people'. Yes – sons of the living God. And the place where I named you 'No more mercy', there I will rename you 'Mercy and forgiveness'.

The rest of this prophecy of Hosea tells how he shows this and proves this in history with Israel. It also shows how he does it with you as well. The twelve tribes of Israel were put on probation for 2,520 years. It started 80 years after Hosea was told by God, first with the ten tribes of Ephraim and then later with the two tribes of Judah. In this twentieth century AD, the 2,520 years is already being fulfilled and we see Israel and Judah back in their land in the same place as promised in Hosea 1:10. But they have still to learn their final lesson.

The Characteristics of the Probation Period

What is the character of that probation period? It is given in chapter 3 of Hosea. It is a remarkable one and history has fulfilled it! Israel was to be stripped of all the forms of religion she once trusted in. She trusted in the outward forms of religion, but not in the spiritual truth. She also ran to other gods and false religions. The Bible describes this as spiritual adultery. It adulterates the truth of God by mixing it with satanic counterfeits. There are those intent on doing this today. They are making a world religion by amalgamating all religions. This syncretism is an adulteration of the true revelation of God in Jesus Christ.

So then, even as Hosea's wife committed adultery with other men, so Israel went in for including in her religion false idols. Idols of Molech with horrible infant sacrifices; idols of Baal whose priests cut themselves with knives until the blood gushed out in their frenzied dances; idols of Dagon, the earth and sea god. They visited the temple prostitutes of false gods until the Lord was sick at heart. They even incorporated immorality as part of their religion.

So then, this religious adultery of Israel was replaced by the probation period of the absence of all these things. In chapter 3 verse 4, God pronounces it: 'The children of Israel will live for a long period without a king'. (That period has been long – over 2,500 years, they have had no king even 2,000 years after King Jesus: 'I will return again to my place, until they acknowledge their offence' 5:15.)

Let us read on. 'And they shall be a long time without a prince and without a sacrifice.' That is true as well. Since Prince Jesus came, they have had no need of a sacrifice. So the temple and sacrifices ended as Daniel prophesied. I quote, 'The Messiah will be cut off, but not for himself'. Yes, it was for others that Jesus the Messiah died, not for himself, but for us.

Then, as Daniel prophesied in chapter 9 verses 24 and 26, the sanctuary of the temple was destroyed in AD 70 and since then Israel has never offered another sacrifice. For nearly 2,000 years sacrifices have ceased. As God told Hosea in this third chapter, *Israel has been without a king, without a country, without a temple and without a sacrifice.* It is amazing because sacrifices for sin were at the very centre of Jewish religion. But now, even in their annual Passover meal, no lamb is sacrificed. God thus shows that the Lamb of God's sacrifice for your sins is sufficient atonement for your salvation for ever.

As Hebrews 10 says, the old temple priests offered sacrifices every day, sacrifices which could never take away sins. They only pointed in type to Jesus who was to fulfil their meaning. Hebrews 10:12–14 says, 'But this man Jesus [because he was man as well as God], after he had offered for all time one sacrifice for sins, he sat down at the right hand of God. Since that time, he waits for his enemies to be made his footstool, because by one sacrifice he has made perfect for ever those who are being made holy.'

What is the next prophecy this remarkable verse gives? We turn back again to Hosea 3:4 and we read that Israel *will be without an image* for that long period of 2,520 years.

Now the remarkable fact is that during this period of probation, Israel has forbidden any carving of the image of man or beast! Look through all the modern sculpture of Israel and all you find is geographical designs. Moreover, for the 2,520 years probation, Israel has forbidden the making of any idols! That too is mentioned in this verse. 'You will be without teraphims' – they had become idols.

It also says they will be without priests. That is the meaning of the word 'ephod'. It was the priests who wore the ephod. That was the ritualistic sacrificial priestly robe.

There is no need now of priests because the Lord Jesus is our High Priest and because no other sacrifices are necessary. His one offering is sufficient atonement for all sinners. So you see how literally this verse, Hosea 3:4, has been and is being fulfilled. Israel was put on probation for 2,520 years. During that time she has been without a king, without a country and, since AD 70, without a temple, without sacrifices, without a priest, without images or idols.

'They Will Return and Seek a King'

But what follows in the next verse? Oh the glory of it! It says, 'Afterwards the children of Israel will return. Hallelujah – have they returned to their land? A member of parliament was asked by a Cabinet minister, 'What proof have you got that the Bible is true?' He answered, 'The Jew – the history of the Jew. A history fully foretold in the Bible by God.' That is a proof he could not dispute!

What is the next stage according to verse 5? It says, 'They will seek the Lord their God.' That stage has not yet begun. Many Israelis are atheists. The terrible atrocities against their nation have embittered them. There are, of course, some Israelis who see that their return to the Promised Land is a fulfilment of prophecy. They are called Zionists. It would surprise you to see their literature which quotes all the prophecies of the Old Testament. There are also those Jews who weep at the Wailing Wall and who read their Scriptures in their synagogues.

Also the New Testament has been translated into Hebrew and is read in schools. Why do so many Jews read the New Testament? They say it is because the New Testament is the book which describes their land when they were last in it. But in reading about their land, they also read about the Lord Jesus Christ. This has been going on for some years now and the Israeli government is alarmed and trying to stop it.

So you see, we are at an exciting stage of prophecy. What is the next stage in that verse, Hosea 3:5? 'They shall seek David their king'. Now, how on earth can they seek David their king? He has been dead nearly 3,000 years! He had been dead for 200 years when God said this to Hosea! Would it be the Son of David – that is, Jesus? He said that when he returns to this earth (I refer to Matthew 25:41), when he returns with all his holy angels, he will set up his throne on earth and judge all nations on how they treated his brothers, the Jews. Is this the time when Israel will seek David their king?

These then are the words of Hosea 3:4 and 5. Another prophet tells you how it will happen. Zechariah quotes God, 'They will see him whom they have pierced.' As the Israelis see Jesus descending from heaven, they will realise with a shock, it is the one they crucified – and the other nations too. The prophecy says they will mourn with deep sorrow and the whole nation will be converted and cleansed at the fountain for forgiveness. The verse in Hosea 3:5 ends here, 'They will fear the Lord and his goodness in the latter days'.

They Are Back in the Same Place

This will be the end of their probation period. This will be when the Lord will say, 'At the place where I said, "You are no longer my people", I will say to you, "You are my people" and at the place where I said "Your name is no more mercy", I will say, "I will have mercy", you shall have forgiveness.'

God's broken home will be mended. The adulterous wife, Israel, so long on probation, will be remarried. She shall say, 'I am your faithful wife'; the Lord will say, 'I am your husband'. Her rebellious children also will say, 'We are your children' and God the Father will say, 'You are my sons'.

What a wonderful denouement, what a grand climax to the painful story of 25 centuries. Israel was embittered by her experiences and learned the hard way. If you are embittered, God says, please learn the easy way. In Hosea 13:9 he says, 'Oh Israel, you have destroyed yourself, but in me is your help. I will be your king . . . I will ransom you from the power of the grave. I will redeem you from death. O death, I will be your plague. O grave, I will be your destruction . . . O Israel, return unto the Lord . . . I will heal your backslidings. I will love you freely.'

Is the Lord saying the same to you? I don't expect you have sinned as badly as Hosea's wife who became a prostitute. I don't expect you have become as bad as adulterous Ephraim who prostituted the truth of God and mixed it with other religions and idols. But perhaps you have had idols in your heart, things you worship more than God and so the Lord has had to give you a probation period as he did to his wife, Israel. It was painful to you and to God. God experienced the sorrow of a broken home, but he says to you, 'Your probation period is over'. Come weeping to the cross, look at him whom you pierced with your sins and hear him say to you: 'Where I said to you, "You are no longer mine", I will say to you, "You are mine".' Where is that place? It is at the cross of Jesus. You come by saying to Jesus, 'You have bought me by your suffering; I am yours.'

GOD'S BROKEN FAMILY

Did you know that there is a clear hint in the prophecy of Hosea that Israel's probation period would last for two millennia between the first coming of Christ and the second coming of Christ? This ties in with the end of the 2,520-year Diaspora which commenced in stages from 603 BC.

You remember that the Bible says, 'A day in the sight of the Lord is as a thousand years and a thousand years as one day' (2 Peter 3). Well, in Hosea chapter 6, the Lord says, 'I will go and return to my place, until they acknowledge their offence and seek my face. In their affliction they will seek me early.' 'Come let us return to the Lord for he has torn us and he will heal us; he has smitten us and he will bandage up our wounds.' Now notice the next words. 'After two days, he will revive us. In the third day, he will raise us up and we will live in his sight . . . his coming is as certain as the morning dawn.'

I like that translation: 'His coming is as certain as the morning sunrise.' It brings out the meaning of the Hebrew more clearly. You see how the return of the risen Christ to heaven is referred to. It says, 'I will return to my place until Israel acknowledges their offence.' Just before his crucifixion, Jesus said to the Jews, 'I will ascend unto my Father . . . and you will not see me again until you say "Blessed is he who comes in the name of the Lord".'

Two Millennial Days

We are approaching the year AD 2000, almost 2,000 years since Jesus said that. Two millennial days are nearly ended. If the Lord comes for the saved seven years before he comes to Israel, his second coming must be near, especially when you realise that owing to a miscalculation of our Western calendar, Jesus was born four to seven years before AD 1.

Why does Hosea chapter 6 say, 'after two days' and then add 'and in the third day'?

I think that the two days mean two thousand-year days and is the time (roughly) between Christ's first coming and his second coming; but the reference to part of a third day takes you back to the time before Christ when Israel was first taken into exile. Israel was exiled over 700 years BC. Both periods end together near the second coming of Christ.

The wording is not precise because you are not intended to make a precise calculation. It just gives the general span of time – about 2,000 years from the Lord's first coming to his second coming and about 2,500 years from Israel's dispersion to her return as a State of Israel. It should remind you that our God is the God of Ages.

> O God our help in ages past
> Our hope for years to come.
> A thousand ages in they sight?
> Are like an evening gone.
> *Isaac Watts*

HOSEA AND THE TWO GREAT REVIVALS

The Former and the Latter Rain

In Palestine there are two rainy seasons. One is in the spring and the other in the autumn. Between them is a long dry season. Rain is refreshing. It is 'revival'. When you are blessed with spiritual revival, you are greatly refreshed (Acts 4:19).

Are there to be two eras of revival? Does this expression about the former (autumn) and the latter (spring) rain refer to revival? We find the expression here in Hosea 6:5. It seems significant that it is associated in the text with the first coming and the second coming of the Lord Jesus Christ. The expression occurs in other prophecies also. Zechariah speaks of the former and the latter rain when the Lord will visit his people with times of refreshing.

The best-known passage about it is Joel chapter 2. The apostle Peter made Joel's prophecy well known when he said that the great outpouring of the Holy Spirit on the day of Pentecost was a fulfilment of one of those rainy seasons. Thousands of people were converted in one day and there was a great time of people turning to the Lord for salvation. Great signs and miracles accompanied the preaching of the gospel.

I have heard some good Christians say that they don't expect another similar outpouring of the Holy Spirit. The days of miracles are past, they say. But is this right? There were two rainy seasons. Is God going to fulfil the symbolism in only one of them or is the second rainy season going to have a spiritual fulfilment as well? If so, the sowing and reaping season represents Christian history. One year's seasons represents the 2,000 years of the Christian era referred to in the preceding verses of Hosea. The year starts with the spring rain, called the latter (winter) rain. And that is what Peter called Pentecost and the year ends with the autumn rain called the early (winter) rain.

It does seem that the revival spoken of in Hosea refers to the end of church history. The second coming has been referred to in the words, 'His coming is as sure as the morning sunrise'. The two millennial days have been referred to – 2,000 years between the first and second coming, and in verse 2 you read that then 'he will revive us'. We have seen that this did refer to Israel as a nation, but it can also refer to spiritual Israel – the Church. But revival does not come automatically. The Lord says that we have to 'cry unto him day and night'.

Revival starts in God's people first and then the Holy Spirit goes out into the community. Refresh your expectancy with the words of Joel 2:28,29:

> And afterwards, I will pour out my Spirit on all people. Your sons and daughters will prophecy, your old men will dream dreams, your young men will see visions. Even on my servants, both men and women, I will pour out my Spirit in those days.

An Answer to Law-breaking, Lust and Murders

Has it puzzled you that whole nations and communities seem quite happy to join in mass religion so long as it does not touch their lives too closely?

In some countries, whole communities turn out in full for religious ceremonies. They parade their images and idols and play their bands, but when religion requires a change of heart, that popularity vanishes.

It was so with Israel. The ritual of religion had full support. Sacrifice of animals was made and services widely attended, but God said this of the nation in Hosea 6:8 onwards:

> The city is full of lawbreaking and polluted with blood. Whole gangs of robbers and thieves wait to mug a man. Even many priests are immoral. I have seen horrible things says the Lord God, prostitution and filth . . . The rulers rejoice in wickedness and the government is full of lies. They are adulterers heated with lust like a baker heats an oven. Ephraim is half-baked. They coo like a dove to a power in the West and give bird calls for help from the threat to the East. But they have not cried unto me. I have redeemed them but they turn my truth into lies.

Yes, they have mixed heathen idolatry with God's truth. Thus reads a modern translation. And how modern its picture!

So what is God's reply to this empty popular religious ritualism? He says in Hosea 6:6, 'I desire mercy and not sacrifice and the personal knowledge of God more than burnt offerings.'

How does this apply to us? There are two things here. Firstly, outward forms of religion should illustrate truth and not error and, secondly, even if outward forms illustrate truth – God's truth – Bible truth – they are not acceptable if they are a pretence of the real thing.

What is the real thing? God pleads in chapter 14:

> O Israel, return unto the Lord thy God, for you have fallen by your iniquity and sins. Take with you words (not empty ritual acts) and turn to the Lord and say to him, 'Take away all my sin and receive me by your grace. Cleanse my lips and I will give my words to your service.'

So you see, it comes down to individual response and immediately the Lord replies in verse 4, 'I will heal your backslidings, I will love you freely, for my anger is turned away.' The ways of the Lord are right and the saved will walk in them.

Corruption Started with the Priests

'When salt has lost its effectiveness, corruption sets in.' The Lord Jesus said this and this is what God was saying to Hosea in chapters 4 and 5.

Why is there no knowledge of God in the land? Why is swearing, lying, killing, stealing and committing adultery breaking all bounds and murder follows murder, God asks. It is because the salt has lost its effectiveness, its savour. You are the salt of the earth, Jesus said about the Church. If you lose your saltiness, a nation goes corrupt. Is your nation corrupt? Is there swearing, lying and killing and no knowledge of God? The fault is that of churches which only half believe the gospel.

And why is the Church unfaithful to God's revealed truth? God makes a statement which many find unwelcome in these chapters 4 and 5 of Hosea. 'My contention is with you, O priest!' and again God says, 'Hear this, O priest! You have been a snare!' Now, I hesitated to give this part of Hosea, but if I didn't, I would not be giving you the whole word. Is the Church full of unbelief? Then it is the priests who have swallowed and disgorged their unbelief. Now of course there are many wonderful, faithful, believing ministers of God's Word, but God's contention is with those who have swallowed unbelief and of course they get the press. Yes, God says he has a contention with them.

Do you know where this disbelief started? It was in many of the theological colleges which teach people who are training for the ministry. Instead of rejecting error, they latched on to the theories of an immoral Paris doctor – a physician. His name was Astruc. He lived 250 years ago. He suggested that Moses never wrote the Pentateuch. Then 100 years later, a German named Wellhausen developed this theory and added unbelieving criticism to the rest of the Bible. All this was founded on ignorance of the ancient literary methods of the ancients.

Did the theologians wipe their hands of it? Certainly not. Like the Athenians of Paul's day, they welcomed anything new and scandalous. It was put into the training courses of many colleges and universities. All reply was stifled and actual evidence for truth was banned. This unbelief then spread to the nominal church and from the nominal church to the nations.

The sowing of unbelief gave germination to cynicism, agnosticism, indifference and then to all kinds of pagan practices. The salt had lost its savour. Hosea 4:4–6 says, 'Like people, like priest . . . My people are destroyed for lack of knowledge. Because you have rejected the true knowledge, I reject you from being priest to me.'

'My contention is with you, O priest!' said God to Hosea. He says it again in our time. For did not Peter say that in the last days sceptical ministers would come and pretend that they don't even see that Christ promised to return literally. They believe that God cannot intervene in his creation. 'My coming will take that unfaithful servant unawares', said Jesus.

But pray for your faithful pastors who believe God's Word. They have a difficult time. You should support them, be loyal to them and encourage them and share their witness.

A Parent's Sad Reflections

It is sometimes said of a person, 'He wears his heart on his sleeve'. He lets people see how he is moved by their troubles – and their mistakes.

In the words God spoke to Hosea, God reveals his heart-throbs. He shows how he is grieved as a good loving parent over his straying, stumbling and rebellious children. He reflects upon all his hopes he had for them when they were young, but how they have turned out such a disappointment. Is that true of you?

He grieves as a parent who remembers how lovely the child looked and he remembers how, when playing with the child, he imagined a happy and wonderful future for him. But now – oh the agony of heart – after giving the grown lad, now in manhood, chance after chance, he has to give him up. 'O how shall I give you up, Ephraim?' he cries. The closing pages of the prophecy are covered with the compassionate heart of the disappointed Heavenly Father. He remembers what hopes he had for Israel. 'When Israel was a child, I called him out of Egypt.' The Lord Jesus had to relive this all over again in his experience on behalf of mankind – on your behalf, when he was a child refugee brought back from Egypt.

Have you gone back to the slavery of Egypt? The Lord weeps until he delivers you again. Listen to his sad reflection over his lost child in Hosea chapter 11:

> I taught you my child to walk in my ways. I put reins under your arms, and you, like a babe, took it all for granted. I lifted you onto your feet with those walking straps like cords of love and I taught you to talk and scooped food into your mouth – the bread of life – the life-giving Word of God. But in your adolescent rebellion, you were bent on contradicting all I say. You became a prodigal son and daughter. And now you are on probation. O son, daughter, how can I give you up! How can I deliver you! How can I let you suffer the fate of Sodom. My heart turns within me. The conflict of love with justice pains me.

Do you know how God resolved that conflict of his love for you with the requirement that justice must be done? God himself in Jesus Christ bore the penalty of justice for your sentence on the cross. Out of that heart tormented with love for you, flowed the blood which can cleanse you from all sin and water of the Holy Spirit to change your nature to the love of Christ.

GOD'S BROKEN HOME RESTORED

So there we have seen how God shared with you his experience of a broken home, a disappointing marriage. His agonies are like the prophet Hosea's. God's people were like a wife who had forsaken him, like a wife who became a prostitute, sharing her love with the enemies of God.

We saw how the children of such prostitution also became unfaithful to the Heavenly Father so that God named them 'not my children', but would one day rename them, 'my own children'. How other children were named 'no longer deserving mercy', but one day, God in his persistent seeking would restore them and he would rename them 'receiving mercy'. But the greatest heart-moving pathos is the Lord's dealing with his people as with a wife. The most remarkable fulfilment of it in history down to our day.

Hosea had to place his prostitute wife on probation. On giving her chance after chance, she now had to prove her change of heart. We saw how this period of probation would last about 2,500 years from the exile or about 2,000 years from Christ's first coming.

Israel's Tribulation

Israel would have tribulation during that probation period. The tribulation spoken of in Matthew 24:21 and in Luke 21:22, 'These be the days of vengeance that all things which are written in the prophecies might be fulfilled . . . for they shall fall by the edge of the sword and shall be led away captive into all nations.'

We saw how that, even as Hosea's prostitute wife during probation, they would no longer have a temple or priests or a king or a country, or animal sacrifices or idols and how that is fulfilled.

The synagogue took the place of the temple and rabbis were instead of priests and the sacrifice of Jesus instead of animal sacrifices. Moreover, in contrast to Israel's former idolatry, all idols are banned in Israel today.

These remarkable words of God to Hosea have been fulfilled to the letter down the years of Israel's probation and now, soon, Israel will be saying, as in Hosea 6:1, 'Come let us return to the Lord, for he has torn us and he will heal us. He has smitten us and he will bandage us up'. God said, 'This hurt me more than it hurt you', and he says the same to individuals. He says the same to you. 'Afterward the children of Israel will return and seek the Lord their God.'

So you have seen that, if you have had the agony of a broken home or children with broken homes, God shares the agony. He will heal your backslidings, he says, he loves you freely.

There will be a happy ending to your story, even as we see God today working out a happy ending for Israel.

S U M M A R Y

WHAT GOD FORETOLD TO HOSEA

Significance missed by most commentaries
- That just as Hosea put his unfaithful wife on probation, so God was going to put unfaithful Israel on probation for over 2 millennial days (6:2), until purified by persecution then they would return to Palestine.

Hosea the first prophet (775 BC)
- Applied warnings of Lev 26 (seven 'times') dispersion.
- Northern 10 tribes, called Ephraim or Israel, were worse than Judah and dispersed first.

Brief prophesied history in chapter 1
- Ephraim will go into captivity before Judah (v 6).
- Judah to be saved (v 7) from Assyria's invasion, by divine intervention not by arms (fulfilled 2 Kgs 19:6–8).
- God would bring them back, even as Hosea would win back his wife. They would return to the Land where God had disowned them (v 10).
- Both Ephraim and Judah would return to the Holy Land under 'One Head' (v 11) in the latter days.

Probation period chapter 3 onwards:
- Purified by persecution.
- Remarkable fulfilment of 3:4–5.
- Israel had existed without king or country without idolatry, without sacrifices (they ended in AD 70), without priests (ended AD 70).
- They are returning to Palestine in the Latter Days.
- Their loving God will welcome back the prodigal Israel.
- 'I will heal their backslidings. I will love them freely' (14:4).

Replacements prepared for the gospel
- Synagogues replaced temple
- Rabbis replaced priests
- Christ's atonement replaced animal sacrifices

8 WHAT GOD FORETOLD TO EZEKIEL
A HAIR-RAISING PROPHECY

In the East there are more dramatic visual aids given than would be used in the West. In Ezekiel chapter 5, God tells Ezekiel to cut off all his hair. The people would watch this with horror because for a prophet to do this is to invite disaster.

So Ezekiel shaved his head to make people look and take notice. It was a sign that God was going to remove beauty and glory from his people. God was trying every means to arrest the attention of the indifferent, to save people from persisting in their sins and reaping the terrible consequences.

Moreover, the prophet tells them that his hair now represents the people of the nation, so what God has told him to do with it shows what the Lord is going to allow their enemies to do with them, unless they repent.

A prophet's hair was his sacred vow to God. So God used it to demonstrate something to his people, which even people today have not learnt. It is all about the span of history of which Ezekiel speaks. In fact, some students are still wrongly taught that Ezekiel refers only to a 70-year exile in his time, but that is only one segment of this prophecy. The whole picture is demonstrated step by step in which God demonstrates two-and-a-half thousand years of history.

So then as they watch, they see Ezekiel get some scales in which to weigh his hair. He then divides the hair into three portions and carefully weighs each third. Horrors! He's thrown the first bundle of hair into the fire! It burns with a nasty acrid smell. Ezekiel turns to the crowd and repeats in a loud voice what God has told him to say: 'As I live says the Lord God, because you have defiled my sanctuary with all your disgusting filth . . . a third part of you will die of disease and famine!'

That is to be the fate of those represented by the first bundle. The prophet then takes the second bundle. The crowd move into a tight circle to see Ezekiel start cutting up the third into bits and pieces with the sharp sword in his hand. Ezekiel straightens his back and shouts: 'A third of you will be killed by the sword in the invasion, unless you repent!'

They did not repent. The horror of the siege of Jerusalem was soon to begin when sadly thousands of stubborn citizens were massacred.

What is he going to do with the third and last bundle? The crowd back away startled as the prophet takes this hair and throws it up into the air. The watchers harden in their unbelief as they see the wind blow the hair in all directions. As it floats away Ezekiel takes his sword and chases the floating hair slashing out at it shouting: 'Thus says the Lord. The remaining third who survive, I will scatter to all the four winds into all nations and the sword will pursue them. Thus you will be dispersed (as Moses said) into all nations.'

Ezekiel quotes Leviticus 26 as God told him:

> I will make you a ruin and a reproach among the nations around you, in the sight of all who pass by. You will be a reproach and a taunt, a warning and an object of horror to the nations around you when I inflict punishment on you in anger and in wrath and with stinging rebuke. I the Lord have spoken. When I shoot to destroy you, I will bring more and more famine upon you and cut off your supply of food. I will send famine and wild beasts against you, and they will leave you childless. Plague and bloodshed will sweep through you, and I will bring the sword against you. I the Lord have spoken.

Terrible words, yet as Amos was told, you will never cease to be a people! But wait. There is a sudden halt to the drama. 'Ezekiel! Stop! Rescue just a few of those hairs which have floated away!'

The prophet obediently stops and picks up some of the scattered hair. He ties the little bundle for safety into the wide sleeves of his gown. It was an Eastern way of preserving something. Was God going to have mercy on a few? Yes, he would bring back to Palestine a small percentage of those who were scattered. This was fulfilled in the return from exile after 70 years, but the rest remained in foreign countries, settling down as worldwide Jewry. Those who returned from exile would be in the Holy Land when Jesus came 600 years later.

Yet again Ezekiel takes all of those hairs from his sleeve and throws even them into the fire. This was fulfilled when those who had returned to Palestine rejected Christ and within that generation the Romans burnt down Jerusalem and scattered them to join those others still dispersed among the nations.

Still the prophetic story is not ended. Chapter 11:6 says that before his glory returns, God will gather Israel back to their own land:

> Thus says the Lord God, although I shall have cast them afar off among the Gentiles, and although I will have scattered them among the countries where they have gone . . . I will gather you from the peoples, assemble you from the countries where you have been scattered, and I will give you back the land of Israel.

This hair-raising experience embraces the whole prophetic story of the book of Ezekiel.

THE ALL-EMBRACING THEME

Ezekiel's hair-raising symbolism was fitted into an all-embracing theme which God gave to Ezekiel. It was the departure and return of God's glory in Israel.

This theme embraces the whole book. First, there is the dazzling vision of that glory, then its departure in chapter 10; its return in chapter 43 to the Mount of Olives on the east side of Jerusalem, then its entrance into the temple. From there, the Lord's glory fills the earth.

Fitted into this comprehensive framework is the prophesied history of the scattering, dispersion and regathering of Israel to Palestine (chapters 36–39) and the military problem and conflict that it creates until the Lord returns to judge the nations (39:21–29).

> Then I will set my glory among the pagan nations and they will see my judgement . . . Also the house of Israel will know that I am the Lord from that day forwards; and the pagan nations will know that the house of Israel went into captivity for their sins . . . now I will bring them back again . . . They shall know that I am the Lord their God, who caused them to be dispersed among the nations, and now have gathered them back into their own land.

Refugee's Visions of God's Glory

What is it which helps people to survive with new hope when disaster seems to have overtaken them? Many people today have been displaced, many have been refugees. Can they have new hope? For Ezekiel it was by giving him a wider overall view of God's vast time plan.

Ezekiel the prophet was a refugee. He was among the first batch about 600 BC. 'He had visions of God' and that is your solution even if you are a displaced person. God showed Ezekiel what it was all about and God can give you a similar insight. In fact, as we shall see as we go through the prophecy, what God showed Ezekiel even concerns you today.

The Israelites had only got what they deserved. They had been warned by God time and time again, but like many another nation they ignored him. The various prophets had pointed out that the warnings of Moses nearly a thousand years before would be fulfilled if they forsook God and his truth. God told Moses that they would be led into exile and now it had happened, but that was not the end of all hope. They were shattered and even angry at what they had brought upon themselves. All had suffered, good and bad. The good were many like Ezekiel and also Daniel, who was also a refugee in the power of a despot tyrant. The visions which Ezekiel had were most remarkable. They showed that God's purposes for the good are not thwarted even by our rebellion. There was still a wonderful future fairly soon and in the distant centuries.

First, Ezekiel was blessed and uplifted by a vision of God himself. The remarkable thing was that it was given even in this foreign land, in captivity (verse 1 says) in Babylon. Even there the majesty of God was seen. 'I was among the captives by the river Chebar in Chaldea when I saw the heavens opened and I saw visions of God' writes Ezekiel.

Yes, God reigns, God rules, God restores! Ezekiel describes the colour and meaning of the majesty of the Lord who changes despair into deliverance and helplessness into hope. But what an understanding of history you will get from the book of Ezekiel. What an understanding of yourself you will get and what an understanding of the glory of the Lord.

What a wonderful vision of God Ezekiel had in the midst of despair, disaster and desolation. Here he was, a refugee in a foreign land 700 miles from home. His home and house were broken, his relatives slain. Others with no faith wept, 'How can we sing the Lord's song in a strange land?', but God was showing Ezekiel how. No land was foreign to God!

The glory of the vision of the glory of the Lord radiated around Ezekiel in that strange land. This sets the theme for the book of Ezekiel. It opens with a chapter on the glory of the Lord with Ezekiel.

The book starts with the glory and ends with the glory. Oh, my friends, let some of this glory enter your soul as we see that the whole 48 chapters are all about the glory of the Lord. You will only understand this book if you understand that. It is the glory which departed in Ezekiel's day and will return in our day. It is the story of the stages by which God's glory will return to this earth.

First then, Ezekiel's soul is filled with the vision of glory even in exile. Then in chapters 9 to 11 he is taken in vision to Jerusalem to see the glory filling the temple. The people are urged to repent, but they refuse, so the glory departs stage by stage, reluctantly. First it lifts up from the ark of the covenant, then it goes out of the sanctuary to the door, then to the east gates, then to the Mount of Olives. Still the glory waits for a response, but it is a rebellious house, says God. 'The land is full of bloodshed and crimes and the city of violence' and even the religious betray my truth. What a picture of today! Great abominations and horrors are driving me far away from my city, God says. The people would not glorify him the easy way, so God is going to purify them the hard way. This goes for any other nation which rejects Christ. They will learn truth and be purified by the fires of tribulation.

So the glory of God departs. The nation is left, a valley of dry bones, until revival comes and life and the glory of the Lord begins to return at the end of the age, in 39:21: 'I will set my glory among all nations'. The glory of the Lord returns from the East (chapter 43) to Jerusalem on the Mount of Olives on the east side.

Let verse 2 thrill your soul. 'The sound of his coming was like the musical rippling of many waters and the earth shone with his glory.' Let the rippling voice of the Holy Spirit make your face shine as the Lord makes your heart his throne.

The Original Vision

The significance of that opening vision in chapter 1 is not always apparent. The Early Church understood it. It is a symbol of the glory of God in his Word, the Bible, centred in the Gospels which are mirrors of Jesus Christ the Lord of Glory.

The first vision of that glory is full of significance. It is of the bright certainty of the fulfilment of God's Word. In fact, when we compare the symbols we see that they depict the four Gospels as a foundation of that Word in the face and glory of Jesus Christ. How is this so?

What was this gleaming bronze upon which the reflecting fire flashed continuously? It was a glorified picture of the meaning of the laver of Solomon's temple. That great bowl of water represented the whole Word of God. James tells us this. Its expanse of crystal-clear water was for the washing by the Word of God.

This huge portable lake was called by Solomon a molten sea. It should have ranked as one of the seven wonders of the world. It is described in 1 Kings 7. The casting of it was an engineering feat in itself. Its rim was 15ft (5m) in diameter from brim to brim, made of solid bronze. How they kept the whole mould heated so that the molten metal would flow in all around equally amazes any bronze founder. The metal was 9in thick and had lilies cast solid around under the lip. This huge weight was supported by twelve bronze oxen facing outwards and ten pedestals. The pedestals were significant and they feature throughout the rest of the prophecy. They were cubic, with four panels. Each of the panels had on it a lion, an ox, an eagle and a man. The significance of these is worked out in Ezekiel and the book of Revelation. These pedestals had bronze wheels 2ft 3in high (68cm). They moved in any direction. So then this masterpiece of engineering and design made this huge heavy bowl of water or sea completely mobile.

The early Christians immediately saw the significance. The four panels represented the four Gospels. Matthew the lion of Judah, Mark the perfect man, Luke the ox slain for sin and John the royal eagle soaring to heights of divinity.

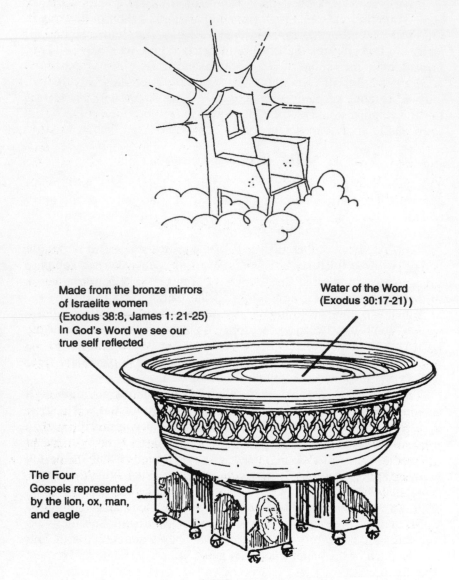

Made from the bronze mirrors
of Israelite women
(Exodus 38:8, James 1: 21-25)
In God's Word we see our
true self reflected

Water of the Word
(Exodus 30:17-21))

The Four
Gospels represented
by the lion, ox, man,
and eagle

Figure 8.1. Ezekiel's vision of a laver in Ezekiel chapter 1 'with the likeness of a throne in appearance like sapphire; and seated above . . . was a likeness as it were of a human form . . . of the likeness of the glory of the Lord' (vv 26,28). See also 1 Kings 7; Revelation 4. This represents the Bible as God's Word speeding to the world in all directions until Christ returns (Ezekiel 43:1–5).

The laver-bowl representing the whole Bible thus rests upon the four Gospel pictures of the likeness of Christ and it is mobile throughout the world. The shining reflection from the altar fire nearby brings light and meaning to all the pages of Scripture by the meaning of the cross, Christ's altar of sacrifice. Christ in all the Scriptures brings glory to God, reflected in the souls of sinners saved by grace. Hallelujah!

God is never defeated. That symbol of the glorious Word centring on Christ fulfilled in the Gospels lifted away from Jerusalem, but it was speeding away into all the world with Christ in all the Scriptures reflected in its mirrors. 2 Corinthians 3:18 says, 'We who with unveiled faces all reflect the Lord's glory, are being transformed into his likeness with ever-increasing glory, which comes from the Lord, who is the Spirit.'

Model Castle Building

Do you remember how you enjoyed building a sandcastle as a child or building one for your child? You saw the castle in your imagination as you dug and carved the sand. Then, of course, came the part that all children delight in, bombarding it until it falls.

In chapter 4, Ezekiel is told to build a model of Jerusalem, then lay a siege against it and lie on his side pretending to be the enemy. This he was to do in public view so that people passing would ask for the reason. Ezekiel was to say that Jerusalem would fall to the enemy if the people did not repent.

God was so anxious to get the message over. He was passionately earnest and urgently concerned to save his people from disaster. Even now he could reverse events if they repented and turned from their wicked ways. If they did not, then the judgement of invasion must be allowed to happen. God would not hold back Satan's evil if the people exposed themselves to it. The prophet was to lie on one side for 390 days, each day to represent a year of devastation for the northern kingdom. Then he was to lie on the other side for 40 days, each day to represent a year of devastation for the southern kingdom.

Year-day Insight

Now there is great significance in this making a day represent a year. God lays down a principle here for interpreting prophecy. Each day represents one year symbolically, but each day represents only one day literally. Many students have not learnt this lesson. *Prophecies concerning future events are usually fulfilled in two ways – symbolically and literally.* If numbers or times are given, these numbers are fulfilled both symbolically and literally. How short-sighted of many to interpret the prophecies one way and not the other. The book of Revelation, for example, was first fulfilled down history in a remarkable way, each day representing a year, but at the end it will be a day equal to a day.

So the principle given to Ezekiel combines with the figures given to Moses to show that the dispersion of Israel throughout the nations would last for over 2,500 years. That has been fulfilled with much sadness. From Ezekiel's time to ours has been over 2,500 years. Israel has been scattered all that time, but is now being regathered. The glory departed, the glory will be returning. God wanted Israel to learn the easy way of repentance, but because they refused, it had to be the hard way. God wants to gather us to himself without the agony, but if we don't respond we have to learn the hard way. Jesus took the hard way to save us from it.

Bad News Brings Good News

So, as soon as the bad news came that Jerusalem had fallen to the enemy, God gave them this good news. It is in Ezekiel, chapter 33 onwards. God can do the same for you. He can turn your bad news into good news. In fact, the Good News – the gospel – is the bad news turned into good news. The bad news is that you are a sinner in God's sight. The good news is that the Lord Jesus Christ atoned for your sins and you can be forgiven.

This picture of the hopeless remnant restored was depicted by the remnant of the prophet's hair which was rescued from that which was scattered to the winds. As I said, the symbol of what happened to his hair was the clue to the whole book of Ezekiel.

From Ezekiel 33 onwards, God speaks of how he is going to take that remnant and make it into a wonderful garment then even the rest of the scattered hair blown to the four winds he is going to weave into his plan and so: 'All Israel will be saved'. 'O the depths of the riches both of the wisdom and knowledge of God.'

So all the prophet's hair which was scattered by the gale to the four winds would be gathered back for the Messiah's second coming and so all Israel would be saved. Chapters 33 to the end are all about that. Stage by stage, the prophesied story of history is written. Let us look at the wonderful story.

THE GOOD SHEPHERD THEME

The very next chapter of Ezekiel (34) tells us of the Good Shepherd. The Good Shepherd is God himself, it says, because the Lord Jesus is God. 'Thus saith the Lord' (v 11) 'I will both search for my sheep and seek them out.' Then in v 16: 'I will seek those who are lost and bring them back again.' Now turn to the words of the Lord Jesus in John 10. He starts by warning the sheep about false shepherds, just as God does in Ezekiel 34. They betray the faith of the sheep. Then comes this tremendous statement in v 14: 'I am the Good Shepherd . . . and I lay down my life for the sheep.'

That is what false shepherds don't do – lay down their life for the sheep. But Jesus has done that for you. It is only because he has died in your place that God can forgive your sins. If you ask him to do this, the Holy Spirit helps you to know him personally.

So Jesus adds a wonderful truth: 'I know my sheep and my sheep know me.'

I have interviewed for radio, born-again Christians from all over the world, from Stone Age people to high technology computer people. They all say, 'Yes, I know Jesus'. This is a fulfilment of Jeremiah 31:34 'In the new covenant they shall all know me from the least to the greatest!'

If you don't know him, it is because you have not asked him into your heart and trusted that his cross saved you. Do so now. Ask him into your heart.

Double Fulfilment

Do you remember that I said many prophecies are fulfilled twice? Usually, first symbolically and then later literally.

In Ezekiel 34 we have such an example. The Good Shepherd of this chapter is fulfilled in the Lord Jesus Christ. He is the shepherd of all who are saved by his death. 'I lay down my life for the sheep,' he said 'and I give unto them eternal life and they will never perish.'

But the literal fulfilment to come is for the nation of Israel. I quote from Ezekiel 34:13,14:

And I will bring them out from the people, and gather them from the countries and will bring them to their own land and feed them upon the mountains of Israel by the rivers and in a good pasture and upon the high mountains of Israel shall their food be; there shall they lie in a good fold and in a fat pasture shall they feed upon the mountains of Israel.

So clearly, Jehovah speaks of our day when Israel is back in their ancient land. Eventually he will be their shepherd.

Some have said that God has finished with Israel. They say he has washed his hands of them. They say that the Church has now taken its place. Examine with me some scriptures which show that this is not so.

In Leviticus 26:42 God says he will not break his covenant with Abraham and Jacob and in v 44 he says: 'Yet for all that, when they are in the land of their enemies . . . I will not destroy them or break my covenant with them . . . I will for their sake remember the covenant with their forefathers.'

God repeats this to Jeremiah in 31:37. He says that even as space cannot be measured so he will never cast away Israel – by no means. Again, Deuteronomy 30 repeats God's warning of 25 centuries in which Israel will be scattered among the nations, but says at the end, 'The Lord your God . . . will gather you again from all the peoples where the Lord your God has scattered you.'

In Paul's exposition of such scriptures in Romans 11, he says that only a remnant – that is a small percentage – of the Jews would become Christians during this Gentile age of the last 2,000 years, but that the whole of Israel would be saved at the end of the age. 'Then all Israel shall be saved', he says in verse 26. He was applying the prophecies of Zechariah 12:10 written five centuries BC, which says that the whole Israeli nation will be converted when the Messiah comes the second time and they will see that it is the one whom they pierced when he came the first time, descending from heaven. Like unbelieving Thomas, they will see the wounds in his hands and feet and say 'My Lord and my God'.

So then Ezekiel 34:13 will be fulfilled, 'I will bring them [the Israelis] into their own land . . . I myself will be the shepherd of my sheep.' So wonderful things are ahead for Israel. Do you remember that vision of the valley of dry bones? That is what follows. Read what God promised and is fulfilling today in Ezekiel 37:14–24:

And I shall put my spirit in you, and you shall live, and I shall place you in your own land: then shall you know that I, the Lord, have spoken it, saith the Lord.

The word of the Lord came again unto me, saying, Moreover, thou son of man, take one stick, and write upon it, 'For Judah and the children of Israel his companions': then take another stick, and write upon it, 'For Joseph, the stick of Ephraim, and for all the house of Israel, his companions': and join them one to another into one stick; and they shall become one in your hand.

And when the children of your people shall speak unto you, saying, 'Will you show us what you mean by these?' say unto them, 'Thus saith the Lord God: Behold, I will take the stick of Joseph, which is in the hand of Ephraim, and the tribes of Israel his fellows, and will put them with him, even with the stick of Judah, and make them one stick, and they shall be one in mine hand.'

And the sticks whereupon you write shall be in your hand before their eyes. And say unto them, 'Thus saith the Lord God: Behold I will take the children of Israel from among the heathen, whither they be gone, and will gather them up on every side, and bring them into their own land: and I will make them one nation in the land upon the mountains of Israel; and one king shall be king to them all: and they shall be no more two nations, neither shall they be divided into two kingdoms any more at all: neither shall they defile themselves any more with their idols, nor with their detestable things, nor with any of their transgressions; but I will save them out of all their dwelling places, wherein they have sinned, and will cleanse them: so shall they be my people and I will be their God . . . And David, my servant, shall be king over them; and they all shall have one shepherd: they shall also walk in my judgements, and observe my statutes, and do them.

Fair Treatment to the Arabs

There is however, at the end of the book, God's instructions for the fair treatment of the Arabs. God says he has the welfare of both the Arabs and Israel at heart, but because it is his land, he gives instructions for settlement in the last days, in Ezekiel 47:18–23 as follows:

> The land shall be an inheritance for Arabs who reside among the Israelis, and be fairly treated as if they were natural-born Israelis; but the boundaries for which Israel is responsible shall be the river Jordan, and the Gaza strip down to the Wadi of Egypt at the south end of the Gaza strip.

God will beat out this area (Isaiah 27:17) and overrule for peace arrangements, to allow Jews to return from other countries. (Two million from Russia? Jeremiah 31:38.) Politicians will have success or failure according to how they fulfil this, but does the context make this apply to our times? God is certainly speaking of these latter days because he describes the coming resurrection of his people in this passage (Isaiah 25:8 and 26:19–21).

God will also make other Arab nations a blessing because in this section of Isaiah's prophecy, he says in 19:24,25:

> In that day Israel will be one of three, along with Egypt and Assyria (Mesopotamia) a blessing in the earth. The Lord of heavenly hosts will bless them, saying: Blessed be Egypt my people, Assyria my handiwork, and Israel my inheritance.

Geological Evidence for the King of Kings

I have referred to God's knowledge of geology shown in the Bible. The implications are obvious. God created the earth and so of course he knows all about the geology. Another implication is that the One who created the continental drift and rift valley and sea levels and earth movements describes them, thousands of years before modern science recorded these things.

Another implication is that God controls future earth movements and geological developments. The scientific knowledge of future geological events demonstrates that God rules in geology as well as in heaven and that he will rule personally on earth.

Why does it prove that God will rule on earth? Because the accurate description of what will happen geologically when Christ comes to judge and reign on earth is a guarantee that God has it all worked out and is fully able to implement it. So what does God tell the Bible prophets will happen geologically to the earth when the Lord Jesus Christ comes with power?

The increased earthquakes today are the continents preparing to do what God tells them when the feet of Christ touch the Mount of Olives at his descent from heaven. The Great Rift Valley described in several scriptures runs through the Jordan Valley, the Red Sea and into Africa. The African continent hinges on this and this rift valley will break through into the Mediterranean Sea through the Mount of Olives past Jerusalem. This will release volcanic fires in the Dead Sea area and rain down fire and sulphur (or brimstone) as it did in Lot's time when Sodom was destroyed. This geological future is described in Ezekiel 38:22 when fire and sulphur will deluge down upon armies invading Jerusalem, then in chapter 47 water will flow into the Jordan Valley from the Mediterranean and Indian Oceans. This will be a new seaway past Jerusalem to make Jerusalem the communication centre of the continents of Africa, Asia and Europe.

This prophecy links up with what God told Joel and also with what he told Zechariah.

Water from the Throne

I have often been asked whether I think chapter 47 of Ezekiel is to be fulfilled literally or symbolically. The chapter is a beautiful picture of the water of life flowing from the throne of God in the temple after the return of the Lord Jesus Christ. The water brings life wherever it flows and as it flows down to the Jordan Valley it gets deeper and deeper. Then it 'heals' the Dead Sea so that fish can live in it.

My answer from Scripture is that, like other prophecies, it is fulfilled spiritually and literally. St John in the book of Revelation applies it spiritually. The water of life flows from the throne of God to everyone who believes. The Lord Jesus spoke of the living water to the Samaritan woman and then to all those who believe on him. He said, 'He who believes on me, out of his inner being will flow rivers of living water.' He spoke of the Holy Spirit who would come and change the heart of the believer and flow out of him to bless others.

But there are details given in Ezekiel 47 which can be fulfilled literally only in the future age. For example, there are geographical and geological details. You are told where the sea level is in the Jordan

Valley. This was measurable and known only 150 years ago. The effect of the Mediterranean Sea flowing into the Dead Sea is described as bringing in sea fish.

What of the fresh water flowing from the limestone of the temple site? Is it possible that water could flow from the Jerusalem heights? The Lord gave me a surprising insight into this. I was studying a Government report on the hydrological survey of Palestine. That means the whole water supply of the Holy Land. I was thrilled to find that the survey found that under the land from Mount Carmel in the north to Beersheba in the south, there was a vast artesian water basin – a vast reservoir of fresh water. It was reported that it would supply Palestine for three-and-a-half years even if there was a drought in which not a drop of rain fell. The Bible was confirmed again. That was why Elijah was able to draw water from the spring in Mount Carmel and why Abraham dug a well at Beersheba. But the most amazing find was that, if there was an outlet broken through at Jerusalem, fresh water would flow out. So Ezekiel 47 can be taken literally. (See 'God is a Geologist' in *Evidence for Truth, Volume 2, Archaeology*.)

But praise God you can prove it true spiritually now. The water of eternal life flows from the Saviour for you. You can drink and find it satisfies and saves you for eternity.

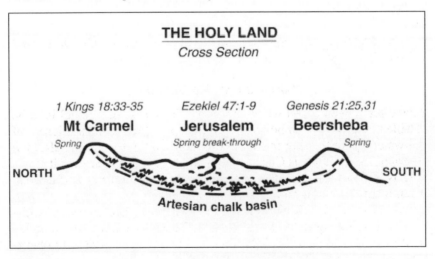

Figure 8.2 Holy Land cross-section showing the hydrological artesian basin under Jerusalem. There is enough fresh water in the Holy Land artesian chalk basin to last 3½ years without rain. Elijah was able to draw water at Mt. Carmel after drought, and Christ's descent to Jerusalem will release fresh water. (Ezekiel 47:1–12)

S U M M A R Y

WHAT GOD FORETOLD TO EZEKIEL

A Hair-raising Prophecy

Ch 5, a comprehensive prophecy from Ezekiel for 26 centuries. Prophet's hair divided into three positions. Represents Israel's future:

- Two portions burnt or slain in the invasion of 603 to 586 (v 2).
- One third of Judah survives, but is scattered to the winds (v 12); 22:15.
- A little hair is rescued from that scattered, symbolising a remnant who would return to Jerusalem after 70 yrs exile (533 BC) (v 3).
- Even these the prophet then throws into the fire. The Romans will scatter them because they reject Christ (v 4).
- Fulfilled by fall of Jerusalem (AD 70).
- All the scattered third will return to Israel at the end of the age. It began in 1917.

Note: Principle that a prophetic day equals one year is in ch 4.

Fits into Theme of God's Glory, which structures the whole prophecy.

- Opening vision of glory ch 1.
- Stage-by-stage glory reluctantly departs as Judah refuses to repent of her cruel, horrible practices and idolatry.
- 1st the glory lifts up from the ark (ch 9).
- 2nd from the sanctuary entrance to the east gate (10:18).
- 3rd from the Mt of Olives the glory departs (11:23).
- Meanwhile:
  - Israel will have sanctuaries (little synagogues) throughout the world (11:16).
  - Israel is left as a valley of dry bones (37:1).
  - Israel is revived and returns as united 12 tribes to Holy Land (37:15–23).
  - When settled they will be invaded (Armageddon?).
  - Israel recognises the Lord and pagan nations are judged (39:21).
  - 'They will see my glory' at the return of Christ.
- 4th the glory returns via Olivet on the East (43:1) cf. Zech 14:4; Acts 1:11,12.
- 5th through the East Gate 'The earth shone with his glory'.
- 6th into the house of the Lord 'Lo! The glory of the Lord filled the house.' 'Son of Man, this is the place of my throne.' (43:5,6) (Matt 25:31,32).

9 WHAT GOD TOLD DANIEL IN THE PUBLIC LANGUAGE
PROPHECY CONCERNING THE GENTILES

'You have interesting feet,' the chiropodist said to me. That surprised me because I thought my feet were quite normal. He brought others to look at them. I was surprised to know that the scars were still discernible from when I trod on a sea urchin on a Grecian shore. You know the sea urchin, that beautiful globular empty shell you see on mantlepieces for decoration. Well, in real life, every hole has a long, sharp, black spike above it. Lots of them broke off in my feet.

Another thing which made my feet interesting was the bruised big toes. This was from climbing Mount Snowdon. I kept banging my boots against the rocks when I took a party of geologists around north Wales.

Daniel's Interesting Feet

I am going to tell you about some interesting feet which will affect your lives. They are the feet of Daniel's dream image. They depict what is happening in the world today. A widely-held view is that these feet have ten toes which symbolise the European amalgamation of sovereignties. Daniel was told by God that this would be the situation just before Christ returned. You can read about it in Daniel 2:41–45.

Now my ten toes are at the end of my feet! Don't laugh. I expect yours are too. And my feet are at the end of my legs – well I should hope so – but God was illustrating that the ten toes of a European amalgamation would be at the very end of history. The rest of the body higher up represented empires before the present European Commonwealth; empires spanning 2,520 years of history, and we are living at the end of history according to Daniel's interesting feet. That makes Daniel's dream image very relevant today. In it, God foretold the history of Gentile empires in Europe down to this day. That is why chapters 2 to 7 are in the Gentile language of Aramaic, and why chapters 8 to 12 are in Hebrew for the Jewish history. It explains what is happening now in Europe and from the west to the east. So let us look at Daniel's strange story to see how it all came about.

Character of the Empires

People are interested in dreams today. Some take a lot of notice of them. In Panama, a familiar greeting is, 'Did you dream well last night?' The Emperor Nebuchadnezzar did not dream well one night. He woke up in a cold sweat. Now he was most impressed by Daniel's interpretation of his dream. Daniel had given all the credit to God and the emperor acknowledged this. He was exuberant and said: 'Your God is the God of gods and the Lord of kings and a revealer of mysteries of the future.'

The colourful despot was ecstatic. He awarded high honours. He made Daniel President of the Central Province of Babylon in which the capital was situated and he made him a university chancellor. We know from the next chapter and history that the empire was highly organised, so it was no empty gesture.

Nebuchadnezzar must have been relieved. The sweat and fear of the nightmare had become a reassuring dream that his empire would not collapse in his day. In that metal statue, God had told Daniel that the emperor was the head of gold. But what empire would it be which was symbolised by the arms and chest of silver?

History tells you that the next empire was composed of two peoples, like the two arms. They were the Medes and the Persians. Their two peoples were united under the one emperor. It was rather like the United Kingdom. Several peoples united under one sovereign. This empire was to rise and fall next, but what was to succeed it?

Daniel was given more private information about this latter kingdom. It would be a Greek empire. This was the bronze waist of the statue. Its warrior would suddenly demolish the Medo-Persian Empire. This warrior turned out to be Alexander the Great. Daniel was told that Alexander would be short-lived and in his place four subsidiary powers would rule his empire. This is symbolised in chapter 7 by the four horns which replaced the single horn. Here again, it is a fact of history that Alexander died after only ten years reign and his four generals divided his empire and each ruled a quarter of it.

Concerning the iron empire of Rome which followed, as prophesied, we have already seen how that divided into east and west, like the two legs of the statue. It then formed into European countries and now into the ten toes of the states of Europe. This could be a great factor in your life.

Politics of the Gentile Empires

'It had a head of gold, but feet of clay.' Have you heard that expression? Any proud scheme of man not founded upon God's truth is doomed to crash. The same applied to the Emperor Nebuchadnezzar's great statue of a man. But what did it mean? God showed Daniel that the four metals of the body and clay feet depicted in the statue were the succession of empires from the sixth century BC down to our times. We have seen how even details about the arms and legs were fulfilled historically.

This statue is rich in other meanings. Consider with me the significance of the metals themselves. Daniel was told that these also had meaning; the gold of Babylon, the silver of Medo-Persia, the bronze of Greece, the iron of Rome and then the mixture of iron lumps and clay lumps.

What did these different materials signify? They signified the type of government in these empires. Nebuchadnezzar – the gold head – was an absolute monarch. No one told him what to do. He told others. He was a despot.

The silver of the Medes and Persians depicted laws which even the emperor had to obey. You may remember that phrase in Daniel, 'The laws of the Medes and Persians which change not'. It was what is called 'an oligarchy'.

The Greek bronze depicted attempts at democracy dominated by the conqueror.

Iron Rome was ruled by a senate, but this senate was often overruled by a dictator, the Caesars. When this empire split up into the kingdoms of Europe, the iron lumps mixed with clay depicted dictatorships mixed with democracies until there would be an amalgam of systems in the states of Europe denoted by the ten toes.

We are moving towards this today. The European Common Market and today's European Parliament is a final state before Christ comes. Why? Because it is in the days of those sovereignties that the uncreated One descends from heaven to rule the world (Daniel 2:42–44).

So what is the lesson of Daniel's statue concerning systems of man's government? Is it not that all fail in some way or other if they are not founded on Bible truth? They fail to bring peace. They fail to share out food, clothing and housing fairly. They fail – why? Because without conversion, man's heart is not right. His nature suffered from that fatal fall. He is motivated by greed, self-interest, pride and fame. It is even corrupt sometimes. There is brutality and lack of love for others. Whenever a nation turns away from the gospel, these things hamper. Many have been noble, good and just, but power has so frequently passed into other hands. Some systems of government are better than others, but ultimately it is the character of the person which matters. Christian revival has, for short periods, uplifted a nation, but

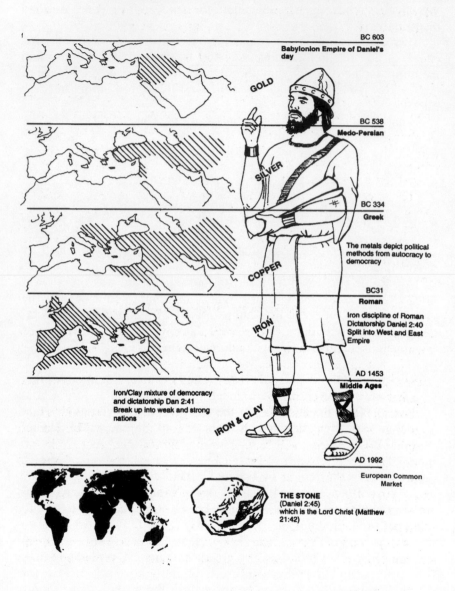

Figure 9.1. Daniel's image from 603 BC to the present day in which the toes represent European sovereignties. The stone strikes the toes 'in the days of these sovereignties' at Christ's return to rule the world.

only to fall back into unbelief. It will only be when Christ comes to reign that we shall see no poor in the land, no greed, no injustice; but fairness and happiness. That is the picture painted in the Bible. Meanwhile, you, as an individual, can make Jesus Lord of your life. Your heart can be an area of Christ's happy reign.

The Uncreated Stone

The stone which no one made! That is the climax to the emperor's dream statue which crashed and was crushed by the stone no one made. That remarkable revelation of world history from Daniel's time to modern times, has enheartened many that 'God is working his purpose out'. Moreover, he is working it out to a happy ending. All systems of government in that series of empires foretold that only when Christ returns will there be peace and justice on earth.

The coming of Jesus Christ is depicted by the uncreated stone. In the words of Daniel explaining this dream to the emperor, it was the stone made without hands. It was a way of saying that this one who would come to replace man's mis-government would be one who was not created. That can only be a divine eternal person; that can only be the Lord Jesus Christ, Son of God.

First Coming or Second Coming?

How do we know that this stone which smashed the image on its feet means the second coming and not the first coming? It is because at Jesus' second coming, he will descend visibly from heaven. That is what the stone did. He did not do that at his first coming. He came then as a baby – as God incarnate.

Another sign that this refers to the second coming is that it is to happen later in history, after the height of Rome's power. The Roman Empire, Daniel said, will have become divided and then split into many European countries and finally an amalgamation of several countries into a States of Europe. It is then, I quote: 'In the days of those powers', that the uncreated stone descends from heaven and smashes the image of man's governmental systems and sets up a kingdom of godliness, righteousness and happiness.

That picture of Christ is full of significance. It is referred to in many scriptures by many Bible writers in both Old and New Testaments:

- He is the foundation stone for salvation;
- He is the stone upon which he who believes will never be ashamed;
- He is the stone which the builders rejected, but who became the head of the corner of the resurrection;
- He is the stumbling stone to those who refuse to be saved by faith.

And the Lord must be referring to Daniel's statue of world empires since he says that, when the stone falls on anyone, it will crush him to pieces.

Yes, it is a sad fact that the time will come for a nation which rejects Christ for the stone to fall on it in judgement. It will also come for a person who rejects salvation. The stone which was intended to be his foundation stone for salvation will fall on him to crush him to powder.

THE TIMES OF THE GENTILES

Did you know that Jesus called the emperor's dream statue in the book of Daniel 'the Times of the Gentiles'?

We have seen that the succession of empires foretold in the emperor's dream statue have been fulfilled down the last 25 centuries. The Babylonian Empire was succeeded by the Persian Empire just as foretold in 538 BC. The Persian Empire was succeeded by the Greek Empire in 336 BC just as foretold. The Greek Empire was succeeded by the Roman Empire in 31 BC just as foretold. The Roman Empire divided into two in AD 325 just as foretold. The divided Roman Empire split into the nations of Europe in the succeeding centuries just as foretold, and now we have seen the European Parliament forming, foretold as the last stage before the second coming of Christ with power.

Yes, it is that succession of empires which is called 'the Times of the Gentiles'. It is the 25 centuries since the Babylonian Empire down to our day which the Lord Jesus Christ calls the Time of the Gentiles. He calls it that in Luke 21:24.

'The Times of the Gentiles' from 603 BC to AD 1992

Note: this was compiled by the author many years before it was fulfilled in the European Single Market on 31 December 1992.

Event: Prophecy (Daniel 2 and 7)   603 BC

Period: 'Times of the Empires' (Dan. 12:7)   2,520-year span

• Babylonian Empire (Gold)   603–538 BC
• Medo-Persian Empire (Silver)   538–334 BC
• Greek Empire (Copper)   334–31 BC
• Roman Empire (Iron)   31 BC–AD 1453
• Mixture of democracies and dictatorships
    (iron and clay)   AD 1453–1992

(Continued)

Event: Home created for the Jews	AD 1917
Period: 30 years (Dan. 12:11)	30-year span
Event: State of Israel (by UNO)	AD 1947
Period: 45 years (Dan. 12:12)	45-year span
Event: European Union of Ten Sovereignties European Single Market signed ('Ten' may refer to ethnic areas, not countries)	AD 1992 31 December 1992.

Period and event to come: The Stone (Daniel 2:45) which is the Lord Jesus Christ (Matthew 21:42) at his second coming, who will crush man's misgovernment in the days of the European United Sovereignties (Daniel 2:42–44). Christ's Kingdom will then fill the earth and bring peace, righteousness and happiness.

Why is it called, 'the Times of the Gentiles?' It is because, during that time, Gentiles have ruled in Jerusalem. That is why. *Its duration is the same period as the dispersion of Israel.* Yes, for the same 25 centuries, the Israelites have been scattered among countries other than their own. That also was prophesied.

Now the Lord Jesus went on to say something very significant. He said that when the Times of the Gentiles are nearing conclusion, the dispersion of Israel would also be drawing to an end. They would see Israel back in God's land. Do you see that today? Then he said, when that happens know that the Kingdom of God is near. What kingdom is that?

It is the same kingdom Daniel spoke of. Remember how he said that God's Kingdom on earth would come in the days of the European powers. That would be at the end of the Times of the Gentiles. Jesus said that when you see these things begin to happen, then know that the Kingdom of God is near. That is after he had spoken about his second coming. This Kingdom of Christ's reign will replace all man-made empires which have gone before. Those human empires were on earth so Christ's Kingdom must be a kingdom on earth to replace man's failures. Indeed, God told Daniel it would fill the earth.

At its inception, Jesus said he would sit on his throne in Jerusalem and all nations would be brought before him to be judged. They would be judged according to whether their policies had resisted the gospel or helped the gospel. When they are judged, Jesus said some will be surprised that they were judged in this way. So pray for your nation and its policies as the Bible says, so that they may find that that day is one of gladness not sadness.

Royal Command Performance Spoilt

Sometimes people get big-headed when people praise them. The tyrant Emperor Nebuchadnezzar did. That head of gold in chapter 2 must have put ideas into Nebuchadnezzar's head. Didn't the head of gold represent himself! Daniel had said so, but why only the head of the statue? He would claim all the statue. He would dominate all Gentile history which it represented.

So a furnace for smelting was built and gold was melted and made to flow into huge moulds. These large gold components were assembled into the biggest image known. It was 90ft high and 9ft wide. Was Nebuchadnezzar only the head of gold? No, he was the whole image of gold. Probably it was an image of himself. All his empire must fall down and worship him. He wanted to exalt himself above God – just like Satan. Satan tried to lift himself above God, but pride was his downfall.

The huge image of Nebuchadnezzar was set up in the largest plain in his province. Millions would be able to assemble around it. Every official in his highly-structured organisation would be there. The crowds stretched back a mile or more, but all would see this shining gold likeness of Nebuchadnezzar, because it rose up high in the middle of the Plain of Dura. The massed orchestra of every type of known musical instrument struck up: that was the signal that everybody must worship the image.

All did, except the Jews. The emperor was furious. He would make an example of Daniel's three friends, Shadrach, Meshach and Abednego.

'You've one more chance!' he shouted at them.

'No go!' they replied calmly. 'The God of Creation will rescue us. Even if he doesn't, we will willingly die for the truth.'

Now the tyrant emperor was not used to refusal. He exploded in fury. His face went from red to scarlet, and from scarlet to purple.

'Heat the furnace seven times as much!' he roared. This was a draught-controlled smelting furnace. The heat became so terrific that the foundry workers shrivelled up and died. Into this intense smelting heat the three believers were thrown. But the only thing the flames burnt were the ropes that bound them. The fires of persecution can set you free! They walked at liberty and a fourth person joined them in the fire. It was the Son of God.

The whole episode was a portent of the fire of persecution which believers would suffer down those 25 centuries of the Times of the

Gentiles. Believers refuse to worship idols, but in the fires the Son of God walks with them.

The idolatrous emperor was humbled. 'Servants of the Most High God, come out of the furnace!' he ordered.

Out they walked. There was not a hair singed, nor a garment burnt. Their bodies were unscathed and there was not even the smell of fire upon them.

'I make a decree!' shouted the emperor. 'No one is to say one word against the God of these believers.'

So down the 25 centuries of the Times of the Gentiles, the fires of martyrdom were to rise at various times. The brave witness of believers was to convert more to God then than in times of ease. As Tertullian said, 'The blood of the martyrs is the seed of the church.'

Seven Years' Madness

When a person gets changed by God, he loves to tell others of his conversion. It was so with the tyrant Nebuchadnezzar. Chapter 4 of Daniel is his amazing testimony. God humbled this man with seven years' madness. It was a peculiar madness too. He thought he was an animal, so do you know what he did? He left his sumptuous feasting table and went out to eat grass on his lawn. Medical specialists call this disease lycanthrope. Yes! Emperor Nebuchadnezzar left his soup and roast duck, left his uniformed servants and lived outside in the rain and dew and crawled on his hands and knees, bent down and with his mouth to the grass chewed it like a cow! He said so in his testimony in Daniel chapter 4.

Why did he admit such humiliation in his written statement? Perhaps he feared worse would happen if he didn't. I think, however, he genuinely wanted to give God the glory, because he writes: 'I thought it good to show the signs and wonders that the High God has wrought towards me.' And he ends: 'Now, I, Nebuchadnezzar, praise and extol and honour the King of heaven, all whose works are truth and his ways just and those who walk in pride he is able to humble.'

Now, how did it all happen? Nebuchadnezzar tells the story himself. He was flourishing in his palace, he says. (Archaeology has unearthed some of the splendours of that palace and the mighty city. The hanging gardens of Babylon were one of the Seven Wonders of the World.) He says how he boasted, 'Is not this great Babylon that I have built by my might and by my honour?'

But he dreamed a disturbing dream one night. He saw a huge tree in the middle of the earth. All life depended upon it. Then an angel came down from heaven and shouted, 'Cut it down, cut off its branches, scatter its fruit, but leave the stump of the trunk in the ground to be wetted by the rain and dew. Let him think he is an animal until seven

'Times' have passed. This is decreed from heaven'.

We shall see the significance of that seven 'Times'. It spoke of the madness of man's ungodly rule during 2,500 years until Christ's second coming.

Daniel was sent for, but he feared to tell the despot what it meant.

'Don't hesitate,' said Nebuchadnezzar, 'I want to know.'

Daniel said that it meant the emperor would go mad and become like a beast, then Daniel, like a good evangelist, implored the emperor to break off his sins by right living and start helping the poor and destitute and so delay the fulfilment of that dreaded day.

For one year, Nebuchadnezzar managed to be a bit different. But it is torture to try and be good if your heart is not right. It is like telling a pig not to foul a palace! No, the heart must be changed. 'You must be born again,' said Jesus. 'If any man be in Christ, he becomes a new creature.'

At the end of one year, Nebuchadnezzar forgot his resolution and started boasting about himself. Immediately, he heard a voice, 'The kingdom has departed from you until you acknowledge that the Most High God rules and gives kingdoms to whoever he wishes. You will eat grass like a cow until seven "Times" pass over you.' It was a prophecy for the world as well as for this tyrant.

Seven Times What?

The tyrant Nebuchadnezzar was made mad for seven 'Times'. Seven times what, people have asked.

There is general agreement that it was seven times 360 – 360 what? It is suggested that they were days. It is thought that Nebuchadnezzar was made mad for seven years. But a year has 365 days, not 360. Where do we get 360 from?

I have already explained to you that archaeology discovered that the ancient Sumerians had a measurement of 360 which they called a 'Time', which probably went back to the days of Noah. So a 'Time' was 360, whether it was degrees or days or years.

With Nebuchadnezzar, it was days. So he was mad for seven times 360 days. That means he was eating grass like a cow for 2,520 days.

But God was also showing that he symbolised the Times of the Gentiles. That is when man's pride and misrule would spoil God's earth for 2,520 years. Yes, years, not days. Ezekiel was told that each day represented a year.

This word 'Time' used by the angel in the dream gave a new significance to the words of the Lord to Moses 800 years earlier. God said to Moses that Israel would be scattered through the world for seven 'Times'. That means 2,520 years. That is the correct length of time between Daniel's day and ours.

This insight should encourage your faith in God's overruling control of history. It highlights the message given to this emperor-tyrant, especially as he was the starting point of the succession of empires down the next 2,520 years. Those four empires were foretold in detail in chapter 2 of Daniel's book.

Nebuchadnezzar's reason returned to him when he understood God's overruling power. Your understanding is also enlightened if you allow God to give you an insight into his prophesied purposes. Daniel 4:34,35:

> At the end of the days, I, Nebuchadnezzar, raised my eyes towards heaven and my sanity was restored. Then I praised the Most High, I honoured and glorified him who lives for ever. His dominion is an eternal dominion, his kingdom endures from generation to generation. All the peoples of the earth are regarded as nothing. He does as he pleases with the powers of heaven and the peoples of the earth. No one can hold back his hand or say to him, 'What have you done?'

BELSHAZZAR'S FEAST

The Writing on the Wall

'It's the writing on the wall!' people sometimes say. They mean, it is a warning that calamity will soon be upon them. This saying comes from that dramatic story of Belshazzar's Feast. Belshazzar and his father had succeeded Nebuchadnezzar to the Babylonian throne.

He had failed to learn his grandfather's lesson. He was as hard a tyrant and sinner as Nebuchadnezzar had been before his change of heart. Now Belshazzar was in the midst of debauchery and feasting. He blasphemed Jehovah by drinking out of the sacred vessels stolen from the temple of Jerusalem. He got his wives and concubines to do the same while he praised his idols.

Suddenly, the fingers of a man's hand appeared and wrote Belshazzar's fate upon the plaster in mysterious words. Only Daniel could interpret them. He rebuked the emperor for his sins and then gave the meaning:

- 'Your days are numbered!'
- 'You have been weighed in the balances and found wanting!'
- 'Your kingdom is fallen to the Medes and Persians!'

The fulfilment was swift. That very same night, Belshazzar was killed. How did such a thing happen so quickly? History tells us. Cyrus made a surprise attack. Belshazzar did not know that his father Nabonidus had already been defeated north of Babylon nor did he did know that the Persians had diverted the river which ran through Babylon. They had dammed up one end and dug a new channel to divert it. Then they marched into the city along the dry bed. So even while Belshazzar was drinking himself drunk, the victorious enemy was marching in. The bed of the river made a good road for their marching feet because the Babylonians had paved it some years earlier with bricks, but they had paved the way to the empire's downfall.

Belshazzar now learnt by hard experience, the truth of the words to his grandfather. 'The Most High rules . . . he gives the kingdom to whoever he will.' He had now given it to Cyrus. God had told Isaiah 200 years before that he would do this. He even named Cyrus before he was born. Why? Because this was the man who was to end the 70 years' exile of the Jews and help rebuild the temple for them. Read the prophecy carefully because sceptics have doubted whether God could foretell the future. Isaiah 44:28, 'I am the Lord of Creation . . . who says to Cyrus . . . he will fulfil all my purpose . . . he will build my city and set my exiles free . . . I have called you by name though you have not known me.'

Why does God foretell what he is going to do in the future? He tells you in chapter 46:10, 'To show you I am God, there is no one else. I declare the end from the beginning and from ancient times, things not yet done. I will accomplish all my purpose and call Cyrus from the East.' This then is the purpose of foretelling the future and the reason for Daniel's prophecies too. It is to show that, despite appearance, God is in control. We shall see how he is working out his purposes today.

Doubters' Debility

In our studies in Daniel, we have some good examples of doubters' debility. Those who criticise the Bible are always wrong in the end. Critics said there were several things which could not be right in the story of Belshazzar's Feast in chapter 5. What were they?

They said that Belshazzar was not the name of Nebuchadnezzar's successor and they said that, if Daniel was promoted to be next to Belshazzar in order of importance, he would not be third ruler in the land as it says; he would be second.

Why did doubters think this? It was because the Babylonian records said that the name of Nebuchadnezzar's successor was Nabonidus, not Belshazzar. (Now, it amazes me how, if there is a disagreement between the Bible and what heathen sources say, critics always say it is the Bible which is wrong and not the heathen sources.) It was soon discovered that the Bible was right. Archaeologists dug up thousands of tablets and found that Nabonidus had made his son co-regent. He shared the kingship with Belshazzar and left him in charge of Babylon while he went out to fight the Medo-Persians. Moreover, that would make Daniel the third ruler instead of the second ruler, because

Belshazzar was second to Nabonidus.

What is the lesson for you and me? Always accept, as Paul says, 'that God is true and every man a liar'. That is rather a blunt way of putting it, but you know what he means. To escape the claims of God upon one's life, people criticise God's Word.

Satan was the first to do this in the Garden of Eden. In tempting Adam and Eve, he said, 'Yes. Are you sure God said you must not eat of the fruit of that tree?' Satan has been putting doubts into people's minds ever since. He is called 'the great deceiver'. Where he has undermined faith in the Bible, he then questions the goodness of God. He said to Eve, 'God is trying to keep something back from you. He knows that you will be like gods if you eat of that tree.' Yes, he tempts you to blame God instead of blaming the devil for all that has gone wrong in the world.

Those tyrant rulers he was puffing up with pride to pretend they were gods.

'Fall down and worship my image,' said Nebuchadnezzar.

'Prayers must be made to me,' said Darius, the Mede.

'Am I not a god?' said that horror, Nero, Emperor of Rome.

Paul prophesied that at the end of the age – that is, these days we live in now – those who did not want to be saved would be open to strong delusion. They would believe Satan's great lie. 'He deceives the whole world,' says the book of Revelation, 'and causes all men to worship the beast.'

Shut Mouths

Have you ever been told to shut your mouth? Rather a rude expression, isn't it? Well Daniel was told not to pray to God, to pray only to King Darius as if he were a god.

Satan is always trying to puff you up with pride. That caused Satan's own downfall in the beginning. That caused Eve's downfall in Eden. 'You will be like gods,' said Satan, 'if you disbelieve and disobey.'

With Daniel it was a clever trick arising out of jealousy, but it manipulated the king's pride. 'Why, you are like a god,' said the king's flatterers. 'Make everyone say their prayers to you.' What was their motive? It was jealousy of Daniel. You see, they knew Daniel would refuse to do this. They knew they couldn't shut his mouth. They were jealous of him because, I quote, 'Daniel became distinguished above all the other presidents and governors because an excellent spirit was in him and King Darius the Mede planned to set him over the whole province'.

Daniel's commitment to God had made him honest and reliable. The corrupt officials tried to make complaints about him. It is the same as the media today nosing into all the secret life of prominent people to discredit them. But about Daniel, they could not find one ground for complaint, so they made his prayer life the target. Darius the king fell right into the trap. He signed the decree to shut the mouths of prayer to anyone except himself. Well of course Daniel was caught praying to God as usual. His habit was to praise and pray three times a day. They couldn't shut his mouth.

His jealous corrupt opponents rushed to the king and told him. Darius knew he was trapped. 'You can't alter the decree,' the officials said, 'because the laws of the Medes and Persians do not change.'

They threw Daniel into a den of lions. The lions were all hungry and ready to crunch his bones. But what happened to the lions? The Bible says, 'God shut their mouths!' Isn't that good! Jealous people had failed to shut Daniel's mouth of prayer, but God shut the lions' mouths for their prey.

Don't let Satan shut your mouth, will you? Do you find it difficult to open your mouth to tell others of Jesus? If so, have a quiet time in God's presence and ask yourself why it is. Try to be honest with yourself. 'Why is it that I find it difficult to open my mouth for Jesus? Is it because I value my own self-esteem more than Christ's?' Be honest with yourself and then think out tactful ways you can witness. Perhaps you thought you had to blurt it all out when the better and easier way is to write a letter or send a cassette of testimonies or just to gossip the gospel in connection with the everyday news and signs.

Given to You to Understand

Quite a remarkable statement was made by the Lord Jesus Christ when he told his parables. He gave a principle which applies to the structure of the book of Daniel. After telling a parable, Jesus drew his disciples aside and said, 'To you it is granted to understand but not unto them'. Why did he say this? It was because it sorted out the sincere from the insincere. To those who really wanted to know deeper truths, God was willing to reveal them.

The book of Daniel is divided into two sections on this principle:

1. The *first six* chapters are *public* explanations of prophetic dreams by public personalities in the public's own Gentile language;
2. The *last six* chapters are *private* insights into visions for the sincere – those who want to understand the deep things of God which he told to Daniel in his own private Jewish language.

They give an insight in greater depth to the remarkable outworkings of

God in future history. Consequently, they are visions given to Daniel himself. That is why chapter 7 starts going back again to the first year of Belshazzar. It starts again with the same empires which were in Nebuchadnezzar's dream – the four empires which were to be the future history from Daniel's time down to our modern times, but it tells you more about them, at a deeper level. This vision in chapter 7 was given to Daniel when the first empire was near to its end.

In this vision, the same four empires and their characteristics are depicted by four very different animals. Their characteristics were well born out by subsequent history. They arose out of the sea of unrest. Verse 3 says, 'Hurricanes had churned up that sea'. The Bible says it symbolises the unrest of the masses. Jesus said that this would again be a feature of the end times before he comes again to judge the world.

WEIRD ANIMALS

On the ancient walls of Babylon, archaeologists have revealed the sculptures or paintings of some weird animals. They are myths of course – lions with wings and suchlike. Daniel chapter 7 has similar creatures. They are visions given to Daniel to represent the characteristics of empires from his time down to ours. There are four main beasts. They correlate to the statue of the empires of Daniel 2.

- The first creature was a **lion with eagle's wings** – that depicted the Babylonian Empire.
- The second was a **lop-sided bear** with three ribs between its teeth – that was the Medo-Persian Empire which was soon to start when Daniel wrote this chapter.
- The third was a **leopard with four wings and four heads** – that was the Greek Empire which started in 333 BC.
- But Daniel was terrified by **the fourth beast of horror** which was different from all the others. It had great iron teeth and ten horns and then a little horn – that is widely held to be the Roman Empire which began in 31 BC. The remnants of that last empire continue down to our times. After that, the glorious coming of Christ is described.

He descends from heaven with the clouds of heaven and is given dominion over all peoples, nations and languages. This is a recurrent theme through the rest of the Bible. Much later, when the Lord Jesus was being accused by the high priest of blasphemy, Jesus quoted this passage. He said: 'You will see the Son of Man come to earth in the clouds of heaven.' The high priest tore his coat in two and shouted, 'Blasphemy – why do we need any more witnesses?'

The high priest had asked him that very straight question, 'Are you the Son of God?' Jesus could not avoid the question because the high priest said, 'I charge you under oath of the living God, tell us, are you the Son of God?' So the Lord replied, 'I am'. Then he went on to refer to himself as the Son of Man. That is the title given by Daniel which I have quoted from this chapter 7.

How extraordinary that the world is to become the everlasting kingdom of one who has a human title – the Son of Man. Yet he is doing divine things – descending from heaven with the clouds of millions of angels. And this Son of Man admits to being the Son of God. So he is both God and Man. Only the virgin conception can account for this when God became man.

Praise the Lord for this assurance for the future. Read God's words to Daniel in 7:13–14:

> In my vision at night, I looked and there before me was one like a son of man, coming with the clouds of heaven. He approached the Ancient of Days and was led into his presence. He was given authority, glory and sovereign power; all peoples, nations and men of every language worshipped him. His dominion is an everlasting dominion that will not pass away and his kingdom is one that will never be destroyed.

The Deflated Lion

Now let us look at those strange animals in more detail. How did their symbols apply to history? The first was like a lion, but it had eagle's wings. Then these great eagle's wings were plucked off. Then the lion stood up on its hind legs like a man and a man's heart was given to it. What did this mean? Well, of course, it referred to the same empire as the head of gold in chapter 2 in Daniel's day, but this time it referred to what had already happened to the Emperor Nebuchadnezzar himself. His wings had been plucked off when God subjected him to seven years' madness. When his sanity returned, his beastliness disappeared and he became more human to his subjects because he began to give God his proper place and openly acknowledged him as, 'the Lord God whose eternal Lordship endures from generation to generation'. He openly praised and glorified the King of heaven 'who lives for ever', he said, 'because everything he does is right and all his ways are just. And I who walked in pride, God was able to humble.' As we noted before, it was when rulers ignored the God of the Bible, that the nature of the beast characterised their dealings, but when God's justice becomes the rule of their life, the injustices and cruelties to other human beings become replaced by the kindness and love of God in the Lord Jesus Christ.

Notice that the wings of this beast were torn off. Sometimes we feel that God has torn off a strip from us. When you feel that, be like

Babylon (Iraq)

Persia (Iran)

Greece

Rome

Figure 9.2. The four weird animals of Daniel 7: a deflated lion with eagle's wings; a lop-sided bear; a flying leopard with four heads; a horror beast.

Nebuchadnezzar: instead of rebelling, ask if God is teaching you something. 'God humbled me,' the emperor said, 'then I began to understand and praise him who lives for ever.'

The Lop-sided Bear

How many mythical animals can you think of? Well, there is the uni-corn – that is, a horse with a straight horn on his nose – quite imagi-nary of course?

Can you think of another horse myth? What about Pegasus, the Greek myth. He has wings. Then we have flying alligators or dragons in various national symbols – all imaginary of course. Strange beasts like these are used in the Bible to illustrate things.

For example, in Daniel 7:5, a lop-sided bear was taken to prophesy the rise of the Medo-Persian Empire continuing until 333 BC. Imagine – Daniel and his lop-sided bear! Why was it lop-sided? Because the Medes were the weaker partners. They became dominated more and more by the Persians. In Daniel's image, the two arms depict the two races, Medes and Persians, united in the emperor. This lop-sided bear had three ribs in its teeth. What did that mean? It meant that Persia would conquer three provinces, which it did. They were Babylon, Egypt and Lydia.

Lydia was a powerful kingdom in what is now western Turkey. Perhaps you remember how Xerxes saw it as a stepping-stone to con-quering Greece. It never happened. In spite of his great armada of boats, his campaign failed. Why? Because God had told Daniel that Greece was to be the next empire, therefore it would not be defeated.

So you see how the Bible is a guide to rulers as well, for the best rulers are those who have been guided by it. That is why the Bible says, 'Pray for your rulers'. Pray that they may seek the Bible's guid-ance because God promises good success and a happy people if they do.

This lop-sided bear, Persia, was told in verse 5, to 'arise and devour much flesh'. Cyrus had success in all other quarters because he acknowledged God's will. He helped to restore Jerusalem. His procla-mation is found at the end of 2 Chronicles 36:22 onwards. It reads: 'The Lord, the God of heaven, has given me all the kingdoms of the earth and he has appointed me to build a temple for him at Jerusalem in Judah. Anyone of his people among you – may the Lord his God be with him and let him go up.'

Flying Leopard!

A flying leopard! Whoever heard of such a thing! Well of course Pegasus was a flying horse, but he was a Greek myth; he was supposed to have flown up to Jupiter and become another star in the sky.

Pegasus was a Greek myth but the flying leopard of Daniel 7:6 was a Greek future conqueror who actually materialised. It was a colourful prophecy of Alexander the Great. He was to fulfil it in another 200 years.

If Alexander was the flying leopard, why did he have wings? Alexander made the fastest conquest of history. This young Greek prince absolutely flew (with his army) across the whole of the Middle East. The mighty Persian Empire quickly collapsed before this sudden impact.

Why did the flying leopard have four wings? Well, that would emphasise the speed of the conquest, but there was another reason. Alexander had four very good generals in his campaign. They were to become more and more enterprising. This flying leopard also had four heads. One head with fangs is frightening enough, but to have four open jaws grinning at you is petrifying. So why four? Well, Alexander died suddenly in the midst of his youth,so his four generals continued to rule the Greek Empire. In fact, they divided it up between them. It was the one who ruled Syria, Palestine and the East that the Bible was most interested in. That was the province about which God was going to tell Daniel a remarkable prophecy – a prophecy whose final fulfilment came in 1967.

This prediction involved the sanctuary of the temple of Jerusalem and we will look at a new type of prophecy that God revealed. It is unfolded in chapter 8.

First, look with me at a further description in that chapter 8 of Daniel of that sudden conquest by Alexander the Great. He is described as the he-goat from the West in verse 5. Now this was an appropriate description for a Greek conqueror. The word goat in Greek is *aegion*. The Greek sea is called the Aegean Sea, meaning Goat Sea. Now read Daniel 8:5: 'Behold a he-goat came from the West (that is, to the west of Babylon) across the face of the whole earth. He had a huge single horn between his eyes.'

With this horn he charged at the ram (that was Persia) with fury and completely demolished him. But when the goat's horn was strong, it was suddenly broken and four smaller horns grew out of the stump. There again is depicted those four generals of Alexander who divided the empire among them. But what of the one who ruled Palestine? Events were to be momentous.

We must learn to look at secular history and see the momentous hidden hand of God.

The Horror Beast

The fourth beast was a real horror. It was fierce and terrifying, tearing to bits its prey with great iron teeth set in powerful jaws. On its savage head it had ten horns. Another little horn grew up and up-rooted three of the other horns. Then this little horn changed into a man's eyes and a mouth with powerful speech. He made war with the saints and martyred them.

The importance of this horror beast is emphasised over the three empires preceding it. Only 6 verses are given to the deflated lion and the lop-sided bear and the flying leopard; but 22 verses are given to describe the future history of the horror beast. Daniel was very upset by it.

God responds gloriously to the beast's challenge. 'One like the Son of Man came with the clouds of heaven . . . and there was given to him dominion, glory and kingship. All peoples, nations and tongues serve him and his rule will be for ever and ever and will not pass away. His rule will never be destroyed' (7:13,14).

The Lord Jesus identified this at his trial before the high priest who said, 'I order you to tell us whether you are Christ the Son of God.'

Jesus replied, 'It is as you say. Hereafter, you will see the Son of Man sitting at the right hand of power and coming in the clouds of heaven.'

The history of this fourth animal would be much longer than the others. Indeed, the Roman 'Empire' lasts from 31 BC to our present day. Daniel's image depicts it dividing into two, like the two legs, then into ten main European Sovereignties. This horror beast also depicts ten states by the ten horns. According to Revelation 13, the crowns will be transferred to them, thus picturing separate powers within the European Community.

Q Why was Daniel so upset?

It was because, under the horror beast, God gave him the picture of the martyrdom of millions of Christians under the Roman Empire down to the Middle Ages.

We saw how an empire collapsed, but God continued his purpose in another. That empire of Persia collapsed as prophesied by Daniel because it no longer carried out God's purpose.

When an empire forsakes God's truth in the Bible, that happens again and again. The Persian Empire was typified by the ram in Daniel 8. It was at the height of strength, but this furious one-horned goat charged at it from Greece and demolished it. That was Alexander the Great at the height of his power. While he was still in his thirties, he died suddenly. This had all been foretold in Daniel chapters 7 and 8.

Why should people die in their thirties? Why does God allow it? John the Baptist died in his thirties. He was executed for giving a faithful witness. How tragic! Even he couldn't understand why Jesus didn't rescue him, but the Lord said his work was done.

The Lord Jesus himself died when only 33, but, as he died, he said, 'It is completed'. What was completed? Your salvation and mine through his atoning death. You can now be saved through trusting that atonement.

THE REASON FOR THE SECRET LANGUAGE

That atonement was symbolised by the sanctuary at Jerusalem. Now, here was the crunch. One of the successors of Alexander's generals was going to defile that sanctuary. And how long would it be before it was cleansed? The question is asked in Daniel 8. This was a deep secret for them and for us. It was a secret to be revealed only to the sincere believer with insight. And that is the reason for two very strange phenomena in the book of Daniel.

Firstly, this section of Daniel's prophecy is written in a different language. Why? It was to keep the secret from pagan, unbelieving eyes. The second phenomenon is this: when they asked, 'How long will it be before fulfilment?' God provided a very special angel whose job was to do the calculations and who had a very special name (see next chapter).

Look first at the special language. As already explained, chapter 8 onwards of Daniel is written in the old Hebrew which was no longer used in his pagan environment. The language which Daniel used in chapters 2 to 7 is in Aramaic. This language was already in use in Daniel's time, as archaeology has shown. That is why the first half of the book is to the general public, but the second half is only to the sincere humble believer.

It is as Jesus said to his followers in Matthew 13. 'I speak in parables because it is not given to the insincere to understand the mysteries of the kingdom, but to you it is granted. You have the privilege of understanding'. Then he drew them aside and told them the meaning of the mysteries. God loves to tell secrets to those who live close to him, to those who are not self-opinionated, but willing to listen.

The Language of Babylon

At one time, the critics said that Daniel could not have written those chapters (2:4 to chapter 7) because the Aramaic speech was not known until later. But there again they were wrong. Archaeology has shown that Aramaic was spoken before Daniel's time. In any case, chapter 1 of Daniel tells you that Daniel and his friends were to be taught

Figure 9.3. Babylon's gate built by Nebuchadnezzar (7th century BC). He boasted of it in Daniel 4:30 before God humbled him.

Courtesy: National Geographic Society

Aramaic as part of their re-education. It was the popular language of Babylon.

Another passage in the Bible also shows that Aramaic was spoken long before Daniel – 200 years in fact. This is in 2 Kings 18:26. It was when good King Hezekiah was besieged in Jerusalem by the triumphant Assyrian armies. The enemy general started shouting threats to the defenders on the walls of Jerusalem in their Hebrew language. He told them that Jehovah could not defend them. He was trying to create a mutiny. The king's messenger said, don't speak in Hebrew but speak in Aramaic (that was the Syrian language) for we understand it. Now, if the Bible says Aramaic was spoken as early as that, I believe the Bible, but archaeology also confirms it. Arthur Gibson of Manchester University shows from the Dere Ala Tablets that Aramaic was known well before Daniel's time.

I won't tire you with further evidence, but it shows how the critics were wrong again in their attempts to discredit Scripture. The use of Aramaic continued right down to the time of Christ. The Lord Jesus spoke and preached in this Aramaic tongue. Can you remember something Jesus said in Aramaic? For a special reason St Mark tells us what these words meant. Can you remember the incident? Jesus said it to a little girl aged 12 in her native language. She was dead, but he said to her, *'Talitha cumi!'* Mark 5:41 tells you it meant 'Little girl, I say to you Arise!' The term Jesus used was a very loving one. Immediately she got up and walked around. Everybody was amazed! Then Jesus showed one of his many acts of thoughtfulness. He knew she was hungry so he said, 'Give her something to eat'.

THE MAIN THRUST OF DANIEL

What is the main thrust of the message to Daniel? It is that **God is Sovereign** or, to use everyday language, man proposes but God disposes.

Whatever interpretation you may give to the symbols and episodes, each one concludes that, however meaningless history may look to the unenlightened, God is overruling to achieve his plan. Look at the assessment at the end of each one. The conclusions reached by each episode are:

- *Daniel's Image* 2:21, 'God removes kings and sets up kings.'
- *Monarch's Madness* 4:32, 'The Most High overrules in the kingdom of men.'
- *Writing on the Wall* 5:21, 'All peoples trembled in fear of your father, but when his heart was lifted up and his spirit was hardened in pride . . . his heart was made like the beasts . . . He lived like a donkey and ate grass like a cow . . . till he knew that the Most High

God rules in the kingdom of men and appoints over it whoever he chooses.'

- *Lion's Den* 6:26,27 (NKJV) 'Tremble and fear before the God of Daniel, for He is the living God, and steadfast forever. His kingdom is the one which shall not be destroyed, and His dominion shall endure to the end. He delivers and rescues, and He works signs and wonders in heaven and on earth, who has delivered Daniel from the power of the lions.'
- *The Horror Beast* 7:21–27, 'He will wear out the saints of the Most High and the saints will be given into his hand for a time, two times and half a time. Then the court shall sit and take away his dominion . . . and the kingdoms under the whole heaven shall be given to the saints of the Most High.'
- *Waiting for the Messiah* 9:24, 'Seventy weeks of years are determined.'

New Testament Applies this Sovereign Teaching

The book of Revelation proclaims this teaching amidst the backcloth of thunder and lightning, roaring seas and scorching sun, earthquakes and the sound of trumpets. The rise and fall of kings and empires is summed up by this comment in Revelation 17:17: 'God has put it into their hearts to fulfil his purpose, to be of one mind in giving their kingdom to the beast, until the words of God are fulfilled.'

Consequently, whether the emperor was good or bad, Peter said in 1 Peter 2:13,14 'Submit yourselves to every ordinance of man for the Lord's sake, whether to the king as supreme or to governors . . . for this is the will of God, that by doing good you may silence the ignorant misrepresentations of foolish men.'

Paul likewise said in Romans 13:1,2, 'Be subject unto the authorities . . . for they are ordained by God.'

Concerning the prophesied future, he wrote, 'He who now restrains will do so until he is removed, and then the lawless one will be revealed whom the Lord will consume away with the breath of his mouth (his inspired Word) and finally destroy with the brightness of his coming.'

SUMMARY

WHAT GOD FORETOLD TO DANIEL IN THE PUBLIC LANGUAGE

The Gentile future and prophesied history of the Four Empires from 603 BC to 20th century AD. Note: the popular Aramaic language was in use well before Daniel's time.

Images of the Empires (Daniel 2)
- **Head of Gold** = Babylon 603–538 BC.
- **Arms and Chest of Silver** = Medo Persia 538–334 BC.
- **Waist of Bronze** = Greece 334–31 BC.
- **Legs of Iron** = Rome 31 BC to 20th century AD.
- Divides into E and W like the legs, then into 10 (toes) at the end (European single market with 10 ethnic groupings?)
- **Uncreated stone** descends from heaven in days of 10 toes and smashes the Image.

Animal Symbols of Empires (Daniel 7)
- **Deflated Lion** = Nebuchadnezzar humbled by madness.
- **Lop-sided Bear** = Persia stronger than Media. 3 ribs. Egypt, Babylon, Lydia defeated.
- **Leopard with 4 wings** = Alexander who dies and 4 generals divide empire.
- **The Horror Beast** with iron teeth. Europe breaks up into 10 'kingdoms'. Little horn propaganda uproots 3 kingdoms. After 3½ 'Times' (1,260 years) Bible read again and gradually corrects errors 7:25,26.
- **Son of Man** descends with the clouds.

God's Sovereignty is the prime teaching in Daniel. 'Man proposes but God disposes.'
- **Each episode reaches this conclusion:** Daniel's image 2:21 'God upsets kings and sets up kings'.
- **Monarch's Madness** 4:32 'The Most High overrules in the kingdoms of men'.
- **Writing on the Wall** 5:21 'The Most High overrules in the kingdoms of men'.
- **Lion's Den** 6:26,27 'God's Kingdom cannot be destroyed.'
- **Horror Beast** 7:21–27 Wears out saints only until 'judgement sits'.
- **Waiting for Messiah** 9:24 Seventy weeks of years determined.

NT applies this sovereign teaching
- **Rev 17** 'God has put it into their hearts to fulfil his will . . . until'.
- **1 Pet. 2:13,14** 'Submit yourselves . . . unto governors as sent by him'.
- **Rom 13:1,2** 'Be subject unto the authorities . . . They are ordained by God'.

10   WHAT GOD FORETOLD DANIEL IN HEBREW CONFIDENTIALITY
PROPHECY CONCERNING THE JEWS

Chapters 8 to 12 in the book of Daniel are an answer to the question, 'When will the sanctuary be cleansed?' This answer involves the Jewish future and is therefore confidential. This is why Daniel was inspired to write these chapters in the old Hebrew tongue which was no longer in general use, but was understood by Jews.

The future fortunes of the Jews and the sanctuary where the temple stood were in an area which was going to be invaded by the Greek king, Alexander the Great, 200 years after God told Daniel about it. That is why the scene is set in the area which was going to be covered by the Greek Empire. This empire was symbolised by the goat which is appropriate because the sea between Greece and Turkey is called the Goat Sea or Aegean in the Greek. After AD 638, this area of the Greek Empire was occupied by Moslem powers who extended their conquests to former Yugoslavia and the Balkans in AD 1453. So these prophecies extend down to our time.

Figure 10.1. The goat with a single horn in Daniel 8:5 depicting the Greek Empire in which territory the temple sanctuary was situated and on which the Moslem mosque was built. The little horn was to grow out of that single horn, i.e. it would spring up from the Near East and Arabia.

The single big, strong horn on the goat symbolised Alexander, God said, who would ram the Medo-Persian Empire at great speed and demolish it. But after only ten years, Alexander would die and his four generals would divide up his empire among them. The single horn is therefore broken off and four smaller horns take its place. The sanctuary was situated in one of the four Greek areas. Eventually, the Seleucides dominated this area. Both Antiochus Epiphanes and Mohammed were descended from the Seleucides. Its cleansing would take many, many centuries.

Keeping a Secret

Can you keep a secret? Perhaps you say, 'It depends on the circumstances'. Does it puzzle you why Jesus sometimes said, 'Don't tell anybody!' and at other times he said, 'Tell everybody!' It all depended on the circumstances.

In some of the prophecies of Daniel, God said, 'Reveal this to the worldly emperor'. In others he said, 'Seal it up – only the humble wise will understand it at the time of the end.'

We have seen that the first half of Daniel's prophecy was written in the common tabloid language of the pagan empire. It was in Aramaic. It told the pagans 'God reigns!' As the second half of Daniel is in the old Hebrew, not understood by the worldly of Daniel's day, what is its message to seekers of truth? It is, 'God reveals, but only to the sincere'. That is why the second half, chapters 8 to 11, is **confidential**.

One way in which God conceals his plans from the casual is by certain mystic figures. We are first introduced to them in Daniel 7:25. It is that strange measurement phrased as 'A time, two times and half a time'. The verse says it is given to believers who are being worn out by their persecutors:

> He speaks words against God . . . He makes war with the holy people of God . . . and wears them out and plans to change times and seasons but this will only be allowed for a time, two times and half a time.

God's Computer Angel

Where is the sincere believer to find a clue to this measurement? It is found in what God tells Ezekiel and also in God's special messenger in Daniel 8:13. In fact, God had his special agents – they were special angels. He had one who gave the mathematics of God's plan in history. His name is Palmoni, which means 'God's wonderful calculator'. It is not translated into the English which is rather a pity. In all versions, it is rendered 'angel'. But no other angel has this name. Only the Authorised Version (King James Version) puts the real meaning in the margin, 'The Wonderful Calculator'. This is the one of whom other angels ask 'How long?' They ask him this in verse 13. Why? Because there has been given a mysterious figure. It is 2,300. What on earth does that mean? Well, you should have asked 'What in heaven does that mean?' because it is God's computer angel who would have told you the answer. As with many prophecies, that figure was fulfilled in two ways. First as 2,300 days; then as 2,300 years. Remember that this is given in the confidential section. The 2,300 years was fulfilled dramatically recently. Why was understanding given to the enquirer? It was because he asked the Lord, 'How long will it be?'

THE SANCTUARY CHAPTERS

Daniel chapters 8 to 12 answer the question, 'How long will the sanctuary be trampled underfoot?' The answer is in 8:14, 'For 2,300 day-years, then shall the sanctuary begin to be cleansed.' As we have seen, the sanctuary is where the temple stood.

The sanctuary was in the Greek Empire area (v 21), which was still in the future when Daniel wrote. The huge ram's horn represented Alexander the Great. When the horn was broken off, his four generals divided up the Greek Empire into four.

One of them governed the Holy Land where the sanctuary was. It is because the sanctuary was in the Greek area that chapter 8 starts with the Greek emperor's invasion to defeat Persia. The starting point for the 2,300 years would commence when Alexander reached Jerusalem in 333 BC. Its terminal year is AD 1967 when Jerusalem was taken and ruled by Israel for the first time since Nebuchadnezzar. One of the first actions taken in Jerusalem was to change the status of the Wailing Wall of the sanctuary. It was declared to be a synagogue. The words of 8:14 in the Hebrew mean, 'Then shall the sanctuary begin to be cleansed'. It was no longer 'trampled under foot'.

Surprising Discovery in Africa

I made a surprising discovery on one of my visits to South Africa. A minister gave me permission to look at a book in his library. He had there a very old commentary on the Bible. It was written by Adam Clarke in 1820. He anticipated that the cleansing of the sanctuary would commence in 1967.

That is exactly what did happen. It was then that the Israelis reached the Wailing Wall and made it into a sanctuary. They pronounced it to be a synagogue with the sacred Torah scroll. Why did they do this? It was the only surviving wall of the original sanctuary area. The only part of the temple sanctuary which survived the Roman destruction in AD 70.

Where did Adam Clarke find that this was prophesied and how did he know that it would be 170 years before it would be fulfilled in our days, long after he was dead ? He found it in Daniel 8:13,14.

I have already introduced you to God's calculator angel. He said that it would happen 2,300 years after the time that Alexander the Great invaded the Persian Empire. He states who this is quite clearly in Daniel 8:21. 'The he-goat is the king of Greece and the great horn between his eyes is the first king.'

Now Alexander, the Greek conqueror, was still 200 years into the future when Daniel was told that. Alexander commenced his invasion from the West in 333 BC, calendar year, so that is near the starting date for the 2,300 years.

Why did this invasion involve the sanctuary at Jerusalem? It was because it was when his empire divided into four. The province which ruled Jerusalem was where the sanctuary was.

Now note the double fulfilment. The text goes on to say that near the end of that Greek rule over Palestine, 'A king of dark countenance will arise'. He will defile the temple. It is generally acknowledged that this was Antiochus Epiphanes who caused the sacrifices to cease in 167 BC. He would fulfil the period of 2,300 in **days**, but the longer fulfilment of 2,300 in **years** is what Adam Clarke foresaw, which began to be fulfilled in 1967 at the sanctuary wall.

The following eye-witness report is by Colin Simpson in Dr Skevington Wood's *Signs of the Times*:

To the Jew, the wall represented the only relic of the nation's sanctuary. On the 3rd June 1967, the Israeli troops fought their way to the wall. General Dayan paused there to pray and give thanks. The ram's horn was blown by a chaplain. Then thousands of soldiers streamed in to wait their turn to kiss the stones. Sweating, and some wounded, they covered their heads with anything, even bits of paper, some borrowed from the reporter's notebook. Many were weeping with emotion . . . It was an electric and disturbing experience. At the wall, General Dayan declared, 'We have returned to our holiest of holy places, never to depart again'.

A special prayer was printed for the wall: 'O mighty God, glorious God, truthful God, perfect God, rebuild thy house soon, rebuild it in our time. As a praise to thee, as a glory to thee, rebuild thy sanctuary in our time . . . rebuild thy sanctuary in our time . . . rebuild soon the temple . . . rebuild speedily thy sanctuary.'

So if ever you visit the Wailing Wall at Jerusalem and you see the scrolls of the Law there and the Jews saying their prayers, let it tell you that you are witnessing momentous events which are in the process of unfolding.

The Sanctuary Cycle

The 'sanctuary cycle', the name given to that period of 2,300 years prophesied in the book of Daniel chapter 8, apparently also has astronomical significance.

A remarkable discovery about the sanctuary cycle was made by a Swiss astronomer. His name was M. de Cheseaux. He discovered that the measurement of 2,300 years was an exact unit of time which the sun and the moon took to complete a certain revolution of events. He says that 2,300 years marks off a unit of time and that 'He who timed the movements of the sun and the moon in their orbits', meaning God, must have inspired Daniel to write this. He said that it was a million to one chance that Daniel would hit on this figure by accident.

Well, you will remember that it was God's calculator angel called Palmoni who gave Daniel this figure in chapter 8 verse 14. Here it is. 'Then I heard Palmoni speaking and another angel said to Palmoni, "How long will it take the vision to fulfil?" and he said, "2,300; then the sanctuary will begin to be restored to its rightful state." '

This period of time runs out at about the same time as that other longer measurement of the seven 'Times' of the Gentiles, i.e. 2,520 years. Why does it? Because the starting point of the sanctuary cycle was later in history. It was at the beginning of the third empire prophesied – the Greek Empire – whereas the Times of the Gentiles started with the first empire of Daniel's image – the Babylonian Empire.

Daniel was mystified – and I expect you are too! So a voice said to the angel Gabriel, 'Make this man to understand the vision'. And he said to Daniel, 'Understand O man, that the vision is all to do with the end times.'

Well, whether or not you understand what the figures mean precisely, you can see what they all say: 'The times are running out'; 'The world's hour is getting late'; 'The midnight hour is approaching.' The cry will soon go out, 'Behold he comes with the clouds of heaven.' Prepare to meet him!

More Information about the Sanctuary Cycle

Someone requested more information about the sanctuary cycle when they heard me speak about it. What is it? What makes a cycle? If you are not interested, then skip these astronomical details. They are contained in Dr Grattan Guinness' learned book, *The Approaching End of the Age* (Hodder & Stoughton, 1878). In it, M. de Cheseaux explains what a cycle is:

A period which brings into harmony different celestial revolutions, containing a certain definite number of each, without remainder or fraction.

He also shows that there are four different kinds of cycle connected with the sun, moon and earth:

1. Those harmonising the solar day and year.
2. Those harmonising the solar year and lunar month.
3. Those harmonising the solar day and lunar month.
4. Those harmonising all three, day, month and year.

M. de Cheseaux adds:

> The discovery of such cycles has always been a great object with astronomers and chronologists. They have considered it so difficult a matter that they have almost laid it down as a principle that it is impossible, at any rate as regards those of the fourth class. Till now, the discovery of a cycle of this kind has been to astronomers, like perpetual motion to mechanics, a sort of philosopher's stone. Anxious to settle whether the thing were really impossible, I began some time ago to try for a cycle of the second kind.

M. de Cheseaux then describes the process by which he was led to the discovery that 315 years is such a soli-lunar cycle, *ten times more exact* than the nineteen-year Metonic cycle in use by the ancients; the sun and moon coming after a lapse of that period, to within 3 hours 24 seconds of absolute agreement, so he proceeds: 'I had no sooner discovered this cycle, than I observed that it was a quarter of the 1,260 years of Daniel, and the Apocalypse, and that consequently, this period is itself a soli-lunar cycle', after which the sun and moon return, within less than half a degree, to the same point of the ecliptic precisely, and that within an hour of each other. That is, after 460,205 days 6 hours, the sun and moon come into conjunction, and in 460,205 days 7 hours 23 mins, *the sun has returned to its exact starting point on the ecliptic* – a period of 1,260 solar years.

According to more accurate modern measures, the repeating 1,260 years differ only by about three hours less. M. de Cheseaux saw that 'time, times and a half' of Daniel 7 meant a period of 1,260 years. It goes without saying that *the biblical period of seven 'Times' (2,520 years) is an equally important and exact cycle in our solar system.* He goes on:

> The relation of this period, assigned by the Holy Spirit as the limit of certain political events, to the most notable movements of the heavenly bodies, made me think it might be the same with the 2,300 years. By the aid of the astronomic tables I examined this latter, and found that at the end of 2,300 Gregorian years, minus six hours fourteen seconds, the sun and the moon return to within half a degree of the place from which they

TURKS MUST VACATE FOR JEWS

Careful students of Scripture, who have reflected at all on these topics, must have observed that in the Book of Revelation there is comparatively little about the Jews and their restoration, that subject having been fully treated in the Old Testament. The Saracenic invasion and the Turkish overthrow are indeed predicted in Revelation, for the Fifth and Sixth Trumpets are universally recognised as prefiguring the sore " woes " which were inflicted on the apostate Christian Church of the East by these desolating Powers. But the Mohammedan conquests are there viewed in connexion with the Christian Churches of the East, and not in connexion with Syria and the Jews. Yet they stand in a most important relation to Israel also, and in *this* connexion they are presented in Daniel viii. It is as the desolater of *Jerusalem*, and the ruler of *Judœa* for twelve centuries, that this Moslem Power principally affects Israel; it occupies the Holy Land and treads down Jerusalem, and has done so ever since A.D. 637, when the Caliph Omar first brought the country under subjection to Mohammedan despotism.

Now just as the Papacy could not be developed while the emperors were ruling at Rome, so the Jews cannot be restored while the Turks are masters in Jerusalem; the one Power must needs fall before the other can rise. The promised land must be freed from Moslem occupation before it can revert to its lawful heirs, the seed of Abraham.

Figure 10.2. Extract from book published in 1886 by Dr H. Grattan Guinness, *Light for the Last Days* (Marshall, Morgan & Scott) in which the author anticipates the pending restoration of Jerusalem to the Jews.

it has been, and is, the obstacle in the way of Israel's restoration. Its removal, under Divine judgment, must therefore figure prominently in prophecies of Jewish restoration in the last times; just as largely as the removal of the Papal Apostasy, under similar judgments, in the predictions of the deliverance of the Gentile Church, prior to the establishment of the kingdom of God on earth.

It should be noted further that both in Daniel and in Revelation this foe is represented as destroyed, not by the brightness of Christ's coming, not suddenly in an hour like "Babylon the Great," but as perishing by inherent decay—"he shall be broken without hand"; "he shall come to his end, and none shall help him"; and under the symbol of the Euphrates, "the waters thereof were dried up." This, as is well known, is, and has been, the characteristic fate of the Ottoman empire. Europe would fain have arrested its decay if she could; she would not suffer any enemy wantonly to attack Turkey; she would not permit it to be roughly overthrown in selfish aggression. From motives of policy she would fain have upheld it in its position, but found it impossible. Corruption and death are working in the body politic; vitality is failing at the centre; and Ottoman dominion must, in spite of every effort, soon cease to exist.

started, and that an hour later the sun has reached its exact starting point on the ecliptic; whence it follows that the prophetic period of 2,300 years, is a cyclical period (also remarkable for the number of its aliquot parts, and for containing a complete number of cycles) and one so perfect, that though it is thirty times longer than the celebrated cycle of Calippus, it has an error of only thirteen hours, a seventeenth part of the error of that ancient cycle.

The exact similarity of the error of these two cycles of 1,260 and 2,300 years, made me soon conclude that the difference between them, 1,040 years, ought to be a perfect cycle, free from all error; and all the more remarkable as uniting the three kinds of cycles, and furnishing consequently a cycle of that fourth kind, so long sought in vain, and finally concluded to be chimerical, impossible to find.

On examination of this period of 1,040 years by the best modern astronomic tables, I found that it was even so. Its error is absolutely imperceptible, in so long a period, and may indeed be accounted for by errors in the tables themselves, owing to the inaccuracy of some of the ancient observations on which they are founded.

As I before said, a cycle of this kind had long been sought in vain; no astronomer or chronologist had been able to light upon one for nineteen centuries; and yet for two thousand three hundred years, there it has been, written in characters legible enough, in the Book of Daniel; legible, that is, to him who was willing to take the trouble of comparing the great prophetic periods with the movements of the heavenly bodies; in other words, to him, who compared the book of nature with the book of revelation.

A copy of M. de Cheseaux's book is kept in the library of the University of Lausanne, and another in the British Museum. It is entitled, *Mémoires posthumes de M. de Cheseaux*. It was submitted to the astronomers of the Royal Academy of Sciences at Paris.

The Greek 'Little Horn'

The 'Little Horn' of the west half of the Roman Empire (7:8) is not to be confused with the Little Horn of the Greek Eastern section. The little horn of 8:9 and his dark or mystic sayings was to be Mohammed (8:23,24). It was this propagating of his religion by the sword which nearly wiped out the Greek Orthodox Church and overran all the area occupied originally by the Greek Empire. Alexander's domains reached from the Balkans to Pakistan and it is mainly that area in which Islam is now strong. As 8:9 says, its expansion was to be overwhelming eastwards and southwards, including the Holy Land. It was on part of the sanctuary platform that the mosque was built in AD 638.

Historic Purpose of the Greek and Roman Empires

In the prophecies God gave to Daniel, we have seen the purpose behind each empire down the last 2,520 years. You see, God didn't foretell the future just to satisfy curiosity. It was to show his purpose behind history.

For example, the Babylonian Empire brought God's judgement upon a nation which was obstinately deaf to his voice. That is typical of most nations at various times.

The Persian Empire restored a remnant of godly people to Palestine after 70 years as foretold by Jeremiah. The temple was rebuilt and so were the city walls. That remnant established Jewry which prepared for Christ's first coming.

The Greek Empire which followed — what was God's purpose for them? Here is a clue! What language is your New Testament written in? I mean the original language in which the Gospels and letters were written? Yes, of course, it was Greek. All translations of the New Testament are translations from the Greek. Now why was that? It was because Greek had become the international language of the day. Whatever the local language may have been, everybody learnt Greek, thanks to Alexander the Great who spread his conquests East and West. Even in Egypt the language became Greek. That is why the Old Testament became translated into Greek 280 years before Christ. By the time of Christ, the Greek version of the Old Testament was widely used even by the Jews. It was from this translation that all the Christians quoted when they wrote the New Testament. The surprising thing is that even when the Greek Empire gave way to the Roman Empire, the international language still continued to be Greek. So Paul and others had this international language to use when they travelled through Europe.

Why did God choose Greek for the gospel message? Many have said it is because it is one of the most expressive and accurate languages of history. Even one of its verbs takes many words in another language to express its full meaning. That is why it sometimes takes more than one modern translation to express the full meaning of a passage.

Now what about the Roman Empire? How did God use that iron empire? Rome's iron might removed all national barriers. Passports were not needed to pass from country to country. Rome's roads, too, took the traveller from one end of Europe to another. Paul was able to travel freely to bring the good news of salvation and so could the other Christians.

Remember that the prophecies of Daniel said that the Roman Empire would later divide up into about ten sovereignties. This it did, so what purpose did God have in that? Was it not so that these

European countries could send explorers throughout the world? Unintentionally that opened up the world for Christians to take the good news. When countries fail to help the gospel, God withdraws his blessing. If we look at history through Bible eyes, we shall understand. Daniel 10:11: 'O Daniel, a man greatly beloved, understand the words that I speak to you.'

DANIEL STRUCTURE

When I was at school, one master made history so interesting that I enjoyed every moment of it. I find that Daniel's prophecies fill history with meaning as God told Daniel all the history of the next 2,500 years before it happened. Daniel tells you his own emotions about it. He says, 'I looked'; 'I saw'; 'I heard a voice speaking to me'; 'Sometimes I was alarmed, anxious, frightened, curious.'

In the prophecy of Daniel, the future history of those 2,500 years are called the 'Times of the Gentiles'. This history is foretold four times. Each time it is from a different angle:

- The first is for the **pagan world** – how it affects them. That is in chapters 1–6.
- The second is how it affects the **Christians**. That is in chapter 7.
- The third prophesied history is about **Israel** – how it affects them. That is in chapters 8–9.
- The fourth outline of future history is for the **modern Christian.** How will it affect you? That is in chapters 10–12.

Special Agents

The last two outlines of history are mostly in the confidential section. So God appoints his special agents to explain the secret meaning and purpose to Daniel and to us believers. As we have seen, those special agents are special angels. The angel named Palmoni is God's mathematician. He gives out all the time measurements for things to happen. The angel called Gabriel tells Daniel about events which will lead up to the Messiah. That is why the same angel Gabriel announced the fulfilment to the Virgin Mary and to Joseph five centuries later.

Then there is a most remarkable angel. He is called, 'The Man clothed in Linen'. His face is as radiant as the sun; his eyes like flames of fire and a golden girdle is around his waist. He explains all of chapters 10 to 12 and brings you down to modern times of science and travel and the (his?) second coming.

These special agents are like those who explain things to John in the book of Revelation; like the angel who explains the meaning of the seven bowls of wrath upon the wicked.

As you look back after 2,520 years, you see how remarkably the four aspects of history have been accurately fulfilled. You may be alarmed to find the pagan aspect has little more now to fulfil, but if you are a Christian, you are uplifted to see the wonderful things in store and you are comforted if you are a Jew that all the suffering will be worthwhile and, if you are an Arab believer, God will say 'Blessed are you my people' (Isaiah 19:25).

Saints Alive!

As I have said, the succession of empires in Daniel chapter 7 is the same as in chapter 2, but it has special reference to how they would affect Christians down the centuries – particularly the fourth empire. That turned out to be the Roman Empire. Daniel was absolutely horrified at what it revealed. The Roman Empire itself would persecute them, but when it split up into ten, there would arise a power which would persecute the true believers worse than any other before it. It would last 1,260 years. Dr Gordon's book, *Behold He Cometh*, explains this.

Notice that when all these tests for the true Christian are over, they will reign with Christ. That is why Paul says, 'Don't you know that the Christians will judge the world?' He was thinking of this passage in Daniel 7:27:

> Then the sovereignty, power and greatness of the kingdom under the whole heaven will be handed over to the saints, the people of the Most High. His kingdom will be an everlasting kingdom and all rulers will worship and obey him.

But when would this be? Does it mean that the spread of the gospel will change the whole world? It could do if it were accepted, but the Bible says that, before Christ's second coming, the world will get worse, so it can't mean that. Jesus himself said that the world's response will be, 'We will not have this man Jesus to reign over us'.

Notice also that in chapter 7 of Daniel, it is his second coming which precedes the reign of Christ on earth. This is clear in verse 13 and is the same as in Daniel 2. I quote, 'One like the Son of Man came with the clouds of heaven . . . and there was given to him dominion, glory and a kingdom that all people, nations and languages should serve him. His dominion is an everlasting dominion which shall not pass away.'

So you see, it is not his birth which is described here but his second coming with the clouds. It is through this second coming that verse 18 says the saints shall reign with him.

You will remember the many passages in the New Testament which say that *after* the resurrection of the believers, Christ will bring them with him to reign on earth. They will be saints alive again!

But who are these saints? In the New Testament, the name is used to mean the saved Christians. It is not used only of outstanding Christians. For example, Paul writes to all the saints at the church of Ephesus, verse 1. Then in verse 13 he says who they are. They are those 'who trusted Christ for salvation after they heard the Word of Truth, the gospel of their salvation; the believers who were sealed as belonging to God.' In Ephesians 2:8, they were those who were saved by 'accepting the free gift of salvation which was by grace and not earned by works'.

Sun and Moon Years

There is another time measurement in Daniel 12 which also shows a remarkable combination of the difference between sun years and moon years.

The Eastern religious people calculate by moon years or lunar years but the Westerners calculate by sun years or solar years. Consequently, Daniel 12 gives the time in moon years when the Jews would be granted a home in Palestine. That date was the Eastern date of 1335. As we have seen, when the Jews were granted this in 1917, the newspapers in Jerusalem included that date on their newspaper headings.

Now, the amazing thing is this: the difference in years between the date measured by the moon and the date measured by the sun is 75 years. This is by adding two figures to the 1,260 years of Daniel 12:7, namely 30 and 45 which Daniel does in verses 11 and 12. These in turn reveal more interesting facts. If you add 30 to 1917, it gives you the year 1947, when the United Nations agreed to a State of Israel which was set up the next year. If you add the 45 as well, that gives you the year 1992, which was the year in which President Clinton was elected and who was more sympathetic to the Jewish needs for settlement than Bush. It was also the year of the establishment of the Single European Market. Jesus said, 'Watch and pray'. So don't only watch – pray as well.

Now, Daniel did just that. When he saw certain dates which applied to his time, he put aside special times of prayer as in chapter 9. What time span did he observe? He saw in Jeremiah's prophecy that the exile would last 70 years. That 70 years was almost up in his day. Here is the passage in Daniel 9:2–5, 17:

> In the first year of his reign, I, Daniel, understood by books, the number of the years whereof the word of the Lord came to Jeremiah the prophet, that he would accomplish 70 years in the desolations of Jerusalem. And I set my face unto the Lord God, to seek by prayer and supplications, with

fasting and sackcloth and ashes; and I prayed unto the Lord my God, and made my confession and said, O Lord, the great and dreadful God, keeping covenant and mercy to them that love him and to them that keep his commandments; we have sinned and have committed iniquity and have done wickedly and have rebelled even by departing from thy precepts and from thy judgements . . . now therefore O our God, hear the prayer of thy servant and his supplications, and cause thy face *to shine upon thy sanctuary that is desolate*, for the Lord's sake.

How then should we pray for our nation?

Abominations and Revivals

Defilement and cleansing at various times is the repeated history of Christianity as well as of the material sanctuary at Jerusalem. That is why revivals are necessary for God's Church. The Church is God's spiritual sanctuary. And the temple of Jerusalem was God's visible sanctuary. Peter wrote, 'You are living stones built into a spiritual house.' The material temple was defiled three times down history as prophesied.

The **first** defilement was prophesied in Daniel 8:23. This sacrilege was committed in 167 BC by a Greek ruler called Antiochus Epiphanes. The prophecy says that he would lift up his heart against God. (Many have done that since.) He would subtly lead many astray by flattery or threats and place an abomination in the temple. But he would be broken by God, not by man. This actually happened. Instead of dying in battle, he died suddenly in Media in 164 BC.

The **second** defilement was when the Roman army destroyed Jerusalem. This was preceded by a sacrilege committed by the Zealots who sacrificed unclean pigs instead of sin sacrifices. The Lord Jesus said that the Christians should read Daniel and understand, so don't be put off by those who despise the prophecies of Daniel. Do as Jesus said, read Daniel and understand it. In Mark 13:14 he said, 'When you see the defiling abomination in that sanctuary, let him who reads Daniel understand.' So that makes it clear that Antiochus Epiphanes did not fulfil all the prophecy of the abomination.

The **third** time was in AD 638. The Mosque of the False Prophet was erected on the site. The New Testament says that the material temple was also a symbol of the spiritual temple in the Church. In 2 Thessalonians 2, this spiritual temple is called the 'Naos'. That is referring to the people who make up the Church. Defilement will come to that, too, the text says. When ambitious men fight for preferment, like Antiochus Epiphanes, their concern for the Bible truth can go out of the window. As Daniel said, 'Truth is cast down to the ground and the anti-God ruler trampled upon it and exalted himself'. We should not be dismayed at this, but pray for the cleansing which revival brings. Revival can save a nation from corruption and revolution.

Did you know that the Evangelical Revival 250 years ago saved Britain from something similar to the French Revolution? That is the opinion of the famous historian J.R. Green. Britain was ripe for revolution. There was agnosticism everywhere. The atheistic sayings of Thomas Payne were on everyone's lips. The Church before the Evangelical Revolution was mainly what was called Latitudinarian – that means they believed very little. The morals of politicians were an open scandal say the historians.

It was at this time that John Wesley was converted in 1738 and then many other clergy were born again by the Holy Spirit. This saved Britain from corruption and cleaned up society. Wesley and others went up and down the land preaching the gospel. The Revival changed thousands of lives of all classes – miners and gentry.

In Parliament, Christians began to pass laws to uplift the poor, to remove exploitation and injustices, to abolish slavery. In those days, the Bible became the most quoted book in Parliament. It happened again in Wales in 1904. It can happen again today if you pray. It starts by cleansing the spiritual sanctuary first.

Revelation about Jesus

'Gabriel, help this man understand.' Daniel was seeking fuller understanding of what that mysterious number 2,300 meant in 8:14. God said, 'Gabriel, help this man understand.'

Why did he ask Gabriel? Because he was going to help Daniel understand about Jesus the Messiah. Why Gabriel? Well, he had a special commission about the Lord Jesus. It was he who later explained to the Virgin Mary and Joseph.

Gabriel helped Daniel to understand that God worked in sevens. Seventy years was the duration of the exile; next it would be 70 x 7 to the first coming of the Messiah, the Prince, he said, as he 'helped that man to understand'. The chosen minority were going back to Jerusalem to rebuild the walls and the temple. The year in which Christ would come would be 70 x 7 years after the command came to rebuild the walls. Now let Gabriel help YOU understand!

That was fulfilled. Seven times seventy is 490 years. The Emperor Cyrus was the first to give command; that was 457 BC. That date brings us exactly to the time of the crucifixion; that is if we reckon in our calendar years by the sun.

But the command was neglected owing to opposition, so a new command was given in 444 BC to Nehemiah but using the same numbers. Now, the Middle East reckons time in lunar years by the moon. They are shorter. Here again, 490 lunar years brings you to the same time – the time of the crucifixion. But is it correct that the timing is to the crucifixion instead of the birth of Jesus? The answer is yes for two reasons. Gabriel said:

1. It would be when the final atonement for sin was made. That would be made by 'the anointed one' whose life would be cut off but not for himself but for others – yes, for you and for me. He would do that after half a week of years' ministry. Half of seven is, of course, 3½ years and that became the length of Christ's ministry before he died for sinners. By the way, the name 'Christ' means 'the anointed one'.
2. The second reason that the timing of 490 years was to the cross is that it fulfilled the symbol of the sanctuary. All the animal sacrifices which took place at the sanctuary only pointed to Christ whose one sacrifice was sufficient for all time.

Now Daniel had been concerned about the defiling of the sanctuary. The angel said, 'Don't worry about that. That is only a symbol. In fact, when Christ has died, it will do away with any need for a sanctuary. For that reason, God will allow the sanctuary to be destroyed again' (8:26). The Roman army will destroy it. Then the need for animal sacrifices will cease for ever. So God will destroy them by the fall of Jerusalem. This happened in AD 70.

The Unseen Enemy

What are the unseen enemies of today? Well, there are satellite spies – they can look down from outer space and see all that is happening on the ground. It is magnified up to see the smallest details. Then there is radar. They are invisible rays. We know of their existence only when we see their findings on the radar screen. Daniel 10 is like a radar screen; it shows up the invisible forces behind the powers of this world.

There was an evil spirit behind the Persian power, verse 13 says. But how do we know that it was an unseen spiritual power? The words merely say, 'The Prince of the kingdom of Persia withstood me'.

Look at who it was against. It was against the angel clothed in linen and against Michael the archangel. They were spiritual beings engaged in a spiritual battle. In Revelation 12 we get a similar picture. Verse 7 says, 'A war arose in heaven, Michael and his angels fighting against the dragon – Satan. And the dragon and his angels fought, but they were defeated and there was no longer any place for them in heaven . . . the dragon is Satan, the devil, the deceiver of the whole world.'

Is that kind of battle still going on? Paul says so. He says in Ephesians 6, 'For we do not fight against earthly powers, but against wicked spirits in high places, against wicked spiritual princes and powers.'

Paul says, 'We fight against them'. Well, how do we fight them when we can't even see them? The answer is in Daniel 10:12. The angel said to Daniel, 'Your words have been heard and I have come to you because of your words.'

What words were those? Prayer. Daniel had put aside three weeks for prayer and, to concentrate on it; he fasted too. Read the passage: 'It was a great conflict . . . In those days, I, Daniel, was fasting for three weeks in prayer.' So, as Paul said later, 'Pray at all times in the Holy Spirit with every kind of prayer and supplication. Be alert and persevere so that there may be openings for preaching the gospel.'

So you see, if barriers are being raised against the gospel, it is revival prayer which is required first. This is not just casual prayer but prayer with intent. 'It is a wrestling,' Paul said, 'a wrestling against wicked unseen spiritual powers.'

The prayers were heard immediately, but the answers were delayed. Those prayers were part of the battle. Always remember that, especially when prayer is difficult. Battle through to victory. Then the same message will come to you, 'Fear not, Daniel, for from the first day that you set your mind to understand and humble yourself before your God, your words have been heard.'

Daniel: Greatly Beloved

For the second time, Daniel is told he is greatly beloved. You are greatly beloved also because the Bible says, 'While you were still a sinner, Christ died for you'. So that love for you was completely undeserved. It was not earned in any way. John says, 'We love him because he first loved us.'

But there are some things which you can do which can increase that love of God in you. First, of course, it is to accept Christ as your Saviour. But, after that, we can learn from the Bible how to please God more and more. Daniel did this. So let's see why God said that Daniel was greatly beloved.

Let me ask you a question. Do you get impatient when a Christian speaks of prophecy? 1 Thessalonians 5 says, 'Despise not prophecies'. One thing which pleased God was that Daniel tried to find out the meaning of prophecies. In particular, he wanted to know the secret of God's timing – those mysterious figures 3½ times and 7 times. Not everybody is interested in that.

Is that why some have no idea of God's timing? Is that why some cannot discern the signs of the times as Jesus commanded? If Daniel wanted to know God's timing, there is all the more reason why we should. Why? Because Daniel was told that the wise believer living at the end time would understand those mysterious figures given to Daniel. As so much time had elapsed, they would need to know the span of God's plan. So if you want to be aware of God's love even more, listen to why Daniel was greatly beloved, in chapter 10:11:

> He said to me, O Daniel, greatly beloved, understand the words which I speak to you . . . From the first day that you set your heart on understanding and humbled yourself in earnest prayer before your God, your words were heard.

Then in verse 14, God's messenger said, 'Understand what will befall your people (the Jews) in the latter days, for the vision is for a long time yet.'

Daniel at Prayer

Then there is the second reason that Daniel was greatly beloved – he linked perception with prayer. That is how you can be very conscious of God's great love for you – link prophecy to prayer.

Daniel read prophecy and found the 70 years exile was terminating – he prayed for three weeks about it. Daniel was then told of the next longer prophecy, 490 years to the Messiah. Daniel prayed about it. Daniel's vision was extended still longer to the end of the age. Daniel prayed about it.

Ancient plays were called Masks; on the ruins of the theatre in Ephesus, there is a stone carving of a mask. Why? Because the characters on the stage wore those masks to disguise their own identity.

The predictions of Daniel chapter 10 are different from all the others before them. How? They foretold events in undisguised language. The other prophecies were masked, so to speak. They were mostly in symbols like the lop-sided bear, the lion with eagle's wings or the metal statue. But, as Dr Basil Atkinson says in *The Times of the Gentiles*, 'This chapter contains literal prophecy of historical events in undisguised language'. It is like Gibbon's history, *The Decline and Fall of Rome*, except that Gibbon wrote it after the events, whereas God told it to Daniel before the events.

Have we any independent opinion on whether chapter 10 is literal history? We have. Even critics have recognised the events and, indeed, you have only to read the history from Persian times onwards to recognise the characters and events.

What are those events? Well, there are too many to rehearse here and I am sure you don't want a history lesson, but you will have heard of the Marathon. That has become very popular to run. It originated in 490 BC when a Greek soldier ran 26 miles from Marathon to Athens without stopping, to tell of the Greek victory against the Persians.

Then you may have seen the monuments in Greece at Thermophylae. The gallant Spartans numbering only 300 held back thousands of Persians at that narrow gorge of Thermophylae – the hot springs.

You would see nothing behind all this history if the Bible didn't reveal to you that it all was the purpose of God, foretold and worked out. Later, in Daniel 10:30, the ships of Kittim are mentioned. That became the name for all naval powers and here refers to Rome which began to exert power. Rome relinked the ruler of Palestine. His name was Antiochus. Out of spite, Antiochus sacrificed pigs on the temple altar and erected an idol of the god Zeus – that was the first abomination.

Then there is Cleopatra – several plays have been made about that Egyptian queen and her affair with Antony. We read about that in verse 6 of this tenth chapter of Daniel:

> After some years, they shall make an alliance and the daughter of the king of the south shall come to the king of the north to make peace, but she shall not retain the strength of her arm.

Then verse 17 describes how the daughter, Cleopatra, was to be given to the Egyptian king. But all this foretold history leads up to the beginning of chapter 12, which speaks of the resurrection of the Lord Jesus Christ.

Your life is a small history – very important to yourself and to God. Is it leading up to an experience of the resurrection power of the Lord Jesus Christ in your life?

DANIEL CHAPTER 12

We are now going to look at the last chapter of Daniel's prophecy, chapter 12. What does the opening to this chapter mean and when was it fulfilled? It reads, 'At that time, Michael, the great Prince, shall arise who has charge of the Jewish people.'

What does that word 'arise' mean? It refers to the resurrection of Jesus Christ. But why should he be called Michael, the great Prince? If we look at Jude verse 9 and compare it with Zechariah 3:2, we see that Michael is identified with the Lord Jesus Christ.

It means that chapter 12 starts with the resurrection of Christ and goes through the gospel age to the time of the believers' resurrection at the end of the age – the time of modern inventions. Actually, this chapter 12 covers the same length of time that Christ's prophecies do in Luke 21. For example, verse 2 goes on to speak of the great time of trouble which will come to the Jews after the resurrection of Christ, which is what Jesus says in Luke 21:23,24:

For great distress shall be upon this people, the Jews. They will fall by the edge of the sword and be led captive among all nations . . . until the Times of the Gentiles are fulfilled.

The Times of the Gentiles – that is what the book of Daniel is all about – those 2,520 years of Israel scattered among the nations! Now, compare those words with the second half of verse 1 in Daniel 12:

And there will be a time of trouble, such as never has been before in the history of the Jewish nation until that time that they shall be delivered. For the Israel nation will be delivered.

What time will they be delivered? Verse 4 says it will be when science and knowledge will have greatly increased and millions of people will be travelling swiftly all over the world.

Well, that is modern times, isn't it? Yes, the inventions of trains, cars and aeroplanes mean that people of today travel swiftly and regularly around the world. More people travel today than ever before. Why, my granny hardly ever went from her village, a couple of generations ago. Now, today, it is commonplace for people to fly abroad for holidays or on business. Whenever you pass a travel agents and see the placards plastered up, let it tell you that it says, 'Daniel's prophecies have come to pass'. 'Knowledge and science shall be increased and multitudes shall go swiftly to and fro.' And verse 2 tells us that the resurrection is near. 'The believers will be raised to everlasting life and the unbelievers to everlasting contempt.'

How Long to the End?

Here comes the question again in the last chapter of Daniel, verse 6. 'How long to the end of these things?' This time, the one answering the question is that wonderful person clothed in linen. It is not God's calculator angel, it is the one who has been explaining things to Daniel for the last three chapters from chapter 10 to 12.

Many have asked the same question since, 'How long will this go on?' What would you have replied to Daniel now that you are living 2,520 years later? Daniel would have been flummoxed to think that he had to wait another 2,520 years before Israel would be delivered and wickedness banished from the earth.

Daniel is told in the last verse. 'Don't you worry Daniel. You will rest in the Lord and then rise to life at the last day.'

Didn't the angel give any clue to the length of time? Oh, yes. He lifted up one hand and said it will be one time plus two times, plus half a time; then he raised up his other hand and said it will be one time, plus two times and half a time.

That is the Times of the Gentiles again. Yes, it totals seven 'Times', but Daniel would not know how long each time would be and so was not discouraged!

But why did the angel divide the period into two separate portions? A very interesting question, with a remarkable answer. You remember how archaeology has revealed that a 'Time' in Sumerian reckoning is 360 years. Seven Times therefore equals 2,520 years. Well, at exactly halfway through that period, the false prophet was prophesied to start, then continue for 1,260 years. The false prophet of the desert (Mohammed) started in AD 622. The era of the false prophet reckoned in lunar years. That is why the Islamic date is in lunar years; in the Middle East, they reckon in lunar years and 1,260 solar years equals 1,335 lunar years. The Middle East date of 1335 was AD 1917. That is the date when the Turks left Jerusalem and Israel was first granted a home in Palestine. This is derived as follows:

Eastern starting date (Hegira) = AD 622
Add 1,260 lunar years in solar years (1222) = AD 1844
Add 30 + 45 lunar years (73 solar years) = AD 1917
See also further details later in this chapter.

Q I am curious to know who the person was who was clothed in linen, and if he is named in Scripture.

He is indeed. A most fascinating question with some remarkable eye-openers which I will deal with later.

The Answer in the End

The last seven verses of the Prophecy of Daniel are an answer to Daniel's question to the angel clothed in linen: 'How long will it be to the end of these wonders?'

What did he mean by 'the end'? The last verse tells you. It was when Daniel and other believers would rise from the dead. Well, that is a long time from Daniel to our days. Yes, that is why the angel said, 'Daniel, be content – you won't understand the figures I am giving you, but the wise living in the end times will understand. But none of the wicked will understand.' Then he lifted up his right hand and showed 3½ fingers and said, 'It will be 3½ times'. So each hand meant 3½ and the two hands meant 7 'Times' altogether. Didn't I say that years earlier Moses spoke of 7 'Times'? I did. It is only in recent years that Christians have known what the figures meant.

They found out in two ways. First, it was through archaeology. Excavations in the Middle East have revealed the method of number-ing dating from just after the Flood of Noah. The Sumerians were very clever mathematicians. They used algebra and square roots and were the first to add up in columns of numbers. But the important thing for prophecy is that they had this period of time called a 'Time'. It was 360. As we have already seen, that is why our circle or compass is still divided into 360 degrees. (Another unit they used was the submultiple 60 and that is why, even today, you have 60 seconds to the minute and 60 minutes to the hour.)

But that number 360 – 360 what? That was the second discovery. In Ezekiel chapter 4, God said that in prophecy, one day equals one year. So that means that 7 'Times' equals 2,520 years, the length of the time that Gentile nations dominate Jerusalem. But notice why the angel lifted up a second hand and said 3½ times – meaning 1,260 years. It was because these lead up to the last days. You see, the last power in Jerusalem dated its years from Mohammed and the important years which ended on those Eastern dates are given in verse 12. They are equivalent to 1917, 1947 and 1992. They are the stages in which God has been establishing Israel in the Promised Land.

Verse 10 says that 'the wicked will do very wickedly, but will not understand'. We certainly have very wicked atrocities today, but don't be disheartened. It says that many will purify themselves and the wise will win many souls to the Lord Jesus Christ.

Christ Appears Before He Was Born

We saw how God commissioned different angels to reveal to Daniel the meaning of various symbols. The last angel to do this was very remarkable. Look what it says about him and see if you can guess his identity. Don't forget, we are in Old Testament times before Jesus was born.

He was a man clothed in linen. Notice how manhood is emphasised. Now, who was that divine being who becomes man? In the New Testament, Revelation 1:13 says, 'There was one like the Son of Man'. Daniel, in the Old Testament, saw that he had a golden girdle around him. The description is the same in the New Testament. Revelation, written *after* Jesus was born, crucified and risen, says, 'He was clothed with a long robe and with a golden girdle around his chest.'

Daniel, writing before Jesus was born says in chapter 10 verse 6, 'His eyes were like flaming torches and his voice like many multitudes'. Revelation 1:14 says, 'His eyes were like flames of fire and his voice like many waters.' Daniel says, 'His face was like lightning.' Revelation says, 'His face was like the sun shining in its full strength.'

Revelation then continues as follows: 'He said, I am the first and the last, the living one. I died and behold I am alive for ever more and I have the keys of death and hell.'

Scripture is suggesting that the one talking to Daniel is the same one who talked to John in the book of Revelation. But in the New Testament, it is Jesus Christ. How can it be Jesus Christ in the Old Testament when it was before he was born? This is the million dollar question. This person appears to be a number of people in Old Testament times right from the time of Abraham, Joshua and others. The explanation that many give is that these were pre-incarnate appearances of the Lord Jesus Christ. They are appearances of Jesus to people before he was born. How extraordinary! How marvellous. Joshua fell down and worshipped him. You must worship God only, the Bible tells you. Daniel fell at his feet. John fell at his feet.

So it looks as if this angel was the divine Lord Jesus himself. It was he who was helping Daniel to look into the future and explain the mystic numbers. Yes, now you understand why Jesus in the Gospels, knew all about the 7 'Times' and called them the Times of the Gentiles. It was he who named them that. That is what the book of Daniel is all about – the Times of the Gentiles.

And the thing is that it was Jesus Christ who gave those mysterious figures to Daniel, 3½ 'Times' plus 3½ 'Times' making 7 'Times'; the 2,520 years are years of the Times of the Gentiles. So he knew what he was saying to the disciples of the New Testament when he spoke of the Times of the Gentiles. They were being fulfilled in those days. They are being fulfilled in our days.

Delayed Answers

Have you brought your shopping list to God? How long is it? Did you forget to bring God's advice notes with it?

It is important to learn the basics of prayer, so look up your advice notes. Prayer is not all one way – thinking about only what you want God to do, instead of what God wants you to do or what is good for you. Prayer is a two-way fellowship with God, a waiting upon God for what is best. There may be some things on your prayer shopping list which will give you indigestion or make you fat and flabby instead of fighting fit. Daniel did not make this mistake. Daniel 9:2 shows that he based his prayers on God's advice list:

> I, Daniel, perceived in the books, the number of years which according to the Word of the Lord, would be 70 years before the end of the desolation of Jerusalem.

He was told in chapter 10 that a *delayed* answer was for a reason. It did not mean God had not heard him. God heard him the moment he started praying, but sometimes the answer was 'no' and sometimes the answer was 'not yet'. For example, Daniel 10:12 says that God heard him the moment he started to pray, but the answer was delayed 21 days.

Daniel was granted his immediate objective. The exile was to end when 70 years were completed. Then the sanctuary would be cleansed and the temple of Jerusalem rebuilt. That was started by Ezra and Nehemiah.

The second objective was the Messiah's coming to cleanse the spiritual sanctuary by his own death. That would take 7 times 70 which equalled 490 years and that was fulfilled.

The third objective was to do with the Wailing Wall. That would be the 2,300 sanctuary cycle years to 1967 when the sanctuary would begin to be cleansed. These were the three objectives of Daniel's earnest prayers.

When Daniel saw that the 70-year exile was almost finished, he didn't say to himself, 'Well it is bound to happen whether I prepare or not.' What did he do? *He made sure that he and his people were right with God so that they would be in on the blessing!*

God has given to you and me an insight into timescales which are being fulfilled in our days for the same reason. It is so that we can be in on the blessing!

Significance of Key Dates

- **1917:** Balfour Declaration drawn up by Britain established rights to Jews for a home in Palestine, but no control over Jerusalem. Turks leave. Tel Aviv established as capital of Israel. This is the starting point for Jews in Israel and occurred 2,520 years after 603 BC, the start of the *Diaspora*.
- **1947:** Way cleared by UNO for State of Israel to be officially created. Implemented in 1948, but still no control over Jerusalem. Visits to the Wailing Wall only permitted on special occasions. This is 2,520 + 30 years after start of *Diaspora*. (See also reference to the year 1947 regarding the purchase of Dead Sea Scrolls, page 210, *Evidence for Truth, Volume 2: Archaeology*.)
- **1968:** 6-day war gives Israel control over Jerusalem for the first time since the *Diaspora*. Israel declares Jerusalem as its capital. Free access to Wailing Wall and some control of the temple site. First synagogue established (at the Wailing Wall) since Jerusalem destroyed in AD 70. Partial fulfilment of the words of the Lord in Luke 21:24: 'And Jerusalem will be trampled by Gentiles until the times of the Gentiles are fulfilled.' This is 2,300 years from the prophet date of 333 BC (Daniel 8:14).
- **1998:** Jubilee year of the new State of Israel. What is significant? Peace initiative stalls . . . Pakistan and India join world nuclear powers (Revelation 16:12?) . . . Failing world economies . . . Power struggles in Russia . . . Conflict between Turkey, Greece and Cyprus . . . Floods, earthquakes, fires, famines . . . Wars, social and

moral disorder . . . Obsession with huge 'idols' paraded during opening ceremony of World Cup in Paris, viewed by nearly a billion people . . . Israel wins Eurovision Song Contest and right to host the contest in 1999, also to be viewed by millions of people . . .

PROPHETIC YEAR-DAY SYSTEM

- Times and seasons God has fixed (Acts 1:7)
- Prophetic year-day   = 360 years (based on Pre-Flood calendar see Volume 1 Ch 13).
- Prophetic month of years   = 30 years
- Prophetic week of years   = 7 years
- Prophetic half-week of years = 3½ years – length of Christ's ministry.
- Prophetic day-year   = 1 year.
- cf. Rev. 9:5,10; 11:3; 12:6,14; 13:5.
- Twice 1,260 = 2,520 days or years (Dan 12:7).

A Time, 2 'Times' and half a 'Time' (3½ 'Times') is 360 + 720 + 180 = 1,260 year-days (Dan 7:25; 12:7,12). This may sound strange to you, but there is no doubt that **God has worked history on this system:**

(1) 603 BC to AD 1917 is 2,520 years (seven 'Times')
- A 'Time' is 360 years, so 360 × 7 is 2,520
- 603 BC (Jew's dispersion) to 1917 (Jew's home) = 2,520 years; Leviticus 26:18,21,24,28
- Plus 30 years = 1947. State of Israel signed in Nov 1947; Daniel 12:11 adds 30 years to 1,260
- Plus 45 years = 1992. Pro-Jew Clinton elected and Single European Market established 31st Dec 1992; Daniel 12:12 adds 45 years to 1,290

(2) 70 weeks of years (70 × 7) = 490 years to the cross. Daniel 9:25
- From 457 BC at Cyrus' command to rebuild (Ezra 1:2) is 490 solar years
- From 444 BC, Artaxerxes' command (Nehemiah 2:1,5) is 490 lunar years

3) 42 months of years is 42 × 30 = 1,260 years
- Popes' temporal power lasted from 610 to 1870 = 1,260 years (Emperor Phocas made pope an emperor in 610. Cancelled in 1870)
- Persecution of those with a testimony and defender of Bible is also 42 months. Revelation 11:2 and 12:14

(4) AD 622 is Moslem start date. 1,335 lunar years after Mohammed equals AD 1917 (which is 2,520 years after 603 BC)

LIGHT FOR
THE LAST DAYS

BY DR. AND MRS.

H. GRATTAN GUINNESS

In 1917 Balfour Declaration opened Palestine to Jews. 1917 was
also Moslem year 1335, see Dan 12:12 (Dr Gratton Guinness calculated correctly 31 years before fulfilment.)

YEAR 1917

the year B.C. 604 witnessed the rise of the typical
Babylon, the supremacy over the typical Israel, what
event is the corresponding year in this time of the end
likely to witness?

        This year has therefore some special
claims to be considered as a very principal starting-point
of the "times of the Gentiles." Measured from it the
period runs out in A.D. 1917, and it is a very notable
fact that a second most remarkable period does the
same. The 1335 years of Daniel xii. 12, the *ne plus
ultra* of prophetic chronology, which is evidently
eastern in character, and consequently lunar in scale,
measured back from this year 1917, lead up to the great
Hegira era of Mohammedanism, the starting-point of
the Mohammedan calendar, the birthday of the Power
which has for more than twelve centuries desolated
Palestine and trodden down Jerusalem.

B.C. 604	2520 solar years	A.D. 1917
	A.D. 622 1335 lunar	A.D. 1917

    The year 1917 is consequently doubly indicated as a
final crisis date, in which the "Seven Times" run out,
as measured from two opening events, both of which
are clearly most critical in connexion with Israel, and
whose dates are both absolutely certain and unquestion-
able.   There can be no question that those
who live to see this year 1917 will have reached one of
the most important, perhaps *the* most momentous, of
these terminal years of crisis.

Figure 10.3. Extract from *Light for the Last Days* by Dr H. Grattan Guinness, published in 1886 by Marshall, Morgan & Scott, where the author predicts the date of the
restoration of the Holy Land of Israel (1917). Note: reference to 1335 years = lunar
years. (See p 263.)

COMPARISON OF PROPHESIED HISTORY OF DAN. 7 WITH DAN. 8 – 10
(down to 20th Century)

ANIMAL SYMBOLS OF *Ch. 7*	*ANIMAL SYMBOLS OF* *Ch. 8 – 10*
Deflated Lion Babylon Nebuchadnezzar	
Lop-sided Bear Persia ← Ch.8 → 3 ribs: Lydia, Babylon, ↓ Egypt	**Ram, two unequal horns.** Medes and Persians defeated by:
Leopard with 4 wings Alexander and his 4 Generals	**He Goat from West** Greece Single great horn = Alexander 333 BC Demolishes Persia Horn broken Alexander died 323 BC 4 horns in his place, 4 Generals
	Little Horn Antiochus Epiphanes occupied sanctuary 2,300 days 167 BC causes sacrifices to cease
Horror Beast Iron = Rome 31 BC Wide conquests **Europe breaks** up into about 10 kingdoms AD 470	**AD 70 Romans cause sacrifices to cease (Dan. 9:26,27)**
Little Horn of Europe uproots 3 kingdoms Lombards, Visigoths, Suabi. Temporal power, AD 610 – 1870 = 1260 yrs Dan. 7:25 for 3½ times (1260) Allows Bible to be read again, this moderates errors.	**Little Horn of the Near East** Mohammed AD 622 Mosque of Oma AD 638 Moslem year 1335 = AD 1917 Dan. 12:12 1967 Cleansing of the Sanctuary begins
Son of Man descends with Clouds	

S U M M A R Y

CONFIDENTIAL HEBREW LANGUAGE ABOUT JEWS' FUTURE

- Temple sanctuary cleansing, chapters 8 to 12 of Daniel.
- God's Computer Angel named *Palmoni* 'wonderful calculator'.
- Sanctuary was in the former Greek Empire (8:21,22).
- Palmoni says 2,300 years before cleansing begins.
- 333 BC to 1967 = 2,300 years.
- Wailing Wall made a synagogue.
- Sanctuary cycle is an amazing cycle (M. de Cheseaux's astronomical discovery).

Three abominations:
1. Antiochus Epiphanes 167 BC sacrilege in temple (8:23).
2. Fall of Jerusalem. Roman and Zealot sacrilege of temple. Jesus and Daniel spoke of another after No. 1 (Matt 24:15).
3. Mosque 'Standing where it ought not' AD 638 (11:31). But some refer it to the tribulation.

Messiah dated 70 weeks of days, i.e. 490 yrs (Dan 9:25,26)

Fulfilled:
- 457 BC Cyrus commands to build temple (9:25 and Ezra 1:2) + 490 **solar** yrs = AD 33 the cross.
- 444 BC Artaxerxes commands building of the walls + 490 **lunar** years = AD 33.
- Christ was crucified in middle of last week of years, i.e. after 3½ year ministry; that reduces AD 33 to AD 30.

7 Signs of Christ's second coming in ch 12
1. When resurrection of believers is near (12:2).
2. Terrible time of trouble (12:1)
3. Increased travel, invention and science for many (12:4).
4. It will be end of 7 'Times' (3½ × 2) (Ch. 12:7) in 20th century.
5. Great increase in wickedness (12:10) but bright witnessing.
6. From Moslem date to blessing for Israel 1335 = 1917. Home for Jews (12:11,12).
7. The wise will understand these figures in the last days (12:9,10).

11 WHAT GOD FORETOLD TO ZECHARIAH
AN ASTONISHING STATEMENT OF THE ADVENT AND THE LAST DAYS

I want to draw out your imagination as we look at the events which led up to the next to last book of the Old Testament. It is the book of the prophet Zechariah – a dramatic book, written 517 BC. *It actually pictures Jehovah being crucified on the cross.* The Hebrew says, 'It is me, Jehovah, whom they pierced' and the whole Israelite nation will be converted when they see it is 'me whom they crucified when I return to the Mount of Olives at the end of the age' (Zechariah 12:10; 14:3,4).

But what was the setting to this book written 2,500 years before the event? The prophecy also describes Jesus riding into Jerusalem on a donkey and being betrayed for 30 pieces of silver, over 500 years before he fulfilled it. Why should this prophecy speak of this?

The prophet, with his companion, Haggai, encouraged the people to rebuild the very temple where this would all happen, five centuries later. Twenty years had passed since people had returned to Jerusalem after the exile and things had ground to a halt – restoration had stopped.

Zechariah was one of the prophets who lived after the exile – it had lasted 70 years. Then a cavalcade had set out from Babylon, 800 miles to the east, to go back to Jerusalem and Zechariah is reminding them that was already 20 years ago. What a size that expedition was! Fifty thousand people accompanied by over 8,000 animals for transport – horses, mules, donkeys, even camels. There were nearly 750 horses, 245 mules, 435 camels and 6,720 donkeys – that is, one animal for every six people. Those people were families, mums, dads and children, yes, and servants – 7,500 servants. They had prospered, you see. When in Babylon, God had told them to settle down there and make money. It was no use wailing and crying over their fate. No use hanging up their harps on the willow trees and sitting down and doing nothing. They had been 70 years in Babylon for their sins in Jerusalem. Now there were riches to be made and God gave the Jews that ability to make good. So now, you see, they were returning 70 years later plus servants, plus silver, satins and salaries!

BACK TO THE PROMISED LAND

These children of Abraham were doing exactly what Abraham did 1,500 years before. They left a comfortable home for a land where the

Saviour would be born – the land of Palestine. All along around that Fertile Crescent, the children would be tripping and singing, quarrelling and playing on that long, long journey – the new children of Abraham to re-establish the Promised Land where the promised Saviour of the world would be born 537 years later.

This migration had its entertainment too. There were 200 singers – men and women musicians. The Jews have always been famous for music. Their music sprang from their worship. They enjoyed their worship! They clapped their hands to the time of their joyful songs of praise like the charismatics. They rapped their tambourines like the Salvation Army. Their teenagers would dance in circles to the rhythm of the psalms and the choirs and orchestra, like the cathedrals who set the tunes with its priests and cantors.

This was all in the spring of 537 BC. The sight of the rubble heap of demolished Jerusalem and the temple did not dismay them. They expected it. They set to, to rebuild their beloved temple with great enthusiasm. This was the task that Ezra, the scribe, called them to, the task the Emperor Cyrus, their liberator, had sent them to, but alas, seven years later he died suddenly and the work slackened.

Then they needed houses to live in and gradually they gave more attention to these than to the temple. Haggai who was Zechariah's fellow prophet had to rebuke them for letting their houses have priority over the Lord's house, the temple. 'Why are you embellishing your own houses with luxurious improvements and not completing the temple?' Let me quote Haggai 1:3–6:

> Then the Word of the Lord came through the prophet Haggai: 'Is it a time for you yourselves to be living in your panelled houses while this house remains a ruin? Now this is what the Lord Almighty says; "Give careful thought to your ways. You have planted much but never have enough. You drink but never have your fill. You put on clothes but are not warm. You earn wages only to put them in a purse with holes in it." '

Then came the opposition. Foreign peoples around who had been imported began to protest. They had rival religions, religions which God said were satanic imitations.

Now that the emperor had died, the authority of the temple builders had vanished and the opposition actually stopped the work. You can be sure that, if God has sent you to do a task, Satan has his plans to stop you. This is what people sometimes forget. So when planning a venture for God, always bind the opposition of Satan.

The Challenge

Thus the opening verses of Zechariah challenge the 20-year stalemate. It reminds the re-established inhabitants that they are in danger of repeating the errors and sins of their fathers. It reminds them that Jerusalem was destroyed and its inhabitants scattered because they ignored God's words. Here is the preface:

> The Lord was very angry with your forefathers. Therefore tell the people, this is what the Lord Almighty says, 'Return to me and I will return to you', says the Lord Almighty. 'Do not be like your forefathers, to whom the earlier prophets proclaimed . . . "Turn from your evil ways and your evil practices." But they would not listen or pay attention to me,' declares the Lord. 'Where are your forefathers now? And the prophets, do they live for ever? But did not my words and my decrees, which I commanded my servants the prophets, overtake your forefathers? Then they repented and said, "The Lord Almighty has done to us what our ways and practices deserve, just as he determined to do".'

That great emigration of 50,000 was impressive, but where were all the rest of their nation? That was only a small fraction of Israel. Where were the other millions?

Zechariah, with other prophets living after the exile, pointed out that God was going to bring all the rest of Israel back at the end of the age. They were to remain among the nations of the world until then. God had also shown this to the prophets before the exile, that only a small percentage would return to re-establish Jewry. Paul the apostle called them 'The Remnant' in Romans 11. God tells Zechariah that even these, resettled in Jerusalem, will be scattered again after they have killed the Good Shepherd. He is divine, next to Jehovah. This is in chapter 13:7,8:

> Awake O sword, against my shepherd, against the man who is close to me, declares the Lord Almighty. Strike the shepherd and the sheep will be scattered and I will turn my hand against the little ones. In the whole land, declares the Lord . . .

As a result of the slaying of the divine Good Shepherd, the people would be scattered again to join the rest of Israel still left in many foreign countries. I emphasise this as many commentators ignore it. Here are the words of the Lord in Zechariah 13:8: 'Two-thirds will be struck down and perish, yet one-third will be left in it.'

Important Spin-off

Even before the exile, God had told the prophets living then that only a remnant would return. The rest would remain among the nations. Had God no future purpose for them? He had indeed – a very important one. It was the establishment of the synagogues throughout the world. They would be local centres for reading the Old Testament

Scriptures. Now that the Jews had no temple, there had to be a substitute. By Paul's time, these synagogues had prepared both Jew and Gentile for the preaching of the gospel. Paul always visited the synagogues first. Those most willing to hear were those Gentiles who had become Jewish converts waiting for the Messiah. God had told Isaiah that this would happen. I quote: 'Arise, shine, for your light has come . . . the Gentiles will come to your light.'

The lesson for you is this: God never abandons anybody. Let that assure you if you are seeking the way back, perhaps after backsliding. You too may have failed to respond to restoration like the larger numbers of Jews who failed to return to Jerusalem. You too may have got too comfortable, too contented with worldly gain, yet now you regret that your priorities were wrong. 'They are those,' said Jesus, 'who were choked with the riches and cares of this life,' yet if you tell God you are sorry, he will forgive, cleanse and restore and even use your wayward experience for others.

So never think God has abandoned you. He seeks you in the Good Shepherd and welcomes you back to full restoration and usefulness.

ZECHARIAH'S WIDENING HORIZONS

'I have been dreaming all night!' Have you heard that exclamation? Perhaps you went to bed full of worries and frustration and you seemed to have a whole series of dreams and nightmares mixed with blissful happy fantasies.

Zechariah went to bed full of worries. He tells you about them in the last book but one in the Old Testament. He had worries about his political friends, worries about his religious friends, worries about his enemies, worries about the ruling foreign power. Their work for God was to rebuild the temple at Jerusalem after the exile, six centuries BC. It had been put off and blocked time and time again. They seemed to make no headway. Zechariah went to bed that night and had as many as eight visions in one night. Those visions changed the whole picture. God had put an entirely different light on things and God can do the same for you, especially if you are worried about building the temple of God.

What do I mean? I mean the spiritual temple – building up a witnessing body of Christian people. God showed Zechariah that it was this spiritual temple of believers that was the main thrust of his plan. But the material temple at Jerusalem was important too.

The ruling powers had followed one reign after another, but still the work on Jerusalem's temple was blocked. Then, when God's servants started to build on the site, the enemies around reported it to the emperor 800 miles to the east. They said, 'If you don't stop this, the Jews will become rebellious again. Once, these Israelites had powerful kings in

David and Solomon. Do you want that threat again?' This report can be found in the book of Ezra chapters 4 and 5. So every time God's servants made another attempt to build, the enemies reported it.

They had reported it to Emperor Cyrus, king of Persia 16 years before. They reported it to Ahasuerus, his successor. They reported it to Artaxerxes and the command came back, 'Stop the work at once!'

Then in 520 BC, in the second year of Emperor Darius, God gave the all-clear!

Perhaps you have had hindrances like that all down the line. In Zechariah's time, the people of God thought they had the go-ahead long before in Cyrus' day. He had given permission so they were not doing anything illegal. But they delayed. Perhaps you thought you had the go-ahead and now you cannot understand why the opportunities keep vanishing.

God's political leader, Zerubbabel, was in despair and the religious priest felt frustrated. Would they never get the work of God established? Would God's Kingdom ever be built to bring salvation, peace and happiness to this world?

Zechariah for Encouragement

It was at this point that the prophet Zechariah had his dreams all night. Well, they were more than dreams. They were visions given by God. They revealed that the building would be successful. Even more important, God was going to build a spiritual temple. They revealed that the Messiah was coming to save. They revealed that the Church, symbolised by Joshua the high priest, needed cleansing. Yes, Joshua was wearing filthy clothes. Cleansing must begin with the Church before God can cleanse the nation. Joel 2:9 says that. 1 Peter 4:17 says that. The high priest symbolised the Church. 'Take those filthy clothes off him!' ordered God. 'If you, the Church, will walk in my ways and if you will perform my service and are faithful . . . then I will remove the iniquity of the land'. And it will not be done by man's might! It is going to be done by spiritual power: 'Not by might nor by power but by my Spirit,' saith the Lord.

Later, in the New Testament, Peter said, 'Judgement begins with the church and if judgement starts with us', says 1 Peter 4:17 'what chance will the ungodly have?'

Those ungodly who scoffed at the disgraceful, soiled, priestly garments, those who welcomed every scandal in order to excuse their own iniquity and who poured out filth day after day in press and pornography – what chance of escape from the anger of God would they have if God starts judging his Church first?

So Zechariah went to bed, his head full of worries and his night was filled with those eight visions! God had a bigger plan, a greater plan, a wider horizon. It scooped in even ungodly opposition. It turned even the wrath of man to the praise of God.

Zechariah's vision promised success in his day, but also reached far beyond to the future redemption of man, then to the return of Christ; to the Kingdom of God on earth when all nations will come to worship the Lord of Hosts, when even the household pots would have Bible texts. The texts would encourage love of the Lord and his good ways. Instead of placards inciting to sin, all advertisements will encourage the enjoyment of purity, self-control and goodness.

In this chapter in Zechariah, we will see the stages revealed by God by which it will be fulfilled even down to our times. Some very, very remarkable prophecies were made which have been fulfilled by Christ and are being fulfilled in these last days.

Zechariah is told, 'Go and tell this to the politician for encouragement! Go tell the priest to strengthen his faith and encourage his cleansing.'

So Zechariah's night of visions is to give courage, resolve and faith to the governor Zerubbabel and the priest Joshua. Now, one of the biggest needs of any personality is encouragement. Encouragement in God's things. The Lord knows this, so he encourages you. Then, when he has encouraged you, he shows you your need of cleansing. He says, 'Your hopes will be built in spite of troublous times, so cleanse your clothes!'

The Eight Visions

- In the *first* vision, Zechariah sees God's Police Patrol. It reports, 'All quiet! Opposition has fizzled out! So build!' They did and finished in four years.
- The *second* vision sees the hunter's trophy horns. The animal heads were trophies of his kills, but they were cut off. This showed that those who hunted down the Jews would be punished. That was fulfilled 70 years later.
- The *third* vision shows the architect planning the foundations.
- The *fourth* vision shows that the real foundation stone represented Jesus Christ, our one and only foundation for salvation that was fulfilled when Jesus died for you on the cross.
- The *fifth* vision shows the witness of the Holy Spirit through the seven church ages which follow after the cross and Pentecost.
- The *sixth* shows a list of sins which curse the earth and oppose the gospel. It is Satan's fight-back.
- The *seventh* shows how the Church, under the simile of the loaf, allowed the woman of Babylon to hide the yeast of false doctrine.
- The *eighth* and last vision is of four chariots bringing the wind of the Spirit of God to north, south, east and west to build the

temple and crown the Priest/King Messiah, for he is King of kings
and Lord of lords.

As we enlarge upon these visions one by one, we shall see the remarkable programme set out for God's victory of truth and happiness in
Zechariah's future. After these eight visions, Zechariah's prophecy
returns to foretell and describe Palm Sunday when King Jesus rode
humbly into Jerusalem on an ass 500 years later; of the Pentecostal rain
of blessing which followed. *Then it turns to our modern times* and
foretells the return of the twelve tribes of Israel to Palestine; of
Lebanon's present anguish and confusion; of Jerusalem being the
insoluble problem today that it is for our modern nations; of the
descent from heaven which Christ will make to Mount Olivet at his
second coming; of the conversion of all Israel when they see his
wounds of crucifixion; and finally of Christ's reign of peace on earth
during the millennium.

So in this summary of Zechariah, what a feast of encouragement
and vision you have for those things which are surely to come to pass.
Why does God give this forward look into the future? It was to encourage Zechariah and us that God has everything in control. God moves
in the storm of unrest and does something which cannot be done in
peace. God moves in the calm of peace and does things which cannot
be done in turmoil.

Heaven's Police Patrol

Have you seen the colourful Canadian mounted police, the Mounties,
riding three or four abreast to survey an area and report back?

Zechariah's first vision was of heaven's police patrol. It was a
mounted police patrol riding through a peaceful green valley of myrtle
trees. The leader rode on a red horse. His three companions rode
abreast behind him. One was on a red horse, the next was on a mottled-
brown horse and beside him was a Mountie on a white horse.

Zechariah asked God what you are probably asking, 'What is all
this about, Lord?' An angel replied, 'I will show you!' God says that
to you when you ask for wisdom. The angel nodded to a man standing
in the wood of myrtle trees and the man answered, 'This is God's
police patrol scrutinising the whole earth.'

Have you noticed that the Bible tells us that God has his intelli-
gence agents throughout the world? It is recorded in various terms,
sometimes like this: 'These are the eyes of the Lord going through the
world' or 'There were creatures full of eyes inside and outside'. That
sounds a bit like closed circuit television observing all the shoppers in
a store, watching for shoplifters.

Do you ever feel that God is just watching you to catch you out?

Some people always feel that way, but, in Zechariah's vision, the Lord was out to give comfort and encouragement. Chapter 1:13 says, 'The Lord gave gracious and comforting words to the angel who talked with me.' He said, 'Cry out! I am very concerned for my people. I am jealous for Jerusalem and Zion.'

I hope you are encouraged to know that the Lord is concerned and jealous on your behalf. But what does jealous mean? The old-fashioned meaning of that word 'jealous' was the feeling of a mother or father for their child. Every instinct is aroused in them to shield or rescue their little boy or girl. The Lord is as sensitive as that about you. In chapter 2 verse 8 he says, 'He who touches you, touches the sensitive pupil of my eye'.

Zechariah was dispirited because his political and religious friends were discouraged over their building project. Their task was to rebuild God's temple and his city. They had been hindered so many times, but now Zechariah, encouraged by the Lord, went to encourage his influential friends.

Not a One-man Job

Perhaps you are discouraged about building the Lord's spiritual temple – the assembly of Christ's saved people. Is it because you are trying to do it all yourself instead of sharing it out with the body of Christ?

Recently, a pastor was discouraged. He had come to the church full of hope for a great work of upbuilding. The months had passed and little seemed to happen, so the pastor was tempted to blame the congregation. His sermons reflected this. Now blame discourages and never does any good.

Some gracious friends pointed out that different methods were shown in the Scriptures. The Scriptures enjoined a shared ministry, not a one-man ministry. Many persons and voices taking part in worship is refreshing whereas one voice doing everything becomes monotonous, however good that voice may be.

Fortunately, that pastor was humble and gracious and shared out the service with the Christians as Paul instructed in 1 Corinthians 12:14. He apologised too and won back the sympathy of his people.

A second thing he learnt was that, to convert people, he had to go where the people were. He had preached to convert people in church but the unconverted were not in church. In some communities they are, of course, but not there. Who was most in touch with those who were not converted? Well, it was his congregation – in their work or with their neighbours. They were the ones who must be strengthened and instructed on how to use their contacts. Neighbours invited in for tea and a chat – chat about the gospel – how the Lord has helped them or listening to attractive cassettes, perhaps of fascinating testimonies.

Another mistake this pastor had been making was that he was doing all the visiting on his own and the congregation expected it, too. This was unscriptural. The Lord sent out his disciples in twos. It is much easier to talk about Jesus if you have another with you.

A further mistake was that the pastor was visiting only his congregation, to keep in their good books, so to speak. The congregation needed to see that they should be helping him. That he, with other Christians accompanying him, must visit 'fringers'. What do I mean? Fringers are contacts who are not converted, relatives of Christians, parents of Sunday School children or mothers and toddlers clubs.

Many of his congregation, too, had cut off their contacts with the unconverted. They had withdrawn into a comfortable huddle and refused even to understand the outlook of the non-churchgoer. It was as if they were saying, 'The unconverted must come our way to Christ.' They must sit in our hard pews, in a service they don't understand and even feel embarrassed by. Non-churchgoers feel at ease in a raucous pub with Bill and Harry, sitting in a circle, but not with the strange reserve of a hard straight-backed pew all facing frontwards. In the club they were Bert and Charlie, but, if introduced at all in church, it was to Mr Roberts and Mr Molyneux and Mrs Green. Goodness, don't these Christians have Christian names? Fortunately much of this has changed now and many churches have refreshments for relaxed chatting after the service.

Where would these non-Christians feel more at home? Well, in the relaxing atmosphere of a house, in a comfortable chair, but not talking about trivialities. Gossip the gospel in a relaxed fashion.

To return to Zechariah's vision about rebuilding the temple, God's mounted patrol returned and reported, 'It's all quiet! All is at rest!' Terrorism has terminated! The hurricanes of hate have blown themselves out! Now the time for God's next stage has come. Arise and build! Build the temple of believers! God does some things in settled state that cannot be achieved in turmoil. He also does other things in persecution which cannot be done in times of peace.

When bad times come, it makes you look at yourself. Do you need to readjust your set ideas? Do you need to reassess your priorities? God sometimes has to do a lot of shaking if a person is set on his own ways. God has brought about a lot of changes in Christian methods today to meet the challenge of scepticism. God's revelation of truth in the Bible is always the same, but the ways of presenting it adjust to the situation.

Jesus said, 'Heaven and earth will pass away, but my words will never pass away.' 'Thy Word is established for ever,' said the psalmist. It is into changing situations that the unchanging Word has to penetrate. Zechariah had seen a time of turmoil in which a very essential work of preparation was shown. Now all was quiet for the next stage

– the building of the temple.

The Lord says to Zechariah, 'Tell them to go ahead and build.' Yes, when people are relaxed then you can build.

Notice how God uses homely illustrations like the next vision. It was a vision of the hunter's trophies. The ornaments of a friend's house can lead to conversation. If you see the heads of animals displayed on the wall, you can note the fierce sharp horns. Zechariah was shown these horns. They must have looked bloodstained to him. He thought of people who had been gored by a bull. 'These represent those who have been cruel to my people,' said the Lord. 'I am sending a carpenter with a saw to saw off those cruel horns.'

In conversation, usually someone says, 'Why does God allow all this cruelty and suffering?' Zechariah is told that the carpenter and the saw represented judgement to come. Never avoid the subject of judgement. Without the Bible teaching of judgement, this is an unjust world. Without judgement for everybody and an afterlife, God would not be a just God. 'Each one of us will give an account of himself to God', the Bible says.

The Branch

In the scripture before us, nations and people will also be judged along with those who destroyed Jerusalem and the temple. You can be a Zechariah to someone today. Opposition will be silenced so, Zechariah, encourage your friends to rebuild! The visions apply this also to the spiritual temple, because in the third, fourth and fifth vision, the Messiah is introduced. Don't forget that this prophecy was fulfilled 500 years later. In this vision in Zechariah 3, the Messiah Jesus would come and be the **chief cornerstone** for the spiritual Church. He is also described as 'the Branch'. The Lord Jesus is described as the Branch by God to many of the prophets. He is the branch from the fallen tree of the royal house of David. He is called the Branch by Isaiah 750 years BC. He is called the Branch by Jeremiah 600 BC. He is called the Branch by Ezekiel in the exile and now is called that by God through Zechariah after the exile in 520 BC.

Zechariah 3:9 says that this branch of David's line will remove guilt in a single day. That was the day of Christ's crucifixion. On that one day Jesus removed the sin of the world. God placed on him the sin of the world, so now everyone who repents and believes can have their sins removed and cleansed for ever.

That is why the stone is also mentioned. The atoning death of the Lord Jesus is the foundation stone for all salvation. By it, the free grace of forgiveness is given. No wonder then that, when this stone is brought forth and revealed, there are joyous shouts of 'Grace! Grace!' unto it.

Amazing Grace! How sweet the sound
That saved a wretch like me.
I once was lost but now am found,
Was blind but now I see.

John Newton

THE FOURTH VISION – THE FOUNDATION STONE

'Where there is no vision, the people perish', says the Bible. We all need that vision renewed from time to time. Do you need your vision renewed? A vision gives encouragement to achieve something noble and not to give up.

The fourth vision of Zechariah gave a surge of hope to two people who felt powerless and dispirited. This vision gave not only a vision of possibility, it was a vision of certainty because God was going to fulfil it in Jesus Christ and that is where we can come in on the blessing.

Jesus Christ was going to be the foundation stone for eternal salvation and the astonishing thing God announced to this man was that Jesus Christ would be a descendant of his. Yes, from this man feeling weak and discouraged, 'From you will come the foundation stone', said God. This was more than the foundation stone of the temple which was being built.

Who was this man? His name was Zerubbabel. The name reveals a wonderful succession of events. His name appeared 500 years later in Matthew's lineage recorded in the New Testament. It was the lineage which led to Christ. It is recorded also in Luke's lineage which led to Christ.

Why was Zerubbabel feeling weak and discouraged? It was not only because his project had failed so far (20 years' attempt to build the temple had achieved little). It was because he had every reason to feel rejected. Why? Because he was only a governor of Jerusalem, yet he was a royal descendant of the mighty king David. He was a political puppet to the emperor of Persia, disposable at any given notice, yet had not God promised an eternal throne to David's descendant?

God showed that this was still to come about. Zerubbabel was worried about the foundation stone and the capstone of the temple that he was building. God promised him success in this and promised that its meaning would be fulfilled in Zerubbabel's anointed descendant. A foundation stone meant the basis and beginning and the capstone meant the completion. Jesus Christ would be both the beginning and completion of our salvation. 'Therefore,' said God, 'shout joyfully to it. Grace! Grace! Marvellous grace' (Zechariah 4:7).

Chief Stone Prophecies

The foundation stone and capstone, Jesus Christ, has featured in Bible prophecy right through from the predictions of Old Testament prophets to the quoting of its fulfilment in the New Testament. The first was by King David 1,000 years before fulfilment. Jesus said that this was by the inspiration of the Holy Spirit. Here is the remarkable prophecy in Psalm 118 verses 14 and 22: 'The Lord is my strength and song and he has become my salvation . . . The stone which the builders rejected has become the chief cornerstone. This is the Lord's doing and it is marvellous in our eyes.'

The Lord Jesus said this would be fulfilled in spite of the unbelief and opposition of man. The next time it was prophesied was by Isaiah about 750 years before it was fulfilled. God said to him in 28:16:

> This is what the Sovereign Lord says: 'See I lay a stone in Zion, a tested stone, a precious cornerstone for a sure foundation; the one who trusts will never be dismayed.'

Paul bangs this home to struggling Christians in Rome. In his letter to them, chapter 9 verse 33, he says that, amidst the scoffing and cynicism of the proud Romans, they did not need to be ashamed. 'He who believes on him shall not be ashamed.' 'I lay in Zion a stumbling stone and rock of offence.' If people do not build upon it by faith as a foundation stone, it becomes a stumbling stone.

The next declaration about the stone of salvation is the passage before us in Zechariah. Peter quotes the fulfilment of it on the day of Pentecost. In Acts 4:8, 'Peter filled with the Holy Spirit said, "Rulers and Elders of Israel, this stone which was rejected by your builders has become the chief cornerstone and there is no salvation in any other name." ' He also quotes it in his first letter, 1 Peter 2:7, 'To you who believe, Jesus is precious, but to those who are disobedient, the stone which the builders rejected has become the chief cornerstone'. Verse 6, 'In scripture it is contained, "Behold I lay in Zion a chief cornerstone, elect, precious, and he who believes on him will not be ashamed." '

Now Joshua, the high priest in Zerubbabel's time, is also discouraged. He too, has his part in the predicted rock or stone of salvation. He represents the Eternal Priesthood of Jesus. Jesus is eternal Priest because his sacrifice prevailed for eternity. Everyone who has trusted in Christ's sacrifice is saved for eternity.

But this Joshua was only an earthly priest and he was very conscious of his unworthiness to be ministering in the holy things of God. Moreover, that inveterate accuser, Satan, was accusing him of his sinfulness.

What should we do if Satan keeps accusing us of sinfulness? Well, of course, acknowledge it with deep sorrow, but turn from sin and to God. Don't deal with it yourself, refer it to God. What does God do in this case? He deals with Satan's accusations. He says, 'Take off those filthy garments from Joshua the high priest and clothe him in my garments of righteousness.' What a picture of the completeness of Christ's salvation for sinners! If we trust his sacrifice, we are not only cleansed, but clothed. Joshua was both cleansed and clothed. How does that operate for us? On the cross, the precious Lord Jesus transferred our sin to himself and transferred his righteousness to us. It was a double transaction and the Lord Jesus Christ was the loser. All the blame became his and all the blessing became ours. So that we not only become saved by grace, but also sanctified by grace. No wonder God told Zechariah to give joyous shouts of 'Grace! Grace unto it'.

Paul gives a rather complicated word to this glorious truth – 'justification'. To simplify the word, make it into smaller words. 'I am justified' means 'Just-as-if-I'd never sinned!'

The high priest, Joshua, not only had his filthy garments taken away, he was reclothed with a clean white garment supplied by God. As Isaiah 61:10 said, 'I will greatly rejoice in the Lord . . . for he has clothed me with the robe of righteousness'. This is our inheritance too. This if often called the wedding garment. Such a garment of beauty was exchanged for filthy rags.

THE LAMPSTAND'S WITNESS (ZECHARIAH 5)

I wonder whether you have seen or read about the beautiful cave paintings in southern France. They are reckoned to be the work of Stone Age men. The animals are drawn with great skill and coloured by blowing powder on to the drawing.

Some are puzzled about how these Stone Age men could see in the dark of the cave. This was solved when stone dishes were found in which oil and a wick had been used. This was surprising. Man had been lighting his way in the dark even from early times.

Oil and wick lamps continued to be very simple down the ages. Even in the time of Moses, they were no more than a bowl on the side of which a wick was draped. It dipped into oil at one end and was lit at the other end. The seven-branched lampstand of Moses' tabernacle was very elaborate in its design, but the lamps standing on the top of each branch were still only simple bowls and lamps which remained simple for another 1,000 years.

We actually have a model in stone of that seven-branched lampstand existent today. It is shown in low relief on the Arch of Titus in Rome and is exactly as described in the writings of Moses 3,500 years ago. This stone carving shows the Roman soldiers carrying out the lampstand at the fall of Jerusalem in AD 70. This again shows the accuracy of Moses' writings, but there is something more important. This lampstand has significance right down to our time.

There are features of Scripture which have a recurring theme throughout the Bible. These features develop with fuller and richer meaning each time they occur. The theme of this lampstand is certainly one of them. We continue in Zechariah's prophecy: the angel woke Zechariah from his sleep to give him his fifth vision. 'What do you see?' he asked. Zechariah said he saw the seven-branched golden lampstand. The angel then showed the next stage in God's plan which it symbolised.

God gave details of its design to Moses for the tabernacle worship in Exodus 25:31. At the time, it appeared to mean nothing more than furniture to give light to the interior of the tabernacle for worship. But as the prophets come and go down the centuries and the New Testament is written, we see deeper truths in its design.

It was very beautifully designed in solid gold. The seven branches were embellished with flowers and almond blossom. At the top of each branch was an oil lamp and each lamp was level horizontally with the others. As Scripture tells you more and more about its symbolic significance, it becomes clear that the golden lampstand typifies the Holy Spirit. That is why in Zechariah 4, we see the vision of the lampstand and then the Lord says that his purpose will be accomplished 'not by might nor by power but by my Spirit says the Lord'. This work of the Holy Spirit is depicted right from the time of Moses down to the last book in the New Testament.

The Holy Trinity in the Tabernacle

Why does the golden lampstand symbolise the Holy Spirit? In the tabernacle, the Holy Trinity is clearly symbolised by the first articles of holy furniture given to Moses to make. God the Father comes first and is symbolised by the ark of the covenant. Jesus Christ is next, typified by the table of shewbread: Jesus Christ is the Bread of Life, so this symbolised the second person of the Holy Trinity. The third item of sacred furniture is this lampstand which symbolised the Holy Spirit. Thus we get Father, Son and Holy Spirit.

Their place in the tabernacle also bore out this meaning. The ark of God the Father was placed beyond the veil – that is, heaven, as Paul tells you. The table of shewbread, Jesus, and the lampstand, the Holy Spirit, are on our side of the veil. In other words, they come into the world. The Lord Jesus came first by the virgin conception and then the Holy Spirit at Pentecost. The Holy Spirit sheds light into a dark world.

Another aspect which symbolises the Holy Spirit is the oil in those lamps. Throughout Scripture, oil signifies the Holy Spirit. The priests were anointed with oil. In the New Testament, the priests are symbolic of all believers – those who have been saved. Why? Because they have been born again by the Holy Spirit and they continue to be blessed and anointed by the Holy Spirit.

Now the Holy Spirit witnesses to the world through those who have been born again. Another point is this. Witnesses always had to be in twos. That is why in this chapter 4 of Zechariah, there are two witnesses standing by the oil lamps of the lampstand. These two witnesses are again depicted in Revelation 11:13. The Lord said:

I will grant to my two witnesses power to prophesy . . . These are the two olive trees and the two lampstands standing before the God of the earth.

This is exactly the description given in Zechariah 4:14:

Do you not know what these are? and I [Zechariah] said 'No Lord'. Then he said to me, 'These are the two anointed who stand before the Lord of all the earth.'

In the illustrations Jesus Christ gave, he often referred to the witness of the saved, meaning to keep our lamp trimmed and shining for Jesus. In Luke 12:35 he said, 'Let your waist be belted for action and your lamps burning and be like men who are waiting for their master.'

And in Matthew 4:21 he asks, 'When you bring a lamp into the house, do you put it under a bucket or under your bed? No! You put it on a lampstand so that all may see.'

No believer should hide his light of testimony. How can you keep your light shining for Jesus? I have just quoted Jesus as saying, 'Keep your lamp trimmed'. Here we turn again to how they trimmed the lamps because this can be a guide to how you can keep your witness bright. We find the instructions in Exodus 30:7. God said the lamp must be trimmed each morning and each evening. This must be done when incense is burnt upon the incense altar before the veil. The incense typified prayer. That is what the New Testament says. So you see, the picture is this: you should have regular prayer times, first in the morning and then at the end of the day in the evening. It is then that your lamp of witness gets trimmed and you are refilled by the Holy Spirit and corrected or directed by instructions from God's Word, the Bible.

This is the secret of shining for Jesus. You shine by the Holy Spirit, not in your own strength.

Do you find it difficult to witness? Perhaps you work among many non-Christians. They are always looking out for faults. That is because the fallen human nature is in revolt against God, so hear these words of encouragement from Jesus in Matthew 10:16–20 (NIV):

I am sending you out like sheep among wolves. Therefore be as shrewd as snakes and as innocent as doves. Be on your guard against men; they will hand you over to the local councils and flog you in their synagogues. On my account you will be brought before governors and kings as witnesses to them and to the Gentiles. But when they arrest you, do not worry about what to say or how to say it. At that time you will be given what to say, for it will not be you speaking but the Spirit of your Father speaking through you.

The book of Revelation opens with a vision of the Lord Jesus walking amidst the seven lamps and he says the seven lampstands are the seven churches, then he says, 'Hear what the Holy Spirit says to the seven churches'. It is widely held that these seven churches represent seven church periods from New Testament times until the second coming of Christ. Until then, the Lord places the responsibility of bringing light to the world by the lamp of witness – lamps filled with the oil of the Holy Spirit and trimmed daily.

This Is Your Life

Once on the television programme *This Is Your Life* was a remarkable missionary to China. She was known as 'the Little Woman'. She was only a chambermaid. Nobody would back her to go to China because she hadn't passed exams, but her heart was so burdened for the Chinese that she was determined to go by herself. She longed that the Chinese should be told of the glorious news of the gospel.

She saved up and bought a railway ticket for the train journey to China from Russia through Siberia to the Chinese border. Then she walked the rest of the way! By caring for the Chinese she led many to find peace and salvation in Jesus Christ and many sad people were made happy. She was brought to the studio on some small pretext and then found that millions of TV viewers were being told of her great accomplishments. God sometimes lifts your interest from a small ambition to something greater.

Zechariah the prophet found this with his interest in rebuilding the temple at Jerusalem. God had given him visions to encourage the workers, but, after those visions, God showed him that there was a more important temple to build. That was a temple of living people. People whose lives had been cleansed and changed and who were telling others of the great news of eternal salvation. But who was going to bring this about? God describes this person. It is the Messiah.

Have you heard the story of the schoolgirl who was asked what she would do if she met the Lord Jesus Christ? They were doing a Scripture lesson in the classroom. The girl said, 'I would take this Bible and give it to Jesus and I would say to him, "This is your life".' She was right. The life of Christ is written by eye-witnesses in the New

Testament and by prophecy foretold in the Old Testament. Yes, Christ is in all the Scriptures. God had told all the earlier prophets what Jesus would be like and what he would do, so how much of the information did he give to Zechariah?

He said in chapter 6 onwards that he would be a Priest-King (6:13); that those he saves would build a spiritual temple. He said that the Messiah would enter Jerusalem riding on a humble donkey, not on a king's war horse (9:9). That was fulfilled on Palm Sunday. God told Zechariah that Jesus would also be a good shepherd, but would be betrayed for 30 pieces of silver (11:12). God also said he would be killed by being pierced (12:10). This harmonises with what God told Daniel 500 years earlier: 'They would pierce my hands and my feet.' Isaiah, 250 years earlier said, 'He was wounded for our transgressions and sins.' So that little girl was right. She would hand the Bible to Jesus and say, 'This is your life'.

HIS FIRST AND SECOND COMING PROPHESIED

Now, I divide Zechariah 6 to 14 into two sections. The first is chapters 6 to 10. These predict details about his first coming and the spiritual kingdom of men's hearts. The second section, chapters 10 to 14 tells of his second coming and the foundation of his earthly kingdom.

It is chapters 6 to 10 which show you that the Messiah would be a Priest-King. To demonstrate this, Joshua (his name means Jesus!) is clothed in priestly garments and a crown is then placed on his head.

God says that he represents the 'Branch', that is the Messiah, and he will be a Priest upon his throne and people from afar will come to build in the temple of the Lord.

What does Peter say about this in the New Testament? 'You come to Jesus, who is a living stone, rejected indeed by man, but chosen of God and precious. You also are living stones, built up into a spiritual house, a holy priesthood to offer up spiritual sacrifices, acceptable to God by Jesus Christ.' Therefore it is contained in the Old Testament scripture, 'Behold I lay in Zion a chief cornerstone elect, precious, and he who believes on him will not be ashamed. To you, therefore, who believe, he is precious.'

Now, the letter to the Hebrews in the New Testament describes the work of the Lord Jesus as our Priest in God's presence. He intercedes for those of you whom he has saved. Listen to the words of Hebrews 7:24 onwards:

> Because Jesus lives for ever, he has a permanent priesthood. Therefore he is able to save completely those who come to God through him, because he always lives to intercede for them. Such a high priest meets our need – one who is holy, blameless, pure, set apart from sinners, exalted above the

heavens. Unlike the other high priests, he does not need to offer sacrifices day after day, first for his own sins, and then for the sins of the people. He sacrificed for their sins once for all when he offered himself.

And Hebrews 9:11,12,24 says:

When Christ came as high priest of the good things that are already here, he went through the greater and more perfect tabernacle that is not man-made, that is to say, not a part of this creation. He did not enter by means of the blood of goats and calves; but he entered the Most Holy Place once for all by his own blood, having obtained eternal redemption . . . For Christ did not enter a man-made sanctuary that was only a copy of the true one; he entered heaven itself, now to appear for us in God's presence.

And again Hebrews 10:11–14 says:

Day after day every priest stands and performs his religious duties, again and again he offers the same sacrifices, which can never take away sins. But when this priest had offered for all time one sacrifice for sins, he sat down at the right hand of God. Since that time he waits for his enemies to be made his footstool, because by one sacrifice he has made perfect for ever those who are being made holy.

PROPHECIES OF ZECHARIAH RELATING TO MODERN TIMES

The last four chapters of Zechariah go on to prophesy what has been happening during the nineteenth and twentieth centuries. How do we know? By looking at the events in chronological order. Both Scripture and history are in the same order of time. There are 13 of them.

So you see these last four chapters of Zechariah reveal the remarkable significance of the events of the times in which we live:

1. 10:1 speaks of revival in the latter rain.
2. 10:10 speaks of the return of Israelis from all over the world. That did not happen even in Christ's time.
3. 11:1,2 speaks of the recent agony of Lebanon.
4. 12:3 says that the problem of Jerusalem will become a burdensome weight for all nations. Any nation which tries to solve the problem while ignoring God's purpose will injure its own cause.
5. 12:3 tells of the last battle of the age when all nations will gather to attack Jerusalem.
6. 12:10;14:4 tells of the sudden appearance of Jesus Christ descending from heaven.
7. 12:12 The Israelis will see it is 'one whom they pierced' (TV close-up?). Every Jew will repent and lament that they rejected their Messiah.
8. Chapter 13 opens with the cleansing of the whole Israeli nation through faith in Christ.

9. Chapter 14 follows up this future history with Christ descending to the Mount of Olives (v 4) to judge the nations.
10. The Mount of Olives splits in two and the rift valley of Jordan and the Red Sea joins up with the Mediterranean, 14:4–8.
11. Then Christ reigns on earth over all the world (14:9).
12. Every nation will send representatives to worship the Lord Christ in Jerusalem (14:16–19).
13. All adverts and newspapers and TV will be cleansed and only propagate pure and wholesome things (14:20,21).

The Warning in Secret Documents

I am going to tell you about the discovery of some secret documents. You may hardly believe it, but I assure you it is true. In the Second World War, a Nazi officer had secret documents to deliver. Instead of flying straight to his destination, he took a short cut over foreign country to visit a friend. He was shot down and taken to the military police. Quickly he flung the document on the fire burning there. They rescued it and beat out the flames. On looking at it, they were astonished to find it had Hitler's plans for invasion of their country. Did they do anything about it? No, they thought it was a hoax. They did not want to believe it so they did nothing about it. They found too late that their country was invaded just as the plans said they would be.

There are secret documents in the Bible. They set out God's plans in the future. They outline all the details of the stages of that plan. It is God's programme for winning back this world from the capture of Satan.

Although the signs are all being fulfilled to show that the programme is under way, there are many who don't believe it. Instead of getting ready, they ignore it to their peril, because it warns the unconverted to seek salvation and tells the Christian to watch, pray and work.

Zechariah is one of the prophets who writes down these plans which God has told him. To Amos, another prophet, God said, 'Truly the Lord God does nothing without revealing his secret to his servants, the prophets.'

We come now to what God told Zechariah about the days you and I are living in. The last chapters of Zechariah are prophecies about the second coming of the Lord Jesus Christ. This is a common pattern in many of the writing prophets. Whereas earlier chapters give details of the first coming of the Messiah, they end with the final triumph of God over evil.

We have read about the regathering of Israel to the Holy Land from all over the world in Zechariah 10:9. We have read, in verse 11, that the sceptre of Egypt will have departed. (Egypt no longer has a king. Those proud pharaohs are a magnificence of the past.) Then chapter 11 opens with the ruin of Lebanon. 'Open your doors O Lebanon.' Lebanon is an open door to powerful intruding devastators. The passage goes on, 'That fire may devour your cedars . . . the glorious trees are ruined, the thick forest has been felled.' When I visited Lebanon, I saw the sad truth. Where once there were the famous cedars of Lebanon, the hills and mountains stood bare and empty. It was symbolic of the fire of war which had terrorised the inhabitants and reduced so many fine buildings to rubble.

The Oracle of the Day of the Lord

These last three chapters of Zechariah are introduced under the heading of 'an Oracle'. What is an oracle? It is a revelation of tremendous happenings. This passage has one recurring phrase throughout. It is the words, 'On that day'. This phrase marks out the passage as one whole and it occurs as many as 14 times.

'On that day!' What day is this? Elsewhere in the Bible it is called, 'the Day of the Lord'. Indeed, that is what it is called in this prophecy of Zechariah 14:1: 'Behold the Day of the Lord is coming'. Peter's epistle comments on this: 'The Day of the Lord will come like a thief.' He also says, 'One day with the Lord is as a thousand years and a thousand years as one day.' In both his letters, Peter too has a characteristic phrase. This has been rendered from the Greek by Baxter as 'An age-long day'. He ends both his letters with it. That phrase, then, the 'Day of the Lord' refers not only to the day upon which God acts in judgement, but also to the period in which he reigns. Indeed, the last three times in Zechariah that the phrase 'On that day' occurs, it does refer to a period of time. I quote, 'The Lord will become king over all the earth' and nations shall go up to Jerusalem to worship the king from year to year. Now King David was *never* worshipped, so what king is this whom it is right to worship? Only King Jesus, because he is divine. The day is near when he will be king over all the earth.

What programme does this oracle say will lead up to such a climax? For the answer, we start at the beginning of the oracle in Zechariah 12:1. It concerns Israel, says the Lord. 'On that day I will make Jerusalem a problem to all the nations around.' Isn't Jerusalem a problem? 'I will make Jerusalem like a huge heavy stone; all nations who try to lift it will hurt themselves.'

We visualise here a group of men trying to lift a large heavy boulder. They all rupture themselves one after another. The nations who try to solve the problem will hurt themselves like this. Why? Because they try to do it their own way instead of inquiring what God's plan is. They use expedience instead of justice and what is politically convenient instead of right dealing. Before the British surrendered the mandate in Palestine, Bevan the politician said, 'I will solve the problem or die in the attempt'. He died in the attempt.

Who is acting for Israel? Verse 1 says it is the Lord who created the heavens and made the earth and created the spirit of man within him. There is authority and power for you. Golda Meier, that famous Israeli Prime Minister said, 'There seems to be somebody acting for us'. That does not excuse any cruel action of course, but she was referring to the miracle of survival.

The next 'On that Day' phrase speaks of the anger of the nations at not being able to solve the problem and their reaction. Next comes an amazing statement. Jerusalem is attacked. The Israelis will pray for deliverance. They pray for the promised Messiah and when he comes they are amazed to see that it is Jesus whom they pierced (12:10). In the Hebrew, the words are, 'They will look on Me whom they pierced' – Jehovah. This says that Jesus is Jehovah!

St John comments on this in Revelation 1:7, 'Behold, Jesus Christ is coming with the clouds and every eye shall see him and all those who pierced him and all the tribes of the earth will wail on account of him.'

So not only will the Israelis wail and mourn when they see Jesus descend from heaven with power, but so will all nations who rejected him. Indeed, it was the Gentiles as well as the Jews who pierced him. But Zechariah 12:10–14 tells you that the distress shown by Israel will be different from that of the Gentiles. They will mourn for Jesus with compassion. They will weep bitterly over Jesus as one mourns over an only child who has died. Their failure to believe in Christ will be felt to be their personal loss. Each family will weep bitterly that they never accepted Jesus as their Messiah and Saviour.

Then the next repeat of the phrase, 'On that Day' in Zechariah 13:1 introduces a flood of blessing for the weeping repentant Israelis. A cleansing fountain of forgiveness will be opened for them. O the wonderful cleansing of the precious blood of the Lamb slain for sinners! 'On that day, says the Lord, there will be a fountain opened for the house of David and the inhabitants of Jerusalem to cleanse them from sin and uncleanness.' They will sing what we believing Gentiles have sung, such as:

What can wash away my sin? Nothing but the blood of Jesus.
What can make me pure within? Nothing but the blood of Jesus.
Oh, precious is the flow that makes me white as snow.
No other power I know, nothing but the blood of Jesus.
Rev R. Lowry

There is a fountain filled with blood, drawn from Immanuel's veins,
And sinners plunged beneath that flood, lose all their guilty stains.
William Cowper

How was that redemption made? Remember that this prophecy was made 500 years before the cross. Verse 6 onwards says it was by wounding God's Good Shepherd. Then comes, in the succeeding verses, a recap of Israel's terrible tribulation down the centuries since rejecting their Good Shepherd. Two-thirds perished. The one-third which survived were refined by their trials as by fire, as silver and gold are refined. That continues until Israel calls on God. He will answer, 'They are my people' and they will say, 'The Lord Jehovah is my God'. Jesus himself said, 'I will not return to you O Israel until you say, Blessed is he who comes in the name of Jehovah.'

In the next and last chapter of Zechariah, there is prophesied the most startling and wonderful climax. It is the descent of Jesus Christ to the Mount of Olives. With him come all the saved and then unfolds the day of God with staggering geological and international implications. 'Prepare the way of the Lord, make straight his paths.'

Earth-shaking Events at Christ's Return

I have already described God's revealed geological knowledge in *Evidence for Truth, Volume 2: Archaeology*, Chapter 2. The earth-shaking events which are to happen at Christ's return are described to Ezekiel in such a way as to show that God knew all about the geology of this globe. It will involve the Great Rift Valley and the movement of continents. It reveals that the increase in earthquakes is the continents preparing to split the moment Christ's feet touch the Mount of Olives at his descent. The dramatic results are described in Ezekiel 47 as well as in Zechariah 14.

Zechariah 14:4 says: 'On that day his feet will stand on the Mount of Olives which lies before Jerusalem on the East'.

Whose feet are these? Verse 3 tells you they are Jehovah's (which is translated 'The Lord'). In the New Testament you are told that they will be the feet of the Lord Jesus Christ. Clearly this implies that Jesus is Jehovah.

Now turn to Acts 1:11 and you read that two angels appeared to the disciples as the Lord Jesus ascended into heaven. They said, 'Men of Galilee, why do you stand looking into heaven? This same Jesus, who is taken up from you into heaven, will come in the same manner that you have seen him go into heaven.'

The next verse tells you they were on the Mount of Olives. So the second coming of Jesus will be in the same way at the same place. Other scriptures tell you that he will descend with the clouds and with the saved. 2 Thessalonians 1:10 tells you that, and so does Jesus in Matthew 24:30. 'Then shall appear the sign of the Son of Man in heaven and then shall all the tribes of the earth mourn and they will see the Son of Man coming in the clouds of heaven with power and great glory.' The next verse tells you the elect (that is, the saved) will be gathered with him. We saw in Zechariah 12 the statement that the nations would mourn to see their judge coming; so the occasion is clearly the second coming of Christ with the saved. Daniel 7 also tells you that the Son of Man will descend with the saints – that is, the saved. Now here again Zechariah 14:5 identifies it as the same occasion: 'Then the Lord your God will come and all the saints with him'. So all these scriptures identify the event as being the second coming of Christ to the Mount of Olives.

It is then that two great geological events will happen of cataclysmic proportions:

- A great rift valley will open up past Jerusalem and link up the Mediterranean Sea with the Red Sea and Indian Ocean.
- Fresh water will be released from an artesian basin which is known to be under Jerusalem.

Now note that these events are associated with the Lord becoming King over all the earth (v 9). Why? Because it will make Jerusalem the maritime centre of the world. In fact Zechariah, like the other prophets, ends with Christ reigning in a millennium of peace for all creation. In the three books of the prophets, Ezekiel, Joel and Zechariah, the millennium is represented as coming after the return of Christ. The order of events is the same in all of them and is as follows:

1. The return of Israel to Palestine.
2. The last war of this age.
3. The return of Christ with power to judge the nations.
4. The establishment of the personal reign of Christ on earth.

The characteristics of his reign are: the abolition of all war and weapons with the worship of Jesus by every nation on earth. Incitement to sin will be abolished and texts encouraging holiness and happiness will appear everywhere. Also, the animal kingdom will be at peace. Animals will not kill each other for food. Paul quite clearly says this in Romans 8. He states that this kingdom on earth will follow the resurrection of the saved at the second coming of Christ.

So all those Old Testament prophets end with a wonderful picture of the final era of peace and happiness. It is Revelation 20 which gives it the name of millennium so it is wrong to say, as some do, that only Revelation speaks of the millennium. It is described in other scriptures as many as six or seven times. This wonderful time will be the result of Christ's second coming.

The question which springs to many minds is, 'Have all these geological events to be taken very literally?' I mean, the splitting of the

Mount of Olives, the formation of the Great Rift Valley and the water flowing out of Jerusalem. Like many prophecies, it will be fulfilled both spiritually and literally.

What evidence do we have that it is to be fulfilled literally? It is the geological events described. They are a literal description of the geological structure of the earth which modern science has discovered. Let me refresh your memories. Verse 4 says, 'The Mount of Olives will be split in two from East to West by a very wide valley.' We geologists now know that this area is at the apex of the Great Rift Valley system. This extends through Africa, up to the Red Sea and up the Jordan valley. This rift is marked by a very wide valley. It is 15 miles wide at the Dead Sea, 100 miles wide at the Red Sea and 60 miles wide through Africa.

What causes a rift valley? It is caused by the continents moving away from each other so that the floor of the valley falls to a depth of several thousand feet. Verse 4 says that this rift valley will extend through that area by a frightening earthquake when Christ's feet touch down on the Mount of Olives. Now, there is a major fault line which runs from east to west between Jordan and the Mediterranean Sea just as described in that verse.

The verse then describes the classical way in which a rift valley is formed. With a shattering roar of sound, the earth mass pulls away southward from the north; a wide section collapses to make the floor of the new rift valley. Read the text, 'One half of the mountain will withdraw northwards and the other half southwards', making a very wide valley.

God Is a Geologist

It is clear from verse 8 that this valley will link up the western sea, i.e. the Mediterranean, with the eastern sea, i.e. the Red Sea linking with the Indian Ocean. This is made clear by a similar prophecy to Ezekiel in chapter 47. There, God describes the sea waters filling up the Dead Sea to sea level. The staggering thing is this. Verse 10 names places which are actually at sea level in the Jordan valley and so does God's words to Joel about the same event in Joel 3:18. The waters from the seas will come up to that level. This again shows remarkable knowledge and could not possibly come from a human mind in those days. These prophecies show that not only will water flow past Jerusalem in a wide maritime canal, it will also bring sea fish into the Dead Sea from the Mediterranean and fishermen will stand on the shore at the new sea level and they will fish for ocean fish (Ezekiel 47:10).

God had revealed these geological events to three of his prophets. They were revealed to Joel eight centuries BC. They were revealed to Ezekiel six centuries BC and they were revealed to Zechariah five centuries BC. So God must be very keen on the geological aspect of his plan.

The second geological event which will happen as a result of Christ's second coming is the release of fresh water from an artesian basin beneath Jerusalem. This too is described by all three prophets. That is what God told Joel. 'A fountain will come forth from the house of the Lord'.

That is what God told Zechariah. 'On that day, living waters will flow out from Jerusalem . . . it shall continue in summer as well as in winter.'

That is what God told Ezekiel. 'He brought me to the door of the temple and behold, water was flowing from below the threshold of the temple. It became ankle deep and knee deep and then waist deep.'

The source of water is based upon geological fact. Research has demonstrated that. What will make those waters flow when Christ comes? The hydrological report actually said it needs the rock to be ruptured. When Christ returns with power from heaven, the rock will rupture literally when his feet touch Olivet. This will release water from the artesian basin. It will also open up that new rift valley canal.

Imagine the tremendously violent earthquake it will make. It will strike terror into the hearts of the ungodly. The passage describes this in Zechariah 14:5. 'And you will run for your life, as you fled from the earthquake in the days of Uzziah.'

The same event is described in Ezekiel 38:18 about the ungodly waging the last battle of the age. 'But on the day that Gog shall come against the land of Israel, says the Lord God, my wrath will be roused . . . On that day there shall be a great shaking . . . and all men that are on the earth will quake at my presence and the mountains will be thrown down and the cliffs shall fall and every wall will tumble to the ground and I will summon every kind of terror upon godless Gog'.

Then comes an interesting note, 'I will rain upon him fire and brimstone.' Brimstone is sulphur. Now where in the Bible did fire and sulphur rain down upon certain wicked cities and destroy them? Yes, it was Sodom and Gomorrah. And where were Sodom and Gomorrah? They were in the Dead Sea rift valley. It was an earthquake which released the burning asphalt and red hot sulphur to rain down on those cities. Doesn't this give extra significance to the warning of Jesus about his second coming? He said, 'As it was in the days of Lot and of Sodom and Gomorrah, so will it be in the day when the Son of Man will come.' The shattering fracture of the earth's crust and the collapse into a new rift valley, will rupture the strata far worse than in Lot's day and blazing asphalt and flashing sulphur and hot melted salt will rain down upon the unbelievers. The molten salt will make many into pillars of salt like Lot's wife.

No wonder Jesus said, 'Remember Lot's wife – do not turn back to the city of destruction like she did.' Sadly, it will be only those who are left behind after Christ's coming who will experience these judgements. Why? Because Christ comes first for his own saved people and then comes with his saved to judge the world. That is why Zechariah 14:4 says he will come to the Mount of Olives with his holy ones. The holy ones are those washed from sin by the blood of Christ.

Remember Lot's wife. She valued this world's goods too much to deny herself and come out for God. As it was in the day of Sodom and Gomorrah, so will it be when the Son of Man, Jesus Christ, comes. Remember Lot's wife. She could not have believed the warning message. There is plenty of unbelief in the world today. People need the evidence of prophecy to convince and bring them to the Lord.

SUMMARY
WHAT GOD FORETOLD TO ZECHARIAH

List of prophecies about Jesus' first coming:
- Palm Sunday: Jesus will ride on donkey to temple now being built (9:9).
- Betrayed for 30 pieces of silver (11:12,13).
- Jesus as God the Good Shepherd (13:7).
- He will be Jehovah whom they crucify (12:10).
- He will be the chief stone of salvation bringing grace (4:7).
- He is the Branch of David's fallen tree (3:8; 6:12).
- He is Priest-King descended through Zerubbabel (6:13; 4:6–10; Matt 1:12).

Events of the last days described in last four chapters:
1. Revival in the latter rain (10:1).
2. Return of Israel from all the world (10:10).
3. Lebanon's agony (11:1,2).
4. Insoluble problem of Jerusalem brings failure to politicians (12:3).
5. Army from all nations will attack Jerusalem (12:3).
6. Christ will suddenly descend to Mt Olivet (12:10;14:4).
7. Israelis will recognise Christ's wounds (TV close-up?) (12:12). 8.Israel's sorrow, repentance and cleansing (12:10–14).
9. Christ will descend to Mt Olivet when city is half taken (14:1–4).
10. Olivet will split in two and rift valley joins up Mediterranean with eastern sea (14:4–8).
11. Christ will judge the world and reign over it (14:9).
12. Every nation will send up representatives to worship Jesus Christ at Harvest Festival time (14:16–19).
13. All adverts, newspapers and TV will be cleansed and only propagate pure and wholesome things (14:20,21).

12　THE PRINCE OF PROPHETS
EVENTS OF THE CHRISTIAN ERA PREDICTED

You will of course immediately recognise that the Prince of Prophets is the Lord Jesus. His major prophecy given on the Mount of Olives is the most remarkable outline of history ever predicted which was to happen between his ascension and his return.

Many events he prophesied are now facts of history and others are unfolding before us, but some people get confused because they say there are all kinds of opinion about application. Others just weigh one opinion against another. This is not the way to get truth from God's Word. We should look for the motives and assumptions behind differing opinions. For example, some don't believe that the Lord Jesus will personally appear in the heavens. Others are more wedded to the passing fashions of theological thought. One such says that all prophecies concerning the nation of Israel are now to be applied to the Christian Church alone. This leads to blindness to the significance of happenings in the Near East today. These mean nothing to them. No wonder the Lord said, 'You observe signs of the weather, but cannot see prophecy fulfilling.' It is true that Christian believers do become spiritual children of Abraham, but Paul, all the prophets and the Lord himself say plainly that it does not negate the promises of God to Israel as a nation.

I was speaking to a Christian the other day who got fixed on an interpretation because it was the opinion of her favourite preacher. 'You must remember,' I said, 'that we can't be right on everything and should be ready to be corrected by Scripture.' We have to beware of hooking on to an interpretation and pinning to it our own pride or self-esteem or loyalty to some society or person, instead of to the Lord. Many cling to a haphazard application because of personal attachment. So, to be subject to the insight of the Holy Spirit, we have to let self be crucified, carefully comparing scripture with scripture. St Paul says in 2 Corinthians 10:5, 'Cast down all theories and every pride that exalts itself . . . and bring into captivity every thought to obey Christ'.

PRINCIPLES FOR RIGHT DISCERNMENT

So you see, it is not just a matter of weighing up man's opinions, but noting carefully the terms of reference in the Scriptures themselves and subjecting even our own pet theories to Christ.

We all know the jokes about a short-sighted swimmer who swam out into a lake to see what the notice said. He found that it said, 'Swimming strictly forbidden!' Or of a diver who dived into the sea before he had read the plaque at the side of the diving-board giving the depth of water. He should have read it before diving in when the tide was low.

The Three Questions

We should not dive into a shallow idea about a text until we have read the terms of reference. What are the terms of reference in what Jesus, the Prince of Prophets, said about the future? Turn with me to Matthew 24. This remarkable prophecy by the Lord himself is also reported in Mark 13 and Luke 21, but we will look now at Matthew 24:3. Here we find that the Lord Jesus answers three questions put to him by the disciples. These then are the terms of reference:

1. When will Jerusalem and the temple be destroyed?
2. What will be the signs of your second coming?
3. What will be the signs of the end of the age?

Now, it is common sense to see that Jesus answers all three questions, yet – would you believe it! – some apply the chapter as if he is replying to only one of those questions and say that it all concerns the second coming only. Some, not wanting to believe in the second coming, say that it all referred to the fall of Jerusalem in AD 70.

As a matter of fact, if we see that the Saviour was replying to all three of those questions, what he said outlines the history of the 2,000 years from his time to ours.

Of course, in the minds of the apostles, all these three things would be associated with the same event. Jesus had just said that the glorious temple would be destroyed. Such a catastrophe and desecration would mean to them the end of the world; especially for those whose reverence was tied to sacred buildings. It does not seem possible to some that truth is more important than temples made with hands. If truth departs from a temple or cathedral or minister, God registers his disapproval very often by some catastrophe and Jesus said this was going to happen to the temple and Jerusalem where the religious authorities rejected the Son of God.

So then, Jesus replies to the first question – when will the temple and Jerusalem be destroyed?

Two Signs for Escape

After a general introduction, Jesus answers that question. He gives the signs and warnings which were fulfilled between AD 66 and 70. Jerusalem was destroyed so thoroughly that, as Jesus foretold, 'There was not one stone left standing upon another'. In fact, the Roman armies were so determined to wipe out Jewry that they ploughed over the whole site and spread the rubble – several yards thick. The observer historians of the time tell us that you would not have known that a city had ever existed there.

So then, verses 15–20 refer to the fall of Jerusalem in AD 70. I will show you, the Lord helping me, that these details were fulfilled to the letter. The two independent historians of the time were Josephus and Hegessippus. They gave most remarkable details which show that not one word or prophecy of the Lord falls to the ground unfulfilled. In fact, the details are such that those of sceptical mind, because they do not believe in prophecy, have said that the Gospels were written after the fall of Jerusalem. But this cannot be, because otherwise the warnings of Jesus would not have alerted the Christians to escape from Jerusalem before the catastrophe, as historians tell us they did.

Next then, let us look at the details prophesied by the Lord Jesus and whose fulfilment is recorded by those secular historians. The first important thing is something which has escaped the notice of any commentator that I have read. It is this. The fall of Jerusalem was in two stages. One stage in AD 66 and the second stage 3½ years later in AD 70. Luke tells us about the first and Matthew and Mark tell us about the second. It is because sceptics have not noticed this that some contradict the other as they are so prone to do.

I will now set out what the Lord prophesied concerning the first stage in the fall of Jerusalem and the fulfilment recorded by historians of the time. Jesus warned Christians to flee from danger on these two occasions when they recognised two different signs that destruction was coming.

At the first sign, they were to flee the whole country before the wars of the Jews started in AD 66. This, Luke records, was when Jerusalem would be surrounded by Roman armies. Look at Luke 21:20, 'When you see Jerusalem surrounded by armies, then know that the destruction is near' or 'has approached'. The Greek word means 'one stage before it has arrived'. At this sign, the Christians were not only to leave Jerusalem, but also all Judea and the whole country to Galilee, because the devastation was to go right through all the towns and villages from the north to the south. They were to flee to the mountains outside their own country.

As I have already stated in Chapter 14 of *Evidence for Truth, Volume 2: Archaeology*, Josephus, the contemporary historian, records what happened in his volume entitled, *The Wars of the Jews*. The Roman garrison for Palestine was at Caesarea on the coast of the Holy Land. News came to the commander about the rioting in Jerusalem, so the commander, whose name was Cestius, marched up with his army and surrounded Jerusalem where the Zealots had gained full control in their rebellion. No one could leave the city and so Christians inside would be trapped as well; so you might ask how the Lord expected the believers to flee if they were trapped? The Christians certainly recognised the warning sign: 'When you see Jerusalem surrounded by armies, then know that desolation is near – escape to the mountains.'

Josephus records the extraordinary thing which happened next. He writes, 'For no reason in the world', Cestius withdrew his forces. Perhaps he thought he needed a larger army. However, whatever the reason, his troops withdrew to Caesarea.

The Zealots hailed this as a triumph and attacked the rear of the army as they went, humiliating the might of Rome, and then returned to the city rejoicing. But not so with the Christians. They recognised the sign and warning and escaped to the mountains of Perea to the east of Jordan.

The commander Cestius sent to Rome for reinforcements and Titus and Vespasian came with a great army and commenced to devastate the whole land starting in Galilee. That is why Jesus had said, 'Woe unto you Chorazin, woe unto you Bethsaida and Capernaum', cities around the Sea of Galilee, 'because you received not the gospel'. And that is why the Christians had to forsake the whole country.

Then for 3½ years, in what was called the Wars of the Jews, the Roman armies levelled to the ground town after town, village after village. They started in Galilee where the Lord Christ had commenced his ministry and within 3½ years had worked down to Jerusalem where Jesus had given the nation its last chance at the Passover 3½ years after the start of his ministry. So within that generation, as Jesus had warned, the nation was judged at the same places over the same period of time.

Actually, Titus and Vespasian had finished devastating the country by the winter of AD 69 and had begun to prepare for the assault on Jerusalem itself. But you will remember that Jesus told the Christians to pray that their escape would not be in winter because of the suffering it would bring to mothers nursing their babies, or on the Sabbath. The Christians must have prayed because just before the advance on the city was to start, unexpected news came from Rome. The tyrant Emperor Nero had died. Immediately, Vespasian was proclaimed emperor by his troops. He returned to Rome and so the campaign was halted until the spring.

It was in the spring that the second stage commenced. During a false peace, Jerusalem had become crowded with Jews from all over the world for the Passover of AD 70. No doubt many Christians had come up with them. It was concerning this second advance on Jerusalem that Matthew and Mark record the Lord's second warning sign. This sign was the abomination in the sacred temple. The Zealots committed a terrible sacrilege within the city just before the Romans closed in to cut off all escape. They sacrificed pigs on the altar. This abomination of unclean animals was immediately recognised by the believers and they remembered the instructions of Christ that they should not lose a moment of time. They were to jump from house top to flat house top. They were not even to descend into the house for luggage. The memoirs of the historian Hegessippus tell of the fulfilment of Christ's words and the obedience of the Christians.

In the nick of time, just before the mighty armies of Titus closed in, and just before the Sabbath, the Christians escaped. After that, sad to relate, not one Jew left the city. The Romans had put up earth barriers around the city to hem them in on every side, just as Jesus prophesied when he wept over the city. 'O hadst thou known the time of your visitation.' All the million or so perished, except for the young men taken off in chains for slavery. The rest were crucified around the walls of Jerusalem. It was hard to find enough wood for all the crosses.

So then, the reply of the Lord Jesus Christ to the first question about the fall of Jerusalem was fulfilled to the finest detail. Now, it is obvious that the Christians could not have escaped if they had not been given the two warning signs before it came to pass, so this defeats sceptics' dating of the prophecy.

We shall see that for the remaining two questions the disciples asked Jesus brought a reply giving prophecies which took 19 centuries to fulfil and which have only reached their final fulfilment in our times.

Other scriptures reveal that there is to be a parallel to the two stages at the Lord's second coming. And even as there were two stages in the fall of Jerusalem in AD 70, so there will be two stages in Christ's second coming. These also will probably be separated by 3½ years. First, he will come for those who belong to him, the saved. Second, he comes with them to Jerusalem.

The first stage of Christ's second coming will be to the air and the saved will rise to meet him. The second stage will be either 3½ years or 7 years later when he continues his descent to the Mount of Olives.

This first stage of his coming will be to take out the believers before the final woes pour out upon the earth. The second stage will be to stop the world destroying itself.

The first stage of his coming will be to judge the Christians for reward. The second stage, probably seven years later, will be to judge the nations of the world.

Prejudice against Prediction

Another error that the Bible warns us against is unbelief that God knows and plans the future. The effects of unbelief in prophecy are widespread. Even many evangelicals have forgotten why the critics have dated the writing of the Scriptures later than the Bible claims. Critics assumed God did not know the future. Although they are theologians, they accept that agnostic assumption. Think of the blasphemy of this. It deliberately contradicts and dishonours the Lord who says in Isaiah 46:10 that he proves he is God by showing that he does know the future. Even many evangelicals forget that the dating of when the Gospels were written is based by sceptics on this agnostic assumption. The Gospels foretell the fall of Jerusalem and Jerusalem fell in AD 70, so they say the Gospels must have been written after that, seeing that they claim to foretell that catastrophe. What a twist that arch-liar has given in persuading university lecturers that the Scripture of truth is a fraud and that the events it foretells were really written after the event and how gullible are so many lecturers and students to accept it. No wonder they come out of college as unbelievers.

Now, the warning in the Gospels to flee from Jerusalem when they see the sign foretold would be no use to Christians if it were given after the event. What is the proof that this prophesied warning was actually given before the fulfilment? It comes again from that secular historian who lived at the time, Josephus. What does he tell us? He tells us that many who were warned by an oracle, forsook the city as sailors would abandon a sinking ship and they escaped to the mountains of Perea, but the other inhabitants, presumably non-Christians, stayed in the city.

This should convince the unprejudiced reader that the warning prophecy was on record beforehand, otherwise it would not have been effective. For the open-minded this is evidence that the Gospels were written before the fall of Jerusalem, not after it. The place of prophecy in its sense of foretelling the future, is therefore important and should not be avoided.

Dr John Robinson showed in his last book, *Redating the New Testament*, SCM, 1976, that the fourth Gospel(that is, St John's Gospel) was also written before the fall of Jerusalem in AD 70. He shows that the Pool of Bethesda, where Jesus healed the paralysed man, was still in existence when John wrote. In AD 70, it was demolished and covered with rubble. The site was not known until recent years.

It is a comment on Peter's words, 'They willingly ignore evidence' for the truth when we find Robinson's book ignored. Yet when he wrote critical books earlier in the 1960s, they were widely promoted in the press, schools and over the air. In fact, they largely contributed to the fall away from faith in the churches of the 1960s onwards.

Scripture says, 'they run greedily into error', and so in Robinson's more recent book, which is constructive and factual, they choose to overlook its truth.

The Second Question

The next question that the Lord Jesus answered was, 'What will be the signs of the end of the age?' The subject of this then is the age and its duration. Jesus replies that the end of the age is not yet. There is a lot to happen before the age ends. The gospel has to be preached to all nations first and other events are to happen.

So, after foretelling the fall of Jerusalem, the Lord deals with the gospel-preaching age which is to follow this catastrophe. In this section, St Luke's record gives different information from that in Matthew and Mark. This is an advantage because one interprets the others. We shall see that many do not correctly analyse this part because they don't place the three reports side by side so that they throw light on each other. It is vital to place the three accounts in parallel if we are to understand Christ's answer. This is an obvious thing to do yet the majority of commentators fail to do it and thus we get confusion of understanding. So open your Bible and keep your fingers in two places, Matthew 24 and Luke 21.

Perhaps you have made (or seen your wife or mother making) sponge cakes. Before the top half is put on, a filling of jam goes on one and cream on the other. When the two cakes are put side by side, you notice that the top and bottom of the cakes are the same. They match up. It is the filling which is different. In all three Gospel accounts of what Jesus prophesied on the Mount of Olives, the top and bottom are the same, that is, the beginning and the end, but the filling in Luke's is different. This particular filling is in verses 22–24.

As you place the accounts side by side (see pages 221–225), you see that the Lord Jesus outlines events which will follow the destruction of the Holy City (v 20 in Matthew and v 21 in Luke). All three accounts agree on this, but then we notice that St Luke's cake filling is different. It gives what happens to the **Jews** scattered throughout the nations, but Matthew and Mark say what happens to the **Christians** during that gospel age. It is a different sandwich filling so to speak. We will turn first to Luke's filling. It is chapter 21 verses 22–24. It is about the scattering of the Jews among all nations and it spans 19 centuries from the fall of Jerusalem down to our times. We read from verse 22: 'For these are the days of vengeance.' Vengeance upon whom? The reply is halfway through verse 23. 'There shall be great distress in the land and wrath upon this people' – that is, the Jews for rejecting the Lord Jesus Christ. This is made obvious in the next verse which says, 'They shall fall by the edge of the sword and shall be led captive into all nations.'

Then the Lord gives the length of duration of that scattering. It will be while Jerusalem is trodden down by the Gentiles and it will be until the times of the Gentiles are fulfilled.

Old Jerusalem was governed by Gentiles (that means non-Jewish nations) until 1967 when the Israelis captured the old city. Yes, during all those 19 centuries when the Jews were scattered around the world, the Gentiles governed their ancient city.

Tribulation for the Jews

This then is the Lukan contribution filling in the middle of the cake: the distress, suffering or tribulation of the Jews up to 1967. It is unique to Luke's record. He alone speaks of the Jewish scattering abroad, but his words join the other two Gospels again on the top half of the sponge cake at the end of that portion representing 19 centuries. He starts with the same words as the other Gospels about the final signs of the age in verse 25. 'Then shall there be signs in the sun and moon and stars', Luke records. Similarly, both Matthew and Mark join Luke here and prophesy about the sun and moon in the end times. Matthew 24:29: 'The sun shall be darkened and the moon will not give her light.'

In passing, this is rather similar to the horrors described in the film *The Nuclear Winter*. The darkening of the sun and moon would certainly give nuclear winter.

So then, we have defined the starting and finishing point of the gospel age. We see that Luke gives what Jesus says about the suffering of God's ancient people, the Jews, so what different aspect does Matthew record was to happen between these two identification points? It is the fortunes of the Christians, not of the Jews given by Luke. That is made clear by the words of Matthew 24:20. 'Pray that your flight be not in winter.' Jesus has been warning the believers to escape and it is in that passage (vv 21–28) that Christians are alerted to the spiritual perils and deceptions which will endanger their witness, because Satan's counterfeits would be so subtle that, if it were possible, it would almost deceive the true elect. The elect in Scripture are, of course, the born-again Christians. This also was fulfilled.

We shall look at these spiritual deceptions and how they nearly wiped out the pure gospel witness down those next 19 centuries, but at this point we should note what Matthew and Mark call this period which is parallel to Luke's scattering and suffering of the Jews.

They call it the tribulation. It was indeed a terrible tribulation for the Jews. They were hounded from country to country down the centuries. But don't jump to conclusions. I am not saying that the Church will go through what is often called the tribulation. I believe it won't.

Figure 12.1. Belsen gas chamber, part of the final stage of the tribulation of the Jews when 6 million Jews perished (Jeremiah 16).

I prefer to call that period **the last woes** after the rapture of the saved. It is the time when the true Church of all born-again believers are removed from the world by being resurrected, then after 3½ years or 7 years, they descend with Christ to stop the world in its death throes.

It is important to see that this use of the word tribulation in Matthew **does** apply to the same period of Luke's scattering of the Jews, for where that scattering starts in Luke, Matthew 24:21 says, 'For then shall there be great tribulation'. And where Luke says the Israelis will return to Jerusalem and govern it, Matthew 24:29 says, 'Immediately **after** the tribulation of those days shall the sun be darkened.'

To recognise that this period of Jewish suffering in Luke's parallel is what is called the tribulation in Matthew will clear away a lot of confusion in the minds of Christians who are keen about the smaller details of the second advent, but it should be remembered that it is the main doctrine of the second coming of Christ which is important, not these details and it is important to preach it because it is a powerful eye-opener to believers and unbelievers on the significance of world events.

Trials for the Christians

So then, we have seen what the Lord Jesus said about the Jewish suffering during over 19 centuries of the gospel era. What does the Lord warn Christians about in that same period as in Matthew and Mark?

First, that there would be many false christs and false prophets. We know from early church history that there were many of these. Satan's favourite trick is to confuse people with false religion. People say, 'Who are we to believe?' God's reply is, 'This is my beloved Son, hear him.' If we humbly read God's Word, the Bible, the Holy Spirit will lead us into all truth. But unfortunately, human nature wants to be confused about religion because one thinks it is an escape from the truth. Consequently, he is wide open to two major deceptions of Satan; 2 Thessalonians 2 tells us that in the latter days, Satan will send the lawless one and, because people refuse to love the truth and be saved, they will be deluded with wicked deception.

So then, after the appearance in the early centuries of many false prophets, the Lord said there would particularly arise the false christ and the false prophet.

In the Middle Ages, the ancient churches of both East and West lost the joyful doctrines of salvation by which the believer is saved for eternity by the one sacrifice of the Lord Jesus on the cross. But we are assured that this eclipse of the gospel would be overcome in two stages according to 2 Thessalonians 2:8. First, by the breath of Christ's mouth. This I take to be by the rediscovery of the Bible. In Revelation

19, it is described as the sword (of the Spirit) which proceeds out of the mouth of the Lord Jesus. During the Reformation and again in recent times, the Bible is being distributed among those who were once denied it. But verse 8 says that all error will not be abolished until the Lord Jesus Christ himself comes and destroys it.

What of the false prophet of the desert? Jesus said in Matthew 24:26, 'If they say to you, behold he is in the desert, do not go out on a pilgrimage.' We know that the rise of Islam wiped out nearly all the Christian Church in North Africa and in other places in the world and even today many who become Christians are secretly put to death.

In spite of these dangers to the witness of the gospel, the Lord assures us in the general introduction to his prophecy that the gospel will be preached to all nations before the end of the age comes.

What else is told us Christians about our part in this age? In this section, the Lord Jesus speaks of the shortening of the age for the sake of the elect. Were it but for this, he said, 'No flesh would be saved'. Certainly, all life is threatened today by nuclear weapons and biological warfare. It is encouraging that this passage implies that life on earth will be saved by the shortening of the last days of this age for the elect's sake. This, I take it, refers to the resurrection of the elect. The living and the dead believers will rise to meet the glorious all-powerful coming of Christ. But for that, life would disappear from this planet.

What a wonderful outline of history the Lord Jesus prophesied on the Mount of Olives. We have seen how he gave us an outline of history from his day to ours. We have seen how Luke's account of the Lord's prophecy interprets Matthew and Mark's accounts. We have seen that we have to place Luke 21 in parallel with Matthew 24, side by side; that this shows us that, at this point, they all report the prophesied fall of Jerusalem in AD 70. Then Luke records what would happen to the Jews for the following 19 centuries, but Matthew tells us what would happen to Christian witness during that time. We have seen that all three accounts join together again to tell us about the second coming of Christ in these last days in which we live.

The grammar construction in Luke's precise Greek also bears out this analysis. The adverbs of time divide out those three sections of history. The first two have been fulfilled and the third is coming to pass in our day. Besides, it is Luke that makes it clear that the opening reply of the Lord Jesus speaks about his second coming because Luke introduces the words, 'Before all these things'. So, before dealing with each of the three questions separately, the Lord Jesus gives a general introduction about the signs of his return and in it, he speaks about world wars of nation against nation and famines and epidemics and earthquakes in many places.

Although the world doesn't realise it, Jesus shows that God has geared the whole programme of history to whether progress is being made in preaching the gospel as a witness to all nations. 'This gospel of the kingdom shall be preached in all the world for a witness unto all nations, then shall the end come.'

Signs and Wonders

Never before in world history have there been world wars which involved the whole population 'nation rising against nation'. We see monuments for the two world wars with long lists of the noble dead in every town and village and we remember them at the eleventh hour on the eleventh day of the eleventh month of the year – Remembrance Sunday. The Lord also said there would be terrible sights and great signs from heaven. Signs from heaven could refer to supernatural signs as well. There have been signs reported in the two world wars as well as at other times. For example, there were many books written about the angels of Mons appearing in the First World War and a ding-dong discussion on whether the troops were dreaming it. The invading armies drove through Belgium to the city of Mons where there was terrible slaughter and the troops trying to halt the advance saw armies of angels helping them. Hundreds of soldiers told us what they saw and it was a topic of conversation for years afterwards.

There was also a vision at the beginning of the First World War of a lamb which was bleeding that appeared above the preacher at an evangelistic campaign. The vision was there for several hours. There was also a sign over London in the last war when the flying bombs started coming over. Some people reported to the press that they had seen a huge angel in the sky holding up his hands as if in protection. The news reporter asked them if they were Christians, but they said they never went to church; they were not believers. So the reporter asked if they had been drinking and they said that the pubs were not open that early. I think there are probably more angelic happenings than we hear of. People don't report them because they are afraid of being laughed at, but great signs from heaven are what the Lord foretold for the latter days.

Then, of course, we know only too well about the terrible famines when hundreds of thousands have died and are dying of starvation. Worst of all, said God to Amos, is the 'famine of God's Word'. In some countries, churches have been closed and gospel preaching forbidden. The Lord also mentions earthquakes in many places. They have greatly increased in the last two decades according to seismological records and these are the geological features of earth preparing itself for the descent of the Lord Jesus to the Mount of Olives. Those who have studied geology will know that earthquakes occur around the world

mainly in the newfold mountain areas. These are where the five conti-
nents push or pull on one another. The three continents of Africa,
Europe and Asia swivel on the Middle East. That is why the fault line
running through the Mount of Olives, east to west, between the
Mediterranean and the Dead Sea will break open and the waters of the
Mediterranean will flow into the Dead Sea, as five of the Old
Testament prophets tell us.

The Last Signs of Christ's Return

The third question which Jesus answers is, 'What will be the sign of
your coming?' All three Gospels report the Lord's answer – in Mark
13:24; Matthew 24:29 and Luke 21:25. 'The sun will be darkened and
the moon will not give its light and the stars will be falling from heav-
en and the powers that are within the heavens will be shaken. And then
shall they see the Son of Man coming in clouds with great power and
glory.' These are the words with little variation in Mark and Matthew.

Luke reports, 'There will be signs in sun and moon and stars.' Luke
adds further details and then joins Mark and Matthew with 'And then
shall they see the Son of Man coming in a cloud with power and great
glory.'

So it is clear that all three join together again in reporting what the
signs will be that Christ's coming is near. All three speak of the sign of
Israel's return under the simile of the fig tree, but again Luke adds
extra signs of the last days.

Let me give you a more literal translation of the Greek of Luke's
additions:

> Upon earth there will be an organisation (*sunoche*) of nations frustrated
> (*aporia*) by the roaring of the sea and surf, men fainting with fear (*pho-
> bias*) and dread at what is coming upon the inhabitants of the earth
> because the powers (*dynameis*) within uranium (*uranos*) will be unloosed.

I have pointed out elsewhere that it is the unloosing of uranium 238
from uranium 235 which is at the basis of all nuclear fission.
Governments are fearful that it might get into the wrong hands, the
hands of a tyrant. There are nearly 4,000 nuclear missiles in the world,
each one many times more powerful than the first nuclear bomb. Just
one of them aimed at one of our greatest cities could wipe it out. This
is where faith in the Lord's return can calm a believer's fear, 'For
except those days shall be shortened [by the Lord's coming], no flesh
shall be saved'.

I have translated *sunoche* as organisation. The word was used of
clubs or organisations, so one would not be overstretching the phrase
by translating it as a United Nations organisation trying to find a solution.

Luke adds words to the effect of, 'Don't you look around in fear. Look up instead, for your Saviour is coming from above. Your redemption is near.'

He is speaking of the redemption of the body by which Paul, his companion, described the body change which will come at the resurrection and rapture. It is Luke's equivalent of Matthew's and Mark's 'Jesus will send out his angels and gather his elect from the ends of earth and heaven'. Luke adds that the believer will escape by standing before Jesus, the Son of Man. That will be at 'the judgement seat of Christ' when he will reward his people for faithful service after their resurrection or rapture.

We have been studying the wonderful prophecy by the Lord Jesus Christ from his day to this – prophecy in the sense of foretelling the future. We have seen how, in the Gospels, he outlined the history of 2,000 years to our days. This is the meaning of Revelation 5 where only the Lamb who was slain was worthy to break open the seals of future history written down in the scroll.

SIX MAJOR SIGNS

Now let us sum up what the Lord Jesus said would happen after the times of the Gentiles when the Israelis ruled in Jerusalem again. I can count six major things which have been happening in the world since that event. Before looking at them, let me explain that the word in the Greek translated 'heavens' is the word which scientists use for the atom from which nuclear fission is triggered off. That means that Jesus was saying that in our days the cause of great fear would be nuclear fission.

The first sign is 'in the sun and the moon and the stars'. Haven't we all become very conscious of astronauts and space shuttles, moon walks and the possibility of star wars?

The second sign is what happens on earth. The words are 'and upon earth an organisation of nations meeting in agonising attempts to find a solution to the problems'. The word for 'an organisation of nations' is translated in the King James version as 'distress', but its primary meaning was an organisation to grapple with a problem like we saw in Bosnia (1993) and the Gulf War (1991).

Isaiah describes the roaring of the seas as symbolic of unrest. Unrest among the masses. Other prophecies enlarge upon this. This is the third sign. Paul says he was told by the Lord that in the last days there would be perilous times – greed for money, blasphemy, child and teenage disobedience, irreconcilable attitudes, forsaking God for pleasure and teachers saying the Bible is full of myths and dabbling in devil-inspired occult. James 5 says that in the last days there will be many crying out against unjust wages.

The fourth sign is given in Luke 21:26. He says that men's hearts will faint with fear through constant reviewing of the threat to the earth's inhabitants.

The fifth sign is fear itself. Nuclear fission has been with us for 40 years and at times fear has been worked up.

The sixth sign is the parable of the fig tree which referred to the Jewish nation, as we have seen. Jesus said that, when once again you see the fig tree (the Jewish nation) no longer withered, but beginning to sprout leaves, know that this time summer is near when it will bear fruit. This means that when Israel is back in the land again as a nation – that is, the buds growing – this time they will become fruitful for their Messiah. They will be convicted and believe on Jesus as their Messiah. It will happen when the Lord Jesus descends to the Mount of Olives. The Scriptures say that they will see him as the one whom they pierced and lament with deep repentance that he was the one they rejected. Zechariah says that there will be the conversion of the whole nation in one day and they will fill the earth with fruit. Isaiah 27:6: 'Israel will bud and blossom and fill the earth with fruit.' It follows the passage about the resurrection of believers and will be during the millennium when Christ reigns on earth after judging the nations.

Jesus said that this would be a sign to let all believers know that his coming is near, that he is even at the door. He said that, in that day, when the door is shut, many will stand outside knocking, but he will say, 'I never knew you, depart from me!' He says this in the parable which follows and then says, be ready, otherwise his coming will catch you unawares.

PROPHECY – CHRIST'S WORDS IN PARALLEL
Source: Revised Standard Version

Jesus Foretells History From His Ascension to His Return

General introduction up to AD 70

MATTHEW 24

[1]Jesus left the temple and was going away, when his disciples came to point out to him the buildings of the temple. [2]But he answered them, 'You see all these, do you not? Truly, I say to you, there will not be left here one stone upon another, that will not be thrown down.'

[3]As he sat on the Mount of Olives, the disciples came to him privately, saying, 'Tell us, when will this be, and what will be the sign of your coming and of the close of the age?'

MARK 13

[1]And as he came out of the temple, one of his disciples said to him, 'Look, Teacher, what wonderful stones and what wonderful buildings!' [2]And Jesus said to him, 'Do you see these great buildings? There will not be left here one stone upon another, that will not be thrown down.'

[3]And as he sat on the Mount of Olives opposite the temple, Peter and James and John and Andrew asked him privately, [4]'Tell us when will this be, and what will be the sign when these things are all to be accomplished?'

LUKE 21

[5]And as some spoke of the temple, how it was adorned with noble stones and offerings, he said, [6]'As for these things which you see, the days will come when there shall not be left here one stone upon another that will not be thrown down.' [7]And they asked him, 'Teacher, when will this be, and what will be the sign when this is about to take place?'

Three questions to answer
1. **The Fall of Jerusalem**
2. **'The Age'**
3. **Signs of the Second Coming**

Note: Luke's adverbs of time (marked *) show that these three events do not happen together. Verses 9, 12, 24, 28 and 31 help to clarify Matthew's and Mark's order of events.

[4]And Jesus answered them, 'Take heed that no one leads you astray. [5]For many will come in my name, saying, "I am the Christ," and they will lead many astray.

[5]And Jesus began to say to them, 'Take heed that no one leads you astray. [6]Many will come in my name, saying, "I am he!" and they will lead many astray. [7]And when you hear of wars and rumors of wars, do not be alarmed; this must take place, but the end is not yet.

[8]And he said, 'Take heed that you are not led astray; for many will come in my name, saying, "I am he!" and, "The time is at hand!" Do not go after them. [9]And when you hear of wars and tumults, **do not be terrified**; for this must **first*** take place, but the end is not yet.'

Prologue

⁶And you will hear of wars and rumors of wars; **see that you are not alarmed;** for this must take place, but **the end is not yet** (*The 3 events do not happen together.*) ⁷For nation will rise against nation, and kingdom against kingdom, and there will be famines and earthquakes in various places: ⁸all this is but the beginning of the sufferings. ⁹"Then they will deliver you up to tribulation, and put you to death; and you will be hated by all nations for my name's sake. ¹⁰And then **many will fall away,** and betray one another, and hate one another. ¹¹And many **false prophets will arise** and lead **many astray.** ¹²And because wickedness is multiplied, most men's **love will grow cold.** ¹³But he who endures to the end will be saved. ¹⁴**And this gospel of the kingdom will be preached throughout the whole world, as a testimony to all nations; and then the end will come.**

⁸For nation will rise against nation, and kingdom against kingdom; there will be earthquakes in various places, there will be famines; this is but the beginning of the sufferings.

⁹"But take heed to yourselves; for they will deliver you up to councils; and you will be beaten in synagogues; and you will stand before governors and kings for my sake, to bear testimony before them. ¹⁰And the gospel must first be preached to all nations. ¹¹And when they bring you to trial and deliver you up, do not be anxious beforehand what you are to say; but say whatever is given you in that hour, for it is not you who speak, but the Holy Spirit. ¹²And brother will deliver up brother to death, and the father his child, and children will rise against parents and have them put to death; ¹³and you will be hated by all for my name's sake. But he who endures to the end will be saved.

¹⁰Then he said to them, '**Nation will rise against nation,** and kingdom against kingdom; ¹¹there will be **great earthquakes,** and in various places famines and pestilences; and there will be terrors and great signs from heaven. ¹²But **before all this*** they will lay their hands on you and persecute you, delivering you up to the synagogues and prisons, and you will be brought before kings and governors for my name's sake. ¹³This will be a time for you to bear testimony. ¹⁴Settle it therefore in your minds, not to meditate beforehand how to answer; ¹⁵for I will give you a mouth and wisdom, which none of your adversaries will be able to withstand or contradict. ¹⁶You will be delivered up even by parents and brothers and kinsmen and friends, and some of you they will put to death; ¹⁷you will be hated by all for my name's sake. ¹⁸But not a hair of your head will perish. ¹⁹By your endurance you will gain your lives.

1. The Fall of Jerusalem
(a) Wars of the Jews Commence

Roman General Cestius surrounded Jerusalem in AD 66 and then withdrew. This was the start of the 3½ years of the Wars of the Jews which devastated the country from North to South. Thats why Jesus said 'don't return to Jerusalem.' Note: Luke gives adverbs of time vv.12,24,28,31. These help to clarify the order of events in Matthew and Mark.

LUKE Continued
AD 66. ²⁰"But when you see **Jerusalem surrounded by armies,** then know that its **desolation has come near.** ²¹Then let those who are in **Judea flee to the mountains,** and let those who are **inside the city depart,** and **let not those who are out in the country enter it again.**

(b) Jerusalem falls

MATTHEW 24	MARK 13	LUKE 21

AD 70: Fall of Jerusalem. [15]"So when you see **the desolating sacrilege** spoken of by the prophet Daniel, standing in the holy place (let the reader understand) (*Passover defiled*), [16]then let those who are in Judea flee to the mountains; [17]let him who is on the housetop not go down to take what is in his house; [18]and let him who is in the field not turn back to take his mantle. [19]And alas for those who are with child and for those who give suck in those days! [20]Pray that your flight may not be in **winter** or on a **sabbath**. (*Vespasian delays in AD 70 his attack until winter has passed owing to the death of Nero.*)

AD 70. [14]"But when you see the desolating sacrilege set up where it ought not to be (let the reader understand), then let those who are in Judea flee to the mountains; [15]let him who is on the housetop not go down, nor enter his house, to take anything away; [16]and let him who is in the field not turn back to take his mantle. [17]And alas for those who are with child and for those who give suck in those days! [18]Pray that it may not happen in winter.

2. 'The Age' AD 70 to 20th cent. (The Church Age)

[21]For then there will be **great tribulation** (*i.e. Jews*) such as has not been from the beginning of the world until now, no, and never will be. [22]And if those days had not been shortened, **no human being would be saved**; but for the sake of the **elect** those days **will be shortened**. *Matthew on how the 20th century affects the Elect.* [23]Then if any one says to you, 'Lo, here is the Christ!' or 'There he is!' do not believe it. [24]For **false Christs and false prophets** will arise and show great signs and wonders, so as to lead astray, if possible, even the **elect**. *Mohammet, AD 622.* [25]Lo, I have told you beforehand. [26]So, if they say to you, 'Lo, he is in the wilderness,' do not go out; if they say, 'Lo, he is in the **inner rooms**,' do not believe it. *Vatican throne is in inner rooms, AD 610.* [27]For **as the lightning** comes from the east and shines as far as the west, so will be the coming of the Son of man. [28]Wherever the body is, there the eagles will be gathered together.

[19]For in those days there will be such **tribulation** (i.e. Jews) as has not been from the beginning of the creation which God created until now, and **never will be**. [20]And if the Lord had not **shortened the days, no human being would be saved**; but for the sake of **the elect**, whom he chose, he **shortened the days**. [21]And then if anyone says to you, 'Look, here is the Christ!' or 'Look, there he is!' do not believe it. [22]False Christs and **false prophets** will arise and show signs and wonders, to lead astray if possible, **the** elect. [23]But take heed; I have told you all things beforehand.

[22]For these are days of vengeance, to fulfil all that is written. [23]Alas for those who are with child and for those who give suck in those days! For **great distress** (*i.e. tribulation of Jews*) shall be upon the earth and **wrath upon this people**; [24]they will fall by the edge of the sword, and be led **captive among all nations**; and Jerusalem will be trodden down by the Gentiles **until* the times of the Gentiles are fulfilled.** *The beginning and end of the Great Tribulation of Matthew 24:21,29 correlate with Luke's dispersion of the Jews v.24 AD 70 and their restoration to govern the city 1967. (Not to be confused with the Tribulation between the Rapture, and Christ's descent to the earth.) This, then, was the 'wrath on this people' for 19 centuries, during 'Times of the Gentiles'.*

3. The last signs to 2nd Coming

MATTHEW 24

29"Immediately **after the tribulation** of those days the sun will be darkened, and the moon will not give its light, and the stars will fall from heaven, and the powers of the heavens will be shaken; 30then will appear the sign of the Son of man in heaven, and then **all the tribes of the earth** will mourn, and they will **see the Son of man coming on the** clouds of heaven **with power** and great glory; 31and he will send out his angels with a loud trumpet call, and they will **gather his elect** from the four winds, from one end of heaven to the other.

32"From the fig tree learn its lesson: as soon as its branch becomes tender and puts forth its leaves, you know that summer is near. 33So also, **when you see** all these things, you know that he is **near, at the very gates.** 34Truly, I say to you, this generation will not pass away till all these things take place. 35Heaven and earth will pass away, but my words will not pass away.

MARK 13

24"But in those days, **after the tribulation** *(after 20 cents. Jewish tribulation Luke 21:22-24)*, the sun will be darkened, and the moon will not give its light, 25and the stars will be falling from heaven, and the powers in the heavens will be shaken. 26And then they will see the **Son of man coming in clouds** with **great power and glory.**

27And then he will send out the angels, and **gather his elect** from the four winds, from the ends of the earth to the ends of heaven. 28"From the fig tree learn its lesson: as soon as its branch becomes tender and puts forth its leaves, you know that summer is near. 29So also, when you see these things taking place, you know that he is near at the very gates. 30Truly, I say to you, this generation will not pass away before all these things take place. 31Heaven and earth will pass away, but **my words will not pass away.**

LUKE 21

25"And there will be **signs in sun and moon and stars**, and upon the earth **distress of nations** in perplexity at the roaring of the sea and the waves, 26men fainting with fear and with foreboding of what is coming on the world; for the powers of the **heavens will be shaken.** 27And then **they will see the Son of man coming in a cloud** with power and great glory. 28Now **when these things begin*** to take place, look up and raise your heads, because **your redemption is drawing near.'**
(Rapture)

29And he told them a parable: 'Look at the fig tree, and all the trees; 30as soon as they come out in leaf, you see for yourselves and know that the summer is already near. 31So also, **when you see** these things taking place, you know that **the kingdom of God is near:****(Millenium)*

³⁶'But of that day and hour **no one knows**, not even the angels of heaven, nor the Son, but the Father only. ³⁷As were the days of Noah, so will be the coming of the Son of man. ³⁸For as in those days before the flood they were eating and drinking, marrying and giving in marriage, until the day when Noah entered the ark, ³⁹and they did not know until the flood came and swept them all away, so will be the coming of the Son of man. ⁴⁰Then two men will be in the field; one is taken and one is left. ⁴¹Two women will be grinding at the mill; one is taken and one is left. ⁴²**Watch therefore**, for **you do not know** on what day your Lord is coming.

³²'But of **that day or that hour no one knows**, not even the angels in heaven, nor the Son, but only the Father.   ³³Take heed, watch; for you do not know when the time will come. ³⁴It is like a man going on a journey, when he leaves home and puts his servants in charge, each with his work, and commands the doorkeeper to be on the watch. ³⁵**Watch** therefore – for you do not know when the master of the house will come, in the evening, or at midnight, or at cockcrow, or in the morning – ³⁶lest he **come suddenly and find you asleep.** ³⁷And what I say to you I say to all: Watch.' *Matt. enlarges upon this by giving 3 parables, ch.25*
1. The wedding at the rapture (1 Cor. 15:23)
2. The reward of saved.
3. Descent to earth to judge nations (Zech. 14:5)

³²Truly, I say to you, this generation will not pass away till all has taken place. ³³Heaven and earth will pass away, but my words will not pass away.

³⁴'But **take heed to yourselves** lest your hearts be weighed down with dissipation and drunkenness and cares of this life, and that day comes upon you **suddenly like a snare**; ³⁵for it will come upon all who dwell upon the face of the whole earth. ³⁶But **watch at all times, praying** that you may have **strength to escape** all these things that will take place, and to stand before the Son of man.' *(The saved will stand before Jesus at the Rapture and thus escape tribulation.)*

SUMMARY

PRINCE OF PROPHETS, THE LORD JESUS CHRIST

Jesus answered 3 questions:
1. Jerusalem;
2. The end of the age;
3. Second coming.

Jesus foretells 20 centuries of history in Matt 24 and 25; Mark 13; Luke 21:

(1) When would Jerusalem fall?
- First the disciples would have a period to witness for Christ.
- Then there would be 2 stages in fall.
- AD 67 When 'Wars of Jews' began. Cestius surrounds city. Christians must flee whole country, because 3½ years war would commence; this is recorded by Luke alone.
- AD 70 Titus would reach Jerusalem at Passover. Christians must flee over roof tops, last minute (Matt and Mark). Jews' tribulation follows and Jerusalem trodden down (Luke 24:24).

(2) The end of the age would not be until 'times of the Gentiles' ended (Lk 24:24).
- Two main apostasies would last 1,260 years and 1,335: one in West 'inner rooms'; one in East 'prophet of desert' (Matt 24:26).
- The Jewish tribulation would last from the fall of Jerusalem until the second coming (Lk 21:22–24, Matt 24:21,29).

(3) Signs of Second Coming
- Space signs (Matt 24:29; Mk 13:24; Lk 21:25).
- Increase in earthquakes, famine and epidemics.
- World wars involving whole populations.
- Organisation of nations to solve problems (Lk 21:25).
- Uranium nuclear fission ('heavens' – Greek *uranos*) (Mk 13:25).
- Phobias and stress at threats and fears.
- Fig tree (Israel) reviving and returning to 'God's Land'.
- Sign of Son of Man coming in the clouds (Matt 25).
- Wedding of bride i.e. the saved (resurrection) (Matt 24:40–42).
- Rewards and places in coming Kingdom.
- Christ's throne on earth to judge nations.
- Kingdom on earth follows (Luke 21:31).

13 THE REVELATION OF JESUS CHRIST (1)
THE ARCH OF CHRIST'S TRIUMPH

At the entrance to Thessalonica in northern Greece, there is an ancient Arch of Triumph. It shows a series of pictures of the Emperor Galerius in AD 310. It was actually his last triumph because he was a cruel persecutor of Christians. Ironically, his huge tomb nearby became a meeting place for Christians and for a thousand years they met to praise and worship the triumphant Christ.

PANELS DEPICT CHRIST'S VICTORY

The last book in the Bible is like an arch of triumph – the triumph and victory of the Lord Jesus Christ. Likewise, there are panels of pictures. Each panel ends in a victory for Jesus. That is why the book is called 'The Revelation' – the Revelation of Jesus Christ. This is what the opening words call this remarkable book: 'The Revelation of Jesus Christ which God gave unto him to show to his servants.'

Did you notice that? God gave it to Jesus so that he could give it to his servants. What is more, there is a special blessing promised to him who reads it aloud (that is what the Greek means) and also a blessing to you who are reading it. One blessing is to see God's hand in history because Revelation foretold history from Christ's day to modern times.

I have said that each panel ends in victory for Jesus. Like that Arch of Triumph, the pictures are very symbolic. We may not understand all the symbols, but the message is clear. It is: Jesus Christ reigns! He reigns in heaven and he will reign on earth.

Look then at Revelation as a series of panels on an arch of triumph and remember that each panel represents a phase in history. Look at how each panel ends:

- The first panel ends in Revelation 3 showing that Jesus triumphs in the **Church**. 'Him who overcomes, I will grant to sit with me in my Throne.' (3:21)
- The second panel ends with triumph over the **Roman Empire**. 'The kings of the earth said . . . hide us from the face of him who sits upon the Throne.' (6:16)
- The third panel ends in triumph over the **world powers**. 'The seventh angel blew the trumpet . . . and great voices said, "The king-

Figure 13.1. Arch of Triumph of Galerius, now the entrance to Thessalonica, Greece. Each panel depicts battles leading up to victory. This is similar to the four panels of Revelation if interpreted as Christ's triumphal arch. Seven episodes in each panel lead to victory for Christ and his faithful ones, in the four main stages of Christian history.

doms of this world have become the kingdoms of the Lord and his Christ and he will reign for ever and ever." ' (11:15)
- The fourth panel ends in triumph over **false religions.** 'His name is called, 'The Word of God' . . . out of his mouth goes a sharp sword

to smite the nations . . . His name is King of kings and Lord of lords. The false prophet which deceived and the beast were thrown alive into the lake of fire and sulphur'. (19:13)

So there we see that this book of God's revelation consists of four highly symbolic panels which end in the universal victory of the Lord Jesus Christ, King of kings and Lord of lords. 'And unto him every knee shall bow and every tongue confess that Jesus Christ is Lord.'

The Arch's Four Panels

When I was looking at the Arch of Triumph erected by conqueror Galerius to record his victories, I noticed there were several panels carved in the sides to show a series of victories which led up to his empire. The last book in the Bible, similar to that earthly arch of victory, has four panels of picturesque symbols. Each panel is a story which ends with the triumph of Christ. This victory over the forces of evil is in four stages which end in the final glorious proclamation. The Lord Jesus reigns and brings blessing to every faithful believer and eventually to the whole world.

As I studied the panels on that earthly triumphal arch, I saw there were some symbols which I didn't understand; but other pictures were quite clear in their meaning. For example, some soldiers were mounted on horses just as in the Revelation panel and at the end of each panel the emperor was in his victory chariot. It is the same in the book of Revelation. The Lord Jesus is on his triumphant throne or in his victory procession at the end of each panel. Then comes the final conquest and his eternal reign.

- The first panel which portrays victory in the Church has **lampstands** as symbols.
- The second panel portraying victory over the Roman Empire has the **seals** and **horses** as the symbols.
- The third, portraying triumph over the whole world has **trumpets** sounding each stage.
- The fourth panel, depicted by the **bowls** (cauldrons) of anger, proclaims the victory of truth over false religions and the unmasking of Satan's deceptions.

Now, each panel is divided into seven – seven lampstands, seven seals, seven trumpets and seven bowls of anger. These four panels and the seven symbols in each sum up the whole book of Revelation.

This story of triumph spans history from Pentecost to judgement day. It is a prophesied history from the cross to the crown. It is God's pre-planned purpose from the beginning of the gospel to the end of

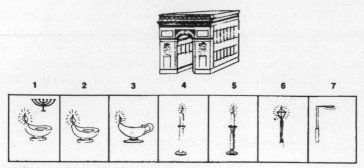

1. Church history AD 96 to 20th Century

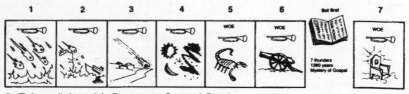

2. Roman history AD 96 to 313

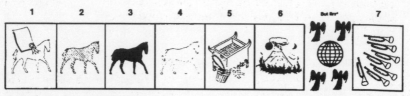

3. False religions 6th Century to Second Coming

4. Reply to false religions 1495 to Second Coming

Figure 13.2. Drawings of the four 'panels' of Revelation's 'Arch of Triumph' as suggested by the author, depicting seven lamps (the Church), seven seals (Roman Empire), seven trumpets (world powers) and seven bowls (divine responses to false religions).

the universe.

To the earthbound thinker, life is a kaleidoscope of catastrophe; but if lifted up to heaven, as John was, each panel of perplexing pictures weaves into a pattern of God's purpose fulfilled and Christ glorified. It moves forward in time until the trumpets blow and the voices proclaim, 'The kingdoms of this world have become the kingdoms of the Lord and of his Christ!'

All evil and wickedness and filth are swept away and thrown into the furnace. All pain and sorrow are turned to joy. How wonderfully each phase terminates in a glorious song by millions of heaven's choristers, for example 15:3:

> They sing the song of Moses and the Lamb saying, 'Great and marvellous are your works, Lord God Almighty. Just and true are your ways O King of the ages . . . All nations will come and worship you.'

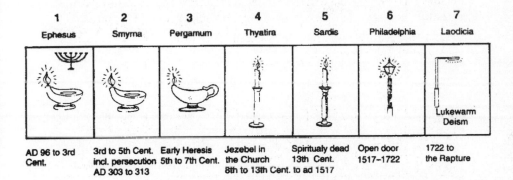

1	2	3	4	5	6	7
Ephesus	Smyrna	Pergamum	Thyatira	Sardis	Philadelphia	Laodicia

| AD 96 to 3rd Cent. | 3rd to 5th Cent. incl. persecution AD 303 to 313 | Early Heresis 5th to 7th Cent. | Jezebel in the Church 8th to 13th Cent. | Spiritualy dead 13th Cent. to ad 1517 | Open door 1517–1722 | 1722 to the Rapture |

Figure 13.3. Panel of the seven lampstands in Revelation's 'Arch of Triumph' depicting the seven Church periods of witness AD 96 to modern times.

The Lampstand Panel

What an insight it is to visualise the book of Revelation as four panels on a triumphant arch. Many of these old arches show the history leading up to each victory. In the book of Revelation, the first panel is a row of seven lampstands. They foretell the history of the Church.

You can guess why lamps should symbolise Christians. The Lord Jesus said a Christian should be like a lamp shining for Jesus. In the tabernacle of Moses, there were seven lamps on a lampstand. Thus, in Revelation, there are seven lamps. The oil symbolised the Holy Spirit. God told Moses that the wick had to be trimmed each morning and each evening. Thus a Christian has to trim his or her lamp of witness each day so that it doesn't give a smoky witness. Start the day with God in prayer and a Bible passage and get strength and guidance. Then ask for fresh infilling by the Holy Spirit because, as Paul says, the Christian is a leaky vessel. Then at the end of the day, look at the past day with God's help. Note the successes and thank the Lord; note the failures and say sorry to the Lord. Thus the daily walk is a light of witness which is trimmed morning and night for bright shining.

All through the Bible, the lamp is a symbol of Christian witness. Jesus asks, 'Do you light your lamp and then hide your light under a bucket?' 'No,' he says, 'you put it on a lampstand to bring the light of truth to others.'

The lamps then, of the first four chapters of Revelation, are Christian witness of the churches by the Holy Spirit down the centuries.

But does the passage support that interpretation? Yes, chapter 1 verse 20 says, 'The seven lampstands are the seven churches'. At the end of each message to one of the churches, the Lord says this: 'Hear what the Spirit says to the churches.'

On that panel with the row of seven lamps, the first lamp shines brightly, but, as you go along the row, the wicks get smokier and smokier until, in the middle, the light has almost gone out. Then comes a revival and the light shines to the world again, but the light of the last lamp is spoilt by unbelief. This was a prophesied history of the Church's witness down the centuries until the return of Christ.

But didn't these churches exist in the first century? Yes, but Jesus says there is also a mysterious interpretation. It confirms that prophecy is fulfilled in two ways – literally, to actual things and symbolically, to the future. There is one interpretation for seven churches in the first century BC and a second interpretation for the Church down the ages. The text tells us this as we shall see.

The Timing

One night, although it was very dark when I was going home, a row of street lamps were spaced along the pavement to light my way until I reached home.

The lamps of church witness in the first four chapters of Revelation are like that. Each lamp represents a period in history during which the Church is lighting the path for pilgrims making for home. Heaven is their home and this home of heaven is depicted after the seventh lamp.

But does the text hint that this is church history from the first century to the second coming of Christ? Yes, Revelation 1:19 does. The Lord Jesus says to John the apostle, 'Write down what you see. It refers to what exists now and also what is to take place later on.'

So then, the first lamp referred to the time when John was writing. The succeeding lamps we take as referring to the following 19 centuries until finally, Christ comes to judge his Church when they rise to meet him. This is symbolised by John being caught up to heaven after the seventh lamp just as the Church will be caught up at the coming of Christ. What is more, the whole book of Revelation covers history (as Jesus said) from when John was writing until the final judgement day described at the end of the book.

I referred to the street lamps on my way home in the dark. The first lamp was shining brightly, but, as I walked along, I found that vandals had damaged the street lamps in the centre. In fact, the one right in the centre was so badly smashed that it had almost gone out. I could hardly see! I nearly tripped up on the kerb.

The Lord said that, down the centuries, the lamps of the Church of the day will suffer. Satan will send his vandals to spoil and smash the witness. In the Middle Ages that lamp was almost completely smashed. The light of truth will grow so dim that many will trip into error and perish in the gutter.

But can't lamps be repaired? Those vandals will even try to stop that! Revived Christians who attempt it will be beaten up by Satan's agents. They will attack them and even kill them and leave them lying in the street. That is what we are told in Revelation 11:4:

> The two lampstands which stand before the Lord of the earth . . . when they have finished their testimony, the beast of the bottomless pit . . . will kill them and their dead bodies will lie in the street called Sodom where their Lord was crucified.

Why did the spiritual vandals attack those making the light shine again? Because the light would show up their errors.

Lampstand Removed

As I was walking down the street where some of the street lamps had been damaged, one lamp-post had been run into by a lorry and demolished.

The Lord Jesus said the lamps of Revelation represented the churches' witness down the centuries. He said to the church at Ephesus: 'Remember how you have fallen. If you do not repent, I will come and remove your lampstand from its place unless you repent.'

I visited the remains of that church. It is near the coast of western Turkey. How sad to see it all in ruins. Not a soul worships there or even lives there. Not a soul gets baptised there even though the baptism trough was there. Three stone steps went down into where the water of baptism should be, but no saved person had been baptised for centuries.

The ruins of that double basilica of Ephesus showed that, in the past, the buildings had to be extended. This was to hold the great crowds of rejoicing witnessing Christians; but now all was silent. The warning of Jesus had been implemented; their lamp of witness was removed. Only the bones of John the apostle rest in the tomb below the iron grid. It was he who wrote down these warnings of Christ. He now awaits the resurrection.

In Revelation 11, the two lampstands of Christian witness also awaited the resurrection. They represented Christians witnessing in Sodom Street. Yes, that is what the text actually says. Their lampstands were smashed in Sodom Street. They were attacked and killed because their words called for repentance. These tormented the unwilling listeners. But they did not wait for the resurrection in vain, for according to verse 11:

> The breath of life from God entered them and they stood up on their feet and great fear fell on those who saw them. Then they heard a loud voice from heaven saying to them 'come up here!' And in the sight of their foes they went up to heaven in a cloud.

Look at the street sign on your road. Does it say 'Sodom Street'? Today, the true Christian is witnessing in Sodom Street. Verse 8 tells you that is symbolic. Are you witnessing in Sodom Street today? You remember all about Sodom in Genesis 19. Sodom was the city which was destroyed by God for homosexuality. Jesus said, 'As it was in the days of Sodom, so shall it be in the day when I return to judge.'

We have all heard of AIDS. Paul calls homosexuality 'shameful acts which get a penalty in the sinners' own bodies'. Some false Christians have excused it. Their lamp will be removed.

Smart Error

Remember how I walked along the street of lamp-posts Those halfway along were damaged by vandals, but the last lamp in the street was very smart. That was because the house on the corner was occupied by a rich household. However, although the lamp was repaired and painted up, the glass on the side near the house was blacked out. Why was that?

It was because the bedroom was near. Those asleep did not want to be awakened by a bright light. What a good picture of a church spiritually asleep and unwilling to be awakened, especially if it clings to error!

A church in error usually has a high opinion of itself. This was so with Laodicea which Jesus rebuked in Revelation 3. That church portrays the seventh and last church of this age. The church of Laodicea was inflated with intellectual pride and unbelief. Jesus accused it of saying: 'I am rich; I have prospered; I have need of nothing!'

But what did Jesus say of it? He said: 'You are lukewarm, spiritually blind and lacking evangelical zeal. You question God's creation, you question whether I am a truthful witness in the Gospel records! I am shut outside your church door.'

Yes, this church represented the seventh and last lamp of witness down the centuries. It exists now in our time just before the coming of Christ to judge his Church. Everyone knows of church leaders who have disbelieved in creation and questioned the accuracy of the Gospel records. To them Christ says, 'I am the true witness'. These are the words of Christ to Christendom of our time, just before his return. This is shown in Revelation 3:21 which refers to the rapture. Here it says that he who repents, he who opens the door to let Christ in, he who overcomes, will rise to meet Christ in the air and will sit with Christ on his throne in heaven.

I have said, a church in error usually has a high opinion of itself. Jesus warned the Church of two major errors which would eclipse the Church's witness – they are ritualism without truth, like the Pharisees and scepticism of the Bible, like the Sadducees.

This last church of the age would suffer greatly from the latter – scepticism of the Sadducees. They did not believe in miracles or the resurrection and they did not accept all of the Bible. They are with us today. That is why the Lord of the Church reminds them that he is the beginning of God's creation and the truthful witness of the Gospels. Jesus described them as like yeast in a loaf being baked. Now, yeast works its way into all parts of the loaf of the Church until the whole is leavened, so today this unbelief has worked its way into almost every level of the Church.

'You are lukewarm!' declares the Lord. In other words, they objected to enthusiasm, they disliked evangelism and they resisted revival. Jesus says, 'It is because I love you that I rebuke you for these things.'

The Lamb Rules History

Have you despaired over history? All the wars and bloodshed; all the cruelty and callousness and the meaninglessness of it all. The book of Revelation gives meaning to world events. There is a vision in chapter 4 in which we see that it is only Jesus who gives meaning to history.

John is given a vision of people weeping over the affairs of men, crying over the apparent meaninglessness of it all. The strong angel presents the scroll of history – the history which is about to be unfolded. Read Revelation 5:3:

> And no one in heaven or on earth or under the earth was able to open the scroll or to look into it and I wept much that no one was found worthy to open the scroll or to look into it. Then one of the elders said to me, 'Weep not. Lo, the Lion of the tribe of Judah, the Root of David, has conquered, so that he can open the scroll and its seven seals.'

So John wept but only until he saw that it was the Lamb of God who gave meaning to history. This we shall see in chapter 6 as the seals of each page of the book are broken.

THE VISION OF GOD'S THRONE

The next scene shows who it was who was able to see history this way. It was those who could sing a new song. You can see God's hand in history only if you can sing the new song of redemption: a new song from a new heart changed by the Lord Jesus. That can be you if you trust the Lord Jesus Christ as your Saviour. He is the Lamb of God who can cleanse your heart and open your eyes to the significance of all that is happening around you. This is what they sing in chapter 5 of Revelation:

> You are worthy to take the book and to open the seals, for you were slain and have redeemed us to God by your blood out of every family and tongue and people and nation. And you have made us kings and priests to our God and we shall reign on earth.

The Lamb gives meaning to history. Perhaps you are concerned for the future and want to change it. Here is what Christabel Pankhurst, leader of the women's suffragette movement said in her book *The Lord Cometh*:

> Like so many others, I have lived in an atmosphere of illusion, thinking that once certain obstacles were removed, especially the disfranchisement of women, it would be full-steam ahead for the ideal social and international order. I have even thought that, after its tragic interruption by the War, the march of progress would, if the Allies were victorious, proceed according to the pre-war programme. But when, in 1918, I really faced the facts, I saw the War was not 'a war to end war' but was, despite our coming victory, a beginning of sorrows. Considering the issues, the events, and the currents and cross-currents of the War, and relating it, also, to the history of times past, and having regard to the way things go and ever have gone, even in times of peace, this is what I realised as I never had realised it before: it is not laws, nor institutions, nor any national or international machinery that are at fault, but human nature itself. I had a sharp and terrible vision of the fact that the same passions, greed, ambitions, that caused past Wars, including that of 1914 would continue to rend and tear the nations. The lust for power, especially for world power, would, I saw, be a continuing curse – world empire being desired and contended for by one claimant after another, whether by some class, some nation, or some race, and whether led by an individual or prompted by a collective will-to-power. Just then, by what seemed a chance discovery in a bookshop, I came across writings on prophecy which pointed out that in the Bible there are oracles foretelling and diagnosing the world's ills, and promising that

they shall be cured. Until that day I had taken the prophecies of the Bible no more seriously than a great many other people still do take them. I had simply ignored them, never thinking that they had any bearing whatever upon the world problems of our time. But now I eagerly followed up the clue which this bookshop discovery had given me. What did I read? That God foreknew, and has foretold in the Bible, the evils of this Age, and their gathering and darkening as the Age draws to its close – above all, that he had promised the return of Jesus Christ, to whom he has reserved the Imperial Sceptre of the world. Thus, world power will cease to be the cause of fratricidal human strife, for it will be exercised in divine love and wisdom by the Son of God. 'Ah! that is the solution!' My heart stirred to it. My practical political eye saw that this Divine Programme is absolutely the only one that can solve the international, social, political or moral problems of the world.

Throne Room of Heaven

I watched the glitter and gold of the Queen opening Parliament. It was relayed on television. First, we saw the golden state coach pulled by powerful horses in colourful harness. Then in Parliament we saw the sovereign on the throne. How the crown jewels flashed with iridescent colour. Around the Queen were gathered her subjects. She held in her hand a document to read out to them. It was the future policy of the Government.

Chapters 4 and 5 in Revelation give us an even more glorious picture. It is a glimpse into the throne room of heaven with all the colour of precious stones and the Majesty of God.

> And lo, a throne stood in heaven with one seated upon the throne and he who sat there appeared like jasper and carnelian and round the throne was a rainbow that looked like emerald.

Notice that, as in other scriptures, God is too holy and dazzling for man to look upon. 'No one can look upon me and live,' said the Lord. So the glory of God can never be fully described.

From the throne came flashes of lightning and the rumbling of thunder and voices as when Moses received the Ten Commandments upon Mount Sinai.

Did you see the Olympic torch placed in its bowl and its flame burn bright and symbolic? Seven torches like these burnt before the Throne of God. But what are these creatures surrounding the Throne? They are full of eyes. Eyes in the front, eyes in the back and full of eyes all around and inside. It seems to say that nothing can escape the scrutiny of God. He is surrounded by screens reporting everything like the nerve centre of TV control. He sees all and controls the universe. Like the Queen, he too holds a document in his hand. It contains his future policy for the universe. Man's government has failed through greed, cruelty and sin. Only the love of the cross will bring goodness and happiness, so the document is handed to the Lamb of God. But, behold, the Lamb is a Lion – the Lion of the Tribe of Judah, the root and family tree of King David.

John is startled at the sight and what does he see? He says, 'He saw a Lamb looking as if it had been slain.' Oh what a moving sight for sinners seeking salvation. The gaping wounds, the thorn-pierced brow, the gashes in hands and feet.

The creatures around the throne sing, 'Holy, holy, holy is the Lord God Almighty, who lives for ever and ever.'

God's subjects then fall down before him. All they have, they owe to him even their crowns, so they cast their golden crowns down before the Throne and worship the Creator of the whole universe.

> Worthy are you, our Lord and God, to receive glory and honour and power, for you created all things, and by your will they existed and were created. (Revelation 4:11)

Symbols of the Gospels

What an inspiring picture we had from Revelation 4 and 5. It was a sight of the Lord God on his Throne in heaven. Jewelled colour sparkled, frightening flashes of lightning preceded the rumbling of things to come. The rainbow of divine promise surrounded the throne as the sovereign Lord God opened his parliament and issued his document for good and happy government for the world and universe.

But what were those mystical living creatures around his Throne, upholding a calm sea of crystal? There were four of them. One like a lion, another like an ox, then one with the face of a man and the fourth like a flying eagle.

The early Christians knew what they represented. They represented the four Gospels. That early discernment was handed down the centuries not only by their writings, but in the stained-glass windows of many a church. Look for them when you enter an ancient church. I

Figure 13.4. The symbols depicted in Revelation 4 and 5 following the panel of the seven lamp-stands. See Figure 8.1.

have yet to tell you of their profound significance. Why did the early Christians think these four living creatures represented the four Gospels of Matthew, Mark, Luke and John?

It was because Solomon's temple and Ezekiel's vision tell you so. They describe the same creatures, the lion, the ox, the man and the eagle and now in Revelation we see them again. But Revelation goes further. It shows their effect on world history.

In Solomon's temple, the great laver or huge bowl of water was supported by these four symbols. Why? Because the Bible tells you that the bowl represents the Holy Scriptures and all Scripture is based upon the life of Christ. That record of Jesus is given to us from four angles. The lion of Judah, a king (Matthew), the manhood of Mark, the ox of atonement by Luke and the divinity of the eagle soaring to heaven by John.

How does the Bible show that this great bowl represents the Scriptures? Because Moses was told to make it out of mirrors and James says that when we look into the mirror of God's Word, it shows up our muddy marks, and the water in the bowl is there to wash away those blemishes. So, as we read the Bible, we should correct the faults in our character.

Why then does this bowl – representing the Bible – have the four Gospels as its base? It is because it depicts Christ in all the Scriptures. Christ is foretold and described in the Old Testament before he came and he is recorded in the New Testament when he came. The Lord Jesus proved that after his resurrection in Luke 24. I quote from verses 25–27 and 44–47:

> Jesus said to them, 'How foolish you are, and how slow of heart to believe all that the prophets have spoken! Did not the Christ have to suffer these things and then enter his glory?' And beginning with Moses and all the Prophets, he explained to them what was said in all the Scriptures concerning himself . . . 'This is what I told you while I was still with you. Everything must be fulfilled that is written about me in the Law of Moses, the Prophets and the Psalms.' Then he opened their minds so they could understand the Scriptures. He told them 'This is what is written; the Christ will suffer and rise from the dead on the third day, and repentance and forgiveness of sins will be preached in his name to all nations, beginning at Jerusalem.'

When Christians are faithful to that gospel, it does and will change society and nations.

THE SEVEN SEALS

Billy Graham is fond of saying that he can 'hear the hoof-beats of the horses of the Apocalypse'. What does he mean? He is looking at all the

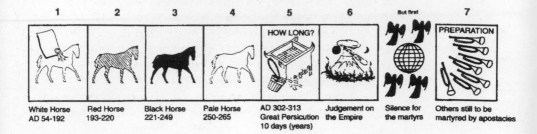

Figure 13.5. Panel of the seven seals in Revelation's 'Arch of Triumph' depicting Christ's triumph over three centuries of **Roman persecution**, AD 96 to AD 313. Note the symbol in seal 5 of prayers poured out, answered when the Roman Empire was christianised.

signs of the times foretold in the Bible and sees that the triumphant coming of Christ is near. Soon he will come to reward the saved and to judge the unsaved.

Those horses of Revelation feature in the first four seals. The Lamb of God breaks these seals to open the pages of history. They appear immediately after the saved are caught up to heaven, just as John was taken up into heaven in his vision.

But you will remember that I have said that Revelation is like most prophecy. It is fulfilled in two ways, symbolically and then literally.

Taken literally, all of Revelation from chapter 6 onwards can be fulfilled in the future. Misapplication of science has imperilled our planet just as Revelation says. The seas can be poisoned and one-third of the fish die. Chemical warfare can destroy the vegetation and trees, germ warfare can inflict humans with terrible sores so that one-third die, nuclear fission can destroy mountains and wreck the continents. Even the disaster of Chernobyl, which means 'bitterness', is mentioned by name in the text of Ukrainian translations, the very place where a nuclear disaster happened. It is in Revelation 8:11, 'A great star fell from heaven blazing like a torch – its name is Bitterness [Wormwood – AV]. Many men died of the bitter contaminated water.' But Revelation has also been fulfilled symbolically in past history. This is a fascinating fact which many expositors ignore.

Where Revelation 3 is taken as the last church period of our times, the rest of Revelation can happen literally in the world's future But those seven churches in chapters 1–3 also actually existed in the first century and so the history depicted in the following chapters also began to happen in John's day of the first century AD and continued to be fulfilled as the centuries passed and made history up to our present times. That means that Revelation 6 to 18 has also been fulfilled symbolically or in parable form. If the first panel of sevens was symbolic past history, then we should expect the other three panels of sevens also to be symbolic past history from the first century to modern times.

Have patience with me and I will show you that this was so. It will help you to understand the book of Revelation better. It will save you from falling into so many of the pitfalls that others have fallen into. It will save you from confusion about the tribulation. It will save you from fanciful interpretations which don't relate to historical facts. It will show you how the cannons and gunfire of the Turks in chapter 9 led to the fall of Constantinople and how that led to the open Bible of the Reformation in chapter 10. It will show you how the Turkish Empire dried up in modern times to leave Palestine free for the return of Israel in the twentieth century.

Above all, remember what Revelation teaches both in the future and in history – Jesus Christ reigns. He opens the pages of history as he breaks the seals, for he alone is worthy because he alone has died to save.

THE HORSES OF THE APOCALYPSE

We shall see in Chapter 16 how the four horses of Revelation 6 will be fulfilled futuristically. Now we will see how they were fulfilled in the Roman history of the first three centuries. They depict the four periods of Rome in which the gospel was first preached.

We have already seen how it is the Lamb – Jesus – who opens each seal. Also it is the living creatures who say 'Come!' The living creatures represented the Gospels, you remember. All the early Church knew that. So then, the fact that it is the living gospel which says 'Come!' shows that you must see how the gospel conquers the mighty Roman Empire itself.

The **first horse is white** and it had a bow and it went forth to conquer. The horse was displayed with the eagle on the Roman war standard. The famous historian, Edward Gibbon, in *The Decline and Fall of the Roman Empire* (1760) describes how the Emperor Nerva from Crete in AD 96 had a bow as his symbol; so we read in Revelation 6:2. This emperor and his successors, Trajan and Hadrian, certainly did conquer. They extended the boundaries into Mesopotamia, Romania; and Hadrian built the famous wall between Scotland and England.

The horse was white, signifying peace and prosperity. Gibbon says that this period from AD 96 to 183 was the happiest and most peaceful period of Roman history.

Why did God allow this? It was when the gospel made its first impact. God arranged that the good news could have free course to get

Figure 13.6. The conquering white horse of Revelation 6:2 with bow and crown.

established from one end of the empire to the other, carried by Christians along the straight Roman roads guarded by soldiers.

That is why it is the living gospel creature representing the gospel which says 'Come!' The Gospels were to invite many to come to the Lord Jesus to be saved. Yet after a hundred years, many failed to respond. Prosperity made them feel no need. So the next Roman period is war. Yes, when Jesus breaks the seal and opens the next page of history, the **second horse is red** – red for war. Revelation 6:4 says, 'He who sat on the red horse took peace from the earth . . . he was given a great sword.'

Gibbon describes how in AD 193, Severus established a military regime. This tyrant attacked public property, broke every principle of law and justice and civil warfare prevailed for 50 years.

Then Jesus breaks a third seal and opens the next page of history. It was symbolised by **a black horse** (Fig 13.8) 'and he who sat on it had a pair of scales in his hands'. A voice said, 'A day's wage for a loaf of bread, but don't hurt the oil and wine'.

Gibbon says, in this period taxation became crushing, food became dear for the poor, but the luxuries of oil and wine were available for the rich. The empire was ruined.

For this period, too, the creature representing the living gospel says 'Come!' Come to Christ, come to value spiritual things. 'Man shall not

Figure 13.7. The destroying red horse of Revelation 6:4 with fire and sword depicting the end of peace.

live by bread alone, but by every word which proceeds out of the mouth of God.'

We come now to **the fourth horse**. This accurately describes the conditions in the Roman Empire from AD 250 onwards.

The Lamb – the Lord Jesus – breaks the fourth seal and so opens this next page of Roman history. This is symbolised in Revelation 6:8 by a pale green horse (that is what the Greek means). I quote: 'He who sat upon him was named death and hell which followed him (Fig 13.9). One quarter of the people were killed by the sword and hunger and death and wild beasts.'

This prophecy was fulfilled to the hilt. Gibbon says that from AD 250 to 265, one quarter of the population died. I quote: 'Furious plagues raged in every city. As many as 5,000 died every day in the city of Rome.'

In Dr Atkinson's book *War with Satan*, Wickliffe Press (1940), page 65 reads: 'From AD 250 onwards, a quarter of the population of the Roman Empire must have perished and its numbers reduced correspondingly. Many people in destitution fled from their homes. Deserted farms were to be found everywhere. Pestilence contributed to the decline.'

He quotes from *Cambridge Ancient History*, Vol. XII p. 268: 'It is

Figure 13.8. The black horse of Revelation 6:5 with scales depicting scarcity and poverty.

easy to see how all this catastrophe and trouble helped forward the gospel. The fearful troubles showed the vanity and failure of earthly government and also tended to soften hearts and turn people everywhere to the rest and peace offered by the Christian gospel.'

This was God's reply to a great outburst of persecution against the Christians. Yet, now, in spite of all the sufferings of martyred Christians, more were converted to Christ than ever before. Also, the plagues and murders made people think of eternity and the wonderful example of Christians being martyred won the admiration of many. They saw the joy with which the saved accepted torture and death with a smile for the Lord they loved.

So you see, this famine and death all worked out for the spread of the gospel. That is why it is the creature of the living gospel who says 'Come!' Come and see what is behind history. People in prosperity felt no need of God, so drought and death threatens. Then they became open to hear the gospel say 'Come!' Actually the words 'and see' are not in the original. It is just an invitation to come.

Come unto me all you who are weary and heavy laden and I will give you rest. Take my yoke upon you and learn of me for I am gentle and lowly of heart and you will find rest unto your souls. (Matthew 11:28–29)

Figure 13.9. The pale (green) horse of Revelation 6:8 with power to bring death.

Blood of the Martyrs

We are seeing how the symbols of Revelation were fulfilled in past history as well as being fulfilled in the future. We are now at the beginning of the fourth century. The horses of the Roman Empire are at an end. These were confined to the first four seals. The horse of famine and death ended in the time of the persecution by Emperor Diocletian. His final attempt to wipe out Christianity was in the years AD 303 to 313. This is called 'the Great Persecution'. The earlier persecutions by the Roman Empire were bad enough, but Diocletian's was the worst and the last. This ten years' tribulation relates to the ten days referred to in the second church period of Smyrna prophesied in Revelation 2:10.

Consequently, **the fifth seal**, following, shows you the triumph of all those who had been martyred for the Word of God and the testimony of Jesus Christ. You see their souls in heaven. Their seals are under the altar and they cry 'How long will it be before the blood of the martyrs brings judgement upon the persecutors?'

A surprising answer is given. This answer opens up an astonishing insight into the uncovering of the rest of history from the fifth century to modern times. Before we look at that, we will see why the martyrs cried out at such horrific slaughter.

Under Diocletian, there was an acting emperor whose name was

Figure 13.10. Galerius' tomb, Thessalonica, Greece. Galerius was probably the cruellest persecutor of Christians. He built this tomb for himself but it became a Christian church when he died in AD 311.

Galerius. Galerius had satanic hatred of all Christians. He thought that if his efforts were cruel enough, Christianity would be wiped out. He was wrong as many a world ruler has been since. In fact, the saying prevailed, 'The blood of the martyrs was the seed of the church' as recorded by Tertullian (c. AD 160–225).

Galerius persuaded Diocletian to issue an edict in AD 303: all churches had to be destroyed and all Bibles burnt. A Christian soldier tore down the edict. He was immediately arrested and roasted alive over a slow fire. A second edict was issued. By this, all clergy and ministers of the gospel were arrested and imprisoned or executed. A third edict was even more ferocious. They were to be tortured to death or renounce and curse Christ. A fourth edict then extended this to all Christians. Here is a quote from history: 'Men, women and children were tortured, scalded or roasted alive. Limbs were pulled out of joint and their flesh was torn by sharp instruments.' In spite of this, Christians willingly suffered for their Lord. For he had suffered for their sins upon the cross.

An example is recorded of a girl aged 17 named Theodosia. She went to a magistrate to plead for three Christians, fully knowing the consequences. She was seized and tortured. The flesh was scraped off the sides of her body. Even in this agony, she witnessed to her Saviour. As she was dying, she was thrown into the sea to drown.

As the pagan public saw these sufferings, it had the opposite effect to that intended. Thousands enquired about the way of salvation. Galerius, cruel persecutor of Christians, built a tomb for himself. It became a church for Christians holding 3,000. (After 1,100 years, it was changed into a mosque.) Then Constantine defeated Galerius. He quickly issued the famous Edict of Milan in AD 313. This liberated all Christians and proclaimed that Christianity was to be the state religion. It is thought that the ancient Hymn of Praise to the Holy Trinity was composed at this time – the Te Deum. It rejoiced in the victory of suffering as thousands of Christians came out of prison.

> We praise you O God; We acknowledge you to be the Lord, the holy martyr; praise you!

The four horses of pagan Rome ended at this fifth seal. How had Christianity conquered Roman paganism – not by the sword, but as Revelation says:

> They overcame by the blood of the Lamb and by the word of their testimony and they loved not their lives unto death.

Surprise Rest 'Until'

We have seen how the fourth horse of Revelation chapter 6 ended paganism in Rome in AD 313. We saw how that terrible time of torture for Christians which lasted for a further ten years ended with the conquest by Constantine the Great. We saw how 'the blood of the martyrs became the seed of the church', because 'they loved not their lives unto death and overcame by the Blood of the Lamb and the word of their testimony'.

Even before the end of persecution, it is recorded that as many as 40 per cent of the empire had accepted Christianity and this was in the face of persecution. Next, the edict of Emperor Constantine encouraged everybody to be Christianised. But there was a surprise coming. We see this in **the fifth seal**; we hear the martyrs in heaven cry out: 'How long, O Lord, holy and true, will you hesitate to judge!'

A surprising answer is given – an answer which pointed to the next twelve centuries. They were told to rest until Christians later in history were also tortured and martyred. Even more were going to be done to death. This time it would be by false religions. This was all part of the satanic hate (in the words of Revelation). The dragon Satan remains furious with those who keep the commandments of God and have the testimony of Jesus Christ . . . 'until their fellow servants and their brothers are martyred as they were' (Revelation 6:11).

After the Roman Empire officially accepted Christianity, more born-again Christians were slaughtered by the false christ and the false prophet than all those killed by the Caesars. Millions were massacred in the name of religion. In one day alone, St Bartholomew's Day, one million French Huguenots were killed. Then, in the East, millions were killed by the Moslem invasions.

Have you noticed that little word 'until'? The souls martyred for Jesus were told to rest 'until'. That word 'until' covers over twelve centuries. During that time, millions more were to lay down their lives for Jesus. Their testimony will warn many of judgement to come. This is depicted by the next seal, after which there is silence – not a two minute silence, but half an hour's silence – a silence in which you can ask yourself the question – a question of values: If we were to sacrifice our lives for the Saviour, would it be worth it? Some of those martyrs only had to curse Christ, worship the emperor and give up their Bible to be burnt. 'But what shall it profit a man if he gains the whole world and loses his own soul?'

Silence for Martyrs

We have been looking at the symbols of the book of Revelation as if the series of sevens are panels on an Arch of Triumph. In this case, they depict the triumph of the Lord Jesus Christ because each of these four panels ends with the triumph of the King of kings and Lord of lords – Jesus Christ.

The panel which depicts the seals ends with the seventh seal showing the triumph of the Lord Jesus over the Roman Empire. When Jesus breaks the seal and opens that page of history, there is silence in heaven for about half an hour.

Sometimes I have been asked, 'What does the half an hour silence mean?' Somebody rudely said, 'it was before the ladies arrived!' Of course it wasn't – I am sure the men do just as much talking!

But another more sensible suggestion was that it was a silence in honour of all the martyrs put to death by the Roman Empire, only it was a half-hour silence instead of a two minute silence.

I like that. It seems fitting because it was in the fifth seal earlier that John was given a picture of the souls in heaven. They were under the altar of sacrifice. They had sacrificed their lives for the sake of Jesus. You will remember that Paul referred to his own martyrdom, 'I am ready to be offered upon the altar of sacrifice'.

But there was another reason for that silence. When Rome was Christianised in the fourth century, the Christians thought that was the final conquest. They thought that the kingdom of this world had become the Kingdom of Christ, as seal number six says. Was not the Roman emperor himself the chairman of their church councils. But then the angels intervene in chapter 7. 'Wait a bit,' they said. 'Don't think the kingdom has been won yet. That won't happen until the rapture of the saved – that is, until the resurrection of those born again. Wait until we have sealed the complete number.'

Now, Ephesians 1:13 tells you what this sealing is. The believer is sealed by the Holy Spirit when he believes the gospel and is saved. Then Ephesians 4:30 tells you that that sealing guarantees that the bodies of the saved will be changed and resurrected at the coming of Christ.

So what is the angel saying in Revelation 7? There are many centuries of history still to come in which millions more will be saved and suffer death for Christ. Not till then will the saved be reaped. That is why we don't hear of the 144,000 again until seven chapters on, in chapter 14. Not until then does the Lord Jesus put in his sickle and reap his wheat. In parables, the wheat always depicts the saved and the Lord is depicted as coming on a cloud with the souls of the saved in heaven to resurrect the living believers still on earth, as 1 Thessalonians 4 says.

What is the trademark of those believers? Revelation 14 tells you. They sing the new song! No unsaved person can sing that! They are those who have been redeemed.

Protection and Deliverance

What a comforting picture for days like these. Today, politicians open-ly talk of the possible destruction of all life on earth. Revelation 7 is preceded by a picture of our planet being threatened with destruction (**the sixth seal**). This destruction is on land and sea and a third of trees are destroyed. But four angels hold back this threat until the number to be saved is completed. Our world is certainly threatened, but it should comfort you to know that God reigns.

In the book of Revelation, there is a pattern – a structure. The whole wonderful book is unfolded upon this structure. For example, after each panel of seven, God gives illustrations or parables to show what the panels mean. Each panel ends in triumph for Jesus Christ.

Now, a word about parables. You should always remember that they are given only as illustrations. They are not given to teach doc-trine. For doctrine we read the clear statements of the epistles and Gospels. How are we to know truth from error? Most errors are found-ed upon an interpretation of a parable. Why? Because people might interpret a parable to support their own fanciful ideas.

Look at the parable following the sixth seal. The picture is of four angels holding back the threatened destruction until the work of the gospel is completed (see Fig 13.5). Nothing is allowed until the saved are safe in heaven.

How do we know this is the correct teaching? It is by interpreting it by other statements of the Bible. Are there scriptures to support this? Does the Bible show that Christ will rescue the saved before the final judgements of this age?

We have seen that a person is sealed by the Holy Spirit when he believes the gospel. In Ephesians 1:13, we saw that those sealed will have their bodies changed and redeemed at the second coming of Christ (Ephesians 4:30). Now, in 1 Corinthians 15:23, we see that only those who belong to Christ will be resurrected at his coming. Some call this 'the Rapture', but the scripture phrase for it is 'The resurrection of those who belong to Christ'.

Now, Revelation 7 depicts the threat of destruction to the earth being held back until the saved have risen to meet Christ and thus escape to safety. Jesus said this in Luke 21:36. He said, 'Escape these terrors by rising up to stand before the Son of Man.' Jesus is the Son of Man. Isaiah 26:19 onwards says the same:

> The dead shall live, their bodies shall rise . . . Come my people, enter your chambers and shut the door behind you. Hide yourself, for a little while until the wrath against sin is past. For behold, the Lord is coming forth out of his place to punish the inhabitants of the earth for their wickedness.

1 Peter 4:17 likewise says that Jesus will reward his Church, first at the resurrection of the saved and then the terrible judgement will come upon the unsaved. Many other texts tell you the same.

Also, you are told as many as seven times in the New Testament that Jesus will come unexpectedly like a thief in the night. The saved will be rescued and the unsaved left.

THE SEVENTH SEAL

After the silence, the angels prepared to blow the seven trumpets. Peace after three centuries of Roman persecution was very welcome, but it is dangerous for Christianity: it gives the opportunity for self-opinionated persons to formulate their theories which become exaggerated into errors. Religion had become a luxury. It was a preparation ground for the sowing of the seeds of apostasy and so the seven angels *prepare* to blow the seven trumpets of the apostasies to follow (Revelation 8:6): this is the time representing propaganda of unbiblical teaching. Thus in the historicist's interpretation, the first four trumpets concern the medieval Church.

It was because Mohammed was at the receiving end of an idolatrous Christianity, from the Eastern Empire, that made him take his strong monotheistic stand. He even concluded, apparently, that the Church's Trinity was Father, Son and Mary because he saw that the Blessed Virgin Mary got most of the worship. So from the seventh century onwards, Muslims demolish the Church of North Africa and the East, regarding Christians as idol worshippers. This is symbolised by the last three trumpets.

Yet idolatry in the Church did not end in spite of this woeful scourge. 'They did not repent of the works of their hands nor give up worshipping idols of gold, silver, bronze and wood' nor of their murders of born-again Christians (Revelation 9:20,21). Deceiving spirits are behind twisted Christianity (cf. Acts 16:16–18).

In the West, biblical faith died. Later, the medieval Church even burned those who translated the Word of God into the vernacular, because medievalism refused to be corrected by God's Word. Ironically, since the Second World War, the very translations made by the martyrs have been adopted by descendants of the same church authorities for public worship, which will gradually restore true biblical faith.

With each corruption of biblical faith, a third of Christianity becomes dead and the 'living water' is poisoned (Revelation 8:7–18). Under those unbiblical religious authorities, millions of Christians were martyred. But their prayers saved the truth from being wiped out (Revelation 8:2–5). This picture is taken from the tabernacle. The incense altar stood before the mercy seat. The incense upon it represented believer's prayers. Answers may be delayed and saved up until the most appropriate time. Then they are poured out with devastating blessing.

'Those Sealed'

During those three centuries of Roman persecution, a larger percentage of Jews were saved than during the centuries since, but even those were small in number (Romans 11:5, 25, 26) compared with the 'great multitude of Gentiles from all nations' whom no man could number, who would proclaim 'salvation through the Lamb' until the earth is harmed at the end of the age by the final judgements (Revelation 7:3).

What is 'the Great Tribulation'?

'Who are these in white robes?' asks the elder in Revelation 7:13.

Be careful with your answer. 'These are those who have come out of the great tribulation.' Notice the definite article 'the' in the Greek for 'the tribulation'. The word 'tribulation' was used by Jesus in Matthew 24, Mark 13 and Luke 21 to refer to the terrible time between the fall of Jerusalem in AD 70 and Christ's return two millennia later. (This is the historicist interpretation.)

This has been a terrible period for Christians and for Jews; see my Chapter 12. But the descriptions in Revelation do not, in my view, refer to the last seven years of this age, which is also sometimes called the 'the tribulation'. The saved will not go through that as their resurrection comes before it when Jesus comes for his own (Isaiah 26:19–21).

THE 144,000

I am thinking of a picture gallery showing all kinds of paintings. Sometimes you see symbolic pictures. They are puzzling and open to all kinds of interpretation. Below some of them, however, is written what the artist had in mind.

Parables are similar. They are pictures of what God has in mind. Because they are open to different interpretations, false teachers base their patent ideas upon them. For this reason, we should always check our interpretation of parables with the clear statements of the epistles.

One symbol which has often been misapplied is John's vision of the 144,000. This is in Revelation 7. John, the apostle, sees the 144,000 in heaven. They are made up of 12,000 from each of the twelve tribes of Israel. Then John sees another great host, more than can be numbered. They too are in heaven because they have washed their robes white in the cleansing blood of the Lamb. (The Lamb of God is Jesus Christ who died to redeem them.)

Figure 13.11. The symbols following the panel of the seven seals in which we see the altar of sacrifices of the martyred Christians and the prayers of the martyrs poured out over the Roman Empire.

Who are the 144,000? What do they stand for? Some false teachers have rushed in and said, 'They belong to our organisation or church, and if you don't belong to us, you will be lost.' Such an application contradicts Scripture. Jesus said, 'It is those who belong to me who are saved.' The 18th Article of the Church of England emphasises this. It condemns those who say that it is membership of a sect which saves a person, 'for holy Scripture gives us only the name of Jesus Christ whereby we must be saved'. So you see, we are not always able to say what an illustration means, but we are able to say what it does not mean. If it contradicts the plain teaching of Scripture, then our application is wrong. Now, it is not possible to say dogmatically what the 144,000 illustrate. They are seen again in Revelation 14. Here it is clearly stated that they were redeemed from the earth, that they sang a new song, that they were pure and that they followed the Lamb in everything. Surely that means they were born-again Christians.

Perhaps they represent Jewish Christians. Paul said in Romans 11 that there would be a limited number of them added to the Church. But the largest percentage to be saved would be Gentile believers. These could be the great host without number from every tribe and nation who were saved by the redeeming blood of the Lord Jesus, which are mentioned after the 144,000.

Sometimes Christ tested his disciples by asking a question. Revelation 7:13 asks John the question, 'Who are these?' I pass that question on to you. 'Who are these?' Whoever you think they are, they have the mark of the following:

1. They cry 'Salvation belongs to our God and to the Lamb.' In other words, they knew they could not save themselves. They trusted that the shed blood of the Lamb had already saved them.
2. In spite of persecution, they were full of praise and worship and their tears were wiped away.
3. They served God all the time, night and day.

The **seventh seal** leads into the seven warning trumpets which are developed further in the next chapter.

SUMMARY

TRIUMPHAL ARCH OF REVELATION

Prophesies world history from 1st century to modern times.

Analysis: Christ's triumphal arch has:
- Four panels.
- Each panel has 7 pictures and ends with Christ's triumph.
- Between each panel there are given symbols to explain meanings of the panels. e.g. Rev 17:1.

1st panel of 7 Lampstands
- Christian witness. Matt 5:15; Zech 4; Rev 1:20.
- 1st to 20th century.
- Christ witnessing amidst 7 church eras.
- Vision of heaven's control room chap 4 and 5.

2nd panel of 7 Seals ·
- Christ's triumph over Rome, chap 6 and 7, AD 62–323
- Symbol of the martyrs, Hebrew and Gentile 7:1–17.
- Short space of peace before apostasies persecute 18:1.

3rd panel of 7 Trumpets
- Persecution by the two apostasies, chap 8 to 10.
- Euphratean power floods out from East, 9:14, sixth trumpet. Causes the Reformation in the West, chap 10.
- Four symbols to interpret the panel, chap 11 to 14.

4th panel of 7 Cauldrons or bowls
- Wrath defeat the apostasies.
- Each cauldron is a reply to each trumpet in panel 3.
- Euphratean power dries up; 16:12 sixth cauldron.
- Visions to explain the cauldrons 'One of the angels of the cauldrons came and said, "Come, I will show you . . ." ' (17:1).

Note: The above is the **historic** (historicist) application of panels 1 to 4. The **futuristic** fulfilment would be during the tribulation. Prophecy is usually fulfilled both ways, i.e. symbolically and then literally (Matt 17:10–13).

14 THE REVELATION OF JESUS CHRIST (2)
SEVEN TRUMPETS AND SEVEN BOWLS

I was watching a pageantry of ancient warfare. The watchman on the city tower suddenly blew his trumpet. It was to warn the whole fortress that the enemy was coming. The defenders were surprised. They thought they had already defeated the enemy in an earlier battle. The enemy advanced to attack the walls. The defenders tipped great iron bowls of scalding liquid upon them. One by one the bowls were poured out and the enemy retreated. This is the picture in the next three chapters of Revelation, from 7 to 9. Seven angels prepare to sound the warning that the battle is not over.

We have seen that the seals of Revelation 6 show a great victory. They depicted how the Roman Empire accepted Christianity by the fourth century. Christians rejoiced that the great battle of martyrdom was over. The battle seemed to be won. The whole population of the empire was actually encouraged to go to church.

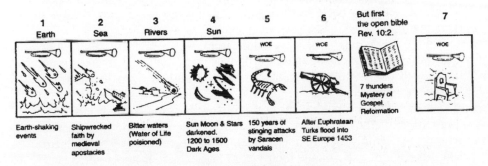

Figure 14.1. Panel of the seven trumpets in Revelation's 'Arch of Triumph' depicting the rise and fall of false religions, 4th century to the End.

THE WARNING TRUMPETS

But heaven saw it differently. The seven angel trumpeters were to sound the warnings one by one. Satan was not going to be defeated as easily as that. The heathen now flooded into the Church. As the centuries went by, their pagan ideas contaminated the truth. Christ offered the water of life; those waters were now poisoned. Chapter 8 verse 10 says a third of these waters were made bitter and many died.

What does this mean – 'many died'? Christ had said that he who
drinks the water of life will live! Eternal life will be theirs. They will
be saved for ever; but now many in the Church lost that assurance of
salvation? They died spiritually. As many as a third of the churchgoers
were not born again. They had not accepted the free gift of salvation!
The water of life was contaminated and poisoned! Many in our churches are like that today. They have no assurance of salvation. Following
that contamination, the fourth trumpet brings darkness. In history, the
dark ages came when the light of the gospel was eclipsed.

Meanwhile, a fresh peril approaches as the next angel sounds his
trumpet. This fifth trumpet was a peril which was to wipe out all the
churches of North Africa (Revelation 9).

You have probably guessed by now that the trumpets are warnings
against false religion. Now look at our own churches. Even in churches where the gospel is clearly preached, there are many who have
never personally received Christ into their hearts as Saviour. It is as
necessary to evangelise your own congregations as it is to evangelise
the world.

The Scorpions (Saracens)

I was in the Oregon desert looking for archaeological clues when out
of a sand hole came a scorpion. I backed away but tried to snap a picture of him on my camera. His tail containing the deadly sting arched
forward over his back towards me and his crab-like claws waved
threateningly.

In the ninth chapter of Revelation, John the apostle is given a snap
picture of a scorpion heralded by the fifth trumpet. It was a warning
that in the seventh century, the Christians of North Africa and the
Mediterranean would be threatened and attacked by a false religion of
the desert. The prophecy was fulfilled by the Saracen invasion. The
way in which they would swarm forward is likened to the way locusts
eat up everything before them. In fact, it takes several animals to
describe them – scorpions, locusts and horses. Their appearance (v 7
says) was like horses arrayed for battle, but they would sting like scorpions and they would afflict them for five months.

Now, five months equals 150 days. God told Ezekiel that each day
represented a year in symbolic prophecy. Did the Saracen affliction
last that long? Here is what Dr Basil Atkinson writes: 'The Saracens
swept through North Africa on horseback like a flight of locusts. Their
conquests lasted from AD 613 to 763.' That is 150 years, just as the
prophecy forewarned. The Saracens' woe commenced in 613 when
Mohammed began to secure converts. They emerged from Arabia as
locusts do and began to settle only when the new capital of Baghdad
was founded by them 150 years later in AD 763 (Hammerton's *Outline*

History of the World).

Their sting was like the sting of a scorpion, verse 5 says, because they tormented the coasts of the Mediterranean. The lives of the Mediterranean peoples were made miserable. There were sudden raids and both rich and poor were carried off to be slaves to work 18 hours a day. They longed for death, as verse 6 says.

What does the sting of a scorpion mean? Throughout the Mediterranean, their activities consisted of raids and then a retreat to a castle on the coasts. But they would *never* take over the government of a country – only sting it, but not kill. They were indeed vandals, just out to destroy, as verse 11 says.

As described in verses 7–9, the Saracens were famed for their beautiful horses. Their dress also is accurately described, their yellow turbans looked like crowns of gold. They had beards like men, but long hair like women. Their leader is described as having come from the bottomless pit and his name means destroyer or vandal – his name is given in two languages, Hebrew and Greek.

What is the significance of that? It was a prophecy that they would overrun Palestine – the homeland of the Hebrews and also the provinces of the Greek Orthodox Church, yet they would not completely kill those churches. It is amazing how the Greek Orthodox congregations managed to survive.

So we see how the prophecies were fulfilled historically. We are also seeing how these prophecies are being fulfilled futuristically today. The vandals are with us again. Vandalism and destruction are committed in modern cities of today. Revelation tells you who instigates it. It is the devil. He is out to destroy. The lawlessness foretold in 2 Thessalonians 2 is all about us. This can happen only when nations abandon their faith in Christ. When they do that, it lets loose the devil. How can it be stopped? Only by spiritual revival.

The Gauntlet

In the Dark Ages, an armoured knight would ride up on his horse and fling down the gauntlet in front of his enemy. It was a symbolic way of challenging the enemy to fight. The actual fight would take place later. So there was the symbol of battle first and the actual battle later.

Most prophecy is similar. It is fulfilled in two ways, symbolically and then literally. This also applies to the book of Revelation. Before we see how it will be fulfilled in the future, we are seeing how remarkably it has been fulfilled in history.

I have said that the trumpets of Revelation depict the deceptions of false religion. Many other godly scholars who believe God's inspired Word seen this and have applied it to past history. The trumpets foretold events from the fourth to the sixteenth century.

A second period of five months is given in Revelation 9:10. This was fulfilled when the Saracens launched a new attack on south-east Italy in 846 and France and, according to *Cambridge Medieval History*, the Saracen power began to decline 150 years later. Two languages are mentioned. They are Hebrew, because this power overran Jerusalem and Greek, because all the area was the area of the former Greek Empire and Greek Orthodox Church.

The Second Woe – The Sixth Trumpet – The Turks

This infliction had hardly died down before a second woe sprang up. The Euphratean power was unleashed (v 12 onwards). The Seljuk Turks entered Baghdad on the River Euphrates in 1055. This sixth trumpet was an even worse blow at Christendom, worse than the Saracen woe (Revelation 9:12). This woe is symbolised by the River Euphrates. The Turkish Empire has often been known as the Euphratean power. That is because they originated from the Euphrates. They were also called the Ottoman Empire. But their attack on European Christianity was to be held back for nearly 400 years, according to Revelation 9:15. Ezekiel said that each day in prophecy represents a year in history and the total of one year and one month and one day and one hour is therefore 396 years.

It was nearly 400 years from the foundation of the Ottoman Empire to their attack upon Constantinople in 1453. This capital of Eastern Christianity fell because the Turks introduced gunpowder and cannon-fire. This is described in Revelation 9:17,18. At Istanbul today, you can see some of these ancient cannons displayed at the railway station. The gun muzzles were shaped like lions and the smoke of gunfire would belch out of their mouths when the cannons were fired, just as described in Revelation 9.

Verse 17 describes gunpowder very accurately 14 centuries before it was invented. From out of the mouths of the cannons 'issued fire, smoke and sulphur'. The *Oxford Dictionary* says, 'Gunpowder, an explosive of saltpetre, charcoal and sulphur'. The word in the Greek for smoke is *kaptos*, which the Greek lexicon defines as from the verb *kaptoo*, to burn to charcoal which gives off smoke. So 'fire, charcoal smoke and sulphur' is a very close identification of the new military machine which fired at the walls of Constantinople (Istanbul), demolishing them after 396 years, thereby breaking through into south-east Europe.

The Ottoman military language is also described in these verses. They numbered their regiments by the term 'myriads' and this is the very word in the Greek of Revelation 9:16. This Turkish military word is used nowhere else in Scripture. Notice the description of these horsemen. They had breastplates of fiery zeal, hyacinth blue and sulphur yellow. This was the well-known armour colour of the Turkish soldiers.

Bible Rediscovered

But Satan overstepped himself. The fall of Constantinople was a rebuke to the Church's idolatry, as God said, but it also caused the Greek Orthodox monks to flee to the West and bring with them the neglected Bible to be read and translated.

Have you had to move house lately? Did you dive into all those old trunks and cases? Perhaps you found letters and books and documents long forgotten.

This is what happened when the Bible was rediscovered and translated. Revelation 10 tells you that this resulted from the tragedy of the fall of Constantinople in 1453. The Turks captured it, but the monks had already moved. They found in their cells old copies of the neglected Bible. When the scholars of the Western Church began to translate them, they found a treasure of truth beyond their wildest dreams. They could rejoice in a complete salvation accomplished by Christ on the cross. No longer did they have to whip themselves with metalled thongs, no longer did they have to wear prickly hair shirts in order to merit salvation. Christ had already saved them. He gave them abundant life as a free gift.

No wonder then that this next phase in Revelation 10:1 is represented by a mighty angel coming down from heaven with a rainbow around him, his face bright as the sun and a little book open in his hand. The Reformation indeed became the time of the open book. People were allowed to read it again. The rainbow around the angel of the open book symbolised God's covenant. The common man once again understood the new covenant spoken of by Jeremiah 31:

> Behold the days are coming, says the Lord, when I will make a new covenant . . . I will put my law within them. I will write it upon their hearts . . . they shall all know me from the least to the greatest, says the Lord, for I will forgive their iniquity and their sins I will not remember any more.

The sweetness of such words would taste like honey, Revelation 10:9 says. It certainly did for those who rediscovered the open Bible at the Reformation.

But the chapter ends with a recommission to bring this good news to all nations. God says, 'You must take the gospel again to all peoples, tribes and nations.' So, after the Reformation, a fresh outbreak of missionary activity was born. One could not keep the good news to oneself. Salvation was as sweet as honey to one's mouth but when the believer had digested it (v 10 says), it became bitter to think of all those who were perishing without this good news – the news that they could be eternally saved by accepting the Lord Jesus Christ into their heart.

Here is the divine commission: 'You must again prophesy to many peoples, nations and tongues and kings.'

The Survival of Christianity

From the time of Constantine, the true biblical witness was not necessarily to be associated with the official Church. Constantine had declared Christianity to be the state religion, but he took the chair at church councils, so bringing a secondary fulfilment to prophecy: 'The outer court of the Temple has been given over to the nations; they will trample the Holy City for 42 months.'

The lampstands referred to are witnessing Christians spoken of by the Lord Jesus, 'Let your light so shine'. They are two because all witness had to be in twos to establish the message. The olive trees were referred to by Zechariah. They supplied oil for the lamps – the oil of the Holy Spirit. That is what you and I need to keep our witness shining bright . . . The devil cannot stop your witness until your work is done. Revelation 11:7 says this: 'When they have finished their testimony . . . the beast shall kill them.' Yes, but not before their work is done.

How is this visitation to be interpreted? Literally or spiritually? In history or in the future? It will be in both ways – Scripture says verse 8 says spiritually, because they witness in a street which is called, spiritually, Sodom and Egypt. So that means it is the witness of all born-again Christians to those who dwell in the ungodly cities of destruction. How long was this witness to be? It says 42 months. That is the same as 1,260 days. As each day equals a year, that meant twelve centuries.

For twelve centuries after Constantine, the ancient churches of the West and of the East strayed further and further away from biblical truth, so born-again Christians were often persecuted for proclaiming it. They witnessed in sackcloth so to speak, until once again the open Bible, portrayed in chapter 10, had its cleansing influence.

Elijah Shall Come

The two witnesses of Revelation 11 will also be fulfilled literally. Elijah will come to prepare for the second coming of Christ.

We have seen that the two witnesses represent Christian testimony after the official Church had strayed from the truth of the Bible from the fourth century onwards. So that was fulfilled in a spiritual sense, as verse 8 said. The two witnesses represented Christians testifying to others.

We will now see that it will also be fulfilled literally, before the second coming of Christ.

One of those witnesses is to be Elijah because, according to 11:5, he will do things which Elijah did in the book of Kings, as did Elisha also. They proclaimed drought and famine on the land for the sins of the nation. They called down fire from heaven. The fire of their words, God's Words, was more powerful than army weapons.

Jesus himself said that prophecies concerning Elijah were fulfilled spiritually, then literally. In Matthew 17, the disciples ask him when Elijah would come. The Lord replied: 'He has come and they have already killed him.' The disciples knew then that he referred to John the Baptist. At his birth, the angel had said that he would come in the spirit of Elijah.

But Jesus went on to say also that 'Elijah will come'. That would be before Christ's second coming. So here again, we get prophecy first fulfilled symbolically in John the Baptist and then, as Jesus said, it will be fulfilled literally in Elijah himself. Indeed, Malachi 4:5 says: 'Behold, I will send you Elijah the prophet before the great and terrible day of the Lord.'

Now, the great and terrible day of the Lord is the judgement of the nations when Christ comes in power. Joel uses the same expression when he describes the blood and fire on earth and the mushroom pillars of smoke of nuclear fission. That was a prelude to the terrible day of the Lord.

Concerning the first coming of Jesus, when he came to die on the cross, the Lord said, 'I have come not to judge the world, but to save the world.' At the second coming he will say, 'I have come for those I have saved and will now judge the world.'

But God is always wanting to give people a last chance, a chance to repent before judgement. So he will send Elijah before that great and terrible day of the Lord comes. Peter writes in his second letter that God is long-suffering and not willing that any should perish, but that all should come to repentance. He says, 'Remember that one thousand years is only like one day in God's sight', so time is extended to give adequate time to turn to God.

Seven Sisters

I often go to view the beautiful cliffs which stretch out towards Eastbourne, on the south coast of England, to see the seven chalk cliffs which are called the Seven Sisters. The cliffs shine white in the sun and the glistening sea laps at their bases. The sea eats away this base so that the chalk rock falls straight down. This leaves the white chalk cliffs always vertical and at the top the fresh grass grows a green carpet right to the edge. This gives the top a wavy green canopy emphasising the seven white humps. These are the Seven Sisters divided by six dips. The last dip before the seventh hump is wider than the others. Indeed, it is called a gap – Birling Gap. When I get to it, I look through it and find the cliffs turn a corner. They start a new series of white cliffs.

Now, in the book of Revelation, the seven seals and the trumpets are like that. In both cases, there is a gap between the sixth and the seventh. Into that gap is put a symbol or vision. This is to give an insight into the next series of sevens to follow. It is as if to say: 'You expected the end to come didn't you, but no, there are another seven to come, before the end.'

This is to keep the Church expectant all down the ages. The Church which no longer expects her Lord to return is a Church which has fallen asleep. So said the Lord in his parable of the ten virgins. But this arrangement in Revelation is a way of showing that a panel of sevens succeed each other in prophesied history, until the final seven which is that of the bowls of anger. They have no such gap. The seventh follows on immediately because at last the end has come.

What symbol was it that was put into the gap of the seventh trumpet? It was the symbol of the opened Bible, the Word of God, once again made available for the ordinary man in the street to read (Fig 14.1). We saw how it was caused by the capture of Constantinople in 1453. What led to this was the Turkish gunfire described in Revelation 9 – the sixth trumpet.

Thus a new phase of history opened up. Bible truth was again to be spread to all nations. The light of the gospel was to shine out to the world again. The course which this would take is depicted in the seven bowls of anger. That is the last panel on the Arch of Triumph which is the book of Revelation.

You remember how the seven trumpets warned the defenders that false religion was advancing to capture the castle of truth. Then the great metal bowls of scalding liquid are poured down to repel the attackers. The bowls are the restoration of truth, step by step. Each bowl of anger is an answer in history to each of the trumpets of warning. For example, the sixth trumpet shows the Turkish power flooding out and, in reverse, under the sixth bowl of anger it is drying up (Fig 13.2). In drying up and withdrawing from the Holy Land in 1917, the way was cleared for God to re-establish Israel in the land of promise. The Lord Jesus said, 'When you see this happen, know that my return is near'.

The Time Factor

We have seen how the two witnesses of Revelation 11 depicted born-again Christians witnessing to false religion before they were killed. The Ottoman Empire burst into south-east Europe at the fall of

Constantinople in 1453. It killed many Eastern Orthodox Christians, but it brought the life of God's breath to Western Christendom. As we have seen, those who fled to the West brought the rediscovered Bible.

Thus, in Revelation 11, the two witnesses were also slain but brought life to Christians in the West. In the West, too, the witness of the Bible-believing Lollards and Waldensians was crushed, but within 3½ years the Reformation was born (= 3½ days, verses 9 and 11).

As usual, after the seventh symbol, there is a series of visions which illustrate the meaning of the preceding panel. It is the same after the seventh trumpet. We are shown remarkable visions, but they all have a common feature which did not occur in the visions after the other sets of seven.

What is that common feature in the seven trumpets? It is a time measurement. The prophecies of the seven trumpets concern a period of 1,260 days. Remember that Ezekiel was told that each day represented one year. So the seven trumpets concern a period of 1,260 years long. It stretches from the fourth to the sixteenth century. The witnesses in sackcloth are Christians witnessing for that length of time. The same time is depicted in the following chapter 12. The woman clothed with the sun has children persecuted for that length of time. The dragon (Satan's false religions) persecutes the saved for that same length of time. Now, I want you to observe that this time period of 1,260 years is repeated four times but only in connection with the rise and fall of false religion. This refers to idolatrous mediaeval Christianity and also includes the rise and fall of the nations which promote the false prophet of the desert. We saw how the Saracens and the Turks flooded over Palestine in the seventh and eleventh centuries, as depicted in the fifth and sixth trumpet. (We noted how this power dried up and withdrew under the sixth bowl in 1917.)

They measure time by the moon and not by the sun. Moon years are shorter than sun years, so to make the 1,260 moon years into sun years, you add 75 years. That makes the Moslem date 1335. We have a dramatic confirmation of that as noted before. When the Turks fled out of Jerusalem in 1917, the newspapers there had this lunar date, 1335, at the top of the front page and, on the other side, the Western date 1917, was printed. It was then that the promised home for Jews was realised in Palestine.

Read what Dr Grattan Guinness wrote in 1886: 'The Jews cannot be restored while the Turks are masters in Jerusalem. Their removal must figure prominently in prophecies of Jewish restoration. Those who live to see the year 1917 will have reached a most important year.'

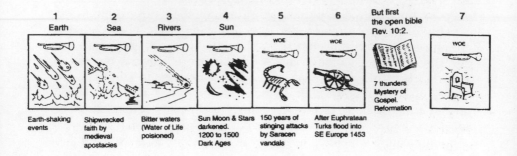

Figure 14.2. The symbols following the panel of the seven trumpets.

Rejected Biblical Christianity

Have you admired the heraldic animals on royal shields? They are, of course, symbolic. One may be a unicorn with a crown on its horn, another may be a lion wearing a crown. Similar imagery is given in the book of Revelation. A dragon represents Satan and horns represent kings, then later there are crowns on the horns. This means that sovereignty is transferred from the Roman Empire to the nations which arise out of it.

The world and the devil do not mind religion, but they intensely dislike biblical truth. That is depicted in the fight of the dragon against the woman clothed with the sun in Revelation chapter 12. Her off-spring are described as those who 'overcame the devil by the blood of the Lamb and by the word of their testimony and they loved not their lives unto death'.

The woman and her offspring escape into the wilderness for 1,260 days. When did this start? The clue is that it commenced when the Roman Empire existed, but continued into the time when that empire had broken up into ten kingdoms – the kingdoms of Europe.

How do we know this? We are told that the dragon had seven heads; this is taken to be the seven hills of Rome; that the crowns were upon those seven heads. This means that Imperial Rome was ruling at the beginning of that persecution. But later, in chapter 13, the beast with seven heads had ten horns, representing the ten kingdoms. These were the countries or language groups into which the empire had split. It was those ten horns which now wore the crowns. The rulership had passed from Rome's seven hills to the kingdoms of Europe (17:9,12).

For twelve centuries, all these powers caused biblical Christians to be rejected. They had a wilderness experience, as the text says. This went on from century to century until some of the kings advocated their cause from the sixteenth century onwards.

So the woman and her children who had a testimony escaped to the wilderness and were protected for 3½ times – that is, the same period of 1,260 years. The dragon – Satan, the devil – was extremely angry that he had not destroyed all the born-again Christians. He is still angry today and he instils that hatred of those who are saved into others, even into unconverted churchgoers.

Hatred or dislike of conversion is part of man's fallen nature. Verse 10 says that Satan accuses the saved falsely. He accuses them day and night and finds it easy to get others to do this. He is the one who causes the unconverted to say that the saved 'are a lot of hypocrites'. But do not be discouraged, because Revelation 12:10 says:

Rejoice then, O heaven, and you that dwell therein . . . for the accuser of our brethren has been cast out, who accused them day and night before our God; and they have conquered him by the blood of the Lamb and by the word of their testimony, for they loved not their lives unto death.

The Deadly Wound

On ancient monuments you get some weird creatures depicted: leopards with several heads, lions with cow horns and bears with iron teeth. These all had symbolic meaning.

In Revelation 13, you are given a description of a very curious creature. He was a make-up of three different animals – the leopard, the bear and the lion. This imagery is taken from Daniel who lived six centuries before Christ. To him, God foretold the succession of empires from Daniel's time down to modern times. These animals represented world empires which followed one another. The first was Babylon, the second Persia, the third Greece and the fourth was a mixture of them all in the Roman Empire.

Dr Atkinson points out in his book, *War with Satan*, that the Roman government was Western, as the Greek Empire had been. It had a mixture of senate and dictator, like the Persian bear and the blasphemous way of the Babylonian lion. This strange beast gets wounded, but then recovers. In fulfilment, the empire ended, but recovered as European countries and finally as the European Economic Community. This is reflected in the control over buying and selling, spoken of at the end of chapter 13. All trade is to be done by numbers. We are rapidly approaching that situation. The use of money is giving way to credit cards with your number on it. Even pots of jam, historically manufactured in every household, are now purchased using a number in code on the label.

In the book of Daniel, it is at this stage that the second coming of

Christ takes place. That means in our times. As he descends to Olivet, then to Zion in Jerusalem, he comes with all the saved. They take over earth's government and, after judgement, they show that the world becomes a happy and just place when the Lord Jesus rules. Appropriately, this is depicted in the next chapter, Revelation 14:1: 'Then I looked and behold, a Lamb stood on Mount Zion and with him those who sang a new song . . . those redeemed from among men.'

But, in preparation, a last chance is given for all nations to hear the gospel. In verse 6, it comes through mid-heaven to every nation, family and language and people. This comes before the final fall of false religion. This comes through radio and television broadcasting today, where the messages bounce around the world from the ionosphere in mid-heaven to every family who tunes in, as the verse says.

The False Lamb

I was looking at one of those triumphal arches again and noticed that between the panels depicting the history of victory, there were other symbols.

It is the same here in the book of Revelation. We have seen how between each panel of seven are symbols which explain the panels. The list of illustrations before the last panel (that of the bowls of anger) ends with the vision of two lambs – the false lamb and the true Lamb of God. These are in chapters 13 and 14. In these chapters, the world finds the false lamb very convincing. The media give him full coverage. Although obviously a religious leader, according to the prophecy, the statements of unbelief are welcome, for it is an excuse to hide from the truth of God. Revelation 13:5 says:

> The animal was given a month uttering haughty and blasphemous words and it was allowed to exercise authority for 42 months. He opened his mouth to utter blasphemies against God, blaspheming his name . . . Here is a call for the endurance and the faith of the saved.

In these chapters, the religious leaders who twist the truth into imitation Christianity also get a good hearing, especially those who imply that religious acts can avoid the need of a new and changed heart. Verse 11: 'Then I saw another animal approved by the earth. He had two horns like a lamb, but he spoke as a dragon.'

The dragon was Satan, the passage tells you, so it was the devil disguised as a sheep. The Lord Jesus warned you about sheep in wolves' clothing and Paul spoke of ministers appointed by the devil to look like ministers of light.

All those whose names were not written in the book of life were deceived. This had also been revealed to Paul in 2 Thessalonians 2. All those who had no love for the truth and didn't want to be saved, were deceived by Satan's strong delusion. But then, in chapter 14, you are shown the true Lamb of God:

> I looked and behold on Mount Zion stood the Lamb. With him were those who sang a new song before the throne. No one else could learn that song except those redeemed from the earth.

Who is this true Lamb of God? It is the Lamb who was slain from the beginning of the earth.

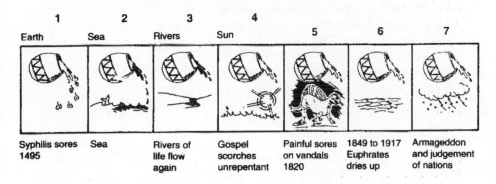

1	2	3	4	5	6	7
Earth	Sea	Rivers	Sun			
Syphilis sores 1495	Sea	Rivers of life flow again	Gospel scorches unrepentant	Painful sores on vandals 1820	1849 to 1917 Euphrates dries up	Armageddon and judgement of nations

Figure 14.3. Panel of the seven bowls in Revelation's 'Arch of Triumph' depicting replies of the bowls to each trumpet AD 1500 to the End. (Mainly to do with apostasy and response to false religions.)

THE SEVEN BOWLS OF ANGER

I was in an old farmhouse and on the wall I saw one of those old large sickles they used to reap the wheat with it. Up until recent times, wheat was always reaped by the hand sickle. In some countries, the sickle is still used. In Revelation 14:14 John describes what he saw:

> I looked and beheld a white cloud and upon the cloud sat one like the Son of Man having on his head a golden crown and in his hand a sharp sickle; and another angel came out of the temple crying with a loud voice to him who sat on the cloud 'Thrust in your sickle and reap, for the time has come for you to reap, for the harvest of the earth is ripe.'

This is yet another vision of the resurrection of the saved at the second coming of Christ. How do we know?

1. Because in all the parables which Jesus told, the wheat represented the saved.
2. Because Paul calls this harvest, the reaping of those who belong to Christ.

3. Because there were three harvests in the Jewish year. This was the second one. The first represented Christ's resurrection (Paul says); the second was the believer's resurrection and the third was all the unsaved for judgement which is the wine press of God's anger at the end of the same chapter.

This harvest, then, is the second – that of the saved. Why does Christ thrust his sickle into the earth while he is still sitting on the cloud? It is because the Bible says that the Lord Jesus will come in the clouds and the believers will rise to meet him in the air. So he reaps his own from the earth and they rise to meet him.

Why does he not descend immediately to the earth? Because many scriptures say that, before he does so, he rewards the saved. After that, he continues his descent to judge the warring nations who would destroy the earth but for his intervention.

So the rewarding of the saved comes first. This is not to decide whether or not they will go to heaven. That was given to them as a free gift when they accepted it at conversion. This reward is for how they have served Christ since their conversion. The man that Paul talks about in 1 Corinthians 3 did not deserve any reward, but he was saved because his foundation was the rock of salvation, Jesus Christ.

Nevertheless, the Bible says, let the coming of Christ be a happy day for those who are saved by free grace and whose work for Christ since has been well done, with the right motives. Here are Christ's own words: 'Then the Lord will say to you, "Well done, good and faithful servant, you have been faithful in little things, take authority over big things in my kingdom".'

The Wine Press of Anger

I was looking at a big old wine press. The grapes would be picked and flung into the press. This was screwed down until the grape juice flowed out, blood red. In ancient wine presses in the Middle East, the wine was trodden out by the bare feet of the workers.

This treading out of the grapes represented the last harvest. In the agricultural year, it came four months after the wheat harvest. In Revelation 14:14, we saw that the earlier wheat harvest was the reaping of the saved at their resurrection. The harvest after that is always a picture of the reaping of the unsaved for judgement and for just punishment. The picture is a terrible one and a warning to get saved before it is too late. The words are terrible. The unsaved are thrown into 'the great wine press of the wrath or anger of God' and blood came out of the wine press.

Now, why is God so angry? It is because he has given every chance for sinners to repent, warning after warning has been given down the centuries and in our lifetime. God's patience and love has allowed his creatures even to torture and kill his Son.

Some might ask, 'Why does God send such terrible punishments?' The picture in verse 20 is of a terrible battle in which blood runs horrifically. It is a judgement of God, but man will have brought it upon himself. All the chapter before it has God warning and pleading with us not to persist in our sinful ways. The Lamb of God has died and risen and ascended and saved. The messengers have issued a world-wide invitation. Indeed, it is a picture of what is happening now. Here is that loving plea in Isaiah: 'Look unto me, says the Lord, all you ends of the earth and be ye saved!'

In Jeremiah's day, God pleads as he gives them a last chance (Jeremiah 5–7):

> If you heed my warning and turn from your cruelty, greed and injustice to the poor . . . If you turn from the devil's religion . . . If you renounce witchcraft and idolatry . . . Then I will save Jerusalem and save you from being dragged away in chains by the invader.

Yes, the judgements of God on earth are often the natural results of breaking his natural laws.

In the case of Revelation 14:20, it is a picture of the slaughter of Armageddon in the final war of the age, then the judgement of all who refuse to have Jesus Christ to rule over them.

God's Reply to Promiscuity

Today, there is a sudden panic about the AIDS disease. In AD 1500, there was a similar scare. For the first time, the dreaded disease called syphilis hit Europe. It killed one-third of the population. This is described in Revelation 16:2. It was the first bowl of anger to be poured on to the earth. It was God's reply to sexual promiscuity. It struck in Rome first (see the quotation below), and came out on the body and limbs in terrible ulcers. The following are some of the fantastic historic details. Ratcliff writes in *Syphilis – History's Worst Disaster* (Harper):

> Rome was among the first victims, thousands died each day. The syphilis epidemic that set Europe afire in 1495 was probably the greatest calamity that ever struck the human race. It was a new disease. Skeletal remains of Europeans showed no signs of syphilis lesions of bones before that. It was no respecter of persons. In Rome, Caspare Torrella, private physician to the powerful and infamous Borgias, had 17 cases to treat in that Papal family alone. Henry VIII of England contracted it, which probably accounts for the still-born children his various wives bore him. People's bodies erupted with ulcers that ate to the bone and became open sores and

ulcers which no one could hide and then blinded, maddened or paralysed. Prostitutes were ordered to stop practising their trade. For seven years, the disease, syphilis, raged, infecting one person in every three. The pure morality of the early settlers of America kept it at bay in that colony. They said that it was a just punishment from God.

The Mark of the Beast

Ratcliff used the phrase, 'infamous Borgias'. It is no wonder that the bowl of wrath was poured out when we read of the activities of the Borgias in Gibbon's well-known *Decline and Fall*, Volume VII, p 300.

> Few know anything of the history of the Popes without having heard the name of Borgia, which has become almost a byword for abominable wickedness. This was a Spanish family, two or three of whose members became Pope. The most notorious was Rodrigo Borgia, whose papal name was Alexander VI (1492–1503). This Pope's daughter, Lucrezia, was the mother of a child whose father there seems evidence to suppose was the Pope himself, her own parent. The Popes kept mistresses as a matter of course, and took them with them when they travelled. Most of the Popes of the fifteenth and sixteenth centuries had illegitimate children [whom they called nephews, from which comes the term 'nepotism' (*Oxford Dictionary*)] on whom they bestowed rich positions.

Gibbon writes that 'Pope John XXIII was so flagrant that the Council of Constance took the matter up. He was accused of piracy, murder, rape, sodomy and incest.'

Yet Rodrigo Borgia, Pope Alexander VI, had the name in Latin on his triple crown, 'Vicar of the Son of God' (*Vicarivs Filii Dei*). The numerical value (based on $i = 1$, $v = 5$, $l = 50$, $C = 100$, $D = 500$) adds up to 666, i.e. 5,1,100,1,5,1,50,1,1,500,1. (Revelation 13:18 states, NKJV: 'Let him who has understanding calculate the number of the beast, for it is the number of a man: his number is 666.) The Pope had a triumphal arch erected under which he processed, which bore the words, 'Caesar was a man. Alexander is God'. Of course, modern popes are good-living men, but they owe the cleansing of their system to the Reformation.

Read this verse in Revelation 16:2: 'The first angel poured out his bowl of wrath upon the earth and there came a terribly bad ulcer upon those who had the mark of the beast.' The word in the original actually means ulcers.

Homosexuality

Today, the scene is the AIDS diseasewhich has contributed to the death of an estimated 12 million people worldwide (1998). You wonder why there is so much alarm! It can spread to the innocents and it has almost a 100 per cent fatality rate. People who should know better condone homosexuality. For example, a London Borough intends to introduce a schools' syllabus to show that homosexuality is normal. This is planned for infant classes as well as all other grades. The UK Government is currently considering plans to introduce a national teaching syllabus which will include homosexual techniques as part of general sex education. (News item in *The New Christian Herald*, June 1998.) So God has got to make a reply to such perversity. The Scriptures clearly state that it is not a normal way of life. Indeed, Scripture warns that sodomy would be a sign of these times before the second coming. But Jesus offers to deliver any homosexual. Many have had their lives changed. 1 Corinthians 6:9 says:

> Do not be deceived. The following will not inherit the kingdom of God: fornicators, idol worshippers, adulterers, lesbians nor homosexual abusers of man with man . . . and some of you were those, but you are washed, you are cleansed, you are saved by the name of the Lord Jesus Christ and by the power of the Holy Spirit of our God.

To be fully delivered, a person must fully and wholeheartedly give himself to Christ, receive his cleansing and change of heart. A change of attitude is also necessary with individuals and authorities who condone homosexual acts. However strong base inclinations may be, Jesus Christ can free us. God makes it quite clear that it is abhorrent to him and that it is a misuse of bodily functions (Romans 1:26–28). The wicked cities of Sodom and Gomorrah were destroyed for homosexuality (Genesis 19); this is the reason it is referred to as sodomy. The words of Jesus indicate that its growth would be one of the signs of his return (Luke 17:26–32).

Water and Light

We have seen that the book of Revelation gives an accurate prophecy of history. This was between the first century and the twentieth century, as well as the future.

We have seen that the symbols of the bowls of anger were a reply from the sixteenth century onwards to what happened under the symbols of the trumpets in the Middle Ages.

We come now to the water of life which was poisoned under the third trumpet, but, under **the third bowl**, the water of life to the believer was restored. Under the fourth trumpet, the light of the gospel was eclipsed in the Dark Ages, but, under **the fourth bowl**, the light of the gospel blazed out again in the Evangelical Revival which won millions of souls to Jesus Christ in the eighteenth and nineteenth centuries.

To those who shunned the gospel, the glare of the truth scorched them, as the text says, 'They did not like the gospel light which showed up their deeds'. As the Bible says, 'They come not to the light in case their deeds are reproved'. Indeed, 'Satan blinded the minds of those who did not believe in case the light of the glorious gospel of Jesus Christ should shine into them.'

Satan actually prepared a strong delusion for them. It was in the nineteenth century that destructive criticism of the Bible arose. This centred mainly on the books of Moses and the atonement which Christ won for sinners. They said that Moses didn't write the Pentateuch and that they could not accept atonement by substitution. The saved protested. That is why in Revelation 15 the redeemed sing 'The song of Moses and of the Lamb'.

Notice several features about this. Chapter 15 says that they were associated with the sending out of the angels with the bowls. Evangelism went on in the last century in spite of the critics' attacks. The critics said that Moses was a fraud. His books were written later. They also attacked the atonement. They questioned God's theory of atonement – how could the blood of the Lamb save sinners, they said. No one could say they were saved! So they cut out all references to the blood of Christ in their hymn books. But verse 2 says the believers got victory over Satan's deceptions.

How did they do that? Verse 2 says they stood firm upon the Word of God. The sea of glass upon which they stood, symbolised the Bible. You remember that this was the temple washing laver (Fig 13.4). It represented the washing by the Word. This laver was supported on stands which represented the four Gospels and signified that Christ was in all the Scriptures. 'Moses wrote about me,' said Jesus. And so the triumphant believers in heaven sang the song of Moses and the Lamb. They believed the Bible from cover to cover and, concerning the blood of the Lamb, they had experience that it had availed for them.

LIST OF EVENTS

Our studies in Revelation will have given you new insight into the meaning of history and the purpose behind it. For example, the removal of the Turkish Empire out of Palestine was a preparation for God's purposes. There we see how the sixth bowl of anger in Revelation 16 referred to this. Turkey was known as the Euphrates power, just as England might have been known as the Thames kingdom.

After the withdrawal in 1917 of Turkey from Palestine in Revelation 16:12, we are given a list of events which would happen next. True to prophecy, they have been happening in modern times.

First, it left a vacuum which could be invaded by the powers of the East.

Second (v 13), there follows great activity by the evil spirits. They take over the media of the world. They are referred to as the mouths of propaganda. The text implies that there would be in our day three main controlling authorities. They would control most of the broadcasting propaganda. One would be the dragon of paganism and atheism; another would be governed by the Treaty of Rome (the headquarters of the beast); and the third would be controlled by the false prophet. The false prophet would no doubt increase in influence through oil revenues.

Next, in verse 14, we are told what the outcome would be. This propaganda over the media will cause the world powers to build up armaments for Armageddon (the last war of the age). The text says that the whole world will be involved. In verse 15, the Lord gives an important notice to the believers. It is that, at this point, the Lord will come. It will be secretly and unexpectedly like a thief for those who are saved – those who wear the wedding garment of salvation. After this, an attack is made on Palestine. This is from the valley of Megiddo in the north, right down to the valley of Kidron outside Jerusalem. Then in verse 17, the bowl of anger is poured out into the air. As a result, verse 21 says, 'great missiles will fall out of the air' and verse 19 says, 'the cities of the nations will collapse and there will be a mighty earthquake'.

Christians will escape all that happens after verse 15, because as verse 15 shows, they will be caught up to meet Christ in the air, as explained in 1 Thessalonians 4 and 1 Corinthians 15. Their bodies will be changed and they will be awarded their place in the coming kingdom.

Events to Come

Take a look into the future, the media says. The year 2000 is getting near! People try to imagine what it will be like, but conveniently they forget the part sin will play. God has all the future wrapped up. World-shaking events are depicted from Revelation 17 to the end. Notice who it is who comes to explain the meaning of the seven bowls. It is an angel of the bowls of anger. He continues to give the meaning of the final chapters of Revelation. The meaning is given in a series of startling visions. Even John the apostle was astonished.

The first vision is of the powers of Europe trying to find a solution to the world's problems but being deceived by false religion. They are allowed by God to go only so far. Chapter 17 verse 17 says: 'For God has put it into their hearts to fulfil his will and to agree to give their kingdom to the beast, until the words of God are fulfilled.'

They will then reap the results of avoiding gospel truth. Chapters 17 and 18 give a picture of the false bride and then, in chapter 19, a vision of the true bride of Christ. Verse 8 tells us about the Lamb's bride: 'It was given to her that she might be clothed with fine linen bright and clean, for the fine linen is the wonderful deeds done by the saved.'

There is an invitation to be among the saved, to be at the marriage supper of the Lamb, because the wedding is coming very soon.

The Lord Jesus showed in many scriptures that it would take place immediately after the saved have been caught up in the air at their resurrection. They will meet their Saviour who is the Bridegroom. It will be such a happy wedding day. Verse 7 says: 'Let us be glad and rejoice and give honour to him; for the marriage supper of the Lamb has come and his wife has made herself ready.'

But don't try to gatecrash! Jesus told a parable of a man who gate-crashed. He tried to get into the wedding without being prepared. He was spotted and thrown out on his neck.

How did they detect him? He wasn't wearing the wedding garment. He must have refused it because the custom was to give all invited guests a wedding garment as they entered. He must have been too proud – thought his own clothes good enough.

It is the picture of a proud man who thinks he is good enough and refuses to accept the free gift of salvation. Isaiah 64:6 says that your good works look like filthy rags to God, so accept the garment of salvation offered freely. Isaiah speaks of this in 61:10: 'I will greatly rejoice in the Lord . . . for he has clothed me with the garment of salvation.'

Summing Up

In the closing chapters of Revelation, we get a dramatic peep into a marvellous future. Before we look at that, we will sum up the traumatic past which leads to that wonderful time ahead for the Christians.

We have seen that the book of Revelation is to be applied literally for the future and symbolically for the past. We have seen how remarkably it predicted the past history in amazing detail. I will recap on that.

The book of Revelation opens by predicting the history of Christian witness. That is the first panel of seven lampstands, the triumphs and failures of the Church. Then follow the usual visions explaining the meaning. These show that history is in the hands of Jesus, the Lamb of God and that he triumphs.

The second panel of sevens – that of the seals – is the history of how the blood of the martyrs eventually won the Roman Empire to accept Christianity by the fourth century. The visions that follow show that the prayers and suffering of Christians were thus answered, but there are perils to come from other quarters.

The third panel is of seven trumpet warnings that the enemy Satan is advancing to attack the citadel of truth in a more subtle guise – that of false religions. The pagan priests who flooded into the churches were not really converted and brought in with them practices which originated from Babylon. The water of life was thus poisoned under the third trumpet and, under the fourth trumpet, the light of truth was obscured; verse 12 says, 'darkened'. These were the Dark Ages, an appropriate name.

Then under the fifth trumpet in the seventh century, comes the attack from the false prophet of the desert. The Saracen invasion wiped out the churches of North Africa during 150 years. The actual duration was foretold. But Satan outsteps himself, for under the sixth trumpet the Turks break into south-east Europe in 1453. This causes the Reformation because the refugee monks brought the Bible to the West and, when translated, it became the open Bible of the Reformation, referred to in Revelation 10.

The fourth and last panel showed how the bowls of anger are poured out upon unscriptural error. These purify the contaminated waters to bring life again – eternal life – and the sunlight of the gospel shines once again.

Under the sixth bowl, the Turkish Empire dries up from Europe and Palestine. It does so in the time-scale accurately indicated, so that God's purposes are fulfilled in his Holy Land before the second coming of Christ.

So this marvellous insight demonstrates how history is in the hands of the Lamb of God. He opens each page of traumatic history and he triumphs over Satan at each main stage. Finally, the kingdom of this world becomes the Kingdom of God and of his Christ.

All faithful believers will also triumph with him and sing, 'Salvation belongs to our God who sits upon the throne and unto the Lamb . . . Worthy is the Lamb who has redeemed us out of every tribe and family and nation . . . Hallelujah, the Lord God, the Almighty reigns.'

SUMMARY

SEVEN TRUMPETS AND SEVEN BOWLS

5th Trumpet Rev 9:1–12

- Saracens almost wipe out the great N African Church; vv 7–9 describe their famed horses, yellow turbans like crowns of gold, man-like beards, but woman-like long hair.
- Spiritual name v 11 in Hebrew because they overran Palestine and in Greek because it was Greek Orthodox Church which suffered.
- Duration 150 years (5 mths v 5) AD 613–763 then settled. Then another 150 years (v 10) AD 846–1096 of fresh attacks on N Mediterranean.

6th Trumpet Rev 9:13–21

- Second great woe, a worse blow to Christianity.
- Turks launched their conquests from Baghdad in AD 1057.
- Restrained from S.E. Europe for 396 years (v 15) until 1453.
- Cannon and gunpowder (new weapon v 17) breached walls of Constantinople. (Gunpowder is made from chemicals of v 17 – saltpetre, charcoal and sulphur.)
- S.E. Europe subjugated. Monks flee to West with old Scriptures.
- Reformation ch 10. Translations from old Scriptures bring an open Bible recommission.
- 'A little book open.' 'Take it . . . preach again to the nations.'

Cauldrons (Bowls of Wrath) reverse the trumpet apostasies

- Reply to 1st Apostasy of Trumpets 1–4 and 2nd Apostasy 5,6.
- Angel of the cauldrons shows John the meaning of everything from ch 15 to 22; cf. Rev 17:1; 21:9; 22:1.
- The false bride in red claiming to be the Church, ch 17 to 19:4.
- The true bride in white 19:5–9.
- The return of her groom, the King of kings 19:11–18.
- The two apostasies finally demolished vv 19–21. Satan chained during millennium 20:1–3.
- Christ's reign for 1,000 yrs.
- Final Judgement Day 20:11–15; Jn 5:29.
- The bride's heaven 21:9 to 22:17.
- The bride's invitation to the wedding 22:17.

15 THE REVELATION OF JESUS CHRIST (3)
THE NEXT CENTURY

What is going to happen in the next century and onwards? What does the third millennium AD hold for the world's future? The last four chapters of Revelation tell us and we are going to examine these purposes of God.

This series of books up to now has shown what God was doing behind the scenes in the past. We have seen how wonderfully all of it was fulfilled, detail by detail. It demonstrated that behind it all, God ruled and fulfilled his plan. This was in spite of the sin and opposition of world powers.

Now, we shall see that God reigns in the future as well. It is a wonderful future which none would have dared to predict. In fact, when we look at space fiction and those ideas, we see how different it would be if man were in control.

The Four Hallelujahs

I will now give you an outline of the wonderful future and then examine the details, especially about what the millennium might mean. Some are not sure what interpretation to put on that.

Our former studies have brought us to the triumph of Christ at the second coming. As a result, we notice that Revelation 19 is full of praise. In fact, its first half could be called 'The four hallelujahs' and there is an hallelujah chorus for each. 'Hallelujah' means, 'praise the Lord'.

At a conference of 30,000 evangelists in Amsterdam, Billy Graham reminded those who had come from all over the world that 'Hallelujah' and 'Amen' were two words which were the same in every language. The two words come together in verse 4, 'Amen, Hallelujah'.

Now look at the significance of those four hallelujahs. Our first hallelujah in Revelation 19:1 is from a great united voice of many people in heaven. Their great volume of sound says, 'Salvation and glory and honour and power are of the Lord our God'. They are in raptures because they have just been raptured in resurrection from the earth.

The second hallelujah is because of the victory of the Lord Jesus Christ over all the world's evil powers and especially over false religion.

The third hallelujah is from those who represent the fulfilment of

Old Testament and New Testament Scriptures and the representatives of the four Gospels. Yes, all God's plan foretold in the Scriptures and proclaimed through Christ will be fulfilled because God is on the throne.

That is why the fourth hallelujah comes in a loud voice from the throne itself:

> Praise our God, all you his servants, you who fear him, small and great. Then I heard what seemed to be the voice of a great multitude, like the sound of many waters and like the sound of mighty thunderpeals, crying 'Hallelujah, for the Lord our God the Almighty reigns.' (Revelation 19:5,6)

THE FUTURE OUTLINED

What does the future hold? Tomorrow's world in the twenty-first century holds people spellbound with its possibilities. The technological developments of the third millennium after Christ are exciting, yet dangerous, because man's greed and callousness could ruin everything.

Do the last four chapters of Revelation say anything about this future? They do. They agree that tremendous things are going to happen in space, but not the sort of things which man thinks. They agree that there are terrible dangers, but not from the hotline between the superpowers, rather from the hotline between God and sinners. Revelation agrees that there are going to be remarkable space platforms, not fed by shuttles from earth, but by the new Jerusalem which descends down from heaven in a new world of bliss for the saved.

This all follows that remarkable event foretold for so long – the catching up of the saved to the sky and the marriage of the Church as the bride to her beloved Saviour, the Groom; something which is soon to happen. I will give you a brief outline of events which follow this second coming of the Lord Jesus. This is how it is given in the last four chapters of the Bible. Its various details are supported throughout the Scriptures.

The marriage of the bride and the Lamb is followed by Christ, the King of kings, descending to earth to intervene in the last battle of the age – Armageddon. The kings of the earth are always against Christ, but are defeated and judged. The beast and the false prophet, who deceived millions, are cast into hell. Satan, who deceived the whole world, is also cast into hell and chained so that the world isn't fooled any longer.

Those who were raised at the second coming of Christ reign on earth with Christ for a thousand years. (We shall discuss opinions of this later.) Satan will be loosed at the end of the thousand years and again lead a rebellion against God. It will be put down quickly.

Then all the unsaved dead will be raised for judgement and all those whose names are not in the Lamb's book of life will be cast into the lake of fire. The whole universe will then be cleansed. All sin and death will be burnt up in the lake of fire.

After this, a new heaven and a new earth will be created in which dwells righteousness. In this heavenly city the saved will be living. They will enjoy the happiness and love of God in fellowship. A wide range of imagery is used to describe the eternal bliss: precious stones, streets of gold, each gate made of one huge single pearl, the light of the Lamb, the love of God, the thousands of the redeemed walking in white.

The last chapter of the Bible – Revelation 22 – is a loving and earnest plea to receive this wonderful salvation. Nothing that defiles will be allowed to enter and spoil that heavenly city.

The Antichrist

The last four chapters of Revelation bring to a climax the drama of history as seen by God. Those final events (soon to unfold) will be dramatic, traumatic and triumphant for good.

Now, let us look at some of the details. Before the marriage of the true bride to her Redeemer Christ, the saved rise from the dead and rejoice to be with their Saviour. But there will be a false bride; there will also be a false christ – the antichrist.

The apostle John makes some revealing remarks in his epistle, about the antichrist. You will find them in 1 John 2:18: 'You have heard that antichrist is coming, so now, many antichrists have come . . . they went out from us but they were not of us.'

Notice two things. First, there is more than one antichrist, but there is to be a great and final antichrist. John says there are various antichrists in history and the Lord Jesus said there would be many false christs. There are today and there have been in the past. But in the last hour, says John, there will be the great antichrist.

The second thing to note is that John says they will be backsliders from the Church. Surprising, isn't it, but you hear them today. These antichrists began to deny that Jesus is the Christ. In what way do they deny that Jesus is the Christ? Chapter 4:2,3 of John's first letter says that the spirit of antichrist is one who denies that Jesus Christ has come in the flesh. Those who deny that this person, the anointed Saviour, has come in the flesh, are antichrist.

How did the Messiah Jesus come in the flesh? It was by the incarnation, by God becoming man by the virgin conception through the power of the Holy Spirit without any human father. Anyone denying this, says John, is antichrist.

Why should the coming world ruler deny these things? Because he wants one world religion. To say that Jesus is the only Saviour appointed and anointed by God is a barrier to the antichrist who wants to make a world religion by amalgamating the religions of the world.

Already, we have churchmen doing just this. They are denying the virgin conception; they are denying that the Lord Jesus is the only Saviour anointed by God. They prefer this mixture of Babylonish religion. Mystery religion, Babylon the Great. Moreover, Revelation 17:8 says that the majority will fall for it. In fact, all whose names are not written in the book of life. Here we turn back to John's epistle. He says that it is only those who were born again by the Holy Spirit who will discern truth from error.

The True Christ

Having been shown the antichrist, we are now shown the true Christ in the symbolism.

The symbolism concerns the descent to earth of the victorious Jesus Christ. This is after he has rewarded the resurrected, saved Christians. He then continues his descent to judge the warring world at Armageddon. This then is his description in Revelation 19:11:

> Then I saw heaven opened and behold a white horse! He who sat upon it is called Faithful and True, and in righteousness he judges and makes war. His eyes are like a flame of fire and on his head are many diadems; and he has a name inscribed which no one knows but himself. He is clad in a robe dipped in blood and the name by which he is called is The Word of God. And the armies of heaven, arrayed in fine linen, white and pure, followed him on white horses. From his mouth issues a sharp sword with which to smite the nations and he will rule them with a rod of iron; he will tread the wine press of the fury of the wrath of God the Almighty. On his robe and on his thigh he has a name inscribed, King of kings and Lord of lords.

Among the many wonderful attributes, did you notice the name by which he is called? It is the Word of God. This reminds us of the opening passage of John's Gospel about the Lord Jesus Christ:

> In the beginning was the Word and the Word was with God and the Word was God; He was in the beginning with God and all things were made by him.

We have also seen in Volume 1 of this series that science has discovered that all life was and is created by words. The Lord Jesus himself issued those words in creation. Now in verse 15, we see that he also issues the words of eternal spiritual life for the soul: 'From his mouth issues a sharp sword . . .'

What is it that we possess from the mouth of Jesus? It is his words in the Gospels and teaching in the epistles. They show us how to be saved and also how to be lost. Now, in this passage, he comes to deal with those who have rejected salvation and are lost. And why are they lost? Because they were willingly deceived by unbelief on the one hand, and false religion on the other. These are represented by the beast and the false prophet. At Christ's second coming, they are thrown into the lake of fire.

The Bible is also described as a sword in Hebrews 4:12: 'For the Word of God is living and active, sharper than any two-edged sword, piercing to the division of soul and spirit, of joints and marrow, and discerning the thoughts and intentions of the heart.'

THE BIBLE'S MOST SOLEMN CHAPTER

We have reached the most solemn chapter of the whole Bible. It is awesome in description. It is fearful in its implication for the unsaved. It is shattering to the forces of evil. It is the 20th chapter of the book of Revelation.

It commences with Satan, the devil, being seized and chained and imprisoned for a thousand years. Earlier in Revelation, we are told that the devil came to do his worst in the last days. That was because he knew his time was short. Now his time is up.

Why is it that our world is so full of violence, cruelty, awful murders, drug addictions – in ways not known before – witchcraft and even devil worship? Because Satan knows he has only a short time in which to do his worst. That is what the Bible says.

Now, in this chapter 20, his time is up. Verse 2 makes clear his identity and names him as the dragon, the serpent or snake, the devil and Satan. Let us look at those four names.

The **dragon** with his judgement is announced in Isaiah 27:1: 'In that day the Lord with his hard and great strong sword will punish Leviathan, the reeling snake the twisty serpent; he will slay the dragon'. Isaiah speaks of another remarkable thing after Satan is chained: Israel becomes a blessing. Verse 6 says, 'Israel shall blossom . . . and fill the whole world with fruit'. Yes, Israel converted at the appearing of the descending Lord will evangelise the world during the millennium after the chaining of Satan. In Revelation 12, it is the dragon who is trying to wreck the world today in his hate and fury.

The next name for Satan is the **serpent,** that old serpent, the one who introduced all the trouble at the beginning of human history. 'He is the father of lies,' said Jesus. 'He is a murderer from the beginning.'

His third name here is the **devil** or the prince of devils. He is the great schemer and organiser of evil, says Ephesians 6:11; the one who craves for worship from those deceived by evil spirits. That is why you get devil worshippers.

Finally, he is **Satan,** which means the accuser. The Bible says he accuses Christians night and day. That is why the moment a person is connected to Christ and changes his ways, many accuse him of being a hypocrite and look for all his faults.

Now notice the irony of Satan's arrest! Who does it? He is arrested not by God, not by God's Son, not by an archangel even, but by an ordinary angel: 'I saw an angel coming down from heaven holding in his hand the key of the bottomless pit and he seized the devil and chained him and threw him into the pit.'

This cruel, cunning devil who aspired to sit on God's throne is arrested by an ordinary angel. That was because the angel was given the authority, the key and the chain and because the time had come.

Satan Chained

When Satan is chained and imprisoned in the pit, the whole earth will be at rest and peace and break out into praise. So says Isaiah 14; so says Revelation 20. The world discovers that it was Satan who instigated all the trouble and tribulation:

'How deeply you are fallen from heaven, O Lucifer, son of the morning!' says Isaiah. 'You said to yourself, "I will ascend unto heaven, I will exalt my throne above the stars of God . . . I will be like the Most High". Yet you will be brought down to hell, to the depth of the pit!'

Now, at the second coming of Christ, Revelation 20 describes this very act. The angel with the key of the pit imprisons him there. For 1,000 years, the world is in peace. Satan's contract had run out. Satan's contract – what do I mean? Yes, I see in Scripture that God had given Satan a contract. In fact, in the temptation of the Lord Jesus, Satan claims that. In Luke 4:6 we read these astonishing words: 'The devil showed Jesus all the kingdoms of the world in a moment of time and the devil said to him, "All this power I will give you and the glory of them, for that is delivered to me and to whoever I wish I give it." '

Surely, you say, that was a false and insolent claim. But no, Jesus doesn't dispute it. In fact, later, he described the devil as 'The prince of this age'. Now, in Revelation 20, 'this age' had ended. Satan's contract had run out.

But why should God give a contract to such an evil being? He wasn't evil when he was created. Ezekiel 28:15 tells us that. Satan was perfect when he was created. It was then that the oversight of earth's development was committed to him. God does not break his word or contract even to the wicked, but he can justly overrule it to bring good out of evil.

When did Satan fall? I suggest that it was in the second day of creation, because that was the only day God did not bless. That was the day the air was made. Satan is described as the prince and power of the air. It seems to me that from then on he began to interfere with God's creation until, at the end of the sixth day, he corrupted man.

Satan is the source of all illness and germs, Jesus said, concerning an afflicted woman suffering from spinal softening. When Satan is chained, disease will disappear, said Isaiah about the millennium. Also, war will disappear, said Micah about the millennium. Savagery in the animal kingdom will also disappear, says Paul when he quotes Isaiah.

Yes, there is a wonderful time coming when Satan is bound. The best is yet to be! That is when Christ comes.

But you can limit Satan's activity now – by prayer, said Jesus. 'That which you bind in heaven by prayer will be bound on earth.'

THE BIBLICAL MILLENNIUM

I have mentioned the millennium. The word is found in Revelation 20. Millennium means 1,000 years and, in Christian circles, it has the connotation of 1,000 years happiness and bliss when all wars will cease – that cannot be said of these times – disease will vanish and there will be righteousness and happiness because Jesus Christ reigns.

When will this be? Before considering that question, I should say that any opinion on this is not essential to Christian doctrine. It is not essential to salvation. Saved Christians have different opinions and so it is more of a sin to quarrel about it than it is to fail to have the right answer. Paul says, 'If I understand all prophecies and have not love, it profits me nothing.' Having said that, I want you to consider with me the scriptures which I think show that *the millennium follows Christ's return and is the result of Christ's return.*

First, the Lord clearly states in Luke 21:31 that his Kingdom comes after his return. The verses before that describe his second coming and the signs which show his coming is near. Then he says, 'When you see these things come to pass, showing the second coming is imminent, know that the Kingdom of God is near.' So then, this Kingdom is still to come after Christ's return – that must be the millennium.

Second, Paul tells us in Romans 8 that the resurrection of the sons of God will be followed by peace and harmony, even in the animal creation. Now the Christian is resurrected at Christ's second coming. The peace and harmony which follows is what the prophets Isaiah and Micah speak of when referring to the millennium.

Third, sometimes it is asserted that the 1,000 years is spoken of only in Revelation 20. Well, while it is true that the length of the period is given there, the characteristics of the millennium are given in many Old Testament passages and by Paul. Moreover, Peter refers to it and says that with the Lord a day is like 1,000 years and 1,000 years are like a day. Also, at the end of both his epistles, he uses a typical Greek phrase: it is 'an age-lasting day'. Now this phrase, 'the day of the Lord' is frequently used by the Old Testament prophets. The New Testament shows it as a 1,000-year day.

Fourth, Isaiah 27 refers to the binding of Satan and that this will be followed by Israel filling the earth with fruit. This gives sense to the way God has been gathering Israel to the Holy Land. Other prophecies tell you that the nation of Israel will be converted immediately they see Christ descend to Jerusalem and see the wounds in his body. The term 'Israel' here cannot refer to spiritual Israel – the Church – because the believers are saved before the second coming.

We shall see that Christian opinion of the first three centuries was in line with the millennium following Christ's return, but remember that, although the Jews will be the missionaries of the new age, the Gentile Christians are the main missionaries for this age.

The Millennium and the Early Church

How are we to come to the right interpretation of less clear texts of the Bible? First, it is no use seeing how many are for and how many are against. You need to look at people's motives for their opinion.

Our question is – does the 1,000 years of peace and righteousness come after the return of Christ or before it? Are we now living at a time when there are no wars and wickedness and when there is no cruelty among the animals or will that be after Christ has returned and judged those things?

Professor Harnack, in his article entitled 'Millennium', in *Encyclopaedia Brittanica,* under 'Person and Work of the Redeemer', reviews all the Christian writers of the first three centuries and finds that they believed that the millennium would come after Christ's return. So why did some begin to change their opinion in the fifth century? It was because, when the Roman Empire made Christianity its state religion, some thought the millennium had already begun – even though Christ had not returned – and that the Church was already reigning on earth.

Augustine in AD 413 was the first to suggest this idea. We saw that the first four seals in Revelation foretold the persecution by the Roman Empire, then, under the fifth seal, all those in heaven who were martyred by Rome asked how long it would be before the persecutors were judged. They were told that there were yet even worse persecutions coming when other Christians would be martyred like themselves in later centuries. But they thought the temporary lull in persecution was the millennium on their doorstep.

So you see, it was not the examination of the text of Revelation 20 which changed its interpretation.

Among the Christian writers of the first three centuries, Harnack refers to Justin Martyr. He lived AD 100 to 165. He was told by a disciple of the apostle John (who wrote Revelation) that the millennium was *after* Christ's return. Then there was another Christian writer named Ireneus who wrote around AD 185. He listened to Polycarp who also knew John the apostle. He too said the millennium would come after Christ's return. Tertullian was another who lived a few years later. He also said the millennium would follow Christ's return.

The Reformers Martin Luther, John Knox, and John Calvin also agreed that the millennium would follow Christ's return and not precede it.

'Some say,' writes Luther, 'that before the latter day the whole world shall become Christians. This is a falsehood forged by Satan that he might darken sound doctrine. Beware, therefore, of this delusion.' And John Knox, the intrepid Scotch reformer, likewise declares: 'To reform the whole earth, which never was, nor yet shall be, till that righteous King and Judge appear for the restoration of all things.' Of the unfitness of the conception of the Kingdom appearing before the King, of the triumph of the saints before the triumph of the Saviour, John Calvin speaks thus: 'Christ is our Head, whose kingdom and glory have not yet appeared. If the members were to go before the Head, the order of things would be inverted and preposterous; but we shall follow our Prince when He shall come in the glory of His Father and sit upon the throne of His majesty.'

The only way in which Revelation 20 could be interpreted differently is to say that the words about the first resurrection relate to when the saved lived spiritually – that is, when they were born again. But that is an unnatural way of applying the words. In any case, the same words refer to the second resurrection, for judgement, which refuses to be interpreted like that.

So the wars and sin of today are not the millennium. When the true millennium comes, sin, Satan and suffering will be banished and the Lord Jesus will be the centre of love and praise (Habakkuk 2:14): 'The earth shall be filled with the knowledge of the Lord as the waters cover the sea.'

The Millennium in the Old Testament

It is not always realised how often the millennium is described in the Old Testament. The beginning of the millennium is described in Joel, Micah and Zechariah, and even Habakkuk, and further details are given by Isaiah and Ezekiel. The last chapter of Zechariah describes the second coming when Jesus descends to the Mount of Olives, east of Jerusalem. It says, 'Then the Lord will become King over all the earth'. Did you notice that this will be *after* the second coming. All nations will then go up year after year to worship the King at the Feast of Tabernacles – that is, the harvest festival in October. There will be texts even on the bells of horse harnesses, 'Holiness unto the Lord', as well as on cooking pots.

Micah 4 has the same picture of all nations beating their swords into ploughshares and of God's righteous law going out to all the nations from Jerusalem.

The beginning of the millennium is described in Joel 3. When the great and terrible day of the Lord comes, the Lord will gather all nations to Jerusalem for judgement. Wickedness will be judged and the world will know that Jehovah is the Lord their God. He then dwells in Zion and Jerusalem is holy.

In various visions in Daniel, the Son of Man comes in the clouds with the saved to rule in the earth. Here again, the reign of Christ on earth is after his second coming. We read in Daniel 7:13,14:

> I saw in the night visions, and behold, with the clouds of heaven there came one like a son of man, and he came to the Ancient of Days and was presented before him. And to him was given dominion and glory and kingdom that all peoples, nations and languages should serve him; his dominion is an everlasting dominion which shall not pass away and his kingdom one that shall not be destroyed.

In Ezekiel, it is after the **last battle** of the age in chapters 38 and 39 that we read in 39:21:

> I will set my glory among the nations and all nations shall see my judgement . . . The house of Israel will know that I am the Lord their God, from that day forward and the nations will know that the house of Israel went into captivity for their iniquity . . . and that I have brought them back from the nations and gathered them . . . into their own land.

After this, the remaining chapters describe the glory of the Lord taking up residence in Jerusalem.

One could go on quoting the better-known descriptions of the millennium in Isaiah. They appear throughout the book – in chapters 2, 11 and 65, e.g. 'In the latter days, out of Zion will go forth the law . . . He shall judge between nations . . . They will not learn war any more . . . The wolf will lie down with the lamb . . . the calf and the lion together and a little child shall lead them . . . for the earth will be full of the knowledge of the Lord as the waters cover the sea.'

Paul takes this literally in Romans 8 and it has never happened yet, so what great news for the believer! These are clear statements that there is a wonderful time ahead after the second coming of our Lord Jesus Christ.

THE RESURRECTIONS

The 1,000 years' peace on earth, which is coming when Christ returns and reigns, is marked in Revelation 20 by two resurrections. The resurrection of the saved marks the beginning at the second coming of Jesus and the 1,000 years ends with the resurrection of all the rest. 'The rest of the dead did not come to life until the thousand years were ended' (v 5).

At the end of the chapter we are told that they are raised for judgement, whereas the saved dead are raised for reward and to reign with Christ for 1,000 years. 'This is the first resurrection', it says, 'Blessed and holy is he who shares in the first resurrection; over such the second death has no power, but they shall be priests of God and of Christ and they shall reign with him a thousand years' (v 6).

Paul refers to this in 1 Corinthians 6: 'Don't you know that the saved will judge the world. Don't you know that you will even judge angels?' he says. Daniel also is told that the saved *share* Christ's reign: 'The kingdoms under the whole heaven will be given to the people of the saved of the Most High . . . and all countries will serve and obey them' (7:27).

Someone asked me why the body and soul of the believer needed to be reunited again. Have you wondered why the resurrection was necessary? It is so that the saved can operate in two dimensions – the spiritual unseen and the earthly and material. In this they are like the risen Christ. During the 40 days before he ascended, he appeared and disappeared at will.

Paul says that Christ was the first fruits of this resurrection body. Next, he says, will be the experience of those who belong to Christ – that is, the saved at the second coming; then he says Christ will reign and put all things under his feet – that is the millennium. He will then deliver the Kingdom to the Father. Then comes the resurrection of the unsaved for judgement and hell's punishment. Then death itself will be abolished. These stages are all marked out by adverbs of time. As Paul and Revelation 20:14 say:

Death and Hades will be thrown into the lake of fire, this is the second death [for those] whose names were not found written in the book of life.

Justice is Done

Henry VIII's flagship, *The Mary Rose*, was raised from beneath the sea after nearly 500 years. It was gruesome seeing the skeletons of the 700 crew and soldiers who were drowned. In Revelation 20, John saw in a vision the awesome spectacle of those who had perished in the seas. They rose up from the oceans. They were to be judged as they stood before the great white throne of the mighty God. Verse 13 says: 'The sea gave up the dead which were in it. Death and the abode of the dead gave up the dead in them and all were judged by what they had done.'

In preceding verses we are told that all others were also raised – both small and great – ordinary folk and world famous personalities. None will get away with it. Justice will be done and be seen to be done! This is the theme which I want you to notice. *Justice will be done.*

Imagine when Hitler will stand before this terrifying assize. Every cruelty that he has been responsible for will be returned upon him. If there are ten million people who have suffered pain through him, then ten million similar pains will be experienced by him.

But the 'small' pains will also be judged and sentenced. As I write, I have just heard of someone who left his car in a position dangerous to the public. When it was pointed out, he said, 'Let them lump it!' Lack of consideration for others will also be judged.

So frightening will be the presence of God that verse 11 tells you that 'From his presence even heaven and earth will flee away'. It is then revealed that full records of everyone's every deed, thought or motive have been recorded. 'The books were opened [v 12] and all were judged according to the records – by what they had done.' This is repeated twice.

It means that no one will be able to say that his sentence is unjust. 'The Judge of all the earth will do right', as Abraham said. The trouble is this: the Bible tells you what the sentence will be. Romans 3:19 says the verdict will be 'Guilty'. Then verse 20 says: 'No human being will be justified in God's sight by his works.'

So then, what is our hope? We read, 'There was another book opened called the book of life.' Yes, there are two records. The **book of works** and the **book of grace**. Time and time again Scripture tells us that, 'By works will no person be saved'. Just one sin will keep you out of heaven, Jesus said in the Sermon on the Mount.

So that is why the book of grace is opened. This is the book of life – open to see if our names are there, because only those recorded there will be saved from the lake of fire and enter heaven. Why is it a book of grace? Because by grace you are saved, the Bible says. Grace means '*gratis*' – something free, unearned and undeserved.

Awaiting Trial

We have been looking at the dramatic and awesome 20th chapter of Revelation. Now we come to a mysterious phrase. It is in verse 14, 'Death and Hades were cast into the lake of fire'.

What does this mean? It means that the remand prison is no longer required. Hades was the place where the souls of the unsaved dead await their trial. They were in jail on remand. The Bible says this is where the souls of the lost go to await the day of judgement. Jesus promised that the saved would not go there. Neither would they come to the judgement.

So, why then is death and the place of the dead abolished? Because remand has given place to sentence. In Revelation 20, the judgement has been pronounced; the sentences are about to be implemented and so there is no more need for the remand jail. Neither will there be any more to die and await judgement, so both death and Hades (the remand prison) are destroyed in the lake of fire.

There will be others also in the lake of fire. They will be the false prophet and the antichrist – the false religions which Satan, the devil, used to deceive all who rejected salvation through God's Christ. There will also be those who avoided salvation. These names were not written in the Lamb's book of life. Time and time again Christ sought them with bleeding feet and hands, but they avoided his offer of life until, at last, opportunity passed and they hear the last words of Christ to them recorded in Matthew 25: 'Depart from me, you who bear the curses; depart from me into the eternal fire prepared for the devil and his fallen angels.'

That is the final and eternal separation. The Bible is consistent in God's teaching of separation. At death, there is separation of the saved from the unsaved. The unsaved go to the remand prison to await trial, but the saved go to be with Christ.

At the resurrection, there is separation. In the first resurrection, the bodies of the saved unite with their souls happily already with Christ to receive reward. In the second resurrection, the dead are raised later to receive punishment for their sins at the great assize. Their punishment is just. It is according to the sins done in the body. Sins of omission as well as commission while they were alive. The lost are then separated for eternity. What was their greatest sin? It was refusal to believe on Christ and give themselves to him. The Lord Jesus said this in John 16, 'The Holy Spirit will convince men of sin because they do not believe on me'.

The Bowls Angel Again

We pass from the sadness of the lost in Revelation 20 to the eternal joy of the saved. Who is it who shows to John this wonderful vision of the eternal joy, the bliss of those who love Christ as Saviour and Lord? Have you noticed who it is? It is an angel of the bowls of anger. How strange – and why?

In our analysis of the structure of the book of Revelation, we saw that the book was planned on a series of four sevens – seven lampstands, seven wax seals, seven trumpets and seven bowls of anger. Each series of seven was interpreted and applied by the visions which followed it. Now, the last series of seven was the seven bowls in chapter 16. This series is followed, as usual, by the visions which interpret them. The visions apply their meaning and that is why it is an angel of the seven bowls who talks to John, the writer, about them.

So then, the first six bowls were about the way in which Bible truth would overcome false religion. Thus the angel shows this to be the collapse of mystery Babylon religion and the judgement of the false prophet. Then the marriage of the bride, the Church, to Christ takes place at the second coming of Christ, then next comes the last war of the age – Armageddon. This is followed by Christ's victory, then the millennium.

All this, the angel of the bowls is saying, interprets the sixth bowl. Look at chapter 16.

Preparations for a world war are in verse 14. Then Jesus Christ comes unexpectedly like a thief in the night for his bride. They are the saved. Then follows the world's last war, Armageddon – in verse 16. The seventh bowl is then poured out and Babylon falls and judgement of the nations follows.

It is after this (in the next chapter) that an angel of the bowls begins to explain the meaning. Revelation 17:1 reads: 'Then one of the seven angels who had the seven bowls came and said to me, "Come, I will show you" ' – show the meaning, that is.

For the rest of the book of Revelation, chapters 17 to 22, we are reminded at various points that it is this angel who is explaining things. He explains the marriage of the bride of Christ; he explains Armageddon; he explains the millennium which follows; he tells of the burning up of all evil in the lake of fire and now in chapter 21, he shows the happiness of the bride, the new Jerusalem. In verse 9, the bowls angel speaks again. He says: 'Come, I will show you the bride, the wife of the Lamb.'

Yes, she is married now. She is the wife (it says) and they lived happily ever after.

All the heartbreak of wooing is over. Paul spoke of it (2 Corinthians 11): 'I betroth you to Christ, to present you as a pure virgin to her husband', afraid that the serpent, Satan, might deceive you by false religion as the snake deceived Eve.

Yes, all those fears are now past. The dangers are over. The Bridegroom has come. The saved and Jesus are now united in love. The saved walk the streets of gold.

What Is He Showing You?

We saw how an angel showed John the wonderful meaning of the seven bowls of Revelation 16. Appropriately, it is an angel of the seven bowls who does this in the last six chapters of Revelation.

He showed John the false bride; he showed John the false christ; he showed John the true bride; he showed John the true Christ – husband to the Church; then comes the marriage, the banishment of rival suitors, the millennium. Then the angel shows John the bride's home, the heavenly Jerusalem and now, in chapter 22, he shows John the river of the water of life.

What is he showing us? He wants to show us something which will bring us eternal happiness. He wants to save us from rival suitors. They often appear as angels of light. Paul warned about this, but they are the pawns of the devil. For, as Paul wrote in 2 Corinthians 11:13,14:

> For such men are false apostles, deceitful workmen, disguising themselves as apostles of Christ. And no wonder, for even Satan disguises himself as an angel of light.

'I am jealous over you', says the scripture. That rival suitor will lead you astray from Christ.

In Revelation 22:1, the angel is showing us the river of the water of life. The angel of the bowls showed that, earlier in church history, the water had been poisoned. False doctrine denied that anyone could drink and know that he was saved for eternity. False doctrine said that it was presumption for anyone to think that the water of life would quench spiritual thirst for ever. Yet Christ had said: 'He who believes on me . . . out of his heart will flow rivers of living water' and this he said about the Holy Spirit who would be received by those who believed in Christ as their own Saviour.

Verse 16 says, 'I, Jesus, have sent my angel to you and the Holy Spirit and the bride say to you, "Come, come, you who are thirsty and take the water of life which is free".'

Dual Interpretation of Scripture

Someone said, 'If there is one thing men learn from history, it is that men never learn from history!' There is something that Christianity doesn't learn from history. It is not to have divisions over non-essentials. One non-essential is whether the book of Revelation is in the past or in the future. In other words, some interpret Revelation as *futuristic* and others interpret it as *historical*. I have been showing that most prophecy is fulfilled in both ways. Historically, it may be fulfilled symbolically and, in the future, literally. An example is that Jesus said John the Baptist was Elijah, symbolically, but Elijah himself was still to come literally.

We have seen how chapters 1 to 17 of Revelation have been fulfilled down the last 19 centuries in most remarkable ways. And we see how it will be fulfilled futuristically. This takes chapter 4 as the resurrection of the saved, then all those chapters from 4 to 19 as referring to the tribulation, which follows the rapture.

The Tribulation

What is this tribulation? Tribulation means a terrible time on earth. It is the result of the restraining power of Christian witness being removed because the saved will have been caught up to meet the Lord Jesus Christ. It will last seven years. Actually, those seven years on earth will not affect the Christians much, because I believe Christians will be in the sky attending prize-giving day and the wedding of the bride to the Saviour. Then, at the end of that tribulation on earth, they will descend with the triumphant Saviour to judge the warring nations in the Holy Land and to set up the millennial kingdom of peace and righteousness on earth.

So then, what happens during that seven years' tribulation on earth? It is the period between the resurrection of the saved until they return to earth with Jesus.

Q Will Christians go through the tribulation?

I am often asked this, so I ought to give you some guidelines here, but whether you agree with me or not, don't let it hinder you from talking to others about the signs of the times.

By the word 'tribulation', people often mean those terrible days in the last few years before the descent of Christ from heaven to judge the nations. The Bible describes these times in many places – lawlessness, lust . . . Scripture speaks of Christ coming FOR his own WITH his own. It seems logical that there will be a space of time between these events, but how long will it be? Will it be short? Will Christ descend to earth's atmosphere, raise the saved – dead and living – to meet him in the air, then continue his descent to earth to judge the nations? It seems not, because there is at least one event to take place between the coming FOR his own and the descent WITH his own. It is called 'the judgement of Christ', for which the word in Greek is '*Bema*'.

> For we must all come to the judgement seat [*Bema*] of Christ to receive the deeds done in the body whether they were good or bad.

The Bema in Paul's day was the local court for the local people, not the great assize. Christ's Bema is for his people. They will not come to the great judgement later on. This is the prize-giving day for the faithful and also to allot position in the coming kingdom (Matthew 25:21). That's why the parable in Matthew 25 of the talent rewards precedes Christ's descent to set up his throne on earth (25:31).

Q How long will this take? And also what will be happening on earth during that time?

Well, the saved won't be on earth, will they? They've been caught up to meet Christ in the air. The restraining influence of Christians will have been removed and so morals and malice will run riot. So whatever the length of time of that terrible period, the saved won't be there, will they? – it's between the return FOR his own and WITH his own.

So why is there confusion? It is due to a misunderstanding of the word 'tribulation' in Matthew 24:29. There we read that the elect (saved) are gathered 'after the tribulation' (verse 31 refers). But what tribulation is this? Verse 12 tells you that it will follow the fall of Jerusalem which happened in AD 70. This becomes clear if you put Luke's report alongside Mark and Matthew's.

Luke makes it clear that it would be tribulation for the Jews. During the last 2,000 years, Jews have been hounded from country to country. For Gentiles, too, many millions of Bible-believing Christians have been slaughtered 'for the Word of God and their testimony' (Revelation 20:4).

Q What scriptures show that Christians will be rescued by their resurrection before the tribulation?

God is telling Isaiah about the resurrection in chapter 25 verse 8: 'He will swallow up death for ever and the Lord God will wipe away tears from all faces.' The following verse applies it to God's people.

In Isaiah 26:19 you read 'Thy dead shall live, their bodies will rise. O dwellers of the dust, awake and sing for joy!' Then the Lord comes for his own and says:

Come my people, enter your chambers and shut your doors behind you; hide yourself for a little while until the wrath is past. For behold! The Lord is coming forth out of his place to punish the inhabitants of the earth for their iniquity.

1 Thessalonians 4:17 and Zechariah 14:5,9 also apply.

Most 'futurists' take the events from Revelation 4 to 19 in chronological order, but this may not be so. The most profitable thing is to note the main trends and to see how very relevant they are to the kind

of world our present times are leading up to. Here they all are.
Devastation through chemical, germ and nuclear warfare is graphically described. Out of these threats to mankind, a world dictator emerges
called the antichrist. The Common Market or World Market system is
pictured when everyone is given a number for trading. The enforce-
ment of a world religion which proposes to amalgamate all religions.
The prophet Elijah and his companion witness to the world, especially
to the Jews. Remember that Elijah is to come before Christ's second
coming. He and his companion will be opposed by the false prophet
and the false christ. In the middle of the seven years, the antichrist will
break his covenant with the Israelis, then openly persecute all who
believe the witness of Elijah and his companion. This opposition will
then break into open defiance of God and his Christ and the last war of
the age will be started by antichrist's fist raised against heaven. These
are the implications applied futuristically.

When we get discouraged by the widespread militant atheism of
today, remember that this challenge is the prelude to the world's most
dramatic victory by the Lord Jesus Christ. He is described in
Revelation 19:11,16. Verses 19 and 21 then show antichrist's challenge:

> And I saw the beast and the kings of the earth with their armies gathered
> to make war against him who sits upon the horse and against his army
> . . . And the rest were slain by the sword of him who sits upon the horse,
> the sword that issues from his mouth; and all the birds were gorged with
> their flesh.

NEW HEAVEN AND EARTH

Do earthquake calamities trouble you? A question which some keep
bringing up is: why does God allow earthquakes? Why does God allow
suffering and death? An answer is given in the last two chapters of the
Bible. Revelation 21 starts off with the statement: 'I saw a new heav-
en and a new earth because the first heaven and the first earth had
passed away.'

What was the matter with the old earth? Why did it have to be
destroyed before 'all tears could be wiped away' as verse 4 says? Why
did heaven and earth have to flee away before 'no more death or crying or any more pain'? It was because Satan, the devil, had interfered
with this present earth.

You may say, 'Yes, I know that the devil brought conflict and death
to the animal kingdom. I know that the Bible says that in the millennium there will be no more nature "red in tooth and claw", but I did not
know that death in the physical world was due to Satan'.

My reply is this. We saw how Satan was made overseer of the earth before he rebelled against God and became the father of all wickedness. Now, according to Ezekiel 28, he began to spoil God's creation in its geological stages. You remember that in God's original creation, he made the land area all one continent (Genesis 1). Geologists have since confirmed that. They have also confirmed that the land area has, since then, split into continents. Did Satan break up that unity? The significant thing is this. Most of all the earthquakes are caused by the continents pushing away from each other. Earthquakes occur all around the world in these continental margins called, in geology, the new fold mountains.

So then, for there to be no more death and pain, sorrow or crying, there had to be a new earth. Notice also that it will be after Satan is banished for ever into the lake of fire. It is after this that God declares in verse 5, 'Behold! I make all things new . . . there will be no more pain, because the former things are passed away.'

The A and the Z

Many people love to visit places of historic interest. They capture something of the history of the past, especially old churches and old cathedrals. You may have noticed in these buildings the letters A and a funny looking O. The O is open at the bottom. Actually, it is a Greek letter called Omega (W) and the A stands for the first letter of the Greek alphabet, Alpha (A). Why are those letters there? It is because in the last book of the Bible, the book of Revelation, these words occur several times: 'I am Alpha and Omega'.

Now these are dramatically significant. They occur in Revelation 21:6. It is the Lord Jesus Christ speaking. Here are his words: 'And he said unto me, "It is accomplished. I am Alpha and Omega, the beginning and the end".'

Now Alpha and Omega are the beginning and end of the Greek alphabet. It is like Jesus saying that he is the A and the Z. But why should the beginning and the ending of the alphabet have anything to do with the beginning and ending of creation? That is what this passage has been talking about. It is because of that staggering discovery made by modern scientists that creation is the result of words.

Life itself is the result of words. It is initiated, programmed and completed by words in every cell of life. Those words are called by the scientist the DNA code. It is in every cell of every plant; it is in every cell of every animal; it is in every cell of every human being; it is in every cell of our own bodies. The DNA code is translated into an alphabet of 64 letters or codons (see Chapter 2 of this book and Chapter 5 of *Volume 1: Science*).

Jesus said, 'I am the Alpha and Omega'. He supplied that original alphabet of life. Biologically, his words are in every cell of your body!

Furthermore, he is the originator of all material existence. All atoms contain particles. They are given all sorts of funny names these days, but these sub-atomic particles are named by the Greek alphabet. They are enumerated from Alpha to Omega.

The Lord Jesus Christ says, 'I am the Alpha and Omega, the beginning and the end of creation'. Do you remember the opening words of John's Gospel: 'In the beginning was the Word [that is, Jesus Christ] . . . everything was made by that Word.'

Did you notice the verse (Revelation 21:6) started by saying, 'It is completed!' Creation was completed, but Jesus goes on to say something else was completed. It was our salvation which he offers free of charge. He says: 'I am the Alpha and Omega . . . I will give to you who are thirsty, the fountain of the water of eternal life, free and without charge.'

Flowing from the Throne

In the Cornish town of Helston, there is a sparkling stream flowing through the main street, down the hillside to the sea which is nearby. In Revelation 22 John writes: 'He showed me a pure river of water of life, clear as crystal, flowing out of the throne of God and of the Lamb'. It was flowing down the main street of the heavenly city. There were trees growing on either side. It symbolised paradise regained because one of the trees was the tree of life. This had been depicted in the Garden of Eden where paradise was first lost.

Much of the last chapters of Revelation is an application of the last chapter of Ezekiel. In the 47th chapter of Ezekiel, we are told that when God reigns, water bringing life to a dead area flows from under the threshold of the temple.

In the prophecy of Ezekiel, this description is given as if it is to be taken literally, but in Revelation 22, it is applied spiritually. Here again is an example that prophecy is often fulfilled in two ways – literally and symbolically.

Why do I think Ezekiel's vision was to be fulfilled literally? Because actual geographical details are given. As I explained in Chapter 8, we are told that the water will come up to sea level in the Jordan Valley; and that the sea water of the Mediterranean will flow into the Dead Sea and bring sea fish. When we compare this with Zechariah 14, we have already seen that this will actually happen when Christ descends from heaven to the Mount of Olives. That mountain will split in half. Then the well-known rift valley system will extend from the Jordan Valley to the Mediterranean Sea. It will open up the widest shipping canal in the world. This will make Jerusalem the maritime shipping centre of the continents. Into this new rift valley will flow the fresh waters from the temple threshold.

When I had the privilege of examining the hydrological survey of the Holy Land it showed that abundant fresh water would flow out of Jerusalem if a rupture in the rocks occurred, releasing copious fresh water now contained in the vast artesian basin under the Holy Land. What a blessing to know that this will be fulfilled spiritually also in the future. Yes, abundant living water will flow out from the throne of God.

Whenever God is on the throne, that brings life. Revelation 22 speaks of when the new heaven and earth has been created in which dwells righteousness. All sin, evil and pain will have been banished for ever. To the saved enjoying that eternal bliss, the water of life sparkling and clear will be a source supplying satisfaction in the love and service of God and of the Lamb, the Lord Jesus Christ.

No Longer Sealed

Sometimes, when a very important letter is sent, perhaps very private and confidential as well, such a letter has a wax seal on the flap. That is so it cannot be opened by anyone without breaking the seal.

In Revelation 5, only the Lamb of God had the authority to break the seals of prophesied history. Likewise, Daniel in the Old Testament is given information about the future, but in Daniel 12:9 he is told to seal up the information, to keep it private and confidential. The reason given for this is to hide from Daniel how long it would be to the end. Daniel didn't understand what he was told, so God said those living in the end times would understand.

Why wasn't it good for Daniel to know? Because he asked how long it would be before the end. He would surely have been discouraged if he knew that it would not be for another 2,500 years. But he is told that the confidential information will be understood by Christians living in these last days. So to Daniel, 'The words are sealed until the time of the end'.

Now, Revelation 22, I believe, is for those for whom the time of the end had come. Jesus said in verse 12, 'Behold I come quickly'. He says that to us living in this end time and so adds, 'Do not seal the sayings of the prophecy of this book for the time is at hand.' So, to us, living in the last days, a special insight was promised which was denied even to Daniel; verse 10: 'The spiritually wise will understand'.

Now, it began to be revealed in the last century to godly Bible-believing scholars such as Dr Grattan Guinness, Dr A.J. Gordon and Dr Clark. It was about time schedules. It was that, in prophecy, one day equals one year. For example, when Israel came out of Egypt, the spies took 40 days to report on the Promised Land. They returned and gave a false report, so God said that for each day as a year, the Israelites would wander in the wilderness 40 years.

Likewise, Ezekiel was told that each day represented a year. So then, Daniel was told, in verse 7, that it would be twice 3½ times. I have been able to show from archaeology that one 'Time' was a Sumerian measurement of 360 year-days; seven 'Times' is 2,520 years. That was fulfilled. Israel was dispersed or scattered among the nations for that length of time, as verse 7 says. Moses also said it would be for seven 'Times' long.

Now, that length of scattering until the regathering brings us to modern times when we see the miracle of Israel's regathering today. This insight would have discouraged Daniel but it encourages believers today. Today, some might be tempted to ask how we can know that prophecy is fulfilling after all this long time.

To us, then, who are living, the Lord can say, 'Behold I come quickly', what was sealed and concealed from Daniel is unsealed and revealed to you who are wise enough to understand.

Washed Robes

A missionary was dying from malaria. As he crawled on his stomach, he gasped out a prayer, 'Please, Lord, heal me!' He had crawled to the side of a small pool and, craving for water, he drank. It tasted horrible, but as he lay there for hours, he drank again and again and, lo and behold, he was getting better! Why? The leaves of the trees around had saturated the pool. Those trees supplied quinine. It was a great discovery for medicine. It was the first great breakthrough in drugs to cure malaria.

In Revelation 21 and 22, trees were growing in paradise for healing and, in 22:14, there was the tree of life. Adam of old had forfeited his right to the tree of life because he sinned and hid from God, but now it was promised to all who washed their robes.

Now a little problem. Someone looking at the King James' Bible will see that version says, 'They who do his commandments will have the right to the tree of life'. That old version is usually very reliable, but here it is not.

What is the reason? In the Greek language, the words 'They who do his commandments' and the words 'They who wash their robes' look very similar. If you look at all modern translations, you will see that they all translate it as 'They who wash their robes will have the right to the tree of life'. Since the King James' version was translated, older documents have been discovered which make this quite clear.

However, anyone who knew the teaching of all Scripture should have known that 'by works no one can be saved'. It is only forgiven people who get to heaven – only those who have washed their robes white in the blood of the Lamb – and, indeed, this is what all the other passages in Revelation proclaim. Ephesians 2:8 tells us, we cannot be saved by works; St John tells us, we cannot be saved by works; St Peter tells us, we cannot be saved by works. We are saved by the blood of Christ. 'You were ransomed not by perishable things such as silver and gold, but by the precious blood of Christ, like a lamb without blemish.'

Revelation 7 tells us the good news that all who John saw in heaven rejoicing around the throne were those who had washed their robes and made them white in the blood of the Lamb. They had come and eaten of the tree of life in the paradise of God. Eternal life was theirs.

Tampering Forbidden

I saw a very old bridge in Cornwall. It had a cast-iron notice on it which must have been left there for curiosity's sake. It said: 'Any person tampering with this bridge will be deported immediately to Australia'.

Well, I had often wanted a free trip to Australia as I have many good friends there, but as the notice must have been at least 150 years old, I didn't think I would test it. In any case, I wouldn't do it because it was wrong.

There is another notice we can read any day. It is far older. It is 19 centuries old and it concerns a really serious offence. Strangely enough, however, many people who consider themselves quite respectable, ignore the warning. It is in Revelation 22:18. It is the Creator speaking:

> I solemnly declare that, if anyone adds anything to what is written in this book, to him God will add the plagues written in this book; and if anyone takes anything away from this book, God will take away his share in the tree of life.

Yet there are today theologians who get publicity or media attention, who do just this. I would tremble to be in their shoes on judgement day. They have spread unbelief among the general public. To reinforce the warning, verse 6 says, 'These words are trustworthy and true'. As the Lord Jesus said in John 17, 'Thy Word is Truth'. Similar warnings against tampering with God's Word, the Bible, are in all its sections.

We have it in what God said to Moses, yet many Higher Critics deny what Moses wrote. The Bible says, 'If they don't believe Moses, neither will they believe even though one rose from the dead.' Christ rose from the dead and they don't believe that either.

Notice that this Bible warning not to tamper with God's Word says that anyone who does, will not have his share in the tree of life. Those who do tamper with it lose their assurance that they are saved – if they had any. In fact, they probably don't like this glorious word 'saved' which is proclaimed in the Bible.

It is so appropriate that the Bible should end with such a warning because everyone who heeds it can have the blessing of the last two verses which end the whole Bible. Have you noticed how the Old Testament ended with a curse – the curse which sin had brought to the world, but the New Testament ends with a blessing given through the Lord Jesus Christ. Here it is: 'The grace of our Lord Jesus Christ be with you all, Amen.'

Yes, sin spoilt God's world through Adam.
The law came through Moses.
But grace and truth came through Jesus Christ.

From hopelessness to hope, from destruction to deliverance is the story of history. It can be the story of many others too, that is why the Bible ends by urging all who hear the message to come and take the water of life offered.

SUMMARY

THE NEXT CENTURY

The Rapture
- Illustrated in Rev 14 is the first resurrection. Those who believed.
- The wheat harvest in spring – Christ's wheat are those who die in the Lord (Rev 14:13–16).
- The grapes and fruit harvest in autumn is the second resurrection, i.e. the ungodly for judgement (14:17–20; 20:5,11–15 [cf. 1 Cor 15:25,26]).
- One of the plagues was destructive Bible criticism (15:3). Victory was gained over them by those who sang the song of Moses and the Lamb, i.e. Moses' writings were genuine and the Lamb's atonement fully effective (says Dr Basil Atkinson).
- Rapture next illustrated in 16:15 before Armageddon in v 16 (cf. Is 26:19–21).
- 'I am coming like a thief.' This simile is used 5 times:
    1. Rev 16:15.
    2. Matt 24:43 'Shall gather his elect'.
    3. 1 Thess 5:2 Children of light should not be surprised v 4,5.
    4. 2 Pet 3:10 'Be blameless' (v 14).
    5. Rev 3:3 unworthy Christians warned as in 1 Cor 3:8–15.
- Rapture next mentioned in 20:6 'This is the first resurrection' (cf. 1 Pet 4:17).

The Millennium Rev 20:2–7
- When? Opinion not essential. Love is more important (1 Cor 13:2).
- Kingdom comes after Christ's return (Lk 31:31; Zech 14:9–12; Joel 3:12–18; Hab 2:14; Dan 7:13,14).
- Peace in creation follows Christian's resurrection (Rom 8:19–23).
- Described in other scriptures 1 and 2 Peter 'age-lasting day' of 1,000 years.
- Is 2:2–4; Mic 4:1–8 Wars cease.
- Is 11:6–9; 65:17–25. Peace among animals.
- Before Christ's return, things get worse, not better (2 Tim 3:13; Lk 21:34–36; Matt 24:12; 2 Thess 2:3–8).

16 THE REVELATION OF JESUS CHRIST (4)
THE FUTURISTIC INTERPRETATION OF REVELATION 6–19

A special blessing is promised in Revelation 1 for those who read and understand the book, so that is why we have felt the thrill of truth in these chapters.

I have shown you how remarkably the book of Revelation has been fulfilled in the history of the last 20 centuries. (This is the historicist interpretation.) But we have seen that prophecy is often fulfilled twice. It is fulfilled symbolically, but it is also to be fulfilled literally and in the future. So happenings today are significant for the future as well as in past history.

The futuristic application of chapters 6 to 19 of Revelation is taken to depict the happenings on earth for seven years of tribulation. It will follow after the saved are taken to heaven and it will end when the Lord Jesus returns to earth with them to judge the nations. What will cause the tribulation?

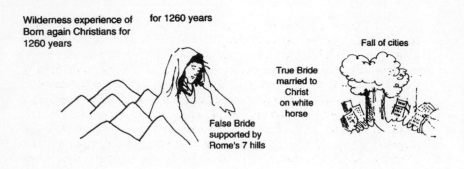

Figure 16.1. The symbols following the panel of the seven bowls depicted in Revelation 17 and 18.

The removal of the saved will allow an outburst of evil in the world. Not only would people be evil, there would also be terrible modern technology to threaten the world's destruction. Only the return of Jesus would save the world later.

SCIENCE AND REVELATION

At one time, the bizarre descriptions in Revelation were thought to be impossible, but Dr R.E.D. Clark has shown the possibility of it all happening if military hardware got into the wrong hands, as many fear that it might. Revelation describes the pollution of the seas. It describes chemical warfare. It describes Chernobyl. It describes what looks like nuclear warfare. Dr Robert Clark, the scientist, described it in his book *Tomorrow's World* (Victoria Institute, 1989). Revelation 6 he thinks describes nuclear warfare and the nuclear winter which would follow. Here are a few passages:

> The sun, we are told, becomes black as sackcloth of hair, a noteworthy expression in view of studies of probable effects of a nuclear war (Sagan). Earlier scientists and military experts had overlooked the fact that nuclear bombing would release a great quantity of black carbon in the form of finely-divided soot, from burning fossil fuels, forests and grasslands, and that this would float about in the mid-troposphere. Here it would absorb radiation from the sun, so becoming warm and remaining suspended for a long time – perhaps a year or more – and so shielding the earth below, which would become colder. Irregular, streaky clouds of soot, blown by winds in the upper atmosphere, will give the impression that the sun has been darkened and is being viewed through a coarse cloth.

Dr Clark thinks that in Revelation 8, acid rain is described:

> After the lapse of a year or two, if present conjectures by scientists are correct, the black pall of soot in the troposphere will begin to dissipate. First in one place, then in another, the clear sky will become visible once more. But this will certainly not happen evenly in all parts of the earth. Slowly the nitrogen oxides will produce nitric acid which will be carried down to earth by rain, but they will have destroyed much of the protective ozone layer in the upper atmosphere, so that when the sun's light reaches the earth, its actinic rays [chemically active radiation] will be intense. Vegetation will suffer greatly from the acid rain, the lightning, and the ultraviolet light of the sun. Grass and similar fragile vegetation will wither but in the forests the actinic rays will reach only the upper branches of the trees and the foliage lower down may well remain green and fresh. Therefore by no means all the trees will be burnt up. As for the grass, it will grow again. It is mentioned later (9:4). Comparing what we have said with the words of Revelation, 'A third of the earth was burnt up and a third of the trees were burnt up and all green grass was burnt up' (8:7), we may see that there is nothing unexpected in the prophecy.'

Is chemical warfare referred to in chapter 16? Read Revelation 16:1–4:

Then I heard a loud voice from the temple saying to the seven angels, go pour out the seven bowls of God's wrath on the earth. The first angel went and poured out his bowl on the land and ugly and painful sores broke out on the people who had the mark of the beast and worshipped his image. The second angel poured out his bowl on the sea and it turned into blood like that of a dead man and every living thing in the sea died. The third angel poured out his bowl on the rivers and springs of water and they became blood.

End Times Tribulation

Does this make you thankful that the return of Christ will be the solution promised by the Bible? Jesus said, 'Those days will be shortened for the elect's sake. But for the shortening of those days, there would be no flesh saved.'

I have sometimes been asked to outline the events of those seven years tribulation on earth. For this, I refer to Dr Hoyt and his book called, *The End Times* (Revell Co, 1981).

He says that the terrible time will be the result of man's sin and rebellion. By forsaking God's laws, mankind will bring these evils upon himself. That is why it is called 'the Consummation'. He then describes the great world dictator who will appear:

> The tribulation period permits the revelation of the great antichrist of the end time (2 Thess. 2:3,4, 6–8). In this man, the mystery of iniquity or lawlessness reaches its fullest development. He is therefore called the 'man of sin' (2 Thess. 2:3) or, 'the lawless one' (2 Thess. 2:8). Sin is lawlessness (1 John 3:4), the very nature of which is to regard self as the highest good and the chief end in life. This one 'opposeth and exalteth himself above all that is called God or that is worshipped so that he, as God, sitteth in the temple of God, showing himself that he is God' (2 Thess. 2:4). This could not take place so long as the true church was within the world, but once the true restraining forces in the church were removed at the rapture, this masterpiece of Satan and man of sin could be revealed. The philosophic trends centring in pantheism (2 Peter 3:3,4), the apostasy in the false church (2 Tim. 4:3,4) and the absence of spiritual influence among professing religionists (Matt. 5:13), will contribute to the revelation of the antichrist and provide a perfect atmosphere for his appearance.

He is described in various other places in Scripture. He will at first be seen as a lamb professing to bring peace and a solution to the world's problems, but he will turn out to be a dragon. Indeed, he will be Satan's masterpiece of deception. He will combine all the world's religions into one. This trend is already with us – multifaith movements to combine all the religions and to obscure the truth that only Jesus Christ can save. Only Jesus has died to save us and to reconcile us to God.

Dr Hoyt there applies the 1,260 days in Revelation literally and says that the antichrist will make a pact with the Jews for 3½ years. 1,260 days equals 3½ years. This would be to bring false peace to Palestine.

The peace will be broken and a worse persecution will break out against the Jews during the last 3½ years. This will lead to the conversion of many. A great number of Gentiles will also be saved and these two groups will become the preachers during the second half of the seven years' tribulation.

At the end of the seven years' tribulation, Christ descends from heaven with great power as described in chapter 19 of Revelation. When Israel sees the wounds in the Lord's body, they will all be converted and weep that this was the Messiah they had rejected. This dramatic descent of Christ will be to stop the last war of the age, the battle of Armageddon.

What of the programme in the seven years tribulation? It is summed up by Dr Hoyt and many others. It is the succession of events given in Revelation chapters 6–18. It starts with the four horses of the apocalypse:

- the white horse of military-enforced peace;
- the red horse of anarchy and the breakdown of peace;
- the black horse of food shortage resulting from anarchy;
- the pale horse of famine and disease.

This is followed by the seven trumpets of pollution and nuclear winter. Terrific armies will be massed in the Euphratean Middle East. Devastation follows because mankind refuses to acknowledge God, but goes in for witchcraft, immorality, murders and demon worship.

Then God sends Moses and Elijah to call men to repentance, but the antichrist kills them. The antichrist also launches a new persecution of Israel. Inspired by Satan, he changes Christianity into a multifaith super-church. A single monetary system will control all trade and spending. No one will be allowed to buy or sell unless he has the trading number of 666.

Then follows the seven last plagues. The military power in the Euphrates dries up and a military bloc of Eastern nations invades the Middle East. There is also invasion from the north of Palestine and a protest from Western powers. The stage is then set for the last war of the age – the battle of Armageddon.

Revelation 16:12 reads, 'And the sixth angel poured out his bowl of wrath upon the great river Euphrates and the water dried up so that the way of the kings of the East might be prepared.'

Then we read in verse 16 how the false prophet and the antichrist muster the world's armies for the battle of Armageddon.

In chapters 17 and 18, God judges all false religion and chapter 19 says it is by the triumphant return of Christ whom the world rejects.

Both the futuristic and the historical application of Revelation 19 ends with the defeat of the antichrist and the false prophet and their banishment to hell. Satan will also be banished to hell. Peace for the world will result. This will all be due to Christ's triumphant return from heaven at the end of the tribulation. Dr Hoyt sums it up as follows:

> The tribulation period will conclude with the demolition of all satanic forces. The satanically-energised human geniuses who head the mass rebellion of mankind at the end of the age, will be taken and cast alive into the lake of fire (Rev. 19:20). The brilliance of Christ's coming will expose the colossal delusion that has been perpetrated on mankind. This will render the beast and his accomplice, the false prophet, inoperative. His legions will desert him (2 Thess. 2:8). Then by his almighty word, Christ will cast these two into the lake of fire without the benefit of formal evaluation . . . Last of all, Satan, that creature who is responsible for the entrance of sin into the world and the calamity that has followed, will be taken and incarcerated in the bottomless pit for a thousand years. (Rev 20:1–3).

It should be remembered that none of those who are saved will see these events on earth. Jesus will, I believe, have resurrected them and taken them to heaven to reward them for their faithfulness.

Correct Interpretation

Now, there are dangers which some fall into when applying Revelation 6 to 18 literally. One is to suggest that there will be several resurrections during the tribulation.

We should never base doctrine on symbols and parables. The straightforward teaching of Jesus' words and Paul's words in 1 Corinthians 15 is that there is the resurrection of Jesus which took place over 19 centuries ago; next will be the resurrection of those who belong to Christ at his second coming and, finally, the general resurrection of everybody else for judgement.

Jesus said none of those who believed the gospel would come to the terrible judgement day. They would be raised at his second coming and the believers still alive would suddenly be given resurrection bodies. John 5:24 says:

> I tell you the truth, whoever hears my word and believes him who sent me, has eternal life and will not come to judgement; he has crossed over from death to life.

Then in verse 29, he refers to these two resurrections and no additional ones. 'Do not be amazed at this, for a time is coming when all who are in their graves will hear his voice and come out – those who have done good will rise to a resurrection of life and those who have practised evil to the resurrection of judgement.' Paul also describes them in several places.

MISLEADING MYTHS

You will have noticed how the last chapters of Revelation emphasise that 'Satan will deceive the whole world' (Revelation 12:9;19:20; 20:3,10).

I have recently reviewed a new book for the Christians in Science organisation. In it are listed many of the myths of anthropology. It certainly is an eye-opener on how in these latter days, 'There will be a strong delusion' (2 Thessalonians 2:9–11) and 'many will turn to myths' and 'turn away from the truth' (2 Timothy 4:4).

Misleading Drawings

Did our hominid ancestors descend from tree climbers or from knuckle walkers? asked Richard Leakey. He then writes in his book, 'We will know only when we find evidence of the very first bi-pedal apes'.

The general public might well say, 'But we thought that a whole succession of apes had been found gradually progressing from knuckle walking, to stooping, then half-erect to upright bi-pedalism. That is the impression we got from R.L.'s drawings on television and his widely circulated book.' They were not told that no fossils supported these imaginative drawings. (See *Evidence for Truth, Volume 1: Science,* p 125.)

The public have been so misled that they do not know that anthropologists confess that all hominids ever found were all upright walkers on two legs (bi-pedalists), although, of course, many are quite confident that some day the in-between 'stooping ape-men' will be found.

Don Johanson found 'Lucy' in the Afar triangle and classifies her as an *Australo-afarenis*. He calls her 'the beginning of mankind, 3½ million years ago'. She was only three and a half feet tall, but even she walked upright like all other hominids. Only bits of Lucy's skull were recovered, the front part was missing, so the size of her brain was not mentioned. Her wisdom teeth were fully erupted and her wide pelvis showed she was a female.

Now, whether we agree or not with such an immense time length does not affect our argument that anthropologists confess that there are no fossils of half-stooping apes.

Like R.L., Johanson also confesses, 'We have no fossils yet that tell us what went on during the in-between time'. By the in-between time he means the vital supposed ape-man period when it is assumed that quadrupedal knuckle-walking apes gradually walked upright.

The Vital Fossil Void

Dr Martin Pickford of Oxford also laments the lack of fossil evidence for this vital stage. *He calls it the fossil void.* Here is what he wrote in the *New Scientist*: 'The fossil void is particularly frustrating because it was during this time that the earliest human ancestor embarked on a vital stage of its journey towards humanity.'

Like Dr Pickford, no shadow of doubt crosses the mind of Don Johanson in his firm faith. With no fossils for the 'in-between time', he finds it easy to picture the process: 'We can picture evolution as starting with a primitive ape-like type that generally, over a long period of time, began to be less and less ape-like and more man-like. There was no abrupt cross-over,' he adds confidently, 'from ape to human, but probably a rather fuzzy time of in-between types. *We have no fossils to tell us what went on during that in-between time.*'

Neither does this 'fossil void' of the most vital question stop others from speculating on how it happened. R.L. gives imaginative drawings of how brachiating proto-hominids descended from the trees to walk upright. Another fossil hunter asks what is it which would make such a creature want to walk upright. He suggests that a series of terrific hurricanes blew down all the trees so that he just had to! But R.L. quotes another suggestion by Rodman and McHenry that it was 'food distances' on the Savanna which caused upright walking on two legs (bi-pedalism) in order to reach widely distributed supplies.

Sir Alistair Hardy of Oxford had still another theory however. He thought that protohominids, as they are called, lived on seashores and developed a taste for oysters. In treading the waves to feel for oysters with their feet, gradually over millions of years they developed bi-pedalism. The picking up of the shellfish developed the opposable thumb of the hominid which enabled him to use tools.

Now all this regresses back to Darwin's 'use inheritance' which the genetics of Mendel the monk showed to be impossible. Only what was already in the genetic code could be inherited. R.L. has a section on molecular biology, but does not survey the full implications of it. Mutations and recombinants cannot account for the radical re-design of the whole of the human skeleton for upright bi-pedal walking. He quotes Lovejoy as saying that 'a drastic anatomical re-building' was necessary. For this reason, anthropologists believed that we did not descend from apes, but from a generalised *ramapithecus* (manlike genus) with equal length limbs and no long arms and fingers for swinging in the trees. The human frame would have vestigial remains if our ancestors had ever gone through such a stage.

I am afraid it makes me ask, 'Is this really science or is it a groping to make the facts fit the theory?' For me, these sceptics are a regression back into Victorian pseudoscience about which the famous Professor Evans-Pritchard wrote in *Theories of Primitive Religion* (OUP, 1965):

> There was no attempt to test theories by unselected examples. The most elementary precautions were neglected as wild surmise followed on wild surmise (called hypotheses). The simplest rules of inductive logic were ignored.

R.L. himself speaks of Dubois who, in 1880, discovered in Java the first specimen now classified as *Homo erectus (upright man)*. He regards this as 'pivotal' for the descent of man, but at the time, it was represented, originally, as a stooping ape-man. He attempts to explain why Dubois hid the leg bones of this creature under the floorboards of his house for 20 years. The real reason, however, seems to be that the leg bones showed that it walked upright in bi-pedal locomotion, but this did not agree with the fashion of theory of the time which even misrepresented Neanderthal man as a stooping ape-man.

This all shows how selective anthropology has been. R.L. also refers to Haekel as a champion of Darwin, but perhaps he does not know that Darwin did not welcome this championship, and refused to allow Haekel to dedicate his book to him. Haekel later admitted that his drawings of supposed recapitulation of embryos in the womb were not true to facts and most anthropologists have since abandoned the recapitulation hypothesis. (See end of p 149, *Evidence for Truth, Volume 1: Science.*)

The Middle East Crossroads

R.L. refers to the Middle East crossroads. He adopts the theory that *homo erectus* moved out of Africa into Europe, Palestine being the bridge. Consequently, he revives the hypothesis that *Homo neanderthalis* interbred with *Homo sapiens* in Palestine. He does not seem aware that Garrod's excavations of the Mount Carmel caves were re-examined and radically revised. Higgs and Brothwell found that the same time gap years separated the Tabun cave of Neanderthal man from the Skhul cave of *Homo sapiens*. This seems conveniently forgotten by a number of anthropologists.

The caves throughout Europe and the Middle East consistently show a sterile stalagmitic layer representing a time when *Homo neanderthalis* disappeared without trace or descendants and that *homo sapiens* was a new start. As a well-known Cambridge anthropologist said

to me, if anyone wanted to believe that modern man was a special creation or a new dispersion, there is nothing in the fossil record to stop
him from doing so.

To do R.L. justice, he shows that more and more anthropologists
are beginning to favour what William Howell called 'the Noah's Ark
Hypothesis', but which is called by other anthropologists, 'the Garden
of Eden Hypothesis'. Genetic sources worldwide reveal that all races
on earth today are descended from one mother. The samples also show
that descent from the one source is in three main branches, i.e. the sons
of Noah. (See Fig 15.1 in *Evidence for Truth, Volume 1: Science*.) The
theories of others ignore this however.

The Great Scientific Soup Myth

Have you heard of the great scientific soup myth? That's what Dr L.R.
Croft calls it. He is a lecturer in biological sciences in the University
of Salford, so he should know what he is talking about.

For some years now, Western universities have propagated the idea
that life could arise by accident. This, it was thought, was by life forming in a soupy type of early sea when the earth was young. They suggested that life's components came together through lightning striking
this soupy sea.

Dr Croft has written a book entitled, *How Life Began*. He shows
that it was scientifically impossible for life to start by accident. He
writes: 'The primeval soup theory has been the greatest scientific myth
of all time.' He goes on to tell you why. But also he reveals, as others
have done, that the atheists in the former Soviet Russia paid for books
to be supplied cheaply in all the Western universities. He says:

> It was suggested by a Russian scientist, Oparin, that the oceans and lakes
> were filled with soup (from which life arose accidentally without a cre-
> ator). I am astonished that Oparin, a dedicated Marxist, could have suc-
> ceeded in converting most of Western society to his belief in the so called
> 'primeval soup'.

The physicist Freeman Dyson remarked:

> The Oparin picture . . . was popular, not because there was any evidence
> to support it, but because it seemed to be an alternative to biblical creation.

This view, according to Croft, was echoed by Sir Fred Hoyle:

> It is remarkable that over the past half century, the scientific world has
> almost without exception, believed a theory for which there is not a single
> supporting fact.

'It is true to say,' says Dr Croft, 'That no other apostle of Marx has been so successful in the promulgation of his gospel of materialism. So it comes as no surprise to find that Oparin was awarded the greatest honour of the Soviet Union.'

It was this atheism that led to the collapse of the Soviet Union. *It is in danger of leading to the collapse of Western society*. It is typified by a young teenager whom I caught breaking a church stained-glass window. 'Why do you do such things,' I asked. He replied: 'There ain't no God mister! That's why!'

As a university biologist, Dr Croft goes on to show how it was quite impossible for life to arise without a creator. Certainly, the primeval soup theory has been the greatest scientific myth of all time.

Sceptics will come in the last days . . . saying 'Where does it promise that Christ will come again, for since our ancestors, everything develops uninterrupted since creation without a break. They willingly forget that God made the heavens and the earth by his words, the continents standing in and out of the water. That water caused the whole world to perish by the Flood. God's Word reserves our present world to be destroyed by fire at the day of judgement when the ungodly will perish. (2 Peter 3:3–7)

This brings us back to the final chapters of Revelation which describe these false teachings and final events, then ends with beautiful pictures of paradise regained.

EPILOGUE TO REVELATION

Supposing someone gave you a precious jewel contained in a lovely jewel-box. Supposing you began to admire the box instead of the jewel – you admired the velvet and the clasp of the box instead of its contents – they would think your appreciation was misguided.

We have reached the end of our exciting discoveries in the book of Revelation, yet we would miss the greatest jewel of all if we thought that foretelling the future was the main value of the book of Revelation. It would be pricing the value of the box above the beautiful jewel which sparkles within it. Whether you understand the prophecies or not, there are greater treasures within that box – treasures of salvation, victory, judgement, praise, worship and, above all, the greatest jewel of all.

Glory of Jesus Unveiled

That Jewel is the Lord Jesus himself and the Father. The book of Revelation brings as much glory to the Lord as any other book in the

Bible. Many people have not understood the symbols of the book and yet they have bathed in the glory which surrounds Jesus and the Father. Their glory thrills the believers and surpasses any uplifting exuberance that created things can give. Even sun and moon pale into insignificance in comparison. Revelation 21:22,23 says:

> I did not see a temple in the city because the Lord God Almighty and the Lamb are its temple. The city does not need the sun or the moon to shine on it, for the glory of God gives it light and the Lamb is its lamp.

We have seen in Revelation how wonderfully the Lord Jesus Christ had all history under his control. He overrules the past and the future and that is wonderful, yet it is the glory of the Lord which shines above mystic symbol. In fact, the book opens with the statement that it is a revelation of Jesus Christ. What is more, it is a revelation to his servants.

Many a person has been transported into a higher degree of adoration of the Lord Jesus because Revelation reveals how wonderful he is. The first chapter is mostly about him. The brilliance of his face and person surpasses even the Transfiguration. He is the Alpha and Omega, the beginning and the end, the first and the last, which is, and which was, and which is to come, the Almighty. It is he who lives and was dead and, behold, he is alive for evermore, Amen, and has the keys of hell and death.

Inspired Worship

There is no other book quite like Revelation to inspire worship and joy. Think of all the songs of joy and praise. Each interlude between the panels gives a fresh outburst of praise by the heavenly host and by earth's redeemed.

Just think how much poorer our hymn books would be if all the hymns inspired by Revelation were to be removed – all those hymns which sing 'Worthy is the Lamb who was slain'. Both old hymns and new songs are full of references from Revelation. 'The Lamb is all the glory of Immanuel's land.' Also, 'Worthy is the Lamb who died, they cried, to be exalted thus; worthy the Lamb, our lips reply, for he was slain for us' (Revelation 5:11–14).

The majesty of God also enhances our praise. He is the Creator. The description is one of colour and covenant for there is a rainbow around the throne and lightnings and thunderings and voices proceed out of it. All creation worships him. They worship him who lives for ever and ever.

'Thou art worthy, O Lord, to receive glory and honour and power;

for you have created all things and for your pleasure they are and were created.'

'The Lord God Almighty reigns!' Revelation shows more than any other New Testament book how to express our worship in love and praise.

Salvation Enjoyed

Listen to the story of some handicapped children. For many weeks, money had been collected so that they could have a holiday in the sun. The workers toiled and collected, then at last the day arrived for their special holiday. Patient anticipation became reality. The television cameras showed the joy of the children as they actually enjoyed the happiness long awaited. The book of Revelation is like those television cameras, taking you to see the saved actually enjoying their salvation.

We do not have to understand the symbols to enjoy the sight of the saved in heaven. In the epistles we learn:

- How to be saved.
- The reason that we can be saved.
- The peril of not being saved.

In Revelation, we see the saved enjoying their salvation, praising their Saviour in overt expressions of love. It is a private viewing:

> After this, I saw a great host which no man could number, of all nations and families and people and languages standing before the throne and before the Lamb clothed with white robes and palm branches in their hands and crying out with a loud voice, Salvation belongs to our God who sits upon the throne and unto the Lamb.

Who are these? asked St John. These are those who have washed their robes and made them white in the blood of the Lamb. On another occasion, they sang a new song before the throne, being those who were redeemed from the earth. On still another occasion, they:

> Sing the song of Moses and the Lamb saying, 'Great and marvellous are your works, Lord God Almighty; just and true are your ways, O King of Saints. Who shall not fear you, O Lord, and glorify your name, for you only are holy; for all nations shall come and worship before you.'

THE REVELATION DRAMA

The great themes of the gospel are fully amplified. They are those which become prominent when God sends revival. They are:

- Man's rebellion and fallen nature.
- The wrath of God against sin, but his love for sinners.
- The need of repentance and faith.
- The good news of eternal salvation through the Lamb who was slain for sinners.
- The reality of Satan behind world events.
- The final judgement and banishment to hell fire of all whose names are not in the Lamb's book of life.
- The persecution of the saved, 'who love not their lives unto death'.
- The victory of the saved 'Who overcame by trusting the blood of the Lamb and by their testimony and God's Word, the Bible'.

All these are graphically illustrated in the book of Revelation.

It is important to know that God has a plan in history which is working towards a divine objective, a climax. Revelation is the climax to the whole Bible. Paradise lost by sin in the first book, Genesis, is paradise regained by the saved through Christ's redemption. The forbidden trees in Eden become trees of healing in heaven.

Revelation is the climax to the love story of the Saviour's wooing and winning the love of the bride, the Church. The story can be traced throughout the Bible:

- The Old Testament prophets speak of the bride clothed in the wedding dress of salvation.
- The Song of Solomon speaks of the bliss of married love.
- John the Baptist declares himself to be the Best Man to give the bride away to the Groom, her Saviour.
- The epistles warn the engaged virgin against rival suitors, namely, Satan and false preachers of twisted gospels, whereas Paul promised the believer to one husband, Jesus Christ.
- The best of human marriage is taken as a picture of the love and oneness of the believers with Christ.

Then Revelation shows the reality of those rival suitors, the opposition to her engagement to Christ, the pain of waiting, 'How long, O Lord?' It shows the attempts of a false bride approved by the world to be an ugly sister. At last comes the joy when she is presented to her beloved Redeemer as a radiant Church. From rejection by the world comes acclaim. The excitement of the wedding day is reflected in Revelation 19:6,7 (NIV).

The Greatest Drama Ever Written

We have seen the book of Revelation as a great triumphal arch upon which all roads of history converge; but it was an arch with a difference. Most triumphal arches record battles and victories of the past. This one foretold the battles and victories of the Christian era which was then future. Upon that arch we have seen the four picture panels of struggle leading to triumph. The lamps are lit, the seals are broken, the trumpets blown and the bowls poured out. The book of Revelation is the greatest drama produced on the stages of heaven and earth that man has seen. Curtain after curtain is raised, scene after scene unfolds the mystery – the mystery of history, the mystery of evil and the mystery of the gospel.

Then comes the climax of the drama. Suddenly, the Saviour is unveiled. This is the meaning of the word 'revelation'. The world sees what is behind these mysteries. The world's Cinderella is to be married to her Prince Jesus, for it is a love story after all. The crowning event is the crowning of the rejected Son of God and his rejected bride, the Church. Invitations to the wedding are sent out by the Holy Spirit. A thousand years' righteousness, happiness and peace consummate in judgement and banishment to the rubbish tip with everlasting destruction of every evil person and spirit.

The final curtain rises on a new heaven and a new earth wherein dwells righteousness and joy and the redeemed radiate the iridescent light streaming from the Father and the Son.

The stage lighting effects for this drama of Revelation are terrific. All the colours of the rainbow are employed and, in the universe, the stars and the sun are the backcloth. Every kind of jewel sparkles. Percussion and sound effects employ thunder and lightning, torrents of hail, earthquakes and stentorian voices – voices of warning, voices of command, voices of accomplishment – until there are heard the gentle voices of the Saviour, his bride (the saved) and of the Holy Spirit urging people to be among the blessed whose names are in the Lamb's book of life and those who are thirsty for the truth to drink the satisfying waters of life which flow from the throne of God.

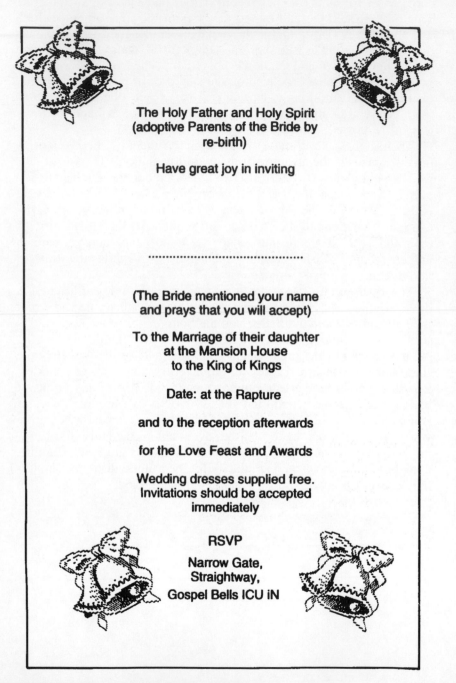

The Holy Father and Holy Spirit
(adoptive Parents of the Bride by
re-birth)

Have great joy in inviting

....

(The Bride mentioned your name
and prays that you will accept)

To the Marriage of their daughter
at the Mansion House
to the King of Kings

Date: at the Rapture

and to the reception afterwards

for the Love Feast and Awards

Wedding dresses supplied free.
Invitations should be accepted
immediately

RSVP

Narrow Gate,
Straightway,
Gospel Bells ICU iN

Figure 16.2. The wedding invitation to all believers.

SUMMARY

THE FUTURISTIC INTERPRETATION

Futuristic application of panels 2 to 4 (seals, trumpets and caul-drons).

- Prophecy often fulfilled both ways (Matt 17:10–13).
- They are to be re-enacted literally during the tribulation (i.e. during 7 years between rapture and judgement of nations).
- Science of destruction has now made it possible (i.e. devastation through chemical, germ and nuclear warfare)
- Appearance of antichrist, world government and multi-faith.
- Elijah comes literally (11:3,6). In John the Baptist, it was spiritually.

A great delusion
- Satan deceives the whole world (Rev 12:9;19:20; 20:3,10).
- Turning to myths in the last days (2 Tim 4:4; 2 Thess 2:9–11; 2 Pet 3:3–7).
- Well-known anthropologists admit no evidence of any stooping ape-men period:
- 'Still to find evidence of very first bi-pedal apes' (yet he draws pictures of stooping ape-men).
- 'We have no fossils yet to tell us of the in-between time (but we can picture it).'
- 'This fossil void is particularly frustrating' (but he assumes that it happened). Dubois 1880, hid leg bones of early man for 20 years (which proved upright walking).

Lessons from Revelation irrespective of interpretation:
- Glory of Jesus unveiled.
- Inspires worship and Christian songs.
- We see the redeemed enjoying their salvation.
- The Lamb controls history.
- Love story of the bride and Christ concluded.

17 HOW THE SECOND COMING WILL AFFECT YOU
THE ORDER OF EVENTS

Now that you have been thrilled by the insights into prophecy, you will want to know how it will happen.

First, I will describe how it will affect you looking at the main facts which all are agreed on. Then we will look at other details which some are not so sure about. I find that often they can be clearly analysed from a humble and consistent examination of the Bible.

Your Seat on the Bench

What then is the clear factor which will make great changes to every-body's life? It is the statement *that Jesus Christ will descend from heaven with great power and glory suddenly to judge the living and the dead.* He will also judge the nations and everyone will have to give an account of their deeds.

This aspect is described in many scriptures. For example, it features in Christ's parable about the sheep and the goats in Matthew 25:31: 'When the Son of Man shall come in his glory and all his holy angels with him, then shall he sit upon the throne of his glory.' Jesus thus applies Daniel 7:13:

Behold one like the Son of Man came with the clouds of heaven . . . and there was given to him a dominion and glory and a kingdom that all people, nations and languages should serve him. His dominion is an everlasting dominion which will not pass away.

Similar statements are made in Daniel 2:44,45 and by Paul in 2 Thessalonians 1:7–10:

This will happen when the Lord Jesus is revealed from heaven in blazing fire with his powerful angels. He will punish those who do not know God and do not obey the gospel of our Lord Jesus. They will be punished with everlasting destruction and shut out from the presence of the Lord and from the majesty of his power.

Paul also says that saved Christians will share Christ's rule and Daniel 7:18 says, 'The saints of the Most High shall take the kingdom and possess the kingdom for ever.' Revelation 20:4 enlarges upon this:

I saw thrones and they who sat upon them and judgement was given to them and I saw the souls of those who were beheaded for the witness of Jesus and for the Word of God . . . They came to life and reigned with Christ a thousand years.

So, if you are saved, that is a wonderful tomorrow for you. Does Paul take this literally? Apparently he does. In 1 Corinthians 6:2, 'Do you not know that the saints will judge the world and, if the world will be judged by you, are you unworthy to judge even the smallest matters?'

That statement quite clearly identifies the saints of Daniel with the rank and file converted Christians. Yes, you will have a seat on the bench of divine law, even if at the moment you are very much aware of your inadequacies.

You may remark, 'But am I a saint? Do I qualify?' In the New Testament, the word 'saint' is used for a person who has accepted the free salvation of Christ. Many of the letters are addressed to the saints – the letters to the Ephesians, Philippians and Colossians are all addressed to the saints who meet together. Ephesians 1:12 says how they became saints:

You trusted Christ . . . after you heard the Word of truth, the gospel of your salvation, in whom also after you believed, you were sealed with that Holy Spirit of promise.

So you see, a saint is a forgiven and cleansed sinner and, as such, you will be with that triumphant host of saints and angels who descend from heaven to Jerusalem.

Your Free Flight!

Isn't it wonderful that, when you accepted the free gift of salvation, you also qualified for a free flight to the Holy Land?

But the statement that you will descend from heaven with Christ to judge the world must assume some previous events. It implies that you will have been caught up to heaven before that. The Scriptures give you the following order of events:

1. You will be given a resurrection body and caught up to heaven to meet your coming Lord. This is often called the rapture.
2. You and all the saved will be the bride at the marriage of Christ and his Church.
3. You will stand at the Bema (courtroom) of Christ for reward for your witness on earth.
4. You will descend with all the saved with the Lord Jesus and the angels to judge the world.

Figure 17.1. The Mount of Olives. Jesus ascended from the top and will return 'in like manner' (Acts 1:11; Zech 14:4). Note the Garden of Gethsemane in the middle foreground of the picture which contains the Franciscan chapel. Some of the olive trees here will probably date back to the time of Christ.

THE RAPTURE

Now we will look at the scriptures which justify those events. Take the first item. The resurrection of the saved or the rapture. Paul calls this 'Our gathering together to Christ'. This is in 2 Thessalonians 2:2: 'Now we implore you brethren, by the coming of our Lord Jesus Christ and our gathering together to him.'

In his first letter to the Thessalonians 4:13–18, he describes that gathering. The souls of the saved who have already died and are with Christ, the Lord will bring with him. Their bodies will be raised and joined with their souls. At the same time, the saved who are still alive will be suddenly changed. Their bodies will be resurrection bodies like Christ's after he rose from the dead.

Will Only the Saved Rise?

But will this resurrection be of saved people only? Some prefer not to be bothered with details and just speak of one general resurrection of everybody, good and bad and that they will receive judgement.

That is sufficient knowledge for a Christian, of course, but I am surprised that no notice has been taken of scriptures which clearly state that Jesus will come first for his own saved people and that the rapture will not include any unconverted people. Take for instance, 1 Corinthians 15:23. Paul gives the order in which the resurrections will take place. First, it was the resurrection of Christ; next it will be those who belong to Jesus, that is, the saved; finally, when Christ has reigned, it will be the resurrection of all the rest for the great judgement day. Each stage is marked off by an adverb of time and introduced by the words, 'Now everyone in his own order'.

Look again at that phrase 'Those who belong to him'. If you belong to him, your resurrection is next on the programme of history. Yes, it includes you if you have repented and believe. That is your happy prospect.

Now match this with what Jesus said in Luke 21:28. Here he speaks of the saved again. He says, 'When these things begin to come to pass, lift up your heads, for your redemption draws near.'

What Redemption Is This?

Were you not redeemed when you accepted Christ? Of course you were! The word redemption refers to the redemption of your body. Why? Because the resurrection of the body is called the redemption of the body in Romans 8:21–23. You are told that creation waits to be delivered from pain and corruption and groans together until the children of God (that is, the saved) have their bodies redeemed from corruption. The phrase used is 'the redemption of the body'.

It occurs again in Ephesians 4:30: 'You are sealed by the Holy Spirit unto the day of redemption.' It means that the Holy Spirit sealed you as belonging to Jesus when you were born again by the Holy Spirit and that guarantees that your body will be redeemed or transformed by the resurrection when Christ comes for his own.

That is why the Lord Jesus says to you that, when you see these signs of the last days, then expect that the redemption of your body is near. Notice when it will happen. It is when the last signs begin to unfold. Why near the beginning? It is because the saved will be snatched away in their resurrection bodies before the final woes – a terrible tribulation which leads to the last war of the age.

The Royal Seal and Guarantee

Have you seen one of those huge royal seals? If you visit a stately home of an old family, they often exhibit a parchment document which pledges certain rights. At the bottom of the document will hang the wax seal imprinted by the royal insignia.

When you accepted Christ as your Saviour, that was when you were sealed as belonging to Jesus. That is exactly what Ephesians 1:13 says:

> You first trusted in Christ . . . after you heard the word of truth, the gospel of your salvation; in whom also after you believed you were sealed with that Holy Spirit of promise, which is your guarantee of inheritance until the redemption (of your body) as Christ's purchased possession.

Isn't that glorious! There is a seal on you. 'This is my property,' says Christ, 'I will rescue it when I come for my own, before the terrible final tribulation of the wicked on earth.'

That is why Paul says that the next resurrection will be of those who belong to Christ. Sadly, the rest are left to the great judgement day of Revelation 20:12. That is why Jesus said, 'He who believes will not come to the judgement day' (John 5:24).

What other scriptures show that Christ will come for his own – for you, if you are saved? Turn to Luke 20:35. Here the Lord is speaking to correct those who had wrong ideas about the resurrection. He said:

> Those who will be accounted worthy to obtain that world and the resurrection from the dead . . . cannot die any more for they are equal to the angels and are the children of God, being children of the resurrection.

When you see that the next big event for you, if you are saved, is the resurrection of those who belong to Christ, you find that other scriptures slot into place. For example, that is why the three parables of Matthew 25 are in significant order. They are in sequence. Jesus has been speaking of the signs of his near return in chapter 24. Then follows the order of events. The first parable is about the ten bridesmaids at the marriage supper of the Lamb when Jesus comes for his own. The next parable is about the talents. This is the reward day for the resurrected saved. They are allotted rewards according to their faithfulness. Now notice the third parable. It is when Christ continues his descent from heaven and sets up his throne on earth. All nations are brought before him for judgement. Accompanying him are all the saints or saved.

This event is described in many scriptures, both Old Testament and New Testament. Daniel 7:13: 'Behold one like the Son of Man came with the clouds of heaven . . . and there was given to him a kingdom which shall not be destroyed.' Then verse 18: 'The saints [that is, the saved] of the Most High shall take the kingdom and possess the kingdom for ever and ever.'

Why Want a Body?

Has the question occurred to you, why it will be necessary for you to have a redeemed and resurrected body? Would it not be sufficient for your spirit to be rejoicing in Christ's presence? After all, Paul said, 'For me to depart this life is to be with Christ which is far, far better'; and the book of Revelation shows you the souls of those martyred for Jesus rejoicing in heaven with wonderful joy and praise.

The answer is that, if you are going to reign with Christ on earth, you need a resurrection body like Christ's. That is so you can operate in two realms, the heavenly and earthly, just as the risen Jesus did during those 40 days before his ascension. The Lord Jesus could appear and disappear, yet his body was real enough for Thomas to put his finger into those wounded hands and Jesus said, 'Look, I am not a ghost', and he ate food with them.

The description of how your body will be redeemed is given in 1 Corinthians 15:51. It will be in a moment, in the twinkling of an eye. Those believers who have died will be raised, never to experience decay again and, if you are alive, your body will be changed into a resurrection body. Death will be swallowed up in victory. It will be so sudden that the word 'atom' is used in the Greek. In these modern days, the world measures everything by atomic time on the Universal Time Clock. (They discovered that Greenwich Mean Time was one whole second out every 100 years!)

Paul then quotes Old Testament prophets. Hosea 13: 'O death, where is your sting? O grave, where is your victory?'; from Isaiah 25:8: 'He will swallow up death in victory and the Lord God will wipe away tears from off all faces.' And chapter 26:19–21: 'Your dead will live, with my dead body they will rise. Awake and sing, ye who dwell in the dust . . . the earth will cast out her dead.'

Then follows a significant statement. It is that this resurrection of the saved will remove them from the earth before the terrible woes and tribulation.

> Come my people [yes, it is those who belong to Christ], enter into your compartments and shut your doors about you; hide yourself as it were for a little moment, until the indignation is passed; for behold the Lord comes out of his place to punish the inhabitants of the earth for their lawlessness. (Isaiah 26:20,21)

THE BRIDE OF CHRIST

Here again, the Old Testament anticipates the New Testament. The prophets agree that it is only the Lord's people who escape the final woes by the rapture or resurrection of the saved. They will enter the many mansions prepared for them. No wonder Jesus said, 'Fear not. In my Father's house are many mansions. I go to prepare a place for you and, if I go to prepare a place for you, I will come again and receive you unto myself.' That word 'receive' was one used for wedding receptions, for the marriage of the bride of Christ.

Ten Bridesmaids

In the Bible, the Church is often referred to as the bride of Christ. The symbol of marriage is used when Christ returns for the bride. How is it then that this parable is about the bridesmaids and not the bride? Is it not to show that some will be left behind at the rapture because they were not saved? Ten bridesmaids are a lot to have at a wedding; usually two or three are enough. I took a wedding once where there must have been ten! When they all walked down the aisle, I wondered when I was coming to the bride.

In the story of the ten bridesmaids, they all turned up to the wedding too early. It was night-time, after eastern fashions and, because they had to wait for the bridegroom, they went into the reception room. Five of them were thoughtless; they had not brought any spare oil in separate containers which was the custom; only five were wise enough to do it.

As they waited, they got more and more tired. They yawned and yawned and fell asleep. Suddenly, they were startled by a shout from the best man. 'It is midnight! The bridegroom is coming! Pull yourselves together and go out to meet him!' In a panic, the ten bridesmaids rushed for their oil lamps. Now, there are one or two things I want to explain to you.

Why were they not pictured by Jesus as the **bride**? The bride represented the saved, the true Church of those born again by the Holy Spirit. My answer is that they were not born again, they were not saved. So they are figured as the **bridesmaids**. They were the fringers, associated with the bride, perhaps even went to church, but they had never accepted Christ as personal Saviour and so they were not ready for his second coming.

Now look at their lamps. The best translations make it clear that none of the ten had oil in their lamps. The custom was to carry oil in a separate vessel, otherwise you would spill the oil out of those rather open clay lamps. That would ruin the lovely dresses. So custom said, carry oil in a separate vessel with your lamp and pour the oil in only when you light up.

The oil represents the Holy Spirit throughout Scripture. So none of these ten were converted. There was no oil in their lamps, but five of them had brought the oil container with them. I suggest that this represents those who knew how to be saved, but had never taken the step. They had not accepted Christ and the Holy Spirit into their hearts. Now, in panic at the signs of Christ's coming, they do so. The five foolish ones are also in panic, but they had not brought the oil containers with their lamps. The text says, they did not know how to be saved. They try to light their wicks, but they flicker out because you cannot shine for Jesus if the Holy Spirit is not in you.

'Go to those who will give you oil,' they are told. They are the saved who will show you how to receive salvation by the Holy Spirit. These five foolish fringers went to enquire, but alas they were too late. The bridegroom, Jesus Christ, had come. The door was shut. The saved, the true bride of Christ, were in heaven safe and rejoicing and the foolish fringers were shut out.

THE BEMA OF CHRIST

If you visit the ruins of Corinth, be sure to see the Bema. It is clearly marked with a notice.

The Bema, as we have already seen, was the local court of justice. Here, the citizens would have their case heard without having to go to the emperor's court in Rome. It was at the local Bema that Paul claimed the right to appear at the final appeal court of Nero.

A number of scriptures talk about the Bema of Christ. The Greek word Bema, means 'seat'. In cities, the area judge had his judgement seat in the basilica or town hall court. It was to Corinth that Paul wrote in 2 Corinthians 5:10:

> For all of us must appear before the judgement seat of Christ in order that each one may receive awards according to the things practised through our body, either good or worthless.

In 1 Corinthians 3:11–15, Paul speaks of a man whose works were pretty worthless, yet because he built upon the foundation of Jesus Christ for salvation, he would be saved, but he would receive very little reward. He would be tested for the motives behind his service.

Some have failed to notice that, whenever judgement for the Christian is mentioned, it is to take place at the Bema of Christ. That will be the judgement seat for Christ's own citizens – citizens of heaven. They will be spared the final judgement of the great white throne. This is what Jesus said in John 5:24, 'He who believes . . . has everlasting life and will not come to the judgement.'

The Bema of Christ will follow the rapture of the saved and the function will be quite different from that of the judgement throne. The Bema will reward Christians for service, but the judgement will give punishment to the unsaved. Let us look at more references to the Bema.

Some disputes are better left for the Bema. Paul says in Romans 14:10 that we should not condemn a brother, 'because we shall all stand before the Bema of Christ', where all the circumstances will be revealed.

At the Bema, salvation is not in question. 1 Corinthians 3:11–15 reads:

> For other foundation can no man lay than that is laid, which is Jesus Christ. Now if any man build upon this foundation gold, silver, precious stones, wood, hay, stubble, every man's work shall be made manifest; for the day shall declare it, because it shall be revealed by fire and the fire shall try every man's work of what sort it is. If any man's work abide which he hath built thereupon, he shall receive a reward. If any man's work shall be burned, he shall suffer loss, but he himself shall be saved.

When you realise the purpose of the Bema, various scriptures fit into place. The Lord Jesus spoke about this Bema in the parable of the talents which follows the marriage parable, and also in the parable of the ten servants who were given money to invest (19:11). In the latter, it is significant that the rewards given are responsibilities in the coming kingdom on earth.

Another incident slots into the fact that only the saved come to the Bema after the rapture in Luke 14:14. Jesus said, don't invite only the rich to a banquet; include the poor and you will be blessed because they can't repay you. 'You will be paid at the resurrection of the just' – that is the resurrection of the justified or saved – in other words, the rapture.

This reward day for service is not the judgement day for the unsaved. The Lord said that the saved would not appear at the judgement (John 5:24,29). In contrast, at the Bema, the saints will receive their positions in the coming kingdom.

All these references to the Bema of Christ should encourage you never to let the Lord down, but to be fully dedicated to work for your Saviour.

Keep Open Your Weather Eye!

Do you watch the weather forecasts? I find that people do all over the world. Jesus said, 'You observe the signs of the weather, yet you do not watch for the signs of my coming. If the sky is red at night, you say that it will be a fine day tomorrow. If the sky is red in the morning, then you say it will be stormy. How is it that you cannot discern the signs of the times?' On other occasions, Jesus said that if you are not watching for the signs of his second coming, then you are asleep. The coming of the Lord will be unexpected, like a thief breaking in.

This analogy of the thief occurs six times in the New Testament and it is always in connection with Christ's servants, in other words, the Christians. Luke 12:37 says, 'Blessed are those servants whom the master finds awake when he comes . . .' Otherwise it will be like a thief in the night. This can be taken therefore as another reference to the rapture of the saved. It is significant that in Revelation 16:15 the alert warning to the coming as a thief occurs before Armageddon in the next verse. This again reinforces those passages which say that the resurrection will take away the saved before the last tribulation. Such things are very relevant in our modern world.

The Real Signs

Let me remind you of some of the signs we looked at. They are:

- Israel (all twelve tribes) restored to the Holy Land;
- the Hebrew language restored;
- the succession of empires ending with the European Common Market;
- Lebanon's agony;
- science and tourism;
- social deterioration;
- spiritism;
- natural signs such as earthquakes, calamities, epidemics;
- the threat of nuclear warfare.

Look at Israel. Jesus likened Israel to a fig tree and said, 'When you see the fig tree beginning to bud, then know that my return is near' (Mark 13:28). Israel has been budding for some years now.

In the Old Testament, God told many prophets that Israel would be scattered for her sins and then brought back to their land. Moses,

Isaiah, Jeremiah, Ezekiel, Daniel, Hosea, Amos, Joel and Zechariah were all told in great detail.

They were told that the exile for 70 years did not fulfil those prophecies. The exile saw only a remnant or small percentage of Judah returning, but even these would be scattered again. When God brings back Israel the second time, Isaiah is told in chapter 11, it will be both Judah and the ten tribes. He said the same to Ezekiel and to Hosea (Ezekiel 37:19–22, Hosea 1:11). It will be all the twelve tribes of Israel. We see this miracle today and they are not called Judah, but Israel. The name on your maps, State of Israel, is a witness to God's hand on history.

A Dead Language Revived

Jeremiah was told that their language would be Hebrew. It is thrilling to see it on every road and shop sign. That language had not been spoken for 2,500 years. This is a remarkable fulfilment of Jeremiah 31:23: 'Thus saith the Lord of hosts, the God of Israel. Yet again shall they use this speech in the land of Judah and in the cities when I bring them again from their captivity.'

Jeremiah was told in Jeremiah 16:16 that they would return in two stages; first as immigrants, then as refugees hounded out of various countries. Hitler's gas chamber massacres were part of that second stage.

Faith in God Restored

Prophecy said they would go back in unbelief, but would be converted when they saw the Lord Jesus descending from heaven to intervene in the last war of the age. 'They shall look on me whom they pierced', said Jehovah in Zechariah 12:10. In that day, all Israel will be grafted back into the stock of their tree. Paul says so in Romans 11:23–26:

> God has power to graft them in again . . . I want you to understand this mystery brethren: a hardening has come upon Israel, until the full number of Gentiles come in, and so all Israel will be saved.

The EEC in Prophecy

An impressive sign to talk about is the European free market. This is widely held as the last stage in the empires listed in the image in Daniel chapter 2. The old Roman Empire will have split up into a Europe of about ten countries or groups. Then Revelation 13 says that all buying and selling will be done by numbers. Everyone will have a number. What number do you have on your plastic card?

A business columnist, Ken Romain, writes:

> The European Community has come a long way since the Treaty of Rome
> . . . Plastic money is another part of the scene. EC member states recently
> introduced a common format for national identity documents but the plas-
> tic bank card could soon become the real passport to 'Citizens Europe' . . .
> In this way, the EC will take a major step towards the completion of an
> internal market for payment systems.

Many students of prophecy have for a long time seen Revelation
13:17 as anticipating that the states which arose out of the old Roman
Empire would have a common marketing system in the last days, 'so
that no man might buy or sell unless he had the mark or the name of
the beast, or the number of his name.'

Science, Technology and the Occult

Science and tourism are another talking point. Daniel 12:4 reads, 'At
the time of the end, many shall run to and fro and knowledge shall
increase.'

What an accurate epitome of our age. Every time you pass a tourist
agent shop, say Daniel 12:4. Every time you walk with others past a
window full of coloured bargain flights to Singapore, Paris or
Australia, say 'Daniel prophesied that'.

Another talking point is this prophesied increase in knowledge. The
word is the same for science. People often remark about all the burst
of inventions during the last 100 years. In the last century, very few
people ventured further than the next village and now we have even
landed men on the moon – which reminds me, Jesus said there would
be signs in the moon.

Sadly, much of that learning is warped as 2 Timothy 3:7 prophesied. They would be ever learning, but never come to the knowledge
of the truth. The social conditions are described in 2 Tmothy 3:1–4:

> Understand this, in the last days, perilous times will come. People will be
> lovers of themselves, lovers of money, boastful, proud, abusive, disobedi-
> ent to parents, brutal, lovers of pleasure rather than lovers of God.

In 1 Timothy 4:1, the rise of the occult is described and the work of
deceiving spirits. There are many other signs and all these have given
rise to a wider *expectancy of the coming of the Lord Jesus Christ.*

THE MILLENNIUM

The general public are now using this word 'millennium' to mean the
thousand years starting in AD 2000, namely, the calendar millennium.
Do not confuse this with the millennium spoken of in Revelation 20.

That millennium speaks of Christ's reign on earth when wars and sin will cease entirely and peace and happiness will be worldwide. The starting date of that period is not known. It could be soon, however, as the signs of its approach described in the Bible are happening around us.

The Bible millennium will be very different from the kind of calendar millennium often dramatised by the media or sci-fi writers. It will turn out to be a very different world from that imagined by the ungodly. Will the phrase in the prayer Jesus taught ever be fulfilled? 'Thy kingdom come, thy will be done on earth as it is in heaven.'

It would be strange if Jesus taught a prayer for which there was not to be a fulfilment. For those who try to spiritualise it, notice that this kingdom is to be 'on earth' in which the perfect will of God is done. 'Your kingdom come; your will be done on earth as it is in heaven.' Can you honestly say that there has ever been such a time in history?

Yet this wonderful time of righteousness and happiness is promised by God four or five times in the Old Testament and two or three times in the New Testament. Many have discussed whether this millennium comes before Christ's return or after it. It is not important doctrinally and Christians should not quarrel over it. Remember 'Though I have the gift of prophecy and understand all mysteries, but have not love, I am nothing.'

However, there are several factors which make it quite clear to me that the millennium will be the result of Christ's coming and therefore will follow it. I have already outlined the reasons in Chapter 15 which I develop further here:

1. Paul says so.
2. The apostle John who wrote Revelation said so to his disciple Papias.
3. The churches of the first three centuries said so.
4. Three of the OT prophets said so.

They all believed that the millennium followed Christ's second coming.

Apostolic Opinion

Let us look at that list. Firstly, St Paul. Where does he show that the millennium follows Christ's return? In Romans 8:18–23 he says that suffering creation waits for the revealing of the sons of God. When is that? It is when the bodies of the saved are redeemed (v 23). We have already seen that Paul uses this phrase to mean the resurrection of the believer's body, when he will be given a new body. This will happen at the second coming of Christ. Creation and the animals were also affected by the fall of Satan and of Adam and still suffer under fierce predators. Isaiah is told by God that in the golden age to come, even the animal kingdom will be at peace. The lion will lie down with the lamb and the baby will not be stung by a wasp (Isaiah 11:6–9). Other features of this golden age will be peace from war and weapons will be beaten into agricultural implements. This is what Revelation 20 calls the millennium. So you see that Paul says that this will follow the resurrection at Christ's second coming. The statement seems quite clear to me. After the resurrection of the sons of God, there will be peace within the animal kingdom.

Secondly, my next evidence that the millennium follows Christ's return is that John, who wrote Revelation 20, said it would. How do we know that?

It was so stated by Papias who was a disciple of John and we have his writings preserved by Eusebius. There were others too who knew St John. Ireneus is one who knew other presbyters who knew John's teaching. They say that John claimed to have been told by the Lord that the thousand years' kingdom on earth would follow Christ's parousia, that is, the second coming.

The Opinion of the Early Churches

Justin Martyr wrote a dialogue with Trypho in AD 153 and he said, 'A certain man among us, John by name, one of the apostles of Christ, in the revelation made to him, prophesied that those who believe in our Christ would reign for a thousand years after their bodily resurrection.' The famous historian Gibbon wrote:

> The ancient and popular doctrine of the millennium was carefully inculcated by a succession of Fathers from Justin Martyr and Ireneus who conversed with the immediate disciples of the apostles.

One of those immediate disciples was Polycarp who quoted a lot of what John taught him. What then changed this opinion? It was Augustine in the fourth century. The action of Emperor Constantine in making Christianity the state religion in AD 323 was such a contrast to centuries of persecution that he thought that Christ's Kingdom had come on earth and therefore that the millennium was being brought in before Christ's return. Later on, Cardinal Manning said that in 'the person of the Pope, Jesus Christ reigned on earth and he must reign till he has put all enemies under his feet'. Later still, the popes were addressed as 'Lord God the Pope'.

Dr A.J. Gordon in his book, *Behold He Cometh,* said this was a mock millennium. Sadly, in the Middle Ages, more Christians were tortured and killed than under any Roman emperor. The estimate is that

50 million Christians were martyred. Wars certainly had not ceased and as someone said, if the devil was chained, he was certainly on a very long chain!

Actually, prophecy showed that the Christian era (that is, the last 20 centuries) would be marked by the two great apostasies – false (medieval) Christianity and the false prophet of the desert. Both would gradually fade out as temporal powers, but their final destruction would be by Christ's return. Until then, they would be fought by the sword of the Spirit, the Word of God. Since the last war, even Roman Catholics have been allowed to read the Bible for themselves. For this we thank God, also for those who have been brought to salvation through it: some are even correcting many Protestant Higher Critics if they deny the resurrection and the virgin birth. (See 2 Thessalonians 2:8, Revelation 19:13–15, Daniel 7:26.)

The Opinion of the OT Writers

Then consider the Old Testament prophets. They all say that Christ's reign on earth will follow his descent from heaven.

Zechariah 14 describes the descent of the Lord to the Mount of Olives (v 4). He is accompanied by all the saints, the saved (v 5). He judges the warring nations. Then verse 9 says: 'The Lord will become King over all the earth' and verse 16 says, 'Everyone who survives of all the nations which came up against Jerusalem, will go up year after year to worship the King, the Lord of hosts', even the common things of life will become holy.

The same picture is given to Ezekiel – chapter 37 describes how the united twelve tribes will return to Palestine. Then a massive invasion will come from the north. It will be defeated by the Lord God who then says in Ezekiel 39:21:

> I will set my glory among the nations and all the nations shall see my judgement . . . The house of Israel shall know that I am the Lord their God from that day forward and that it was I who brought them from the peoples and gathered them from their enemies' lands.

Surely that could be true only if it is referring to the millennium when both Gentiles and Israel would see God's judgement? The eight chapters of Ezekiel which follow, depict the millennium in which the name of Jerusalem will mean 'The Lord is there'.

Isaiah gives a similar succession, after the resurrection of the Lord's people in chapters 25 and 26. That 'twisty snake and dragon' in chapter 27, the devil, is punished as in Revelation 20, then in verse 6, 'Israel shall blossom and put forth shoots and fill the whole world with fruit.'

Joel gives a similar picture in chapter 3. The Lord brings all nations down to the valley of Jehoshaphat by Jerusalem for judgement (v 2). 'There will I sit to judge all the nations' (v 12). 'You will know that I am the Lord your God who dwells in Zion.'

It is in the context of all these prophets that Jesus said in Matthew 25:31, 'When the Son of Man comes in his glory and all the angels with him, then he will sit on his glorious throne. Before him will be gathered all nations.'

To answer those who think that the millennium is mentioned only in the book of Revelation, the following are 13 passages from the Old Testament about the millennium, recorded from God by eight different prophets, with two passages from the New Testament:

- Micah 4:1–4, 'They shall beat their swords into ploughshares and their spears into pruning hooks. Nation will not take up sword against nation, neither shall they learn war any more'(4:3). Also, there will be no poverty any more and everyone will have his fair share of God's goods. The basis of this happiness will be 'All nations will worship the Lord'.
- Habakkuk 2:14 says, 'For the earth will be filled with the knowledge of the glory of the Lord as the waters cover the sea.' Yes, you will really experience that!
- Numbers 14:21 declares to Moses, 'As truly as I live, says the Lord, all the earth will be filled with the glory of the Lord.' Yes, that glory will fill your soul!
- Zechariah 14:16 shows that this will be the result of all nations going up year by year to Jerusalem to worship the King, the Lord of Hosts. Advertisements will incite people to purity and godliness and even common kitchen pots will promote holiness to the Lord. What a change from today's advertisements!
- Joel 3:18 says that the house of the Lord will be a fountain of blessing and Ezekiel 47 says it will bring life to all.
- In three separate passages in Isaiah, we read that long life will be a common experience and the animal kingdom will be at peace. 'The wolf and the lamb will feed together; the lion will eat straw like the ox . . . They shall not hurt or destroy' (Isaiah 65:17–25). 'The leopard will lie down with the kid and the calf and the lion and the fatling together and a little child shall lead them' (Isaiah 11:6–9; Romans 8:18–24).
- 'It will come to pass in the latter days . . . many peoples will say, Come let us go up to the house of the Lord . . . that he may teach us his ways . . . for out of Zion shall go forth the law and the Word of the Lord from Jerusalem' (Isaiah 2:2–4).

Jerusalem, the Centre of the World

Yes, Jerusalem will be the centre of the world and, to implement that, a wide sea channel will open up between the Mediterranean and the Red Sea, passing Jerusalem. This information is given to three prophets, i.e. Ezekiel 47, Joel 3 and Zechariah 14. Ships will bring worshippers from afar and so will aeroplanes. 'Who are these that fly like a cloud and like doves to their windows – the ships of Tarshish [the western end of the Mediterranean Sea] to bring your sons from afar?' (Isaiah 60:8)

All this is called the millennium in Revelation 20. Then, at the end, comes the final judgement and, after the judgement, the eternal state of bliss for all those whose names are written in the book of life. It is an awesome sight we get of the great white throne on which God is seated and from whose face heaven and earth fly away. It should be noted that, at this judgement throne, it is justice which is meted out. All are judged according to the deeds done in the body. No one will be able to grumble and say that justice is not seen to be done. In every case, the punishment will fit the crime, but only the saved, whose names are written in the book of life, will enter the glories of heaven.

To be saved and to be there will be worth all that you have suffered. Let the description of the praises of those there ring in your ears. Let the love and adoration of Jesus and the Father thrill your heart. Let the choruses of hallelujahs inspire every fibre of your being as you join in the Revelation jubilation:

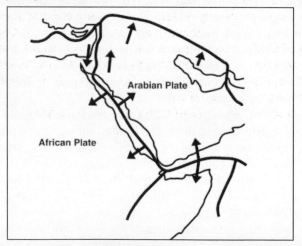

Fig. 17.2 Map showing how Lebanon and Israel lie alongside a tectonic boundary between the African and Arabian plates (solid lines). The arrows show direction of movement which will result in faults appearing at right angles to the main fault line in this region. The continents are preparing for the return of Christ when the Dead Sea rift valley will break into the Mediterranean Sea. Zechariah 14:8 says this will occur at the Mount of Olives. With acknowledgement to *New Scientist*, 16th August 1997.

And I heard as it were the voice of a great multitude and as the voice of many waters and as the voice of many thunderings, saying, Alleluia! for the Lord God omnipotent reigns. Let us be glad and rejoice and give honour to him. They sang the song of Moses and the song of the Lamb, saying, Great and marvellous are your works, Lord God Almighty; just and true are your ways O King of saints!

CONCLUSION

At the end of a fascinating teaching session, the Lord Jesus asked this question: 'Have you understood all these things?'

The disciples replied 'Yes, Lord.'

'Then you are like a seeker of treasure who takes out of his casket jewels new and old.'

Certainly, from resources new and old, God has provided abundant evidence of all his truth as we have seen. In his Word and works, he has given more than anyone could have dared to hope for. In his graciousness he has given us an insight into his plans down the ages, through trauma to happy climax. He has alerted us against subtle deceptions by those 'who twist the Scriptures to their own destruction' in St Peter's words.

From **science** correlated with the Bible, I have shown you the genetic fingerprints of the Creator, substantiated by accredited scientists. From the 'precious stones' and tablets of **archaeology** you have seen that the Bible dates match up its history and culture with a remarkable store of excavated artefacts and new material from my researches. From **prophecy** by scholars new and old, together we have peered into that casket of jewels and precious stones and seen there reflections of God's detailed plans for past, present and future.

Yes, Jesus said, 'Every student who is instructed in the kingdom of heaven is like a faithful steward who brings out of his treasure chest, precious stones, new and old'.

So go out strong in the Lord with faith and with facts.

SUMMARY

SECOND COMING ORDER OF EVENTS

General agreement upon the following:
- Lord Jesus will descend from heaven to judge living and dead, and to judge nations (Matt 25:31, Dan 7:13, 2:44, 2 Thess 1:7–10).
- Christians will share his rule (Dan 7:18, Rev 20:4, 1 Cor 6:2).
- Christians will descend with him, so how then did they get to be with him? By **resurrection.** Sometimes called the **rapture**:
- 'He who believes will not come to the judgement, but will rise at the resurrection of the justified' (Jn 5:24,29).
- Paul says, only those who belong to Christ will be raised (1 Cor 15:23).
- The rest will be raised later (Rev 20:5).
- The saved dead will rise and those living will change to new bodies (1 Cor 15:51–54, 2 Thess 2:1, 1 Thess 4:16,17).
- The Church is the bride of Christ (Eph 5:21–30).
- But when will she be married to him? It is after the rapture (2 Thess 2:1, Lk 17:34,35, 1 Thess 4:16,17).
- Christ and the saved will set up a just and happy rule on earth.
- Paul (1 Cor 15:23–27), Dan (7:13,14,27), Is (2:1–5), Zech (14:9–21), Rev (20:5,6) all agree, but when?

The order of events is in Matthew 25 as follows:
- The marriage (vv 1–3) cf. Jn 3:29, 2 Cor 11:2–4, Eph 5:21–30, Rev 19:6–9.
- The reward giving (vv 14–30); called 'Bema' in many scriptures (2 Cor 5:10).
- The descent with Christ to judge the nations (vv 31–51; Dan 7:18, 1 Cor 6:2).

The Bible Millennium Revelation 20.
- Described in: Is 11:6–9; 65:17–25; Ez 48:35; Joel 3:12–18; Zech 14:16–21.
- When? Rom 8:19–23 says it will be after new bodies are given to the saved.
- Early Fathers agree: all Christian writers in the first 4 centuries taught this and Papius, St John's disciple, says John taught it.
- At the end of the millennium, the unsaved dead will be raised for judgement (Jn 5:29; Rev 20:5,11–15).
- Finally the whole Kingdom is delivered up to the Father after the universe has been cleaned up (Rev 21:27 to 22:5; 1 Cor 15:27,28).